SHICHIHENGE

15

Tomoko Hayakawa

Translated and adapted by
David Ury

Lettered by
Gabe Levine

Ballantine Books · New York

A Del Rey Manga/Kodansha Trade Paperback Original

Published in the United States by Del Rey Books, an imprint of The Random House Publishing Group, a division of Random House, Inc., New York.

DEL REY is a registered trademark and the Del Rey colophon is a trademark of Random House, Inc.

Publication rights arranged through Kodansha Ltd.

First published in Japan in 2006 by Kodansha Ltd., Tokyo as *Yamatonadeshiko Shichihenge.*

ISBN 978-0-345-49919-6

Printed in the United States of America

www.delreymanga.com

9 8 7 6 5 4 3 2

Translator/Adapter—David Ury
Letterer—Gabe Levine

Contents

A Note from the Author

♥ IN THIS VOLUME, THERE'S A STORY I WAS THINKING OF SAVING FOR THE END OF THE SERIES. I'M SURE THERE ARE SOME PEOPLE OUT THERE WHO ARE WONDERING "IS THE SERIES GONNA END SOON?" BUT I'M STILL GOING STRONG. I'M NOT SURE WHEN IT'LL END, BUT I HOPE YOU'LL ALL KEEP READING IN THE MEANTIME.

—**Tomoko Hayakawa**

Honorifics

Throughout the Del Rey Manga books, you will find Japanese honorifics left intact in the translations. For those not familiar with how the Japanese use honorifics and, more important, how they differ from American honorifics, we present this brief overview.

Politeness has always been a critical facet of Japanese culture. Ever since the feudal era, when Japan was a highly stratified society, use of honorifics—which can be defined as polite speech that indicates relationship or status—has played an essential role in the Japanese language. When addressing someone in Japanese, an honorific usually takes the form of a suffix attached to one's name (example: "Asuna-san"), is used as a title at the end of one's name, or appears in place of the name itself (example: "Negi-sensei," or simply "Sensei!").

Honorifics can be expressions of respect or endearment. In the context of manga and anime, honorifics give insight into the nature of the relationship between characters. Many English translations leave out these important honorifics and therefore distort the feel of the original Japanese. Because Japanese honorifics contain nuances that English honorifics lack, it is our policy at Del Rey not to translate them. Here, instead, is a guide to some of the honorifics you may encounter in Del Rey Manga.

-san: This is the most common honorific and is equivalent to Mr., Miss, Ms., or Mrs. It is the all-purpose honorific and can be used in any situation where politeness is required.

-sama: This is one level higher than "-san" and is used to confer great respect.

-dono: This comes from the word "tono," which means "lord." It is an even higher level than "-sama" and confers utmost respect.

-kun: This suffix is used at the end of boys' names to express familiarity or endearment. It is also sometimes used by men among friends, or when addressing someone younger or of a lower station.

-chan: This is used to express endearment, mostly toward girls. It is also used for little boys, pets, and even among lovers. It gives a sense of childish cuteness.

Bozu: This is an informal way to refer to a boy, similar to the English terms "kid" or "squirt."

Sempai/Senpai:
This title suggests that the addressee is one's senior in a group or organization. It is most often used in a school setting, where underclassmen refer to their upperclassmen as "sempai." It can also be used in the workplace, such as when a newer employee addresses an employee who has seniority in the company.

Kohai: This is the opposite of "sempai" and is used toward underclassmen in school or newcomers in the workplace. It connotes that the addressee is of a lower station.

Sensei: Literally meaning "one who has come before," this title is used for teachers, doctors, or masters of any profession or art.

-[blank]: This is usually forgotten in these lists, but it is perhaps the most significant difference between Japanese and English. The lack of honorific means that the speaker has permission to address the person in a very intimate way. Usually, only family, spouses, or very close friends have this kind of permission. Known as *yobisute*, it can be gratifying when someone who has earned the intimacy starts to call one by one's name without an honorific. But when that intimacy hasn't been earned, it can be very insulting

THE wallflower

YAMATONADESHIKO SHICHIHENGE

ヤマトナデシコ七変化♡

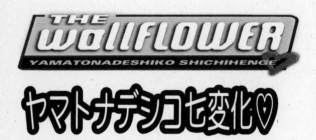

CONTENTS

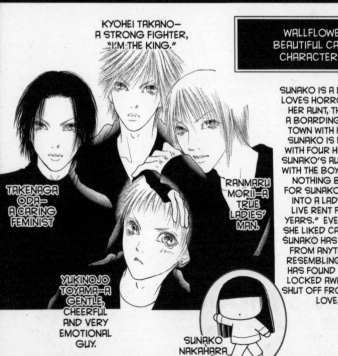

KYOHEI TAKANO—
A STRONG FIGHTER,
"I'M THE KING."
RANMARU MORII—A TRUE LADIES' MAN.
TAKENAGA ODA—A CARING FEMINIST
YUKINOJO TOYAMA—A GENTLE, CHEERFUL AND VERY EMOTIONAL GUY.
SUNAKO NAKAHARA

WALLFLOWER'S BEAUTIFUL CAST OF CHARACTERS (?)

SUNAKO IS A DARK LONER WHO LOVES HORROR MOVIES. WHEN HER AUNT, THE LANDLADY OF A BOARDING HOUSE, LEAVES TOWN WITH HER BOYFRIEND, SUNAKO IS FORCED TO LIVE WITH FOUR HANDSOME GUYS. SUNAKO'S AUNT MAKES A DEAL WITH THE BOYS, WHICH CAUSES NOTHING BUT HEADACHES FOR SUNAKO. "MAKE SUNAKO INTO A LADY, AND YOU CAN LIVE RENT FREE FOR THREE YEARS." EVER SINCE THE GUY SHE LIKED CALLED HER "UGLY," SUNAKO HAS CUT HERSELF OFF FROM ANYTHING REMOTELY RESEMBLING LOVE. SUNAKO HAS FOUND TRUE HAPPINESS LOCKED AWAY IN HER ROOM, SHUT OFF FROM THE WORLD OF LOVE, BUT . . . ?

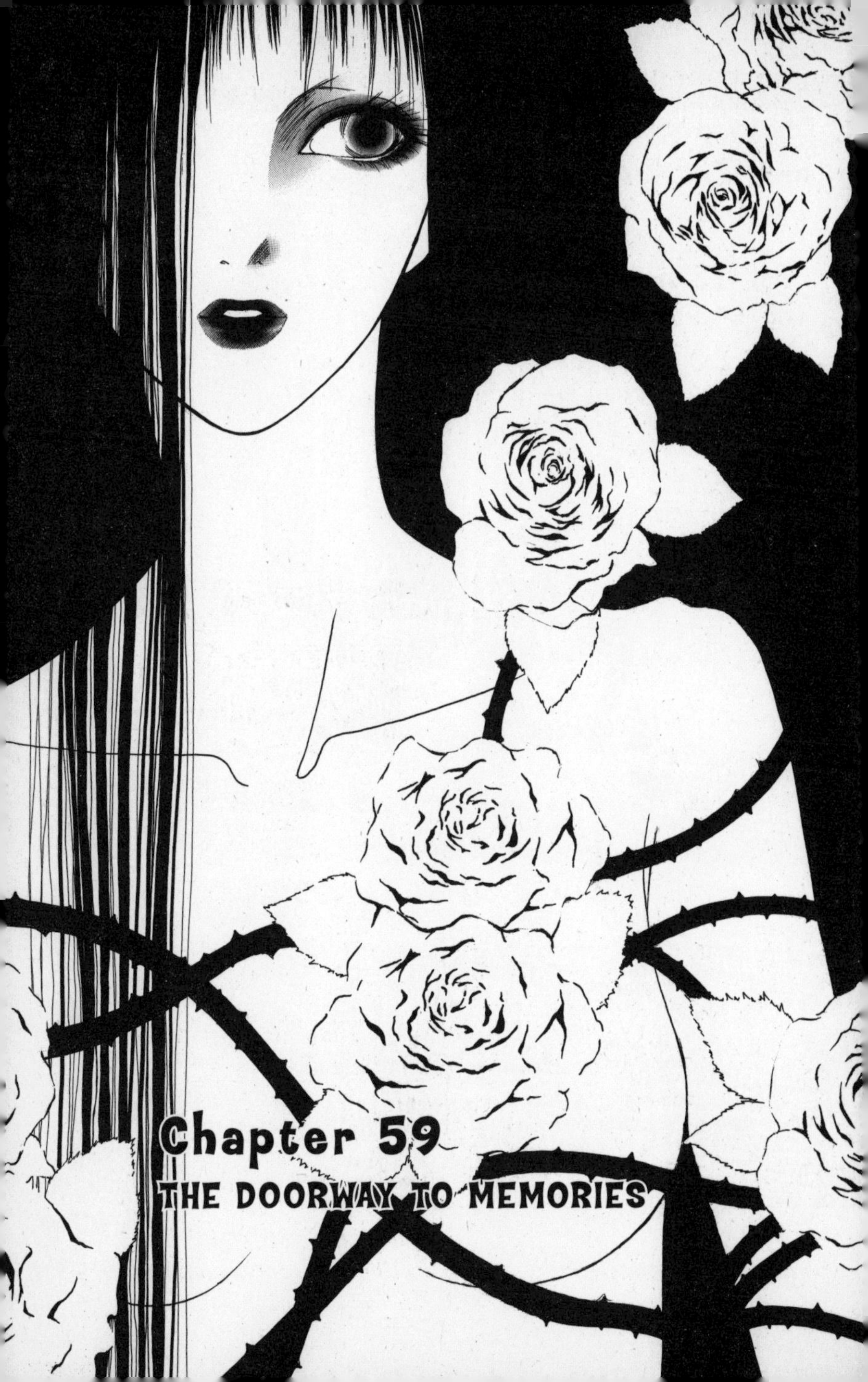
Chapter 59
THE DOORWAY TO MEMORIES

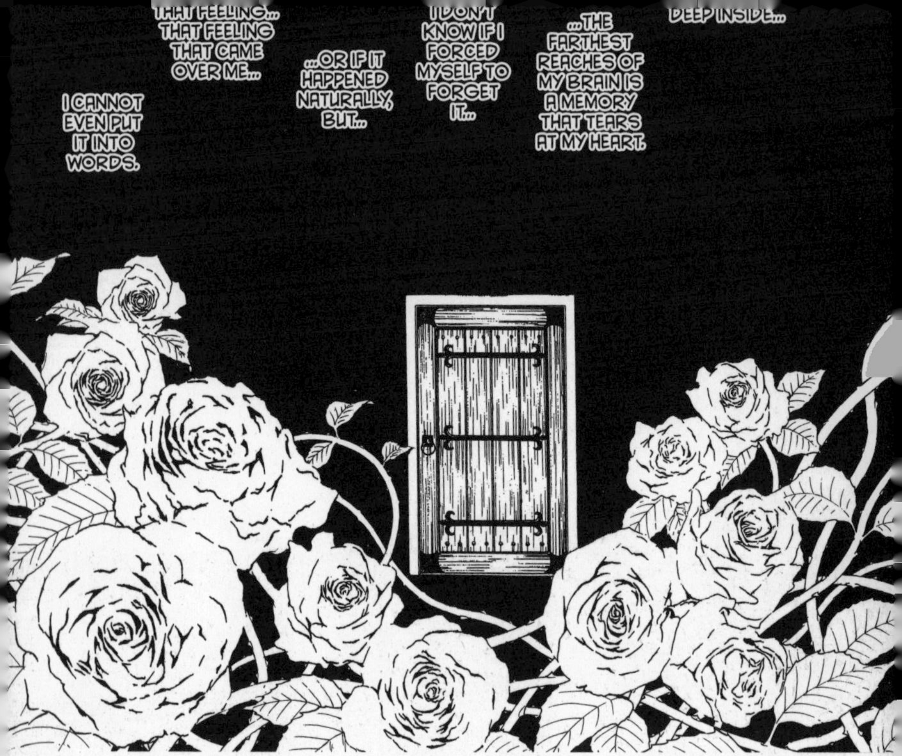
DEEP INSIDE...
...THE FARTHEST REACHES OF MY BRAIN IS A MEMORY THAT TEARS AT MY HEART.
I DON'T KNOW IF I FORCED MYSELF TO FORGET IT...
...OR IF IT HAPPENED NATURALLY, BUT...
THAT FEELING... THAT FEELING THAT CAME OVER ME...
I CANNOT EVEN PUT IT INTO WORDS.

BEHIND THE SCENES

MY EDITOR TOLD ME "YOU NEED TO MAKE SUNAKO GROW." BUT I COULDN'T FIGURE OUT HOW TO MAKE HER "GROW," SO I JUST KEPT PUTTING IT OFF.

I GUESS THE PROBLEM WAS THAT I WAS THINKING TOO HARD ABOUT THE CONCEPT OF "GROWTH." I THOUGHT MAYBE I SHOULD MAKE SUNAKO CONFRONT HER PAST.

. . . BUT WHETHER OR NOT THIS RESULTED IN GROWTH??? I DON'T KNOW.

I PICKED UP A FASHION MAGAZINE TO USE AS REFERENCE FOR THE "MIXER" SCENE. WOW!! PEOPLE SURE DO PUT A LOT OF EFFORT INTO TRYING TO BE POPULAR. I JUST DON'T HAVE THE MOTIVATION TO PUT FORTH THAT KIND OF EFFORT . . . GUESS IT'S THE END FOR ME.

I DON'T THINK THOSE KINDS OF "HOT FASHIONS" AND "HOT MAKEUP TECHNIQUES" WOULD LOOK GOOD ON ME ANYWAY.

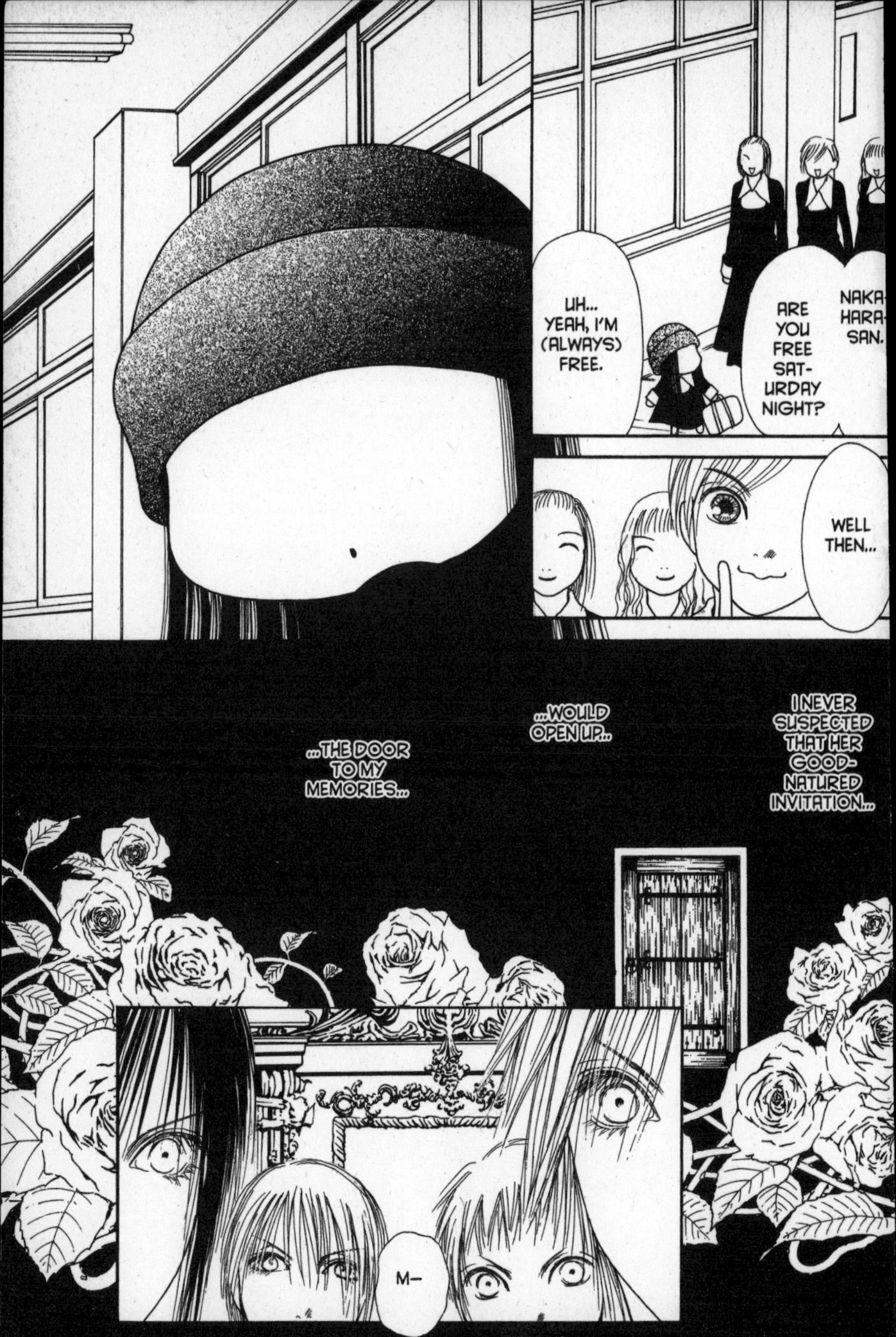
NAKA-HARA-SAN.
ARE YOU FREE SAT-URDAY NIGHT?
UH... YEAH, I'M (ALWAYS) FREE.
WELL THEN...
I NEVER SUSPECTED THAT HER GOOD-NATURED INVITATION...
...WOULD OPEN UP...
...THE DOOR TO MY MEMORIES...
M–

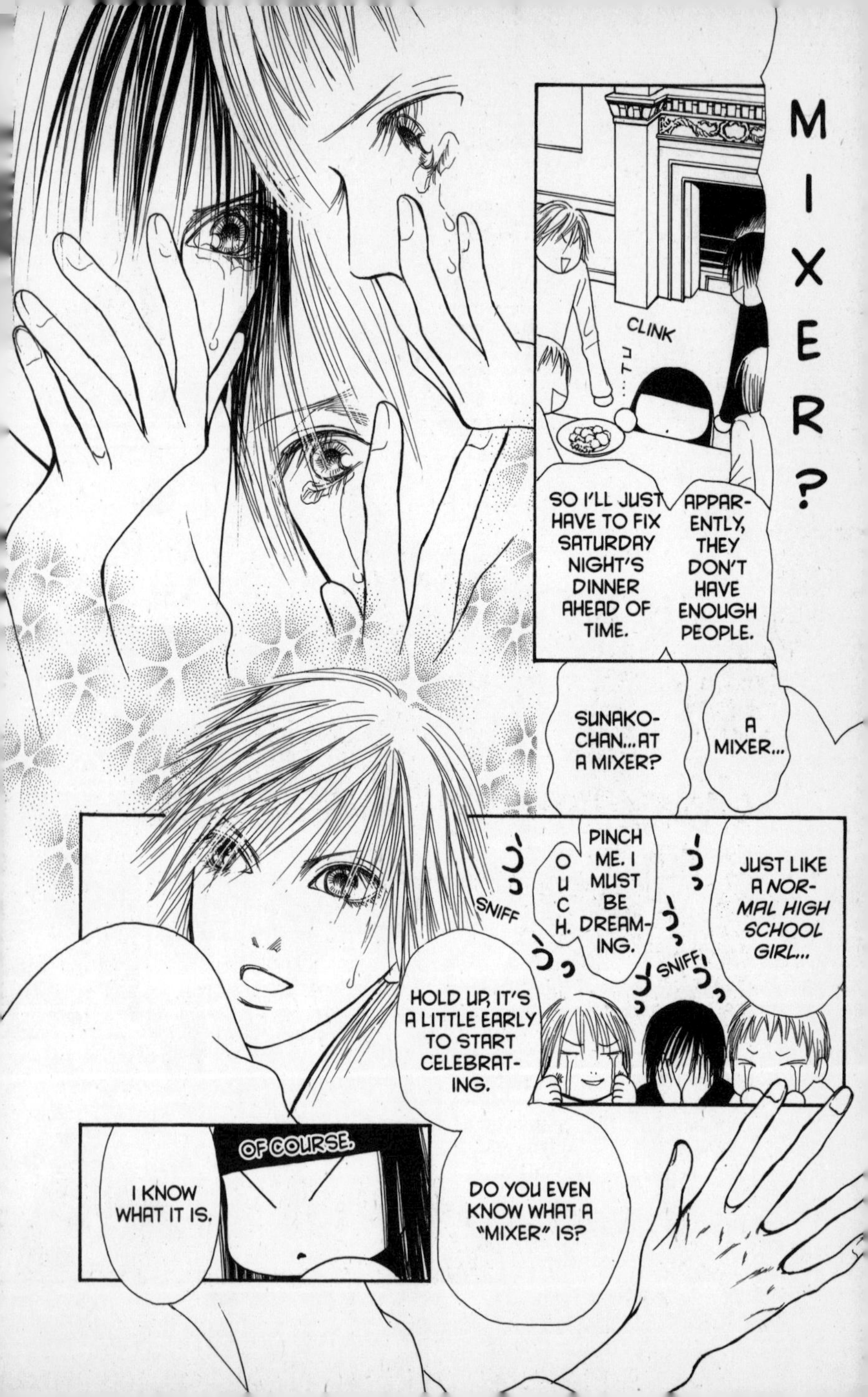
MIXER?
APPARENTLY, THEY DON'T HAVE ENOUGH PEOPLE.
SO I'LL JUST HAVE TO FIX SATURDAY NIGHT'S DINNER AHEAD OF TIME.
CLINK
A MIXER...
SUNAKO-CHAN...AT A MIXER?
JUST LIKE A NORMAL HIGH SCHOOL GIRL...
SNIFF
PINCH ME. I MUST BE DREAMING.
OUCH.
SNIFF
HOLD UP, IT'S A LITTLE EARLY TO START CELEBRATING.
DO YOU EVEN KNOW WHAT A "MIXER" IS?
OF COURSE.
I KNOW WHAT IT IS.

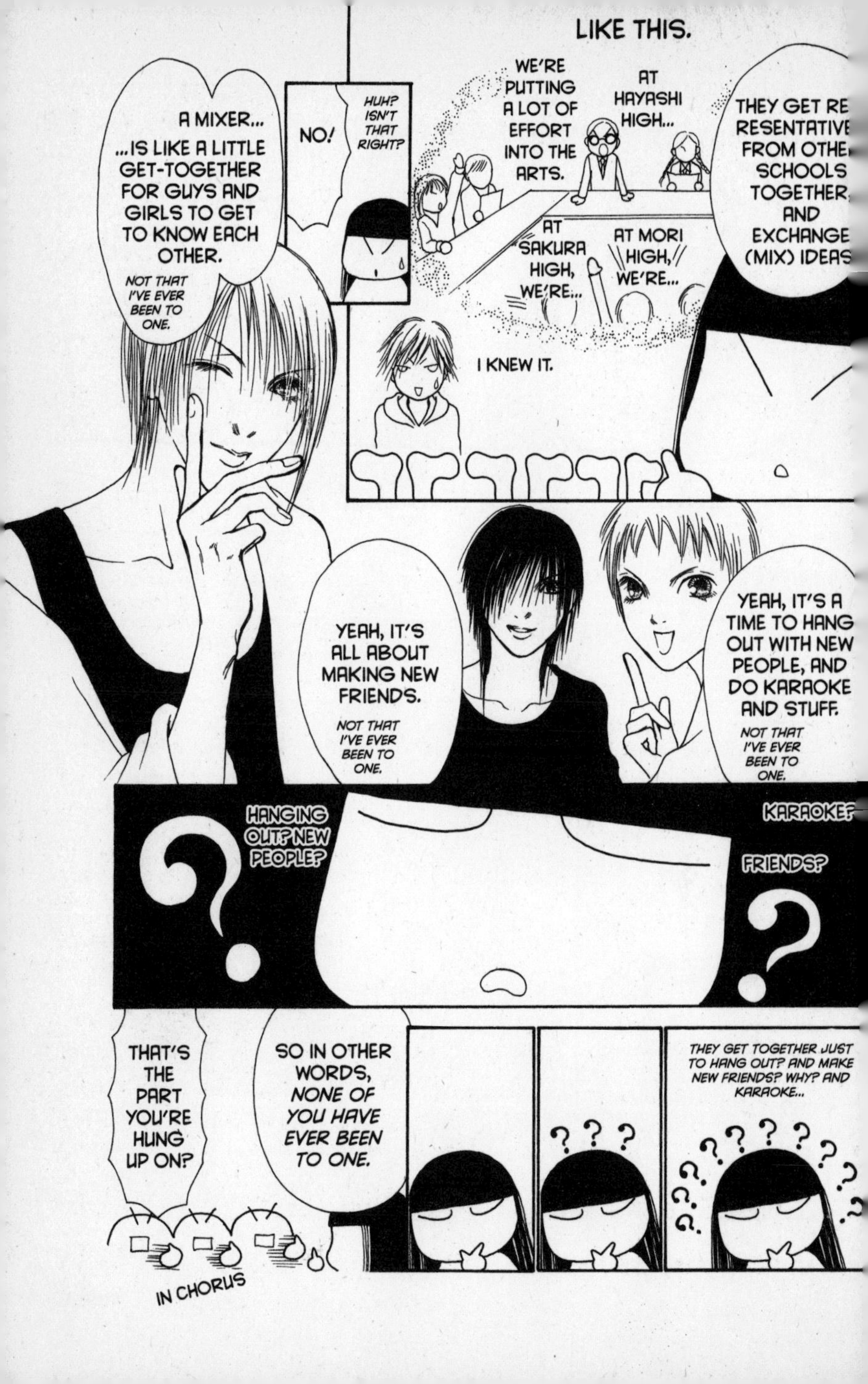
LIKE THIS.
THEY GET RE RESENTATIVE FROM OTHE SCHOOLS TOGETHER AND EXCHANGE (MIX) IDEAS
AT HAYASHI HIGH...
WE'RE PUTTING A LOT OF EFFORT INTO THE ARTS.
AT MORI HIGH, WE'RE...
AT SAKURA HIGH, WE'RE...
I KNEW IT.
HUH? ISN'T THAT RIGHT?
NO!
A MIXER...
...IS LIKE A LITTLE GET-TOGETHER FOR GUYS AND GIRLS TO GET TO KNOW EACH OTHER.
NOT THAT I'VE EVER BEEN TO ONE.
YEAH, IT'S A TIME TO HANG OUT WITH NEW PEOPLE, AND DO KARAOKE AND STUFF.
NOT THAT I'VE EVER BEEN TO ONE.
YEAH, IT'S ALL ABOUT MAKING NEW FRIENDS.
NOT THAT I'VE EVER BEEN TO ONE.
KARAOKE?
FRIENDS?
HANGING OUT? NEW PEOPLE?
THEY GET TOGETHER JUST TO HANG OUT? AND MAKE NEW FRIENDS? WHY? AND KARAOKE...
SO IN OTHER WORDS, NONE OF YOU HAVE EVER BEEN TO ONE.
THAT'S THE PART YOU'RE HUNG UP ON?
IN CHORUS

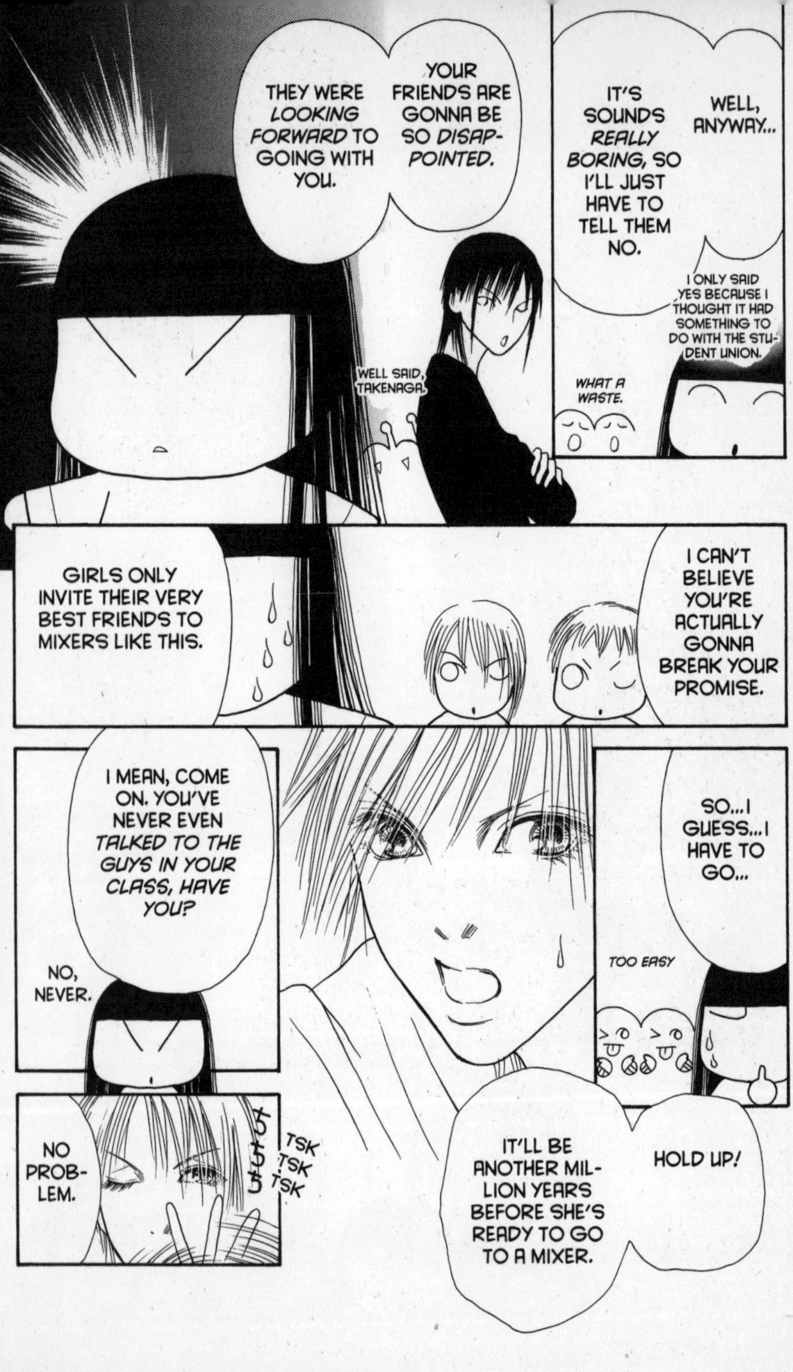
WELL, ANYWAY...
IT'S SOUNDS *REALLY BORING,* SO I'LL JUST HAVE TO TELL THEM NO.
I ONLY SAID YES BECAUSE I THOUGHT IT HAD SOMETHING TO DO WITH THE STU-DENT UNION.
WHAT A WASTE.
YOUR FRIENDS ARE GONNA BE SO *DISAP-POINTED.*
THEY WERE *LOOKING FORWARD* TO GOING WITH YOU.
WELL SAID, TAKENAGA.
I CAN'T BELIEVE YOU'RE ACTUALLY GONNA BREAK YOUR PROMISE.
GIRLS ONLY INVITE THEIR VERY BEST FRIENDS TO MIXERS LIKE THIS.
SO...I GUESS...I HAVE TO GO...
TOO EASY
HOLD UP!
IT'LL BE ANOTHER MIL-LION YEARS BEFORE SHE'S READY TO GO TO A MIXER.
I MEAN, COME ON. YOU'VE NEVER EVEN *TALKED TO THE GUYS IN YOUR CLASS, HAVE YOU?*
NO, NEVER.
NO PROB-LEM.
TSK TSK TSK

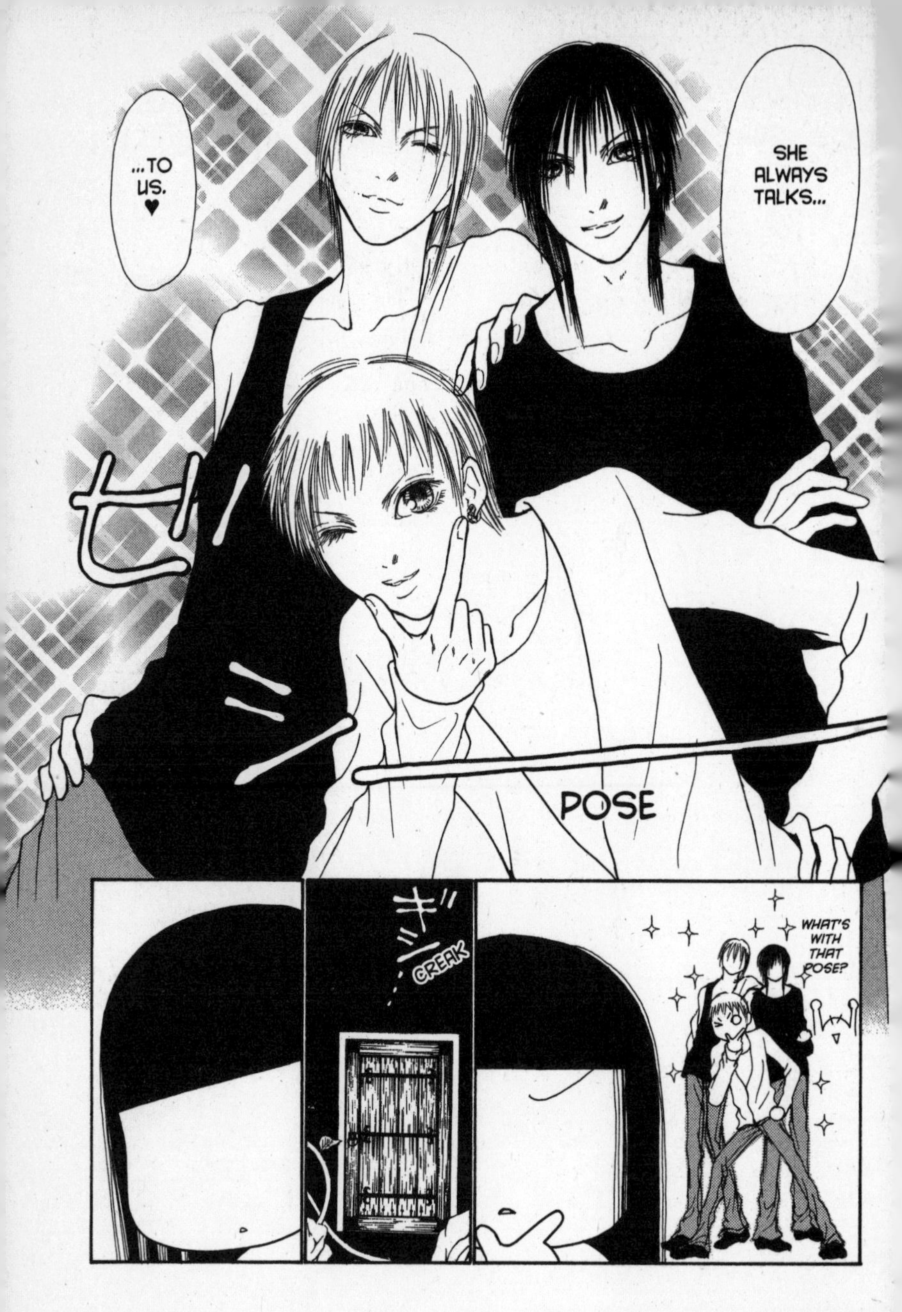
SHE ALWAYS TALKS...
...TO US. ♥
POSE
WHAT'S WITH THAT POSE?
CREAK

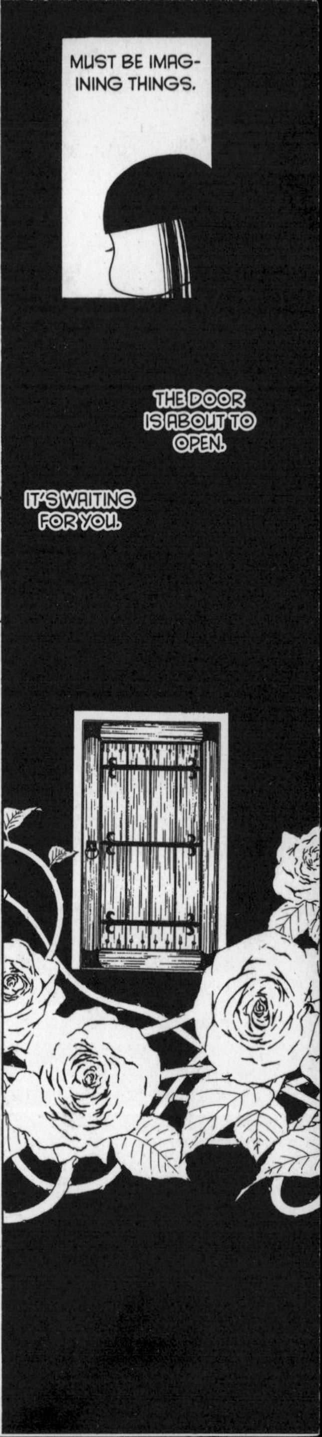
MUST BE IMAG-INING THINGS.
THE DOOR IS ABOUT TO OPEN.
IT'S WAITING FOR YOU.

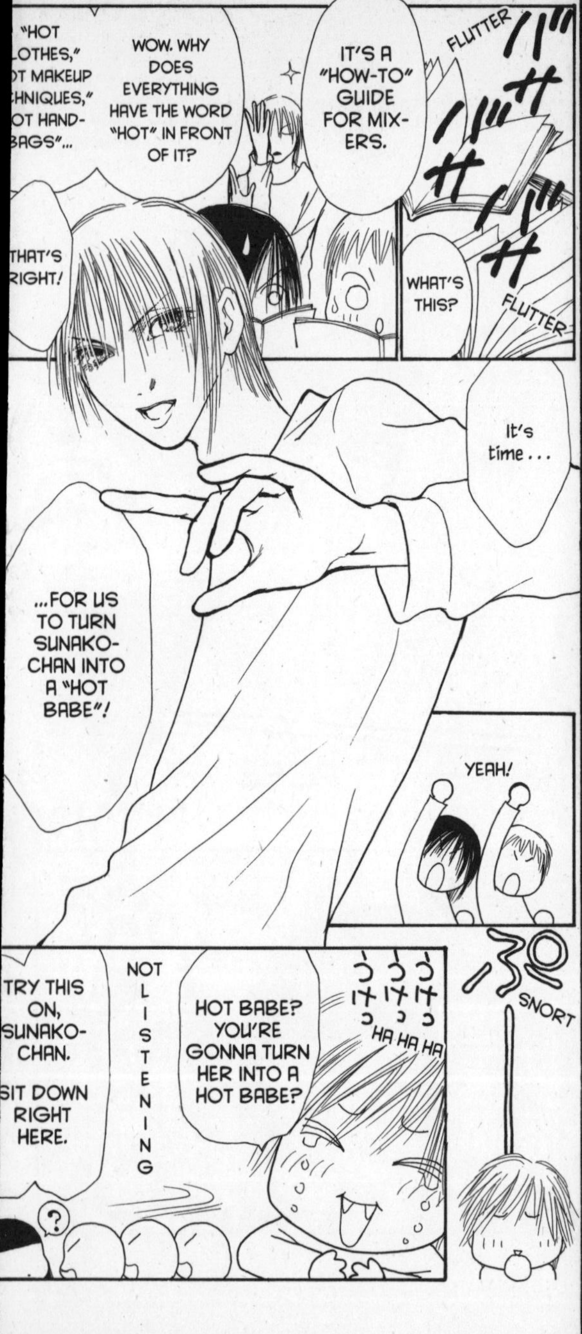
FLUTTER
FLUTTER
WHAT'S THIS?
IT'S A "HOW-TO" GUIDE FOR MIX-ERS.
WOW. WHY DOES EVERYTHING HAVE THE WORD "HOT" IN FRONT OF IT?
"HOT LOTHES," OT MAKEUP CHNIQUES," OT HAND-BAGS"...
THAT'S RIGHT!
It's time . . .
...FOR US TO TURN SUNAKO-CHAN INTO A "HOT BABE"!
YEAH!
SNORT
うけっ うけっ うけっ
HA HA HA
HOT BABE? YOU'RE GONNA TURN HER INTO A HOT BABE?
NOT LISTENING
TRY THIS ON, SUNAKO-CHAN.
SIT DOWN RIGHT HERE.
?

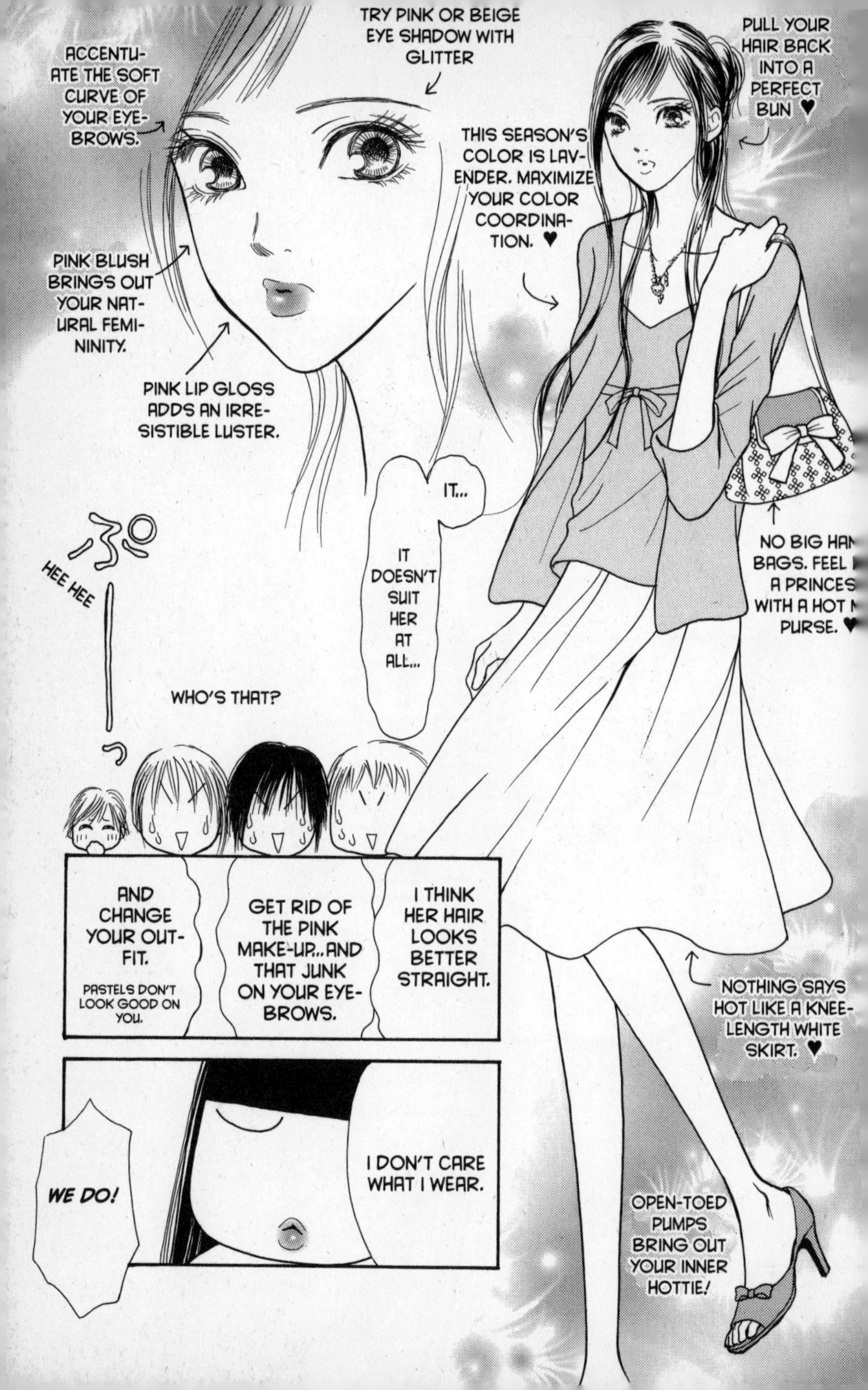
PULL YOUR HAIR BACK INTO A PERFECT BUN ♥
THIS SEASON'S COLOR IS LAVENDER. MAXIMIZE YOUR COLOR COORDINATION. ♥
TRY PINK OR BEIGE EYE SHADOW WITH GLITTER
ACCENTUATE THE SOFT CURVE OF YOUR EYEBROWS.
PINK BLUSH BRINGS OUT YOUR NATURAL FEMININITY.
PINK LIP GLOSS ADDS AN IRRESISTIBLE LUSTER.
NO BIG HAN BAGS. FEEL A PRINCES WITH A HOT PURSE. ♥
IT...
IT DOESN'T SUIT HER AT ALL...
HEE HEE
WHO'S THAT?
NOTHING SAYS HOT LIKE A KNEE-LENGTH WHITE SKIRT. ♥
OPEN-TOED PUMPS BRING OUT YOUR INNER HOTTIE!
I THINK HER HAIR LOOKS BETTER STRAIGHT.
GET RID OF THE PINK MAKE-UP...AND THAT JUNK ON YOUR EYEBROWS.
AND CHANGE YOUR OUTFIT.
PASTELS DON'T LOOK GOOD ON YOU.
I DON'T CARE WHAT I WEAR.
WE DO!

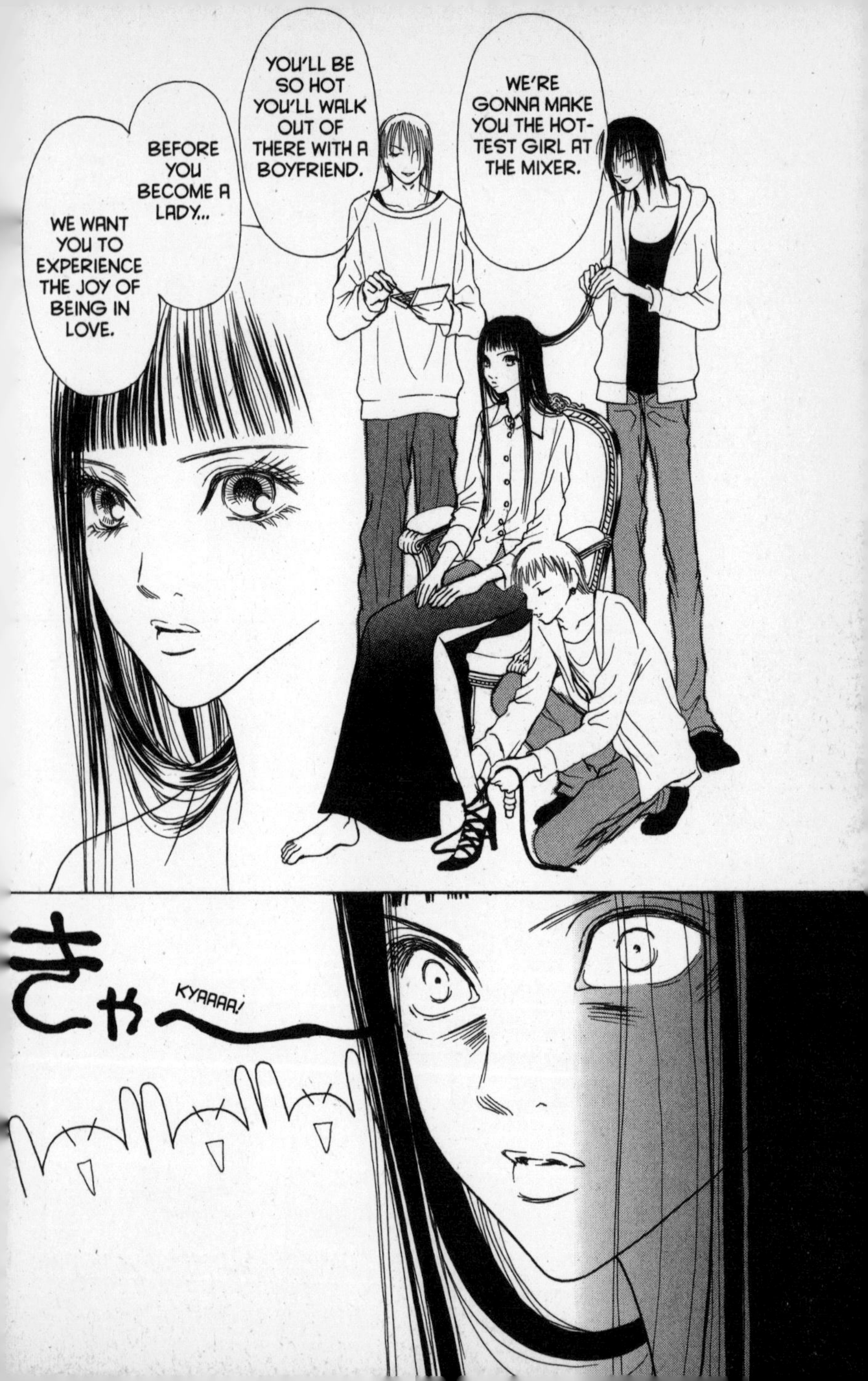
WE'RE GONNA MAKE YOU THE HOT-TEST GIRL AT THE MIXER.
YOU'LL BE SO HOT YOU'LL WALK OUT OF THERE WITH A BOYFRIEND.
BEFORE YOU BECOME A LADY...
WE WANT YOU TO EXPERIENCE THE JOY OF BEING IN LOVE.
きゃ〜
KYAAAA!

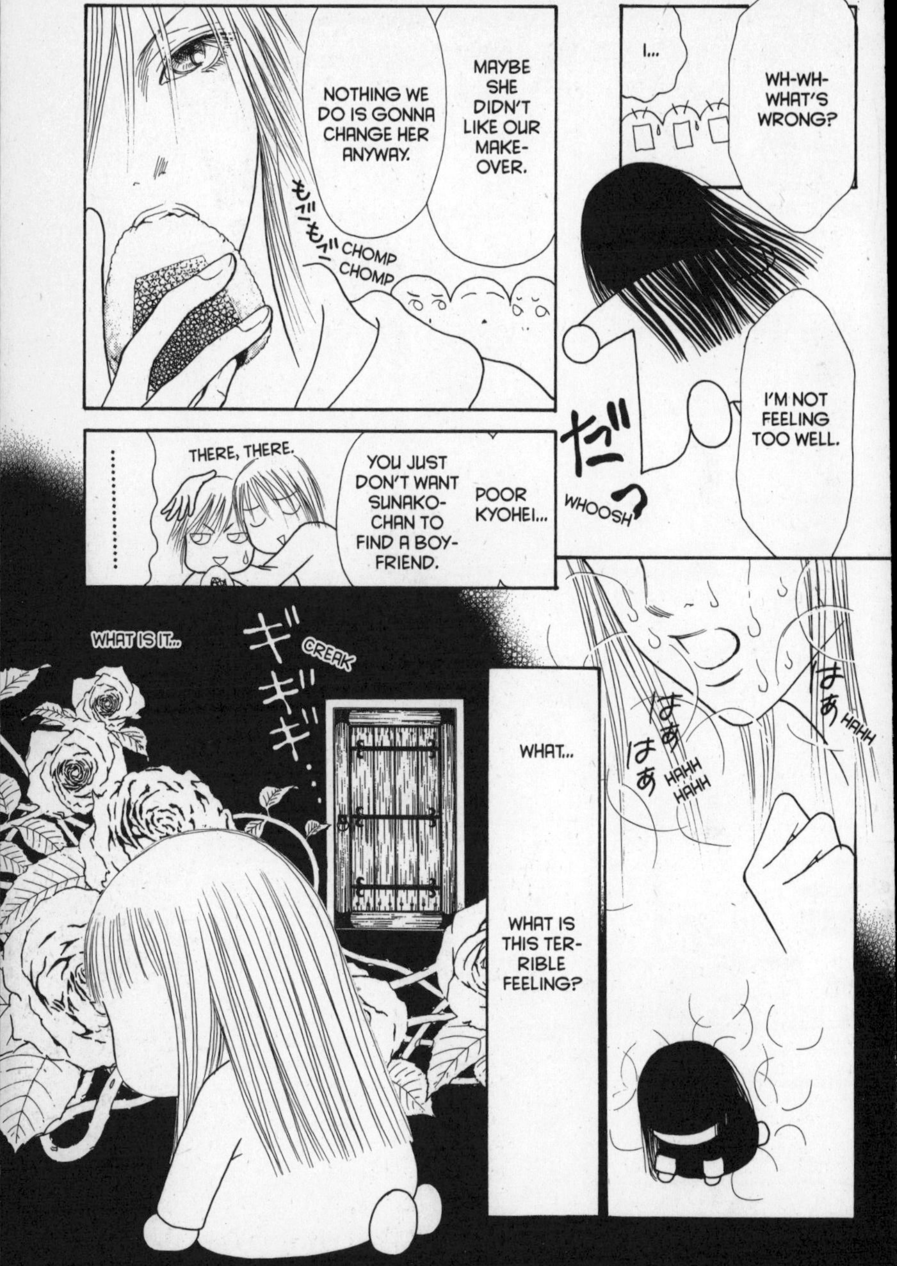
WH-WH-WHAT'S WRONG?
I...
I'M NOT FEELING TOO WELL.
だっ
WHOOSH
MAYBE SHE DIDN'T LIKE OUR MAKE-OVER.
NOTHING WE DO IS GONNA CHANGE HER ANYWAY.
もごもご
CHOMP CHOMP
POOR KYOHEI...
YOU JUST DON'T WANT SUNAKO-CHAN TO FIND A BOY-FRIEND.
THERE, THERE.
....
はあ
HAHH
はあ はあ
HAHH HAHH
WHAT...
WHAT IS THIS TER-RIBLE FEELING?
WHAT IS IT...
ギギギ...
CREAK

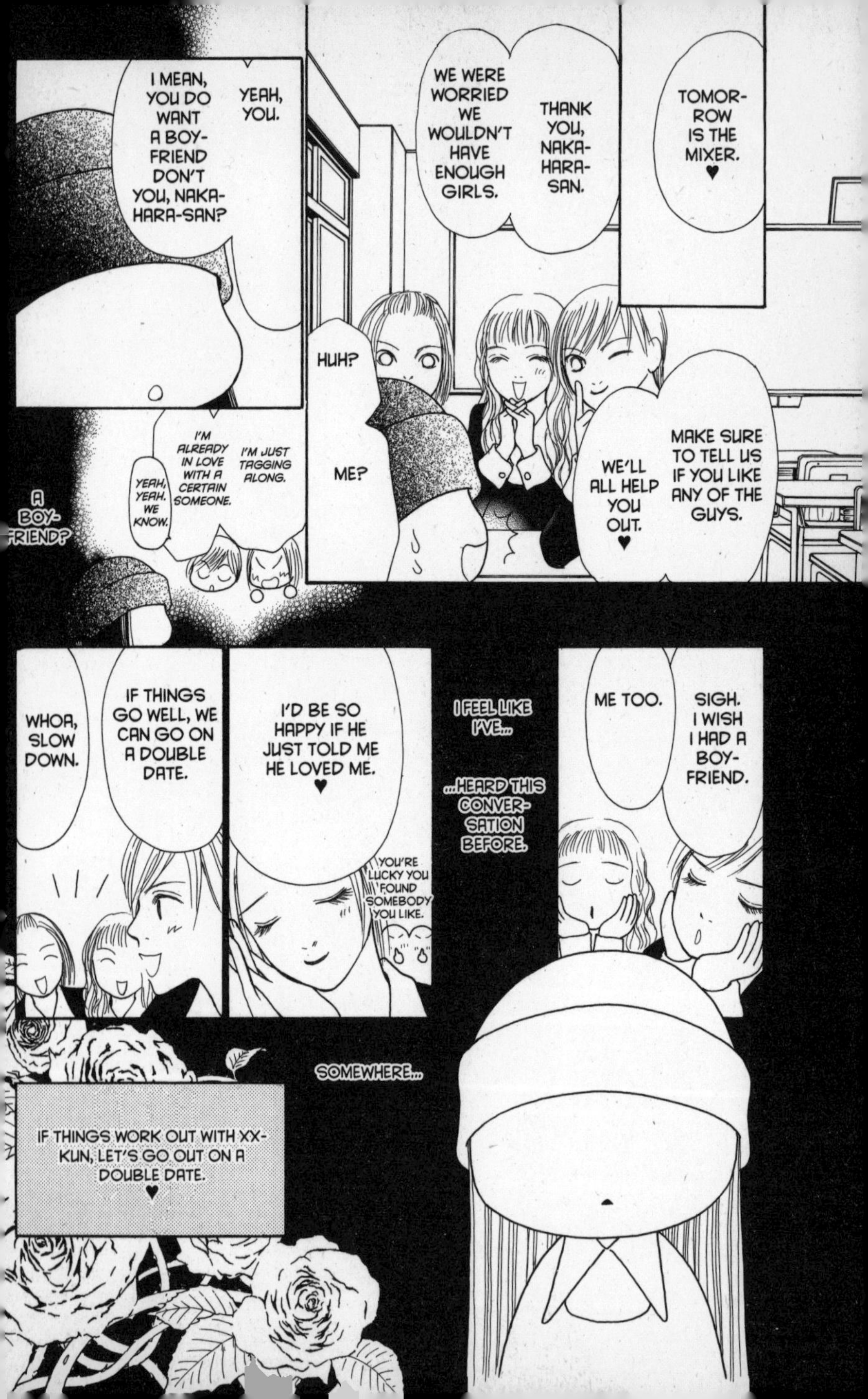
TOMORROW IS THE MIXER. ♥
THANK YOU, NAKAHARA-SAN.
WE WERE WORRIED WE WOULDN'T HAVE ENOUGH GIRLS.
MAKE SURE TO TELL US IF YOU LIKE ANY OF THE GUYS.
WE'LL ALL HELP YOU OUT. ♥
HUH?
ME?
YEAH, YOU.
I MEAN, YOU DO WANT A BOYFRIEND DON'T YOU, NAKAHARA-SAN?
I'M JUST TAGGING ALONG.
I'M ALREADY IN LOVE WITH A CERTAIN SOMEONE.
YEAH, YEAH. WE KNOW.
A BOYFRIEND?
SIGH. I WISH I HAD A BOYFRIEND.
ME TOO.
I FEEL LIKE I'VE...
...HEARD THIS CONVERSATION BEFORE.
I'D BE SO HAPPY IF HE JUST TOLD ME HE LOVED ME. ♥
YOU'RE LUCKY YOU FOUND SOMEBODY YOU LIKE.
IF THINGS GO WELL, WE CAN GO ON A DOUBLE DATE.
WHOA, SLOW DOWN.
SOMEWHERE...
IF THINGS WORK OUT WITH XX-KUN, LET'S GO OUT ON A DOUBLE DATE. ♥

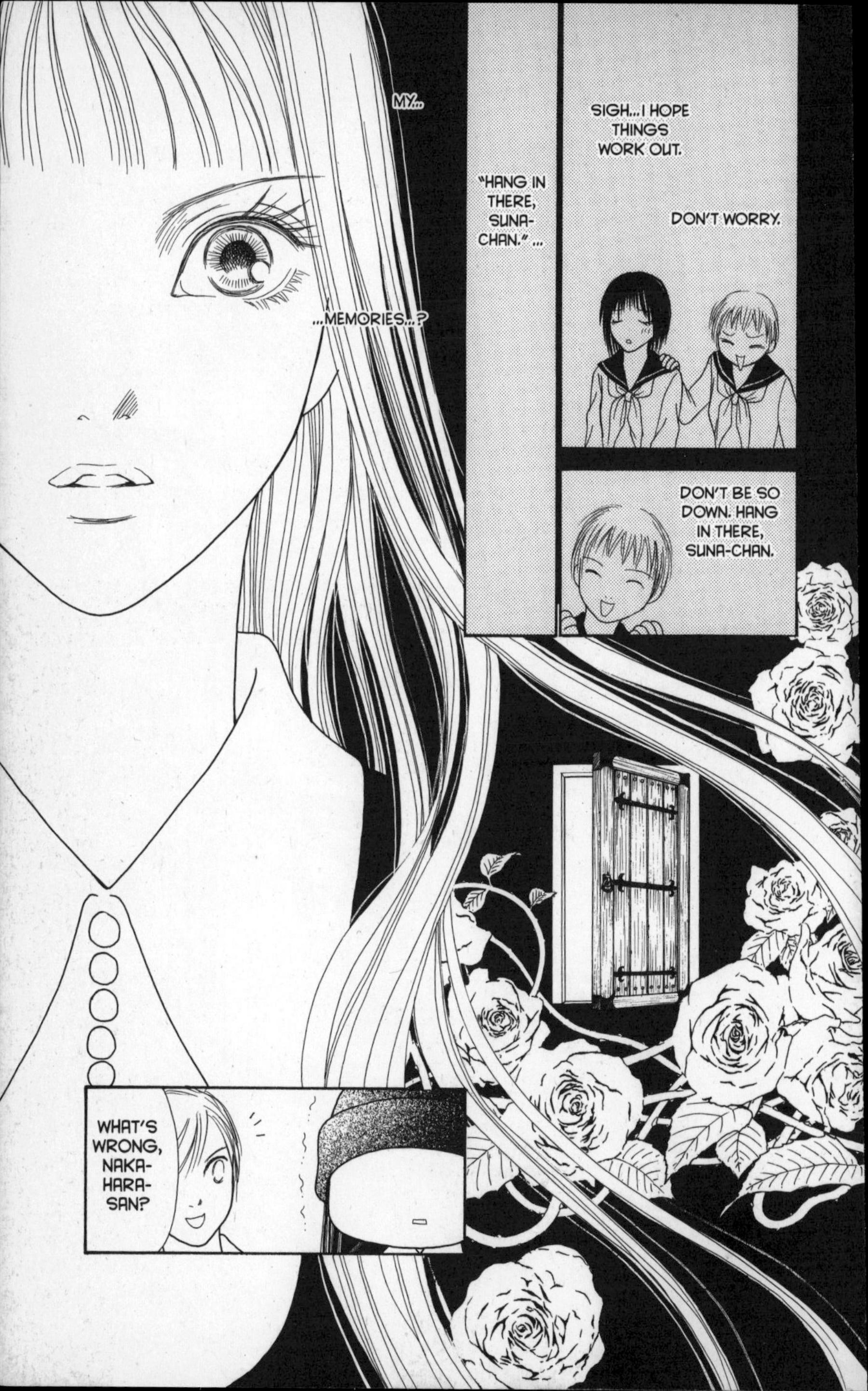
SIGH...I HOPE THINGS WORK OUT.
DON'T WORRY.
DON'T BE SO DOWN. HANG IN THERE, SUNA-CHAN.
"HANG IN THERE, SUNA-CHAN." ...
MY...
...MEMORIES...?
WHAT'S WRONG, NAKA-HARA-SAN?

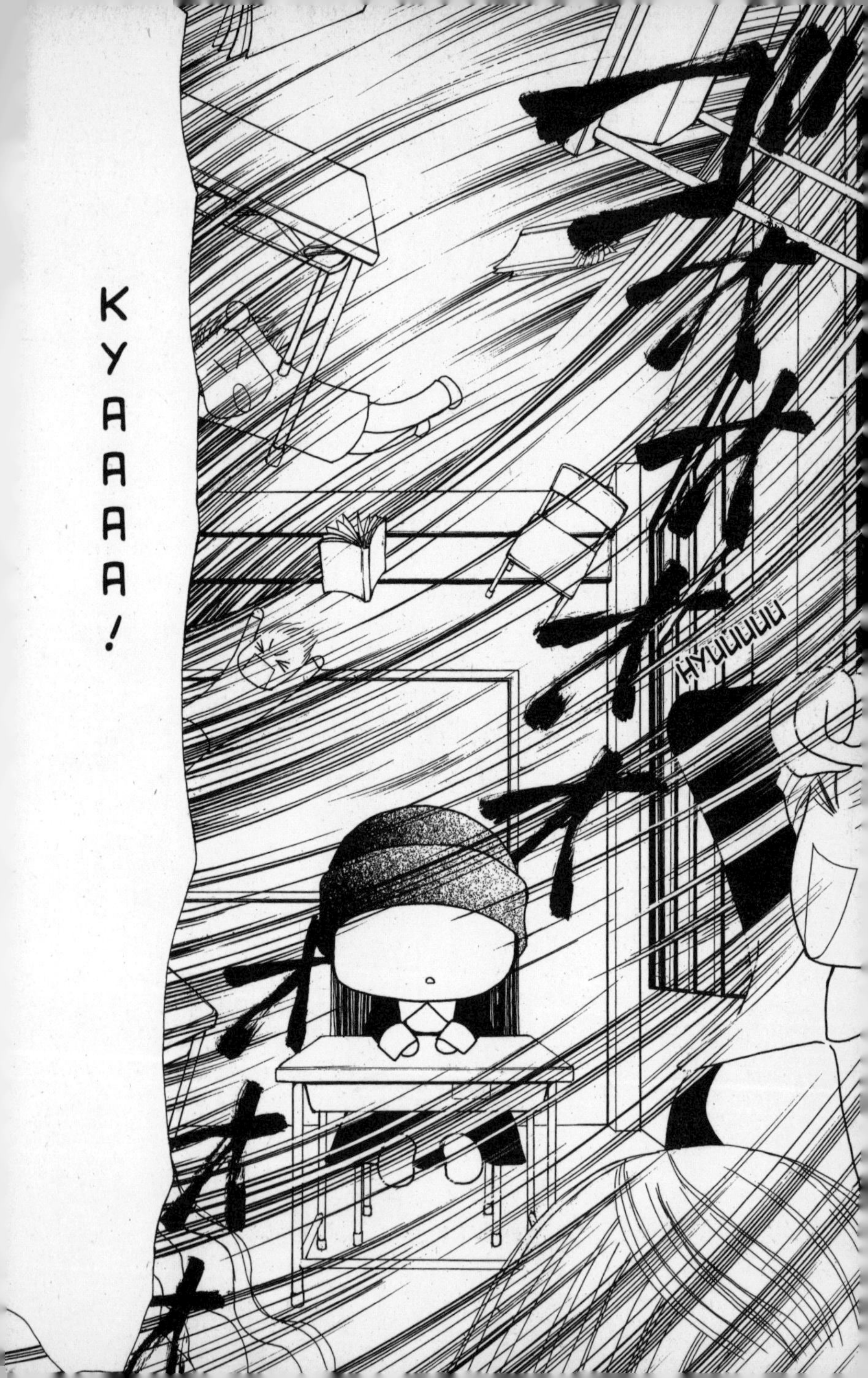
HYUUUUU
KYAAAAA!

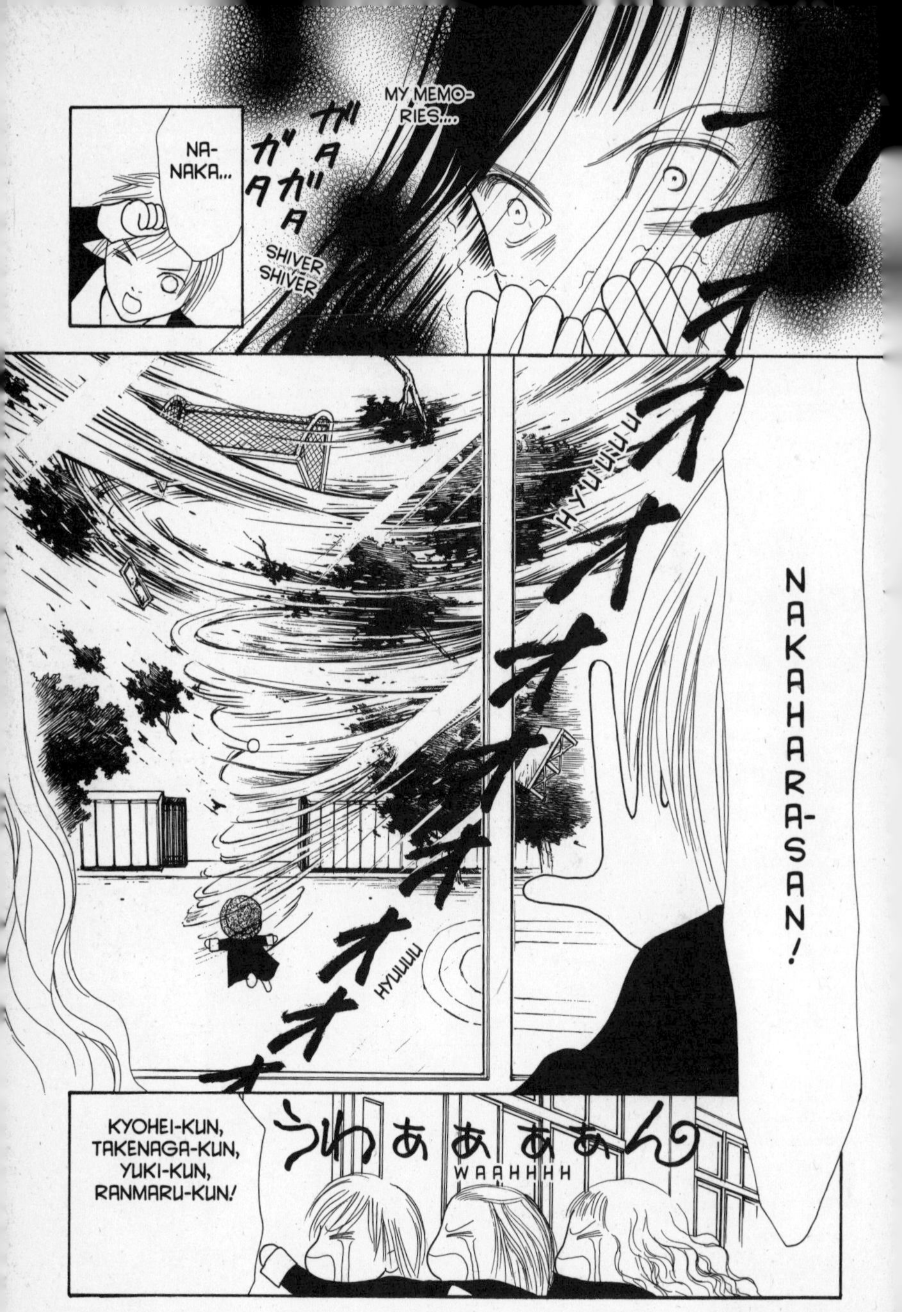
MY MEMORIES...
ガタガタガタ
SHIVER SHIVER
NA-NAKA...
NAKAHARA-SAN!
HYUUUUU
HYUUUU
うわあああああん
WAAHHHH
KYOHEI-KUN, TAKENAGA-KUN, YUKI-KUN, RANMARU-KUN!

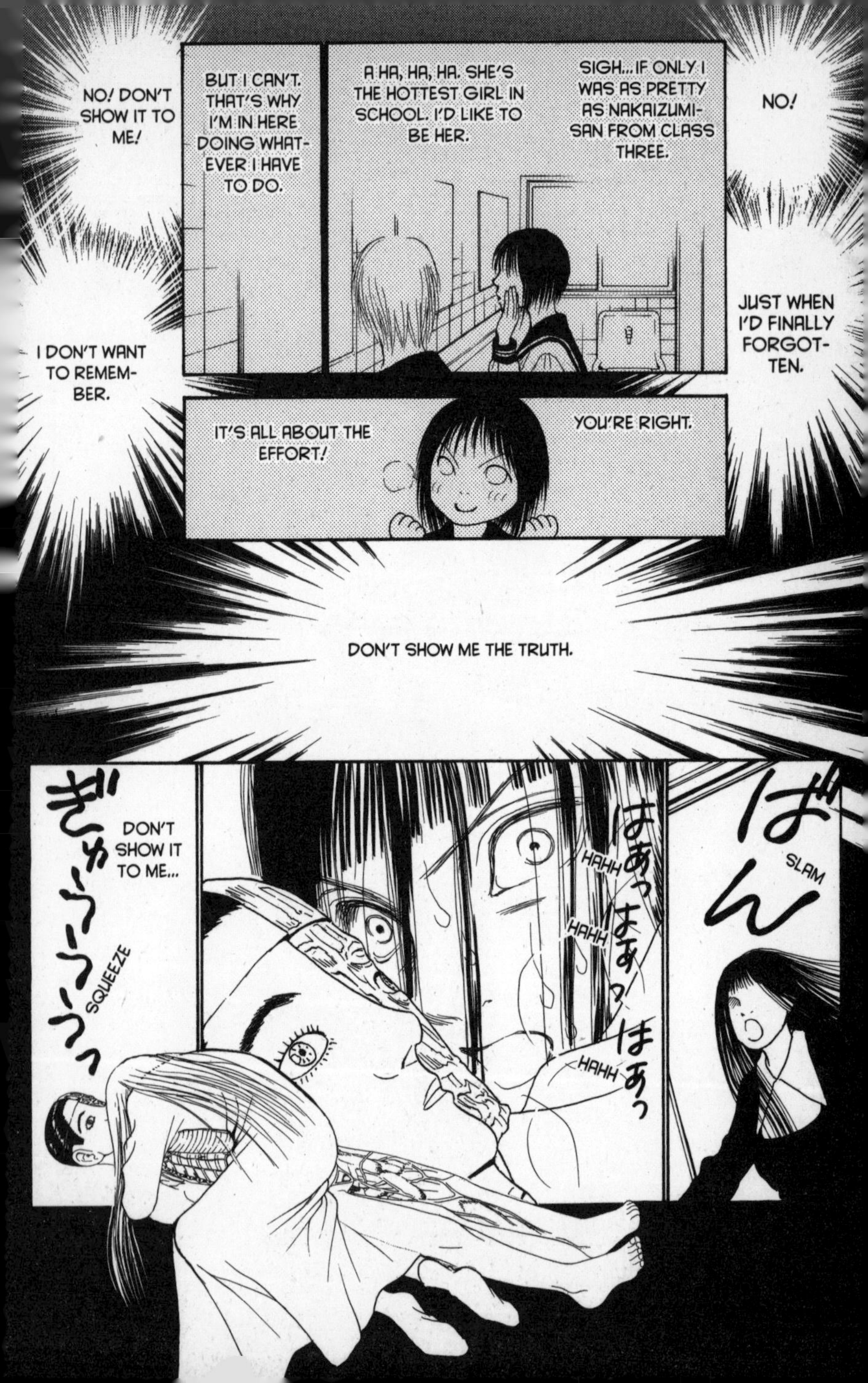
NO!
SIGH... IF ONLY I WAS AS PRETTY AS NAKAIZUMI-SAN FROM CLASS THREE.
A HA, HA, HA. SHE'S THE HOTTEST GIRL IN SCHOOL. I'D LIKE TO BE HER.
BUT I CAN'T. THAT'S WHY I'M IN HERE DOING WHATEVER I HAVE TO DO.
NO! DON'T SHOW IT TO ME!
JUST WHEN I'D FINALLY FORGOTTEN.
YOU'RE RIGHT.
IT'S ALL ABOUT THE EFFORT!
I DON'T WANT TO REMEMBER.
DON'T SHOW ME THE TRUTH.
SLAM
HAHH
HAHH
HAHH
DON'T SHOW IT TO ME...
SQUEEZE

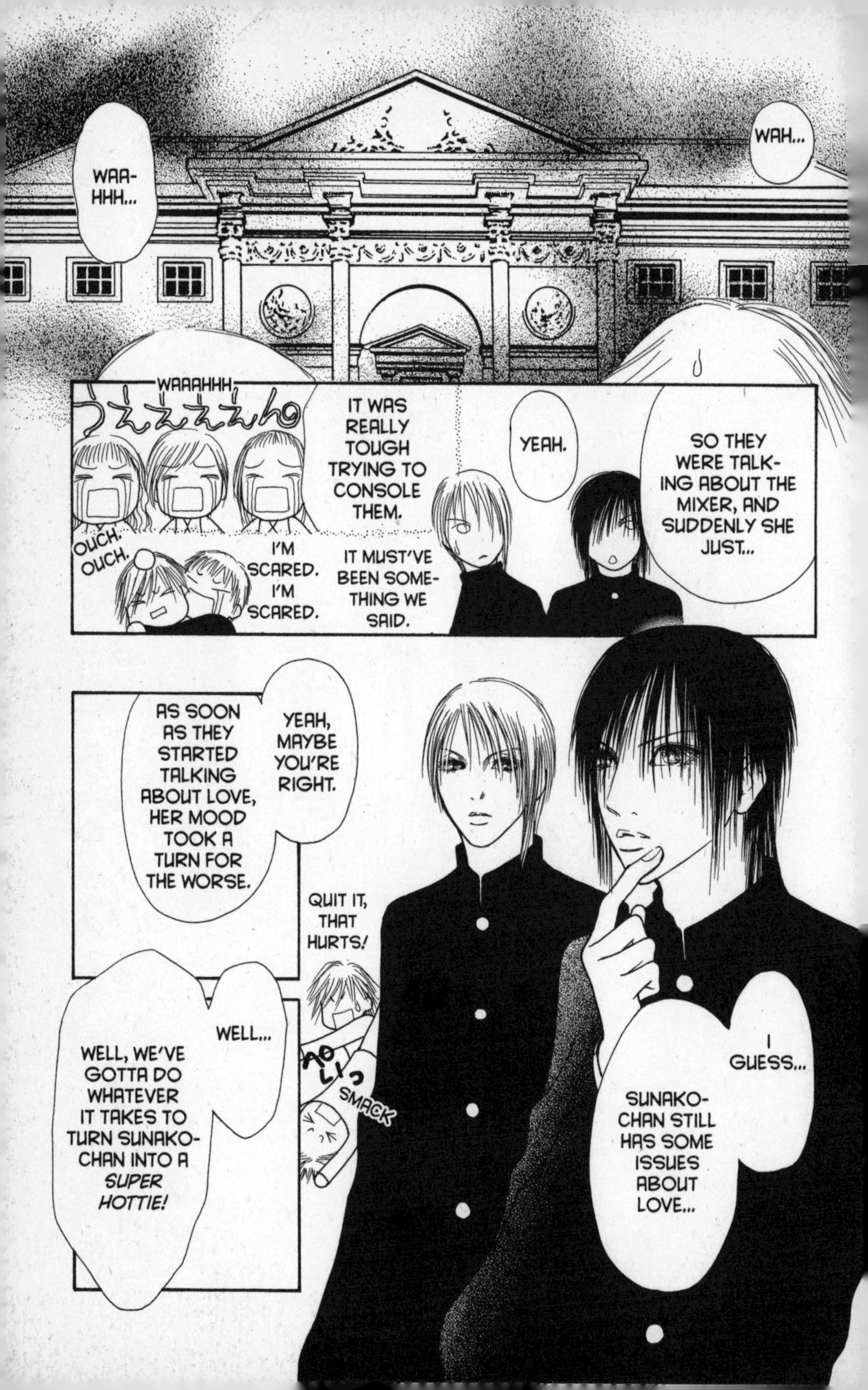
WAH...
WAA-HHH...
SO THEY WERE TALK-ING ABOUT THE MIXER, AND SUDDENLY SHE JUST...
YEAH.
IT WAS REALLY TOUGH TRYING TO CONSOLE THEM.
IT MUST'VE BEEN SOME-THING WE SAID.
WAAAHHH
I'M SCARED. I'M SCARED.
OUCH. OUCH.
I GUESS...
SUNAKO-CHAN STILL HAS SOME ISSUES ABOUT LOVE...
YEAH, MAYBE YOU'RE RIGHT.
AS SOON AS THEY STARTED TALKING ABOUT LOVE, HER MOOD TOOK A TURN FOR THE WORSE.
QUIT IT, THAT HURTS!
SMACK
WELL...
WELL, WE'VE GOTTA DO WHATEVER IT TAKES TO TURN SUNAKO-CHAN INTO A *SUPER HOTTIE!*

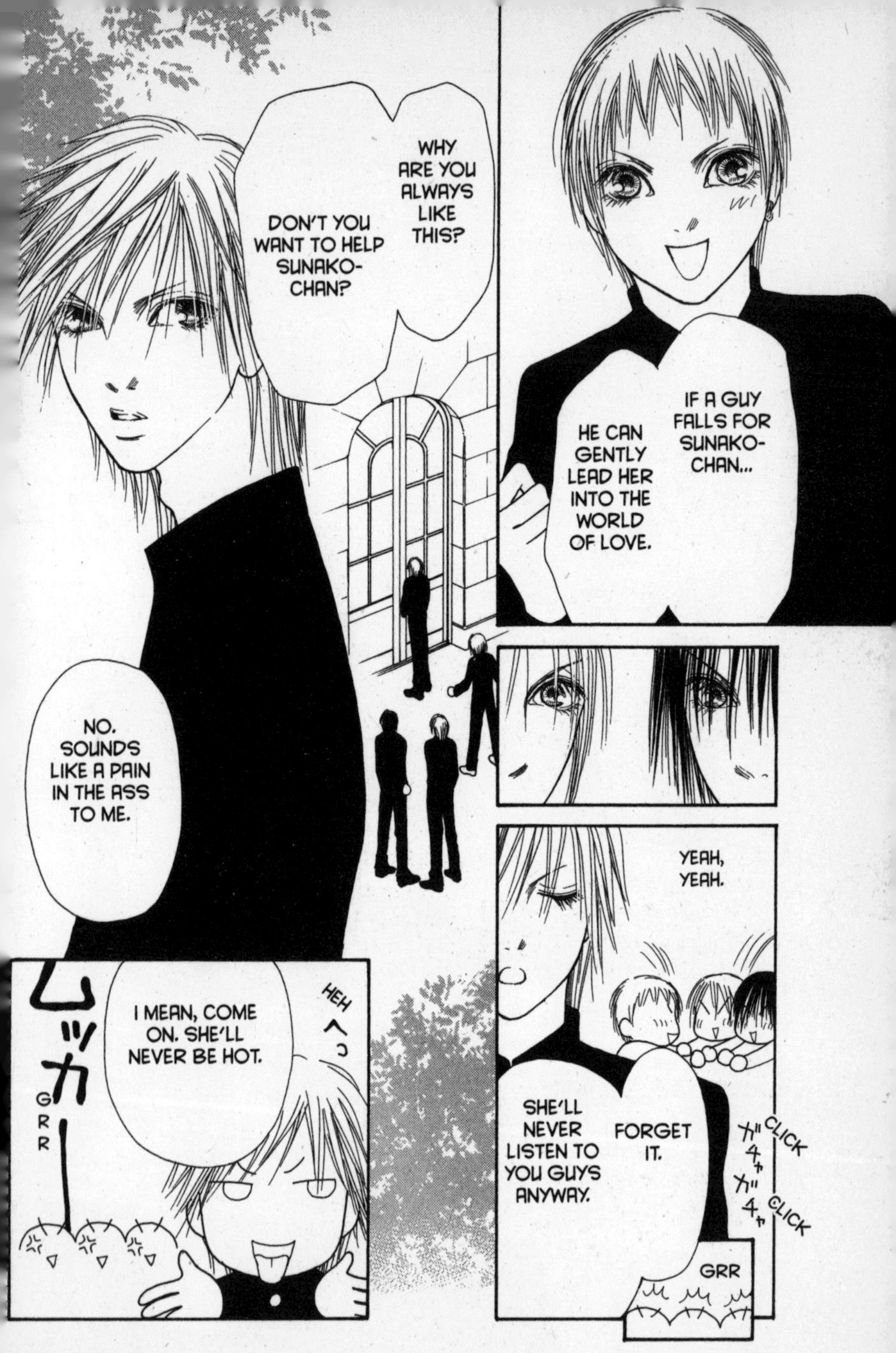
IF A GUY FALLS FOR SUNAKO-CHAN...
HE CAN GENTLY LEAD HER INTO THE WORLD OF LOVE.
YEAH, YEAH.
FORGET IT.
SHE'LL NEVER LISTEN TO YOU GUYS ANYWAY.
ガチャガチャ
CLICK
CLICK
GRR
WHY ARE YOU ALWAYS LIKE THIS?
DON'T YOU WANT TO HELP SUNAKO-CHAN?
NO. SOUNDS LIKE A PAIN IN THE ASS TO ME.
HEH
へっ
I MEAN, COME ON. SHE'LL NEVER BE HOT.
ムッカー
GRR

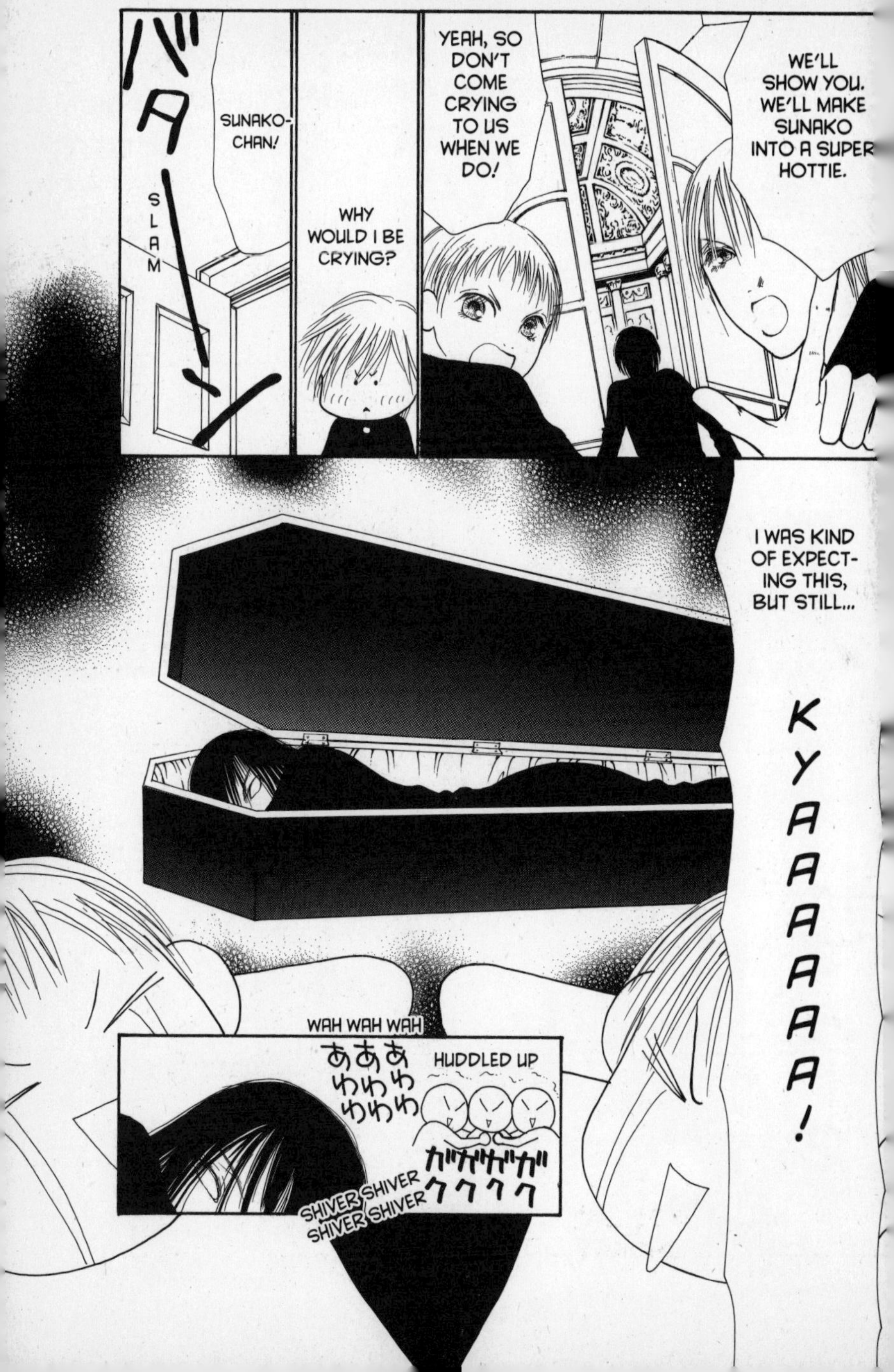

WE'LL SHOW YOU. WE'LL MAKE SUNAKO INTO A SUPER HOTTIE.
YEAH, SO DON'T COME CRYING TO US WHEN WE DO!
WHY WOULD I BE CRYING?
SUNAKO-CHAN!
バタン
SLAM
I WAS KIND OF EXPECTING THIS, BUT STILL...
KYAAAAAAA!
WAH WAH WAH
あああ
わわわ
わわわ
HUDDLED UP
ガガガガ
クククク
SHIVER SHIVER
SHIVER SHIVER

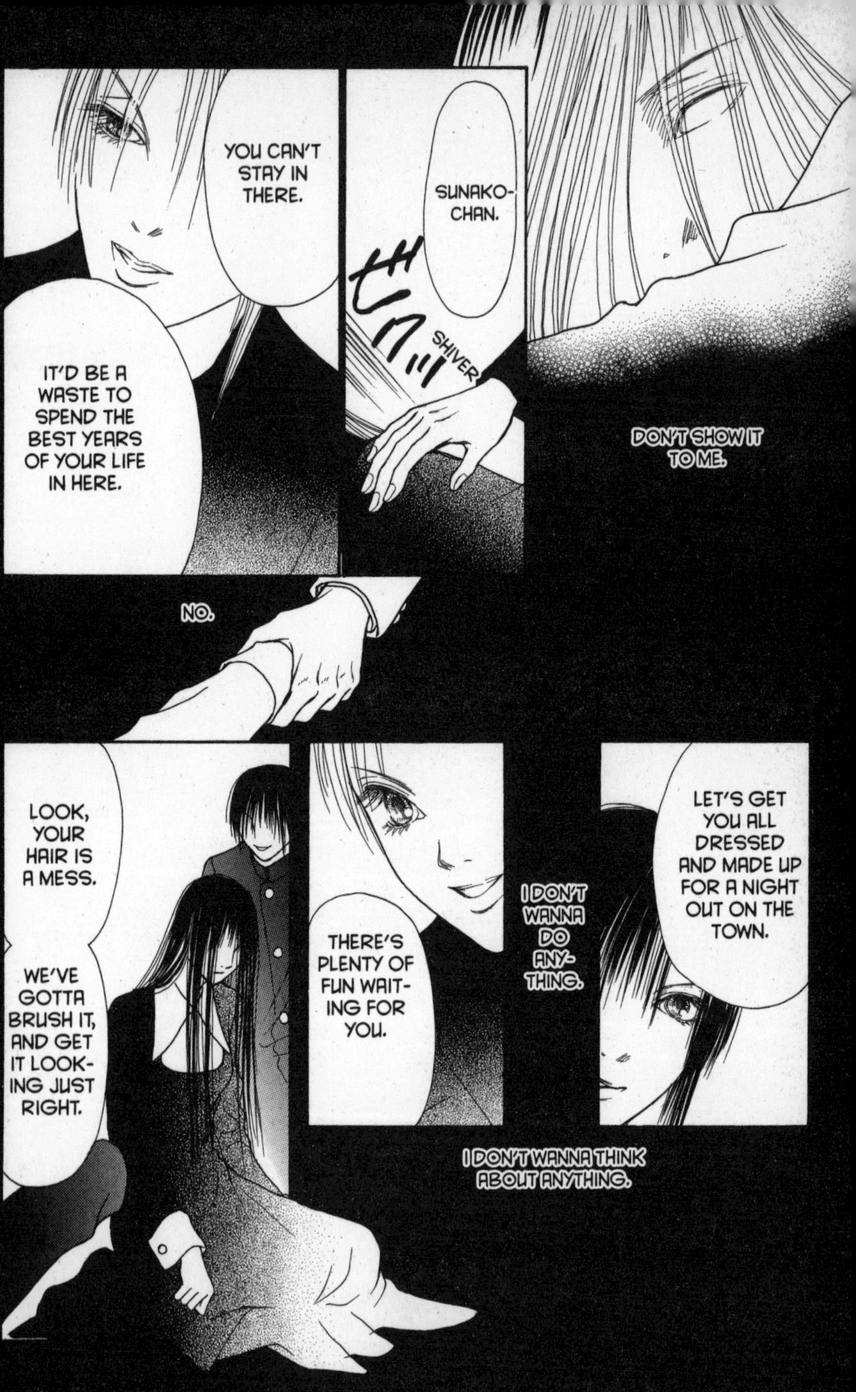
DON'T SHOW IT TO ME.
SUNAKO-CHAN.
SHIVER
YOU CAN'T STAY IN THERE.
IT'D BE A WASTE TO SPEND THE BEST YEARS OF YOUR LIFE IN HERE.
NO.
LET'S GET YOU ALL DRESSED AND MADE UP FOR A NIGHT OUT ON THE TOWN.
I DON'T WANNA DO ANY-THING.
THERE'S PLENTY OF FUN WAIT-ING FOR YOU.
LOOK, YOUR HAIR IS A MESS.
WE'VE GOTTA BRUSH IT, AND GET IT LOOK-ING JUST RIGHT.
I DON'T WANNA THINK ABOUT ANYTHING.

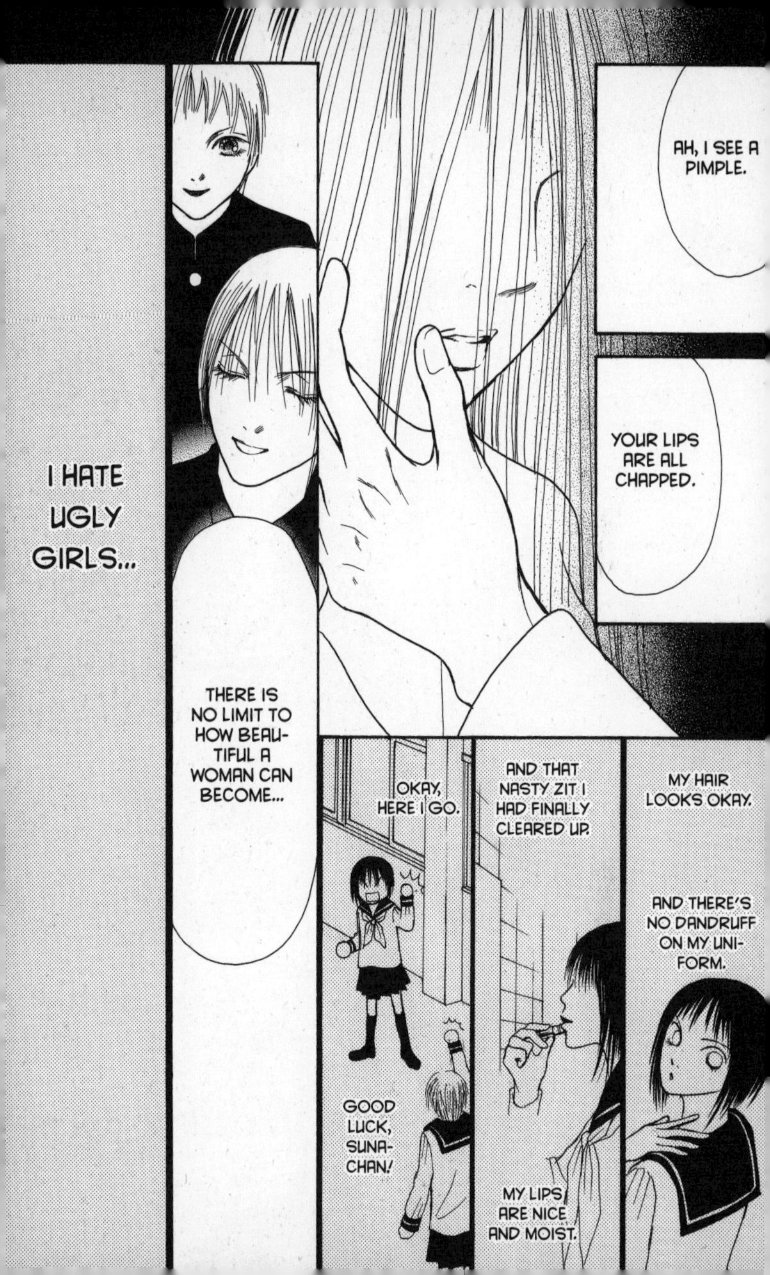
AH, I SEE A PIMPLE.
YOUR LIPS ARE ALL CHAPPED.
MY HAIR LOOKS OKAY.
AND THERE'S NO DANDRUFF ON MY UNI-FORM.
AND THAT NASTY ZIT I HAD FINALLY CLEARED UP.
MY LIPS ARE NICE AND MOIST.
OKAY, HERE I GO.
GOOD LUCK, SUNA-CHAN!
THERE IS NO LIMIT TO HOW BEAU-TIFUL A WOMAN CAN BECOME...
I HATE UGLY GIRLS...

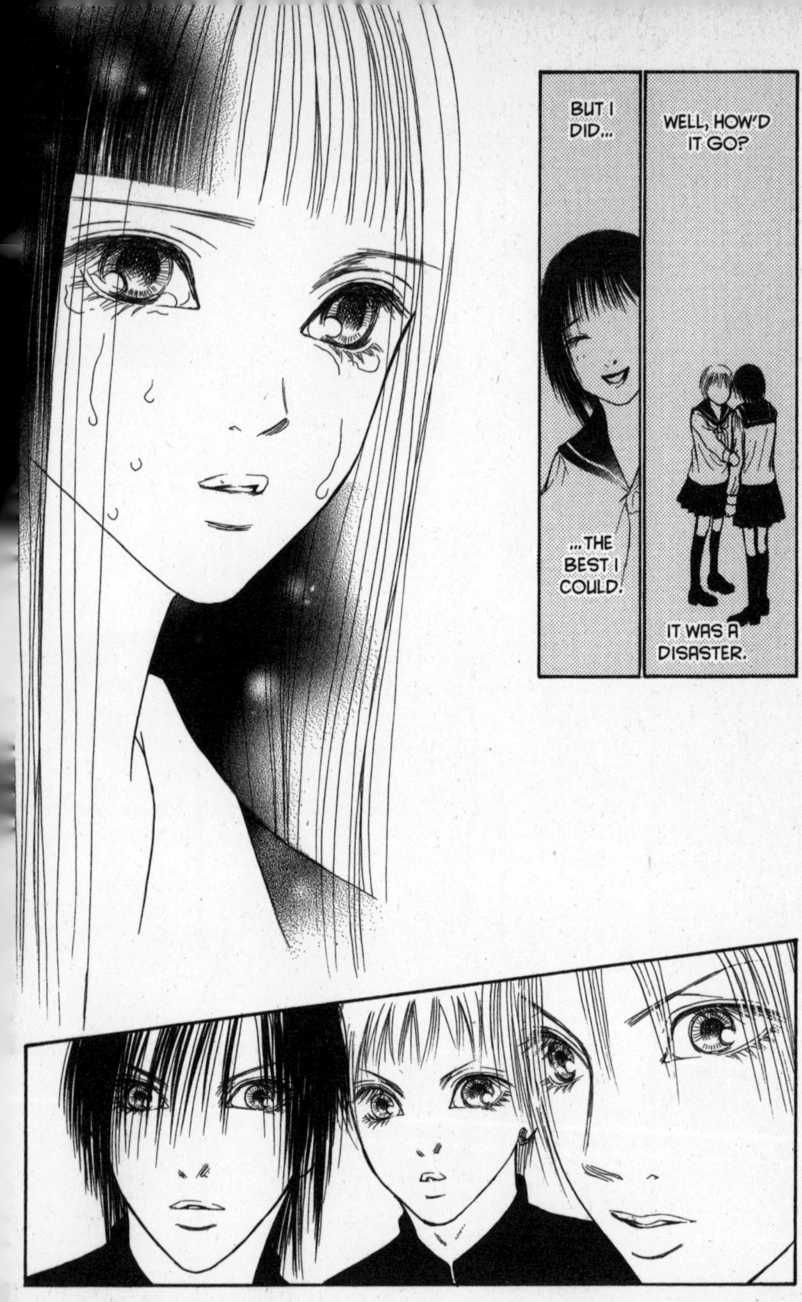
WELL, HOW'D IT GO?
IT WAS A DISASTER.
BUT I DID...
...THE BEST I COULD.

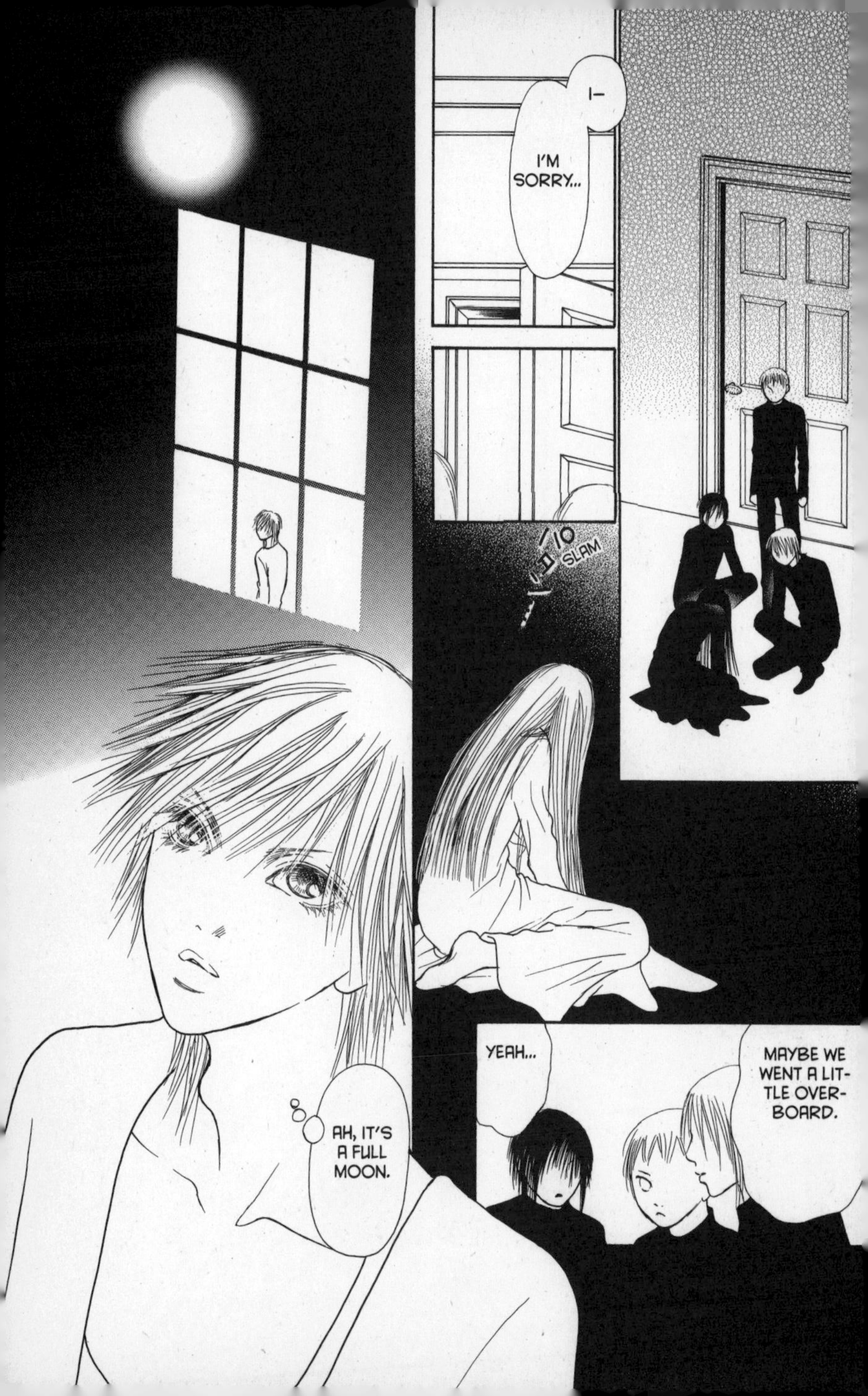
I—
I'M SORRY...
SLAM
MAYBE WE WENT A LITTLE OVERBOARD.
YEAH...
AH, IT'S A FULL MOON.

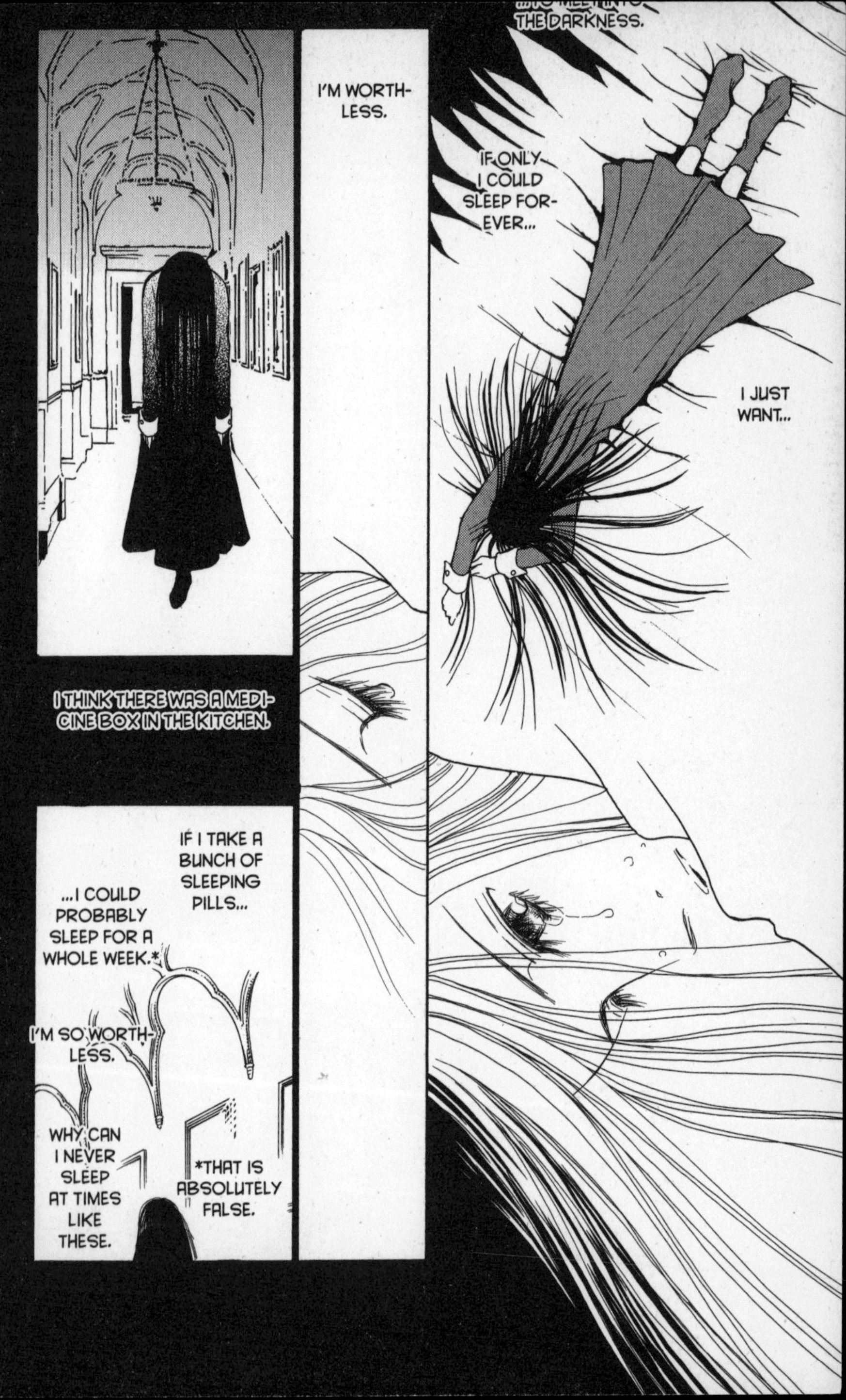
THE DARKNESS.
IF ONLY I COULD SLEEP FOR-EVER...
I JUST WANT...
I'M WORTH-LESS.
I THINK THERE WAS A MEDI-CINE BOX IN THE KITCHEN.
IF I TAKE A BUNCH OF SLEEPING PILLS...
...I COULD PROBABLY SLEEP FOR A WHOLE WEEK.*
I'M SO WORTH-LESS.
WHY CAN I NEVER SLEEP AT TIMES LIKE THESE.
*THAT IS ABSOLUTELY FALSE.

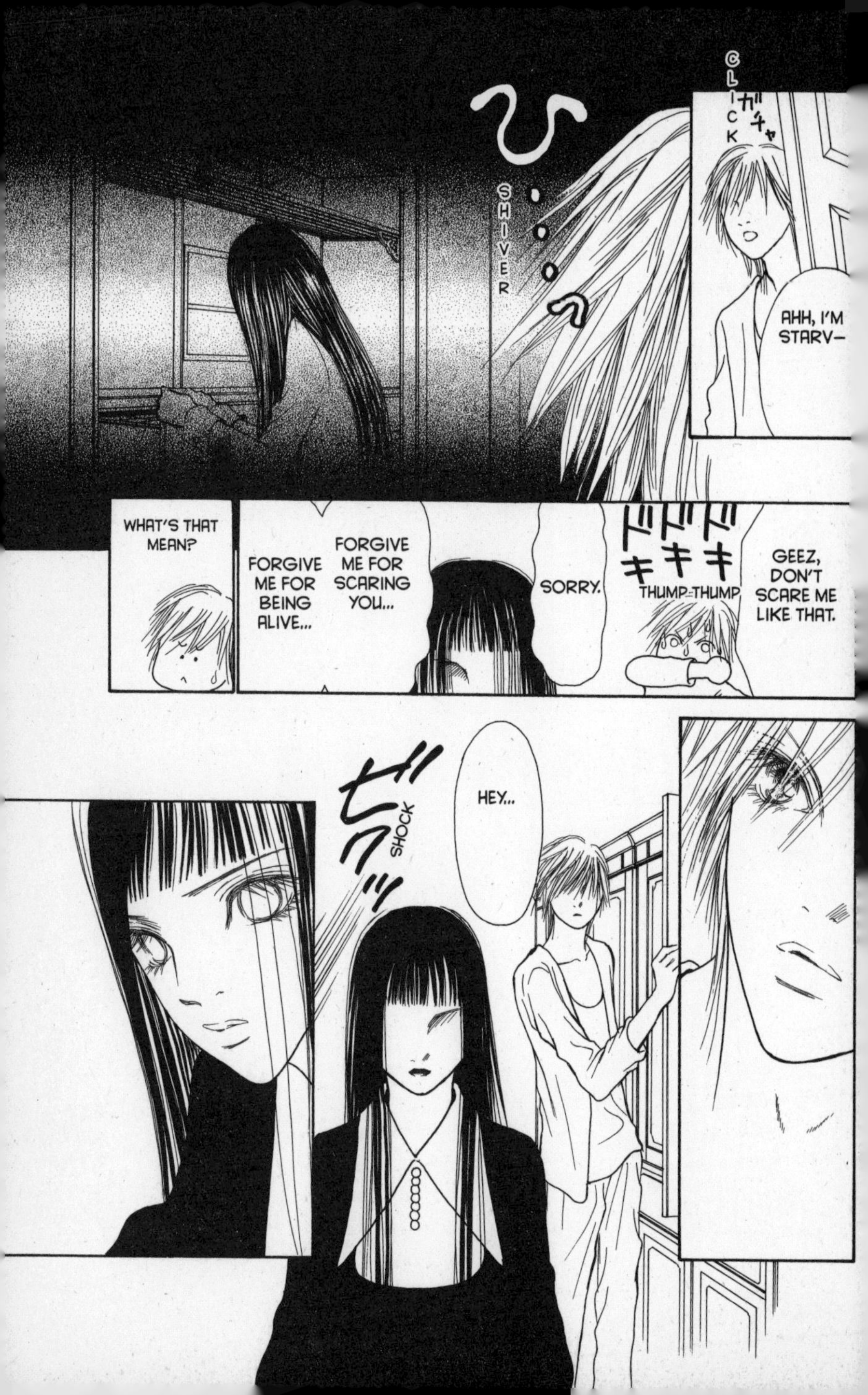
CLICK
ガチャ
AHH, I'M STARV—
SHIVER
GEEZ, DON'T SCARE ME LIKE THAT.
ドドド
キキキ
THUMP-THUMP
SORRY.
FORGIVE ME FOR SCARING YOU...
FORGIVE ME FOR BEING ALIVE...
WHAT'S THAT MEAN?
HEY...
SHOCK

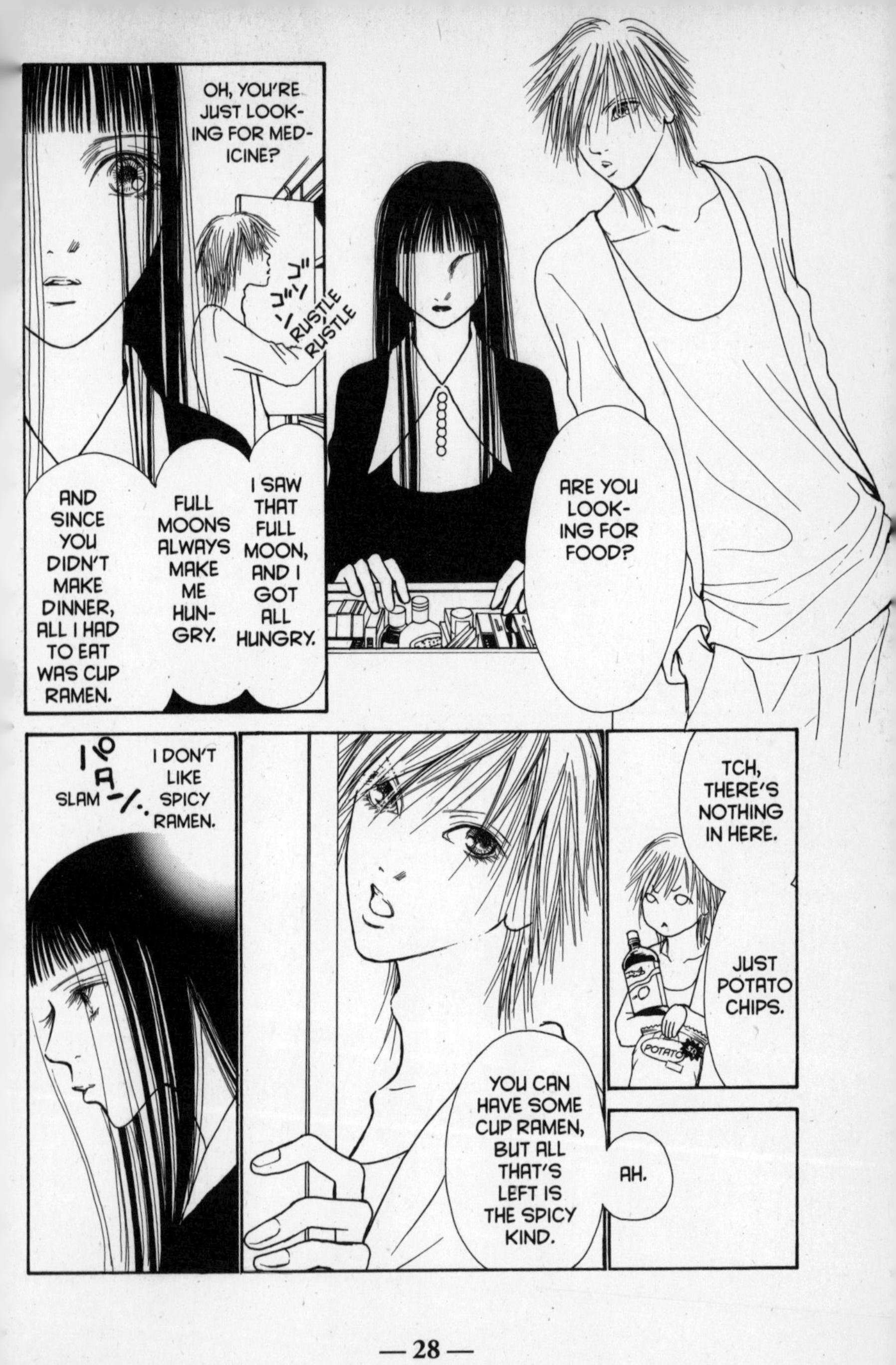
ARE YOU LOOKING FOR FOOD?
OH, YOU'RE JUST LOOKING FOR MEDICINE?
RUSTLE RUSTLE
I SAW THAT FULL MOON, AND I GOT ALL HUNGRY.
FULL MOONS ALWAYS MAKE ME HUNGRY.
AND SINCE YOU DIDN'T MAKE DINNER, ALL I HAD TO EAT WAS CUP RAMEN.
TCH, THERE'S NOTHING IN HERE.
JUST POTATO CHIPS.
POTATO
AH.
YOU CAN HAVE SOME CUP RAMEN, BUT ALL THAT'S LEFT IS THE SPICY KIND.
SLAM
I DON'T LIKE SPICY RAMEN.

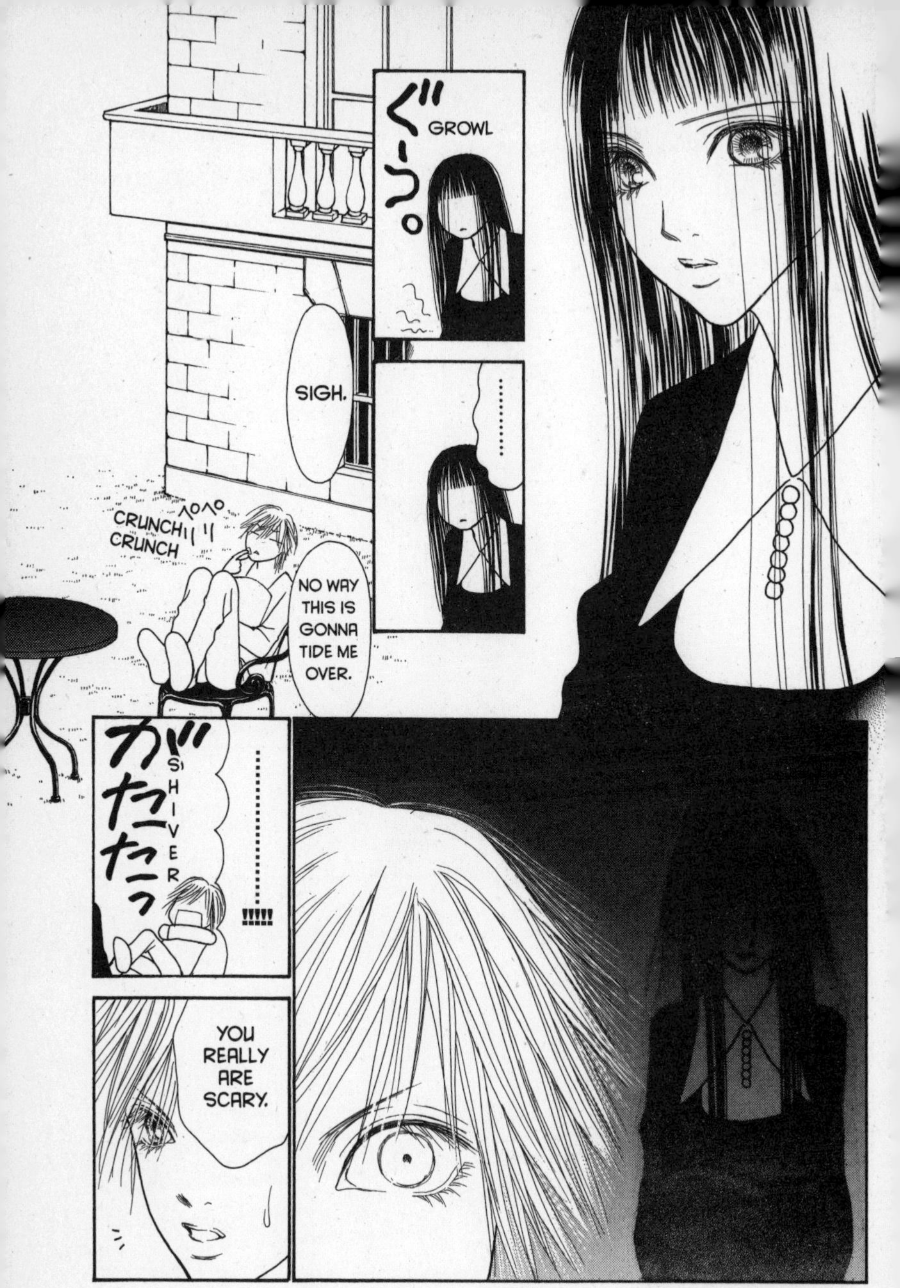

ぐぅ。
GROWL
......
SIGH.
CRUNCH CRUNCH
NO WAY THIS IS GONNA TIDE ME OVER.
がたたっ
SHIVER
......
!!!!!
YOU REALLY ARE SCARY.

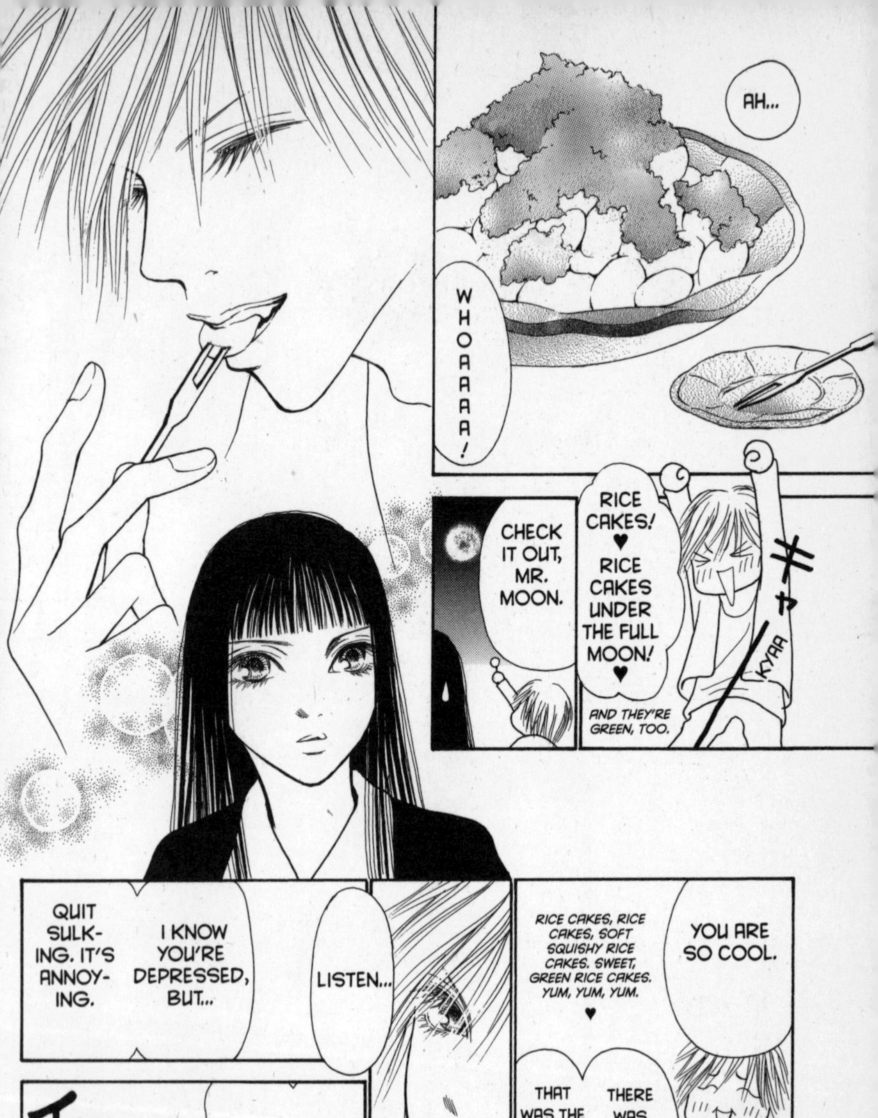
AH...
WHOAAAAA!
RICE CAKES! ♥ RICE CAKES UNDER THE FULL MOON! ♥
キャ KYAA
AND THEY'RE GREEN, TOO.
CHECK IT OUT, MR. MOON.
YOU ARE SO COOL.
RICE CAKES, RICE CAKES, SOFT SQUISHY RICE CAKES. SWEET, GREEN RICE CAKES. YUM, YUM, YUM. ♥
THERE WAS NOTHING IN THE CUPBOARD.
THAT WAS THE BEST I COULD DO.
NO SWEET BEANS OR ANYTHING.
LISTEN...
むぐ CHOMP
I KNOW YOU'RE DEPRESSED, BUT...
QUIT SULKING. IT'S ANNOYING.
EXCUSE ME FOR SULKING
EXCUSE ME FOR BEING ALIVE.
イラ〜〜ッ GRR

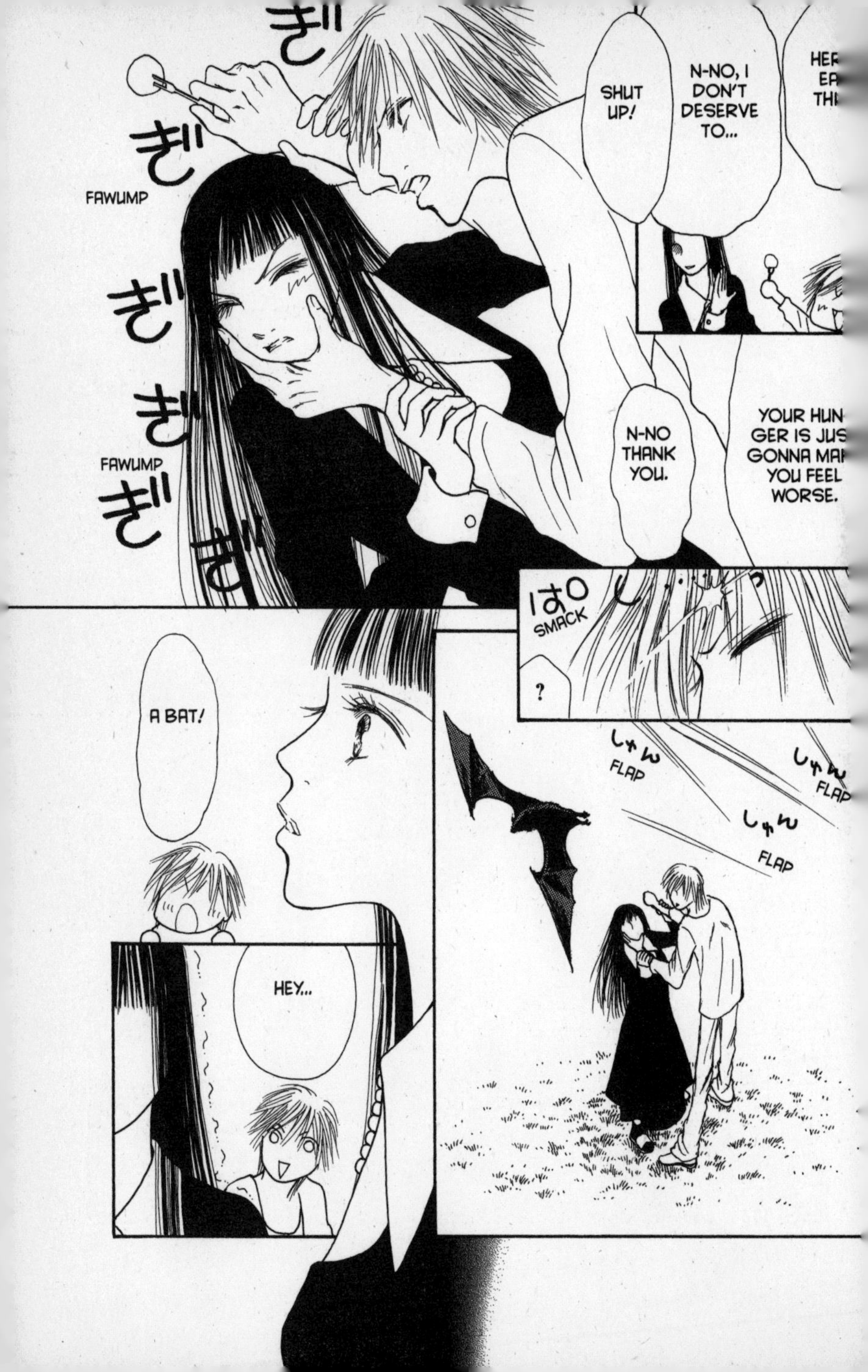
N-NO, I DON'T DESERVE TO...
SHUT UP!
YOUR HUN-GER IS JUS GONNA MA YOU FEEL WORSE.
N-NO THANK YOU.
ぎ
ぎ
FAWUMP
ぎ
ぎ
FAWUMP
ぎ
はっ
SMACK
?
しゅん
FLAP
しゅん
FLAP
しゅん
FLAP
A BAT!
HEY...

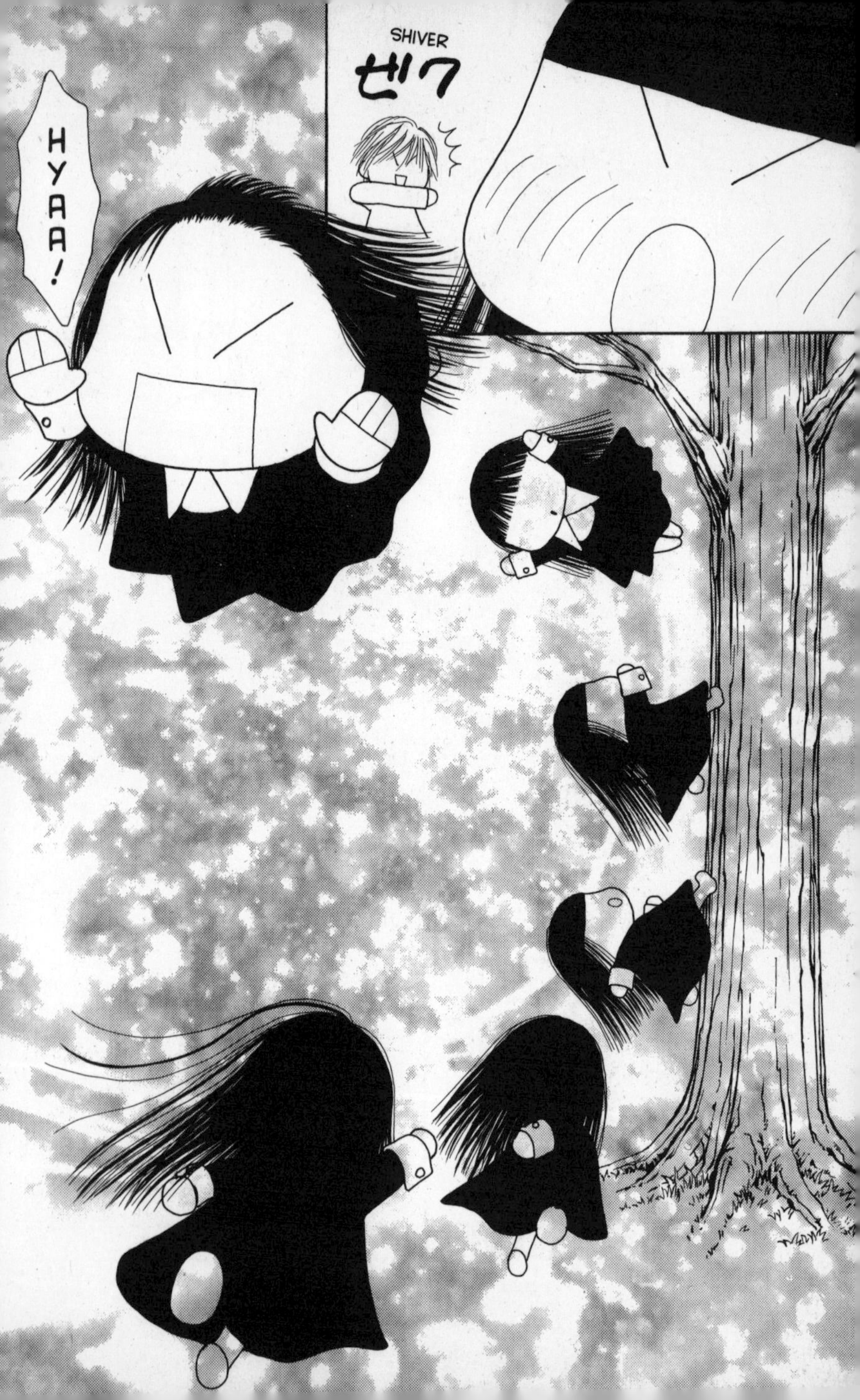
SHIVER
ゼワ
HYAA!

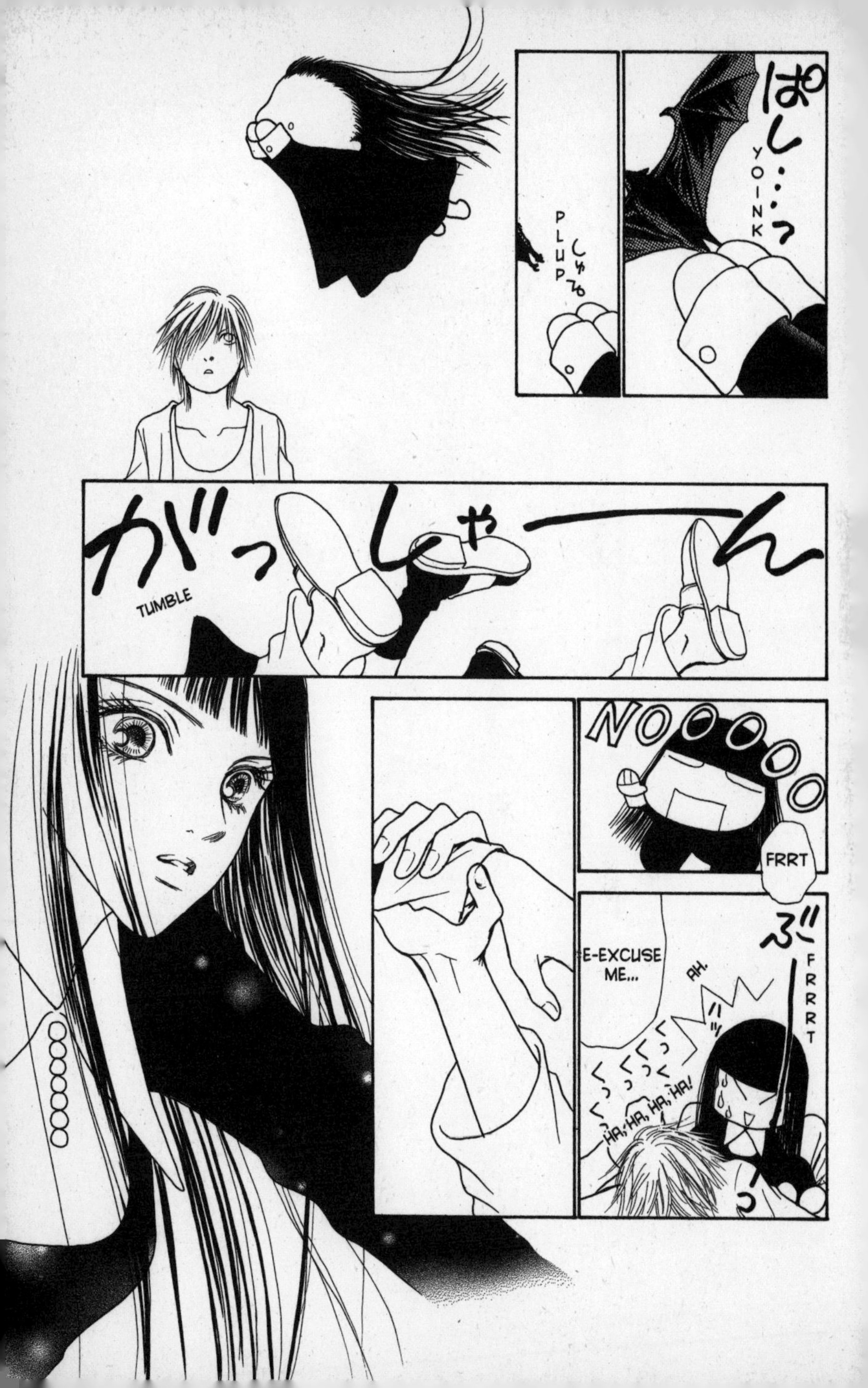
ぱし…っ
YOINK
しゅるっ
PLUP
がっしゃーーん
TUMBLE
NOOOOOO
FRRT
ぶ
FRRRT
ハッ
AH.
E-EXCUSE ME...
くっくっくっくっくっ
HA, HA, HA, HA!

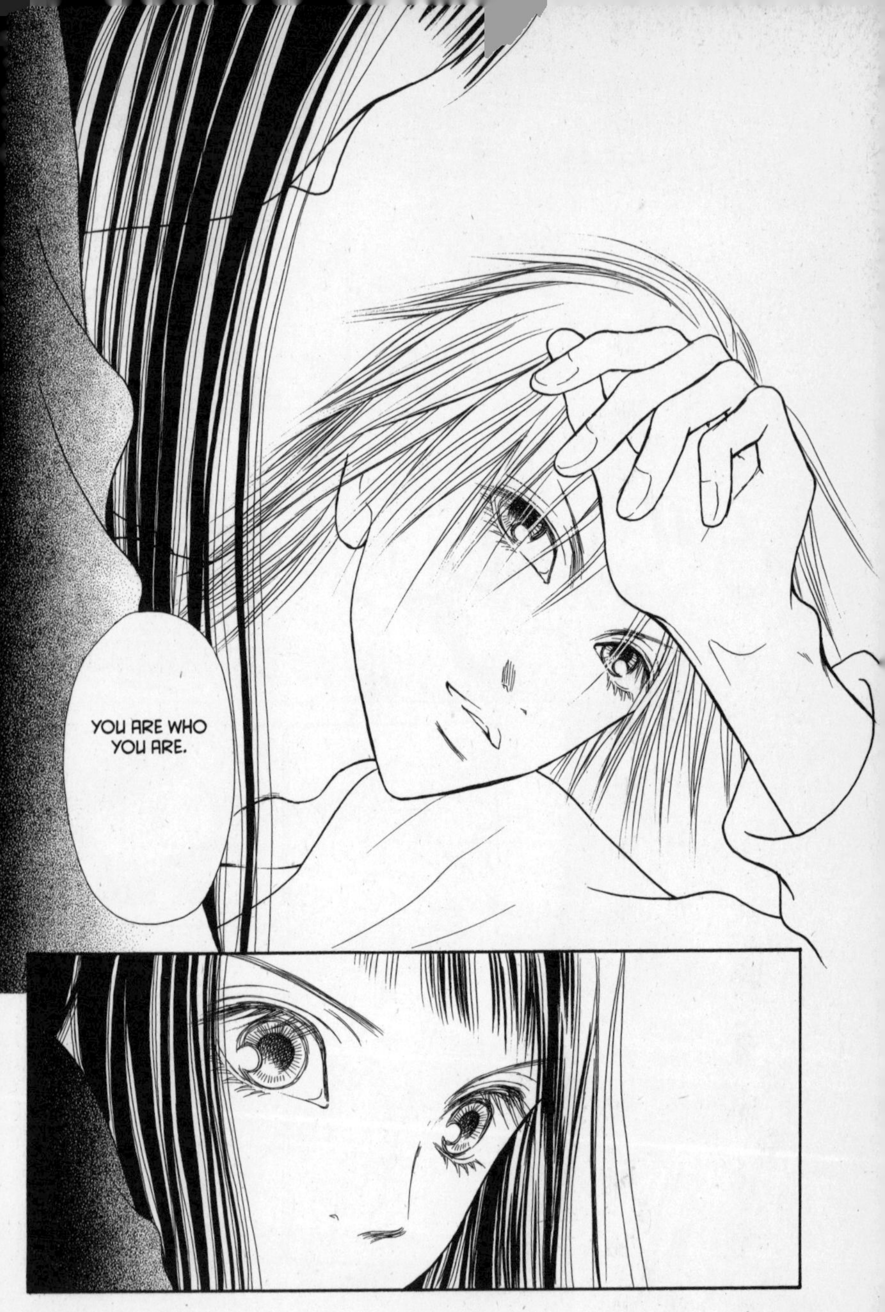
YOU ARE WHO YOU ARE.

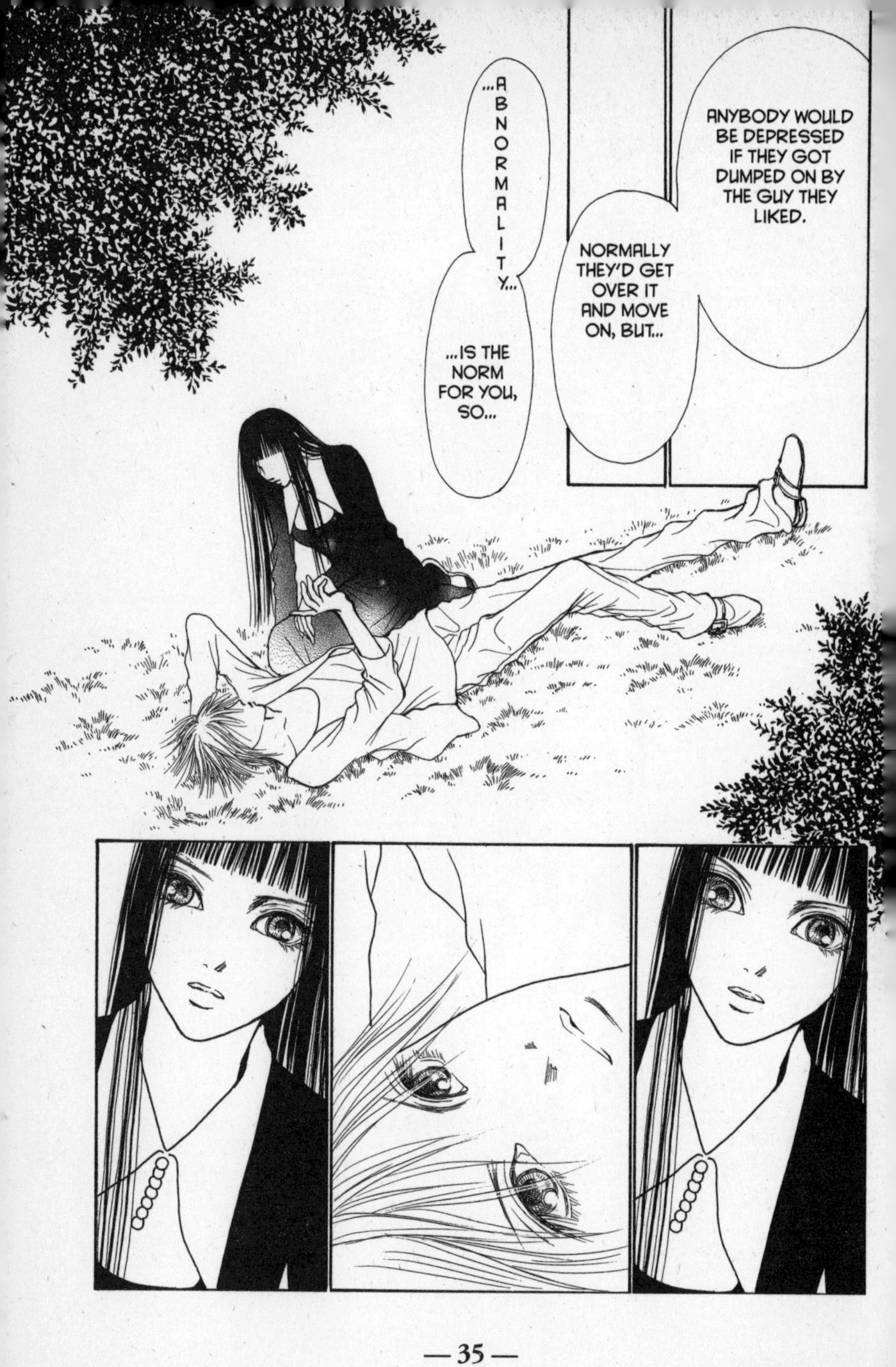
ANYBODY WOULD BE DEPRESSED IF THEY GOT DUMPED ON BY THE GUY THEY LIKED.
NORMALLY THEY'D GET OVER IT AND MOVE ON, BUT...
...ABNORMALITY...
...IS THE NORM FOR YOU, SO...

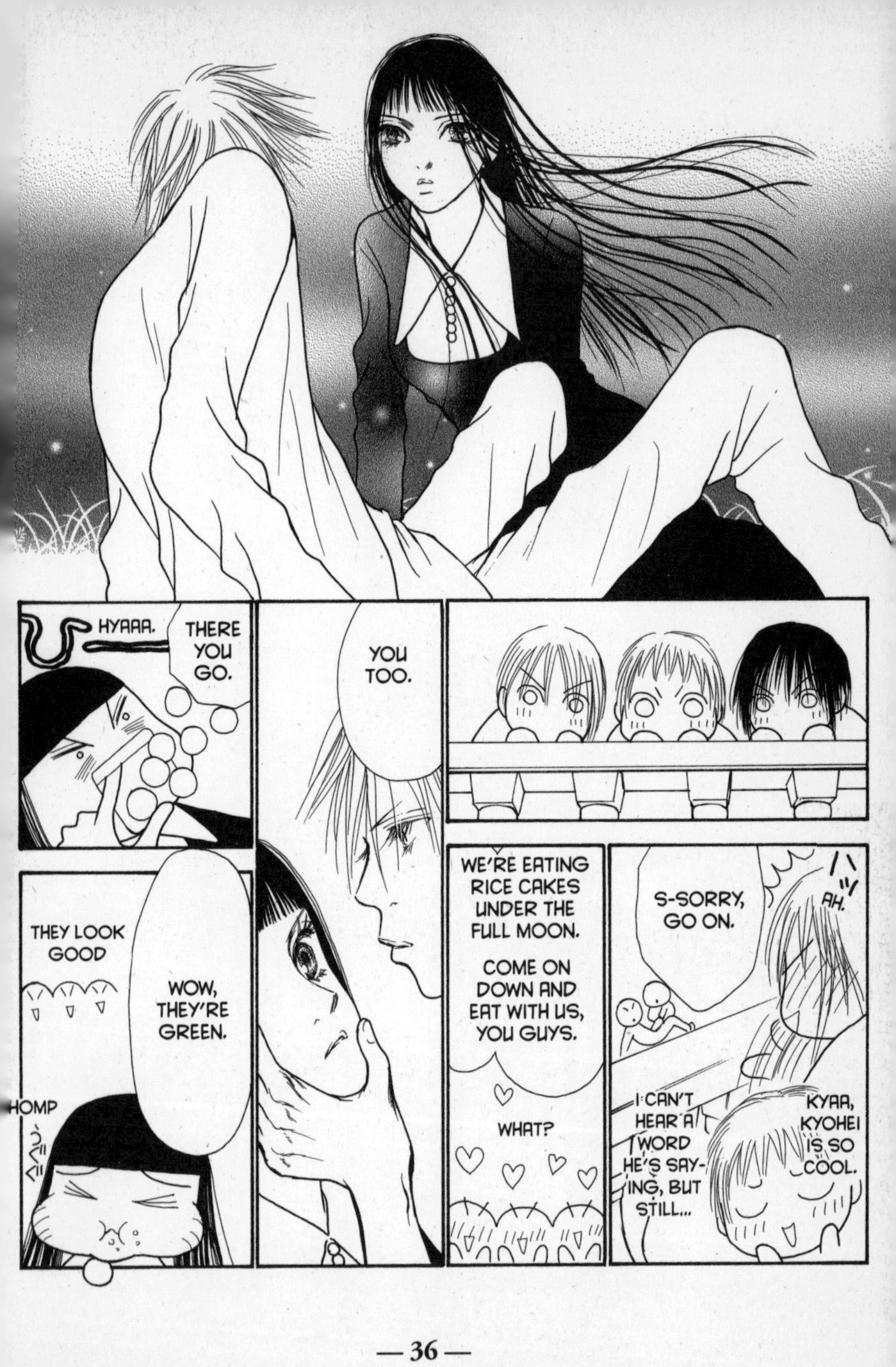
AH.
S-SORRY, GO ON.
KYAA, KYOHEI IS SO COOL.
I CAN'T HEAR A WORD HE'S SAY-ING, BUT STILL...
WE'RE EATING RICE CAKES UNDER THE FULL MOON.
COME ON DOWN AND EAT WITH US, YOU GUYS.
WHAT?
YOU TOO.
THERE YOU GO.
HYAAA.
WOW, THEY'RE GREEN.
THEY LOOK GOOD
HOMP

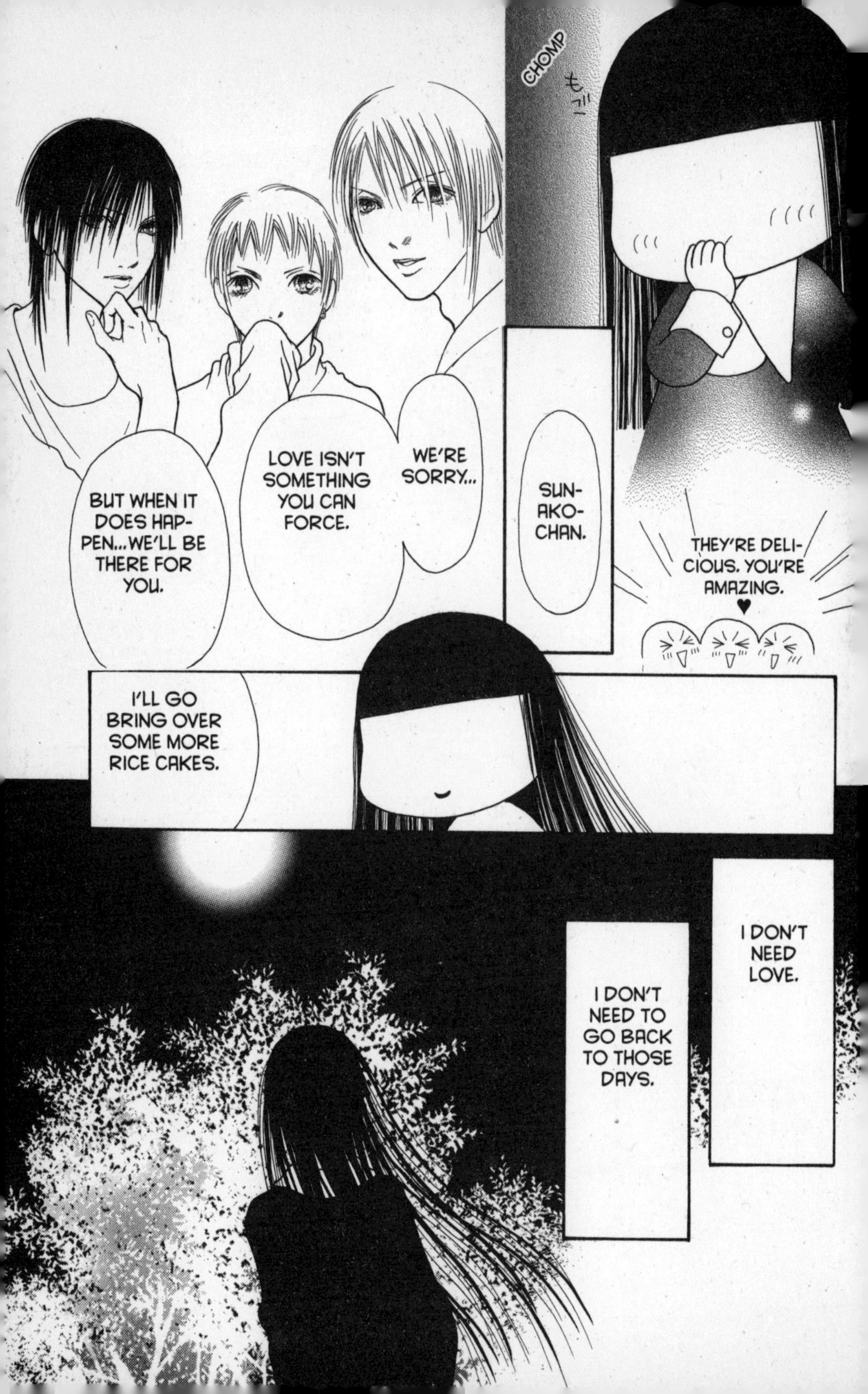
CHOMP
もご
THEY'RE DELICIOUS. YOU'RE AMAZING. ♥
SUN-AKO-CHAN.
WE'RE SORRY...
LOVE ISN'T SOMETHING YOU CAN FORCE.
BUT WHEN IT DOES HAP-PEN...WE'LL BE THERE FOR YOU.
I'LL GO BRING OVER SOME MORE RICE CAKES.
I DON'T NEED LOVE.
I DON'T NEED TO GO BACK TO THOSE DAYS.

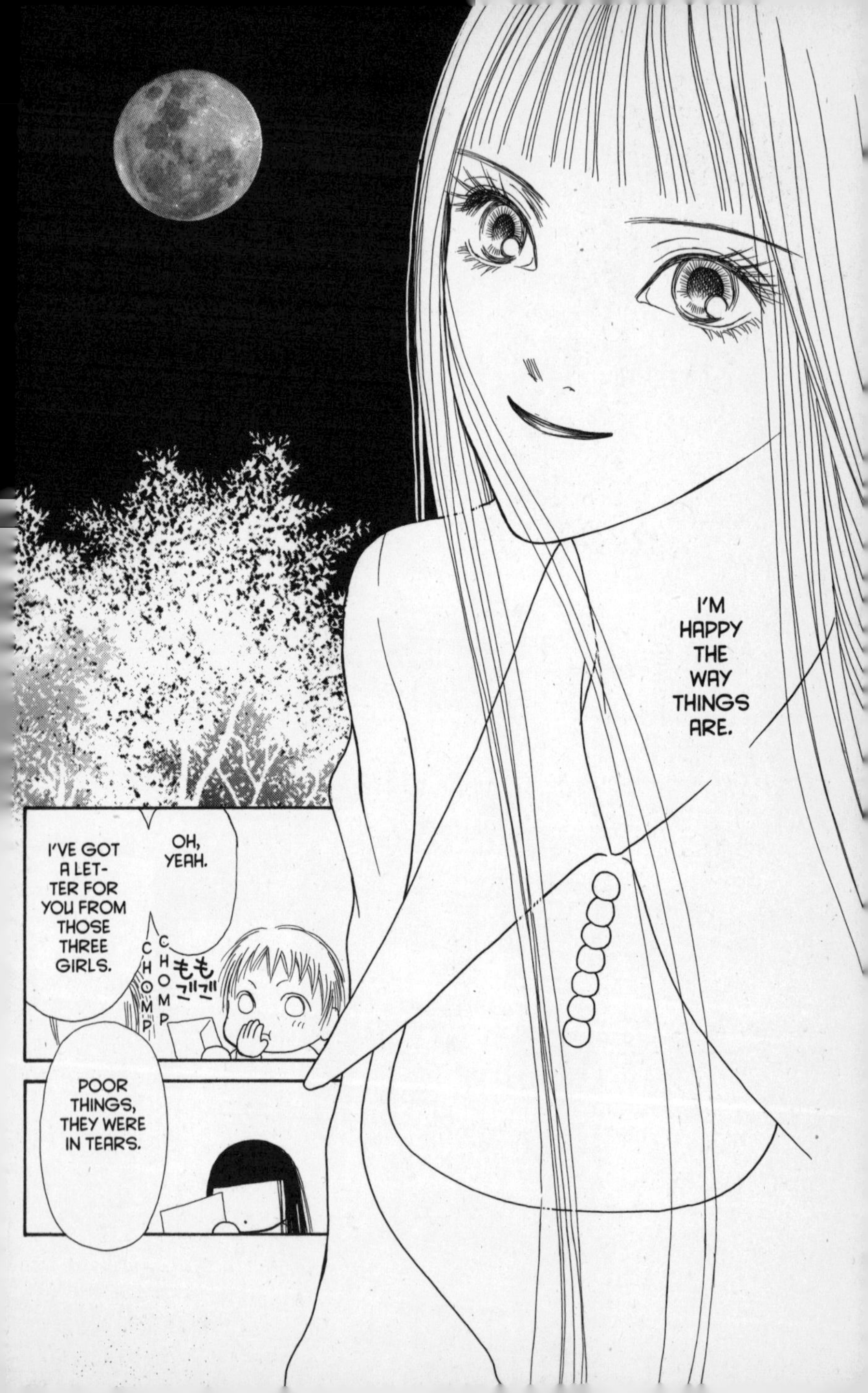
I'M HAPPY THE WAY THINGS ARE.
OH, YEAH.
I'VE GOT A LET-TER FOR YOU FROM THOSE THREE GIRLS.
CHOMP CHOMP
POOR THINGS, THEY WERE IN TEARS.

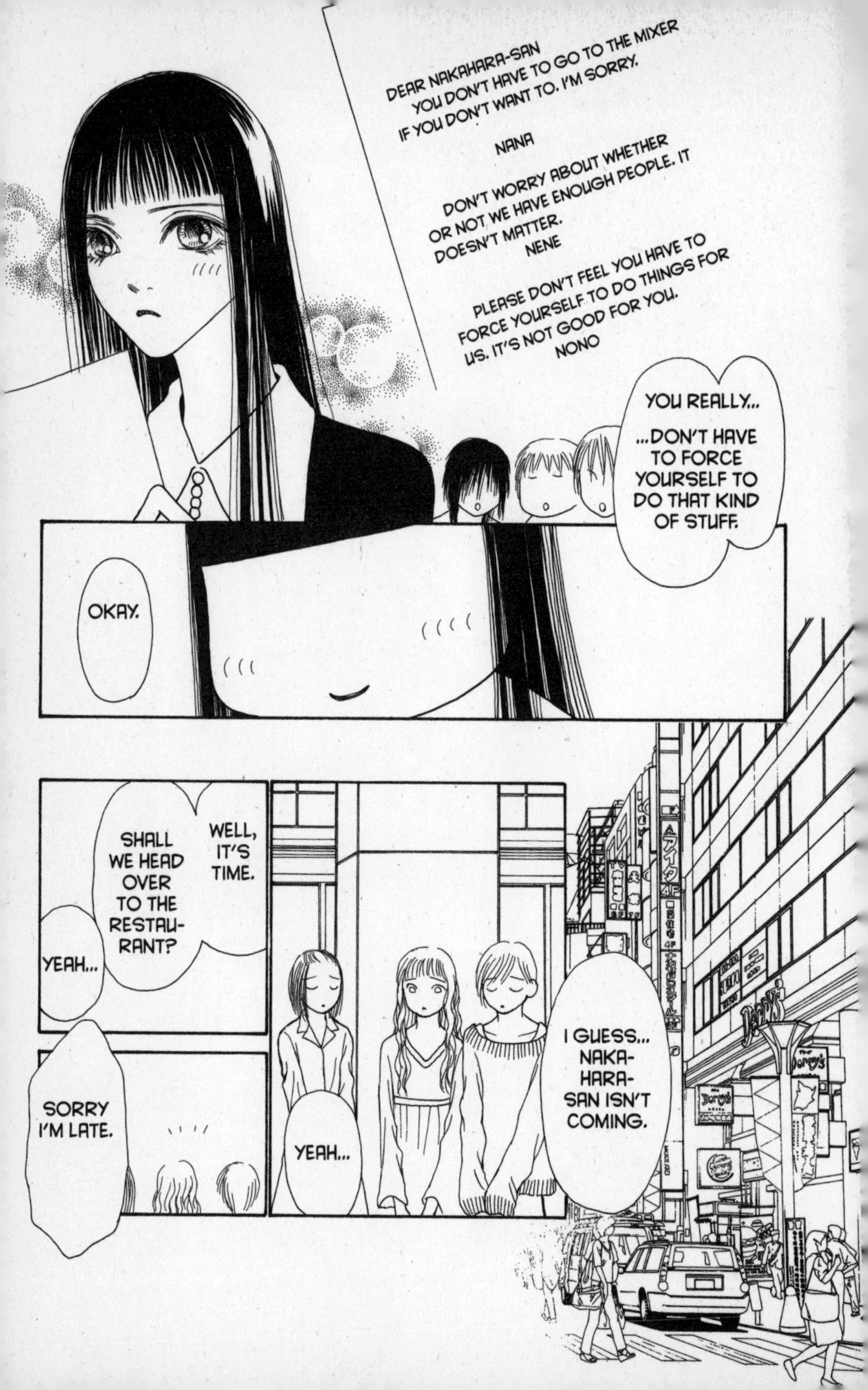
DEAR NAKAHARA-SAN
YOU DON'T HAVE TO GO TO THE MIXER IF YOU DON'T WANT TO. I'M SORRY.
NANA
DON'T WORRY ABOUT WHETHER OR NOT WE HAVE ENOUGH PEOPLE. IT DOESN'T MATTER.
NENE
PLEASE DON'T FEEL YOU HAVE TO FORCE YOURSELF TO DO THINGS FOR US. IT'S NOT GOOD FOR YOU.
NONO
YOU REALLY... ...DON'T HAVE TO FORCE YOURSELF TO DO THAT KIND OF STUFF.
OKAY.
I GUESS... NAKA-HARA-SAN ISN'T COMING.
YEAH...
WELL, IT'S TIME.
SHALL WE HEAD OVER TO THE RESTAU-RANT?
YEAH...
SORRY I'M LATE.

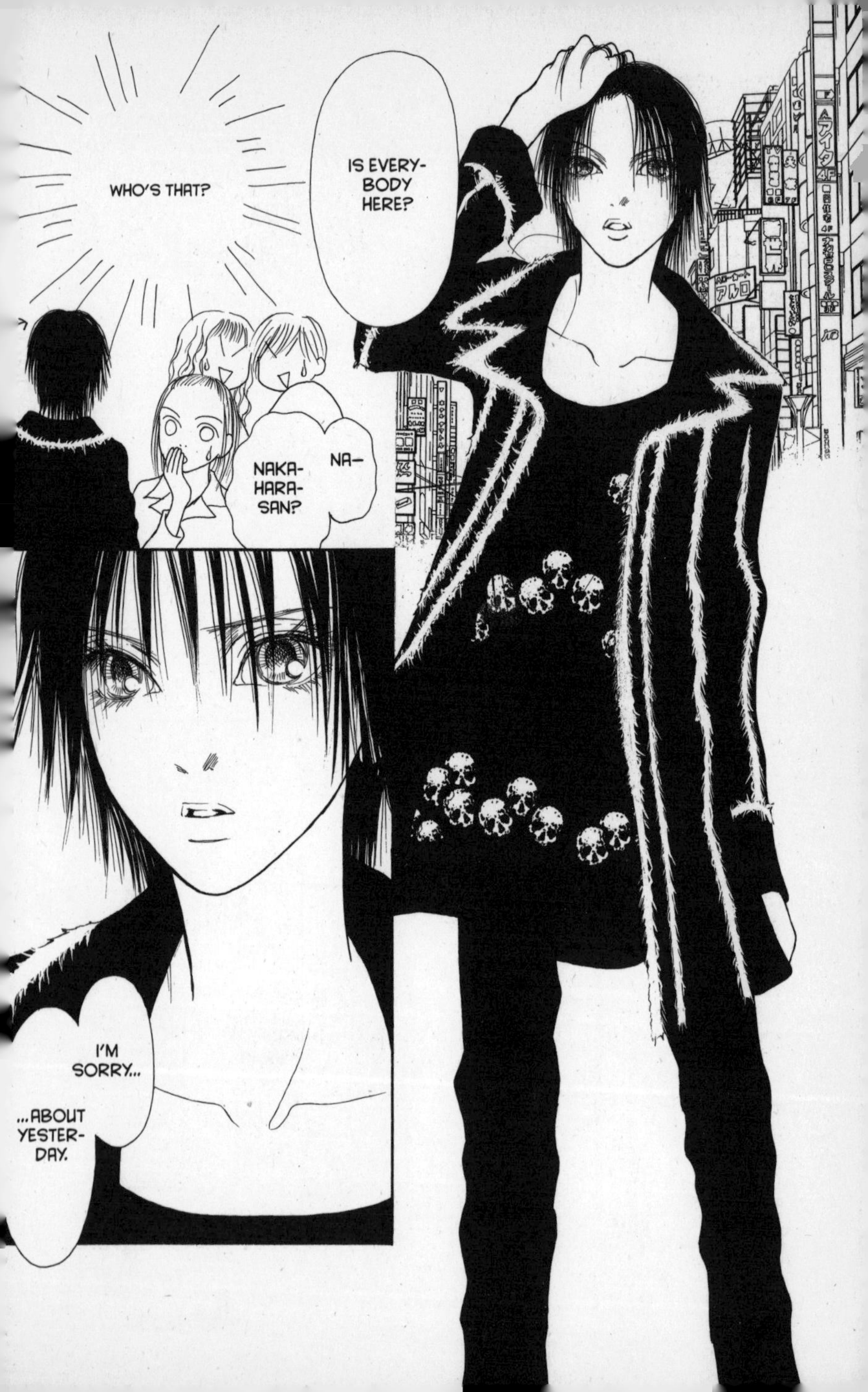
IS EVERY-BODY HERE?
WHO'S THAT?
NA-
NAKA-HARA-SAN?
I'M SORRY...
...ABOUT YESTER-DAY.

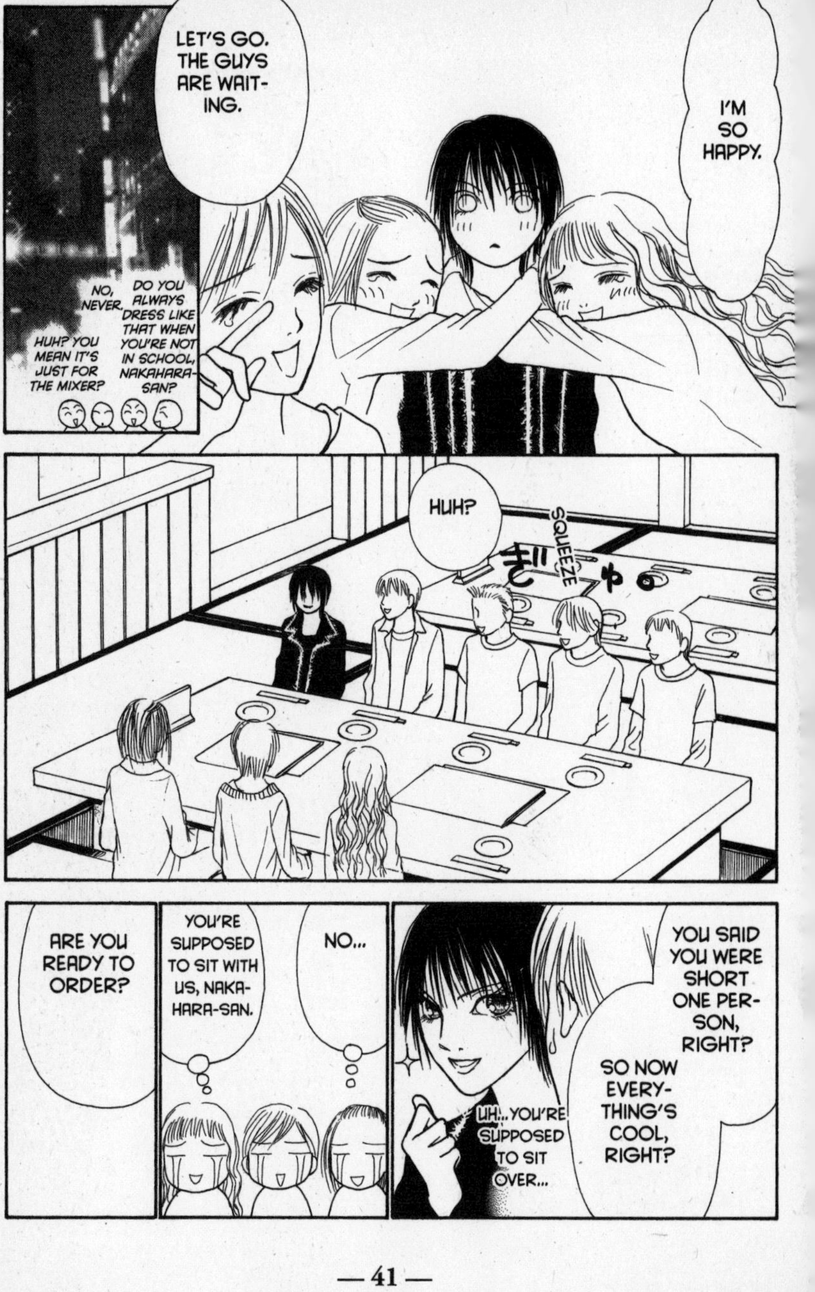
I'M SO HAPPY.
LET'S GO. THE GUYS ARE WAIT-ING.
DO YOU ALWAYS DRESS LIKE THAT WHEN YOU'RE NOT IN SCHOOL, NAKAHARA-SAN?
NO, NEVER.
HUH? YOU MEAN IT'S JUST FOR THE MIXER?
HUH?
SQUEEZE
YOU SAID YOU WERE SHORT ONE PER-SON, RIGHT?
SO NOW EVERY-THING'S COOL, RIGHT?
UH... YOU'RE SUPPOSED TO SIT OVER...
NO...
YOU'RE SUPPOSED TO SIT WITH US, NAKA-HARA-SAN.
ARE YOU READY TO ORDER?

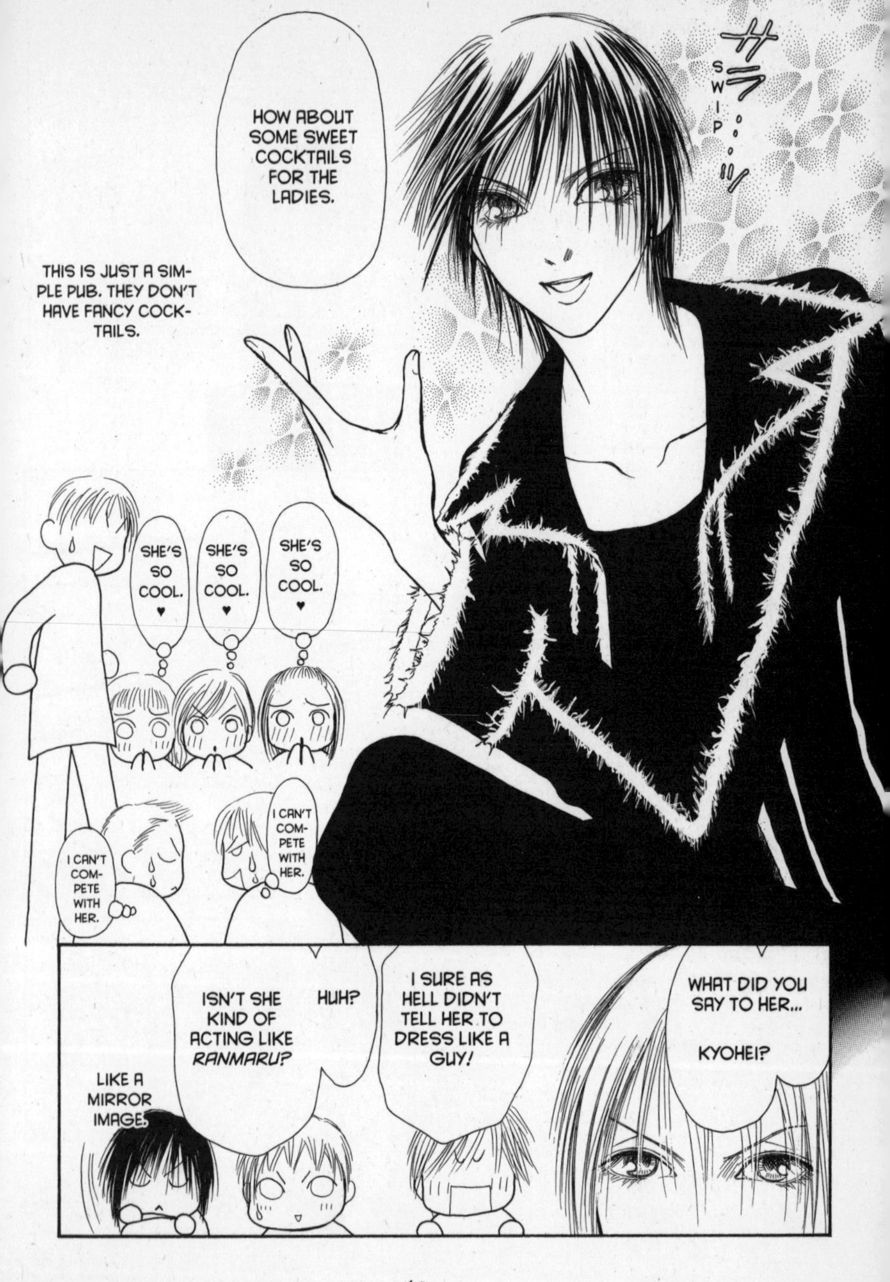
サラ
SWIP...!!
HOW ABOUT SOME SWEET COCKTAILS FOR THE LADIES.
THIS IS JUST A SIM-PLE PUB. THEY DON'T HAVE FANCY COCK-TAILS.
SHE'S SO COOL. ♥
SHE'S SO COOL. ♥
SHE'S SO COOL. ♥
I CAN'T COM-PETE WITH HER.
I CAN'T COM-PETE WITH HER.
WHAT DID YOU SAY TO HER...
KYOHEI?
I SURE AS HELL DIDN'T TELL HER TO DRESS LIKE A GUY!
HUH?
ISN'T SHE KIND OF ACTING LIKE *RANMARU*?
LIKE A MIRROR IMAGE.

Chapter 60
TWIN RHAPSODY

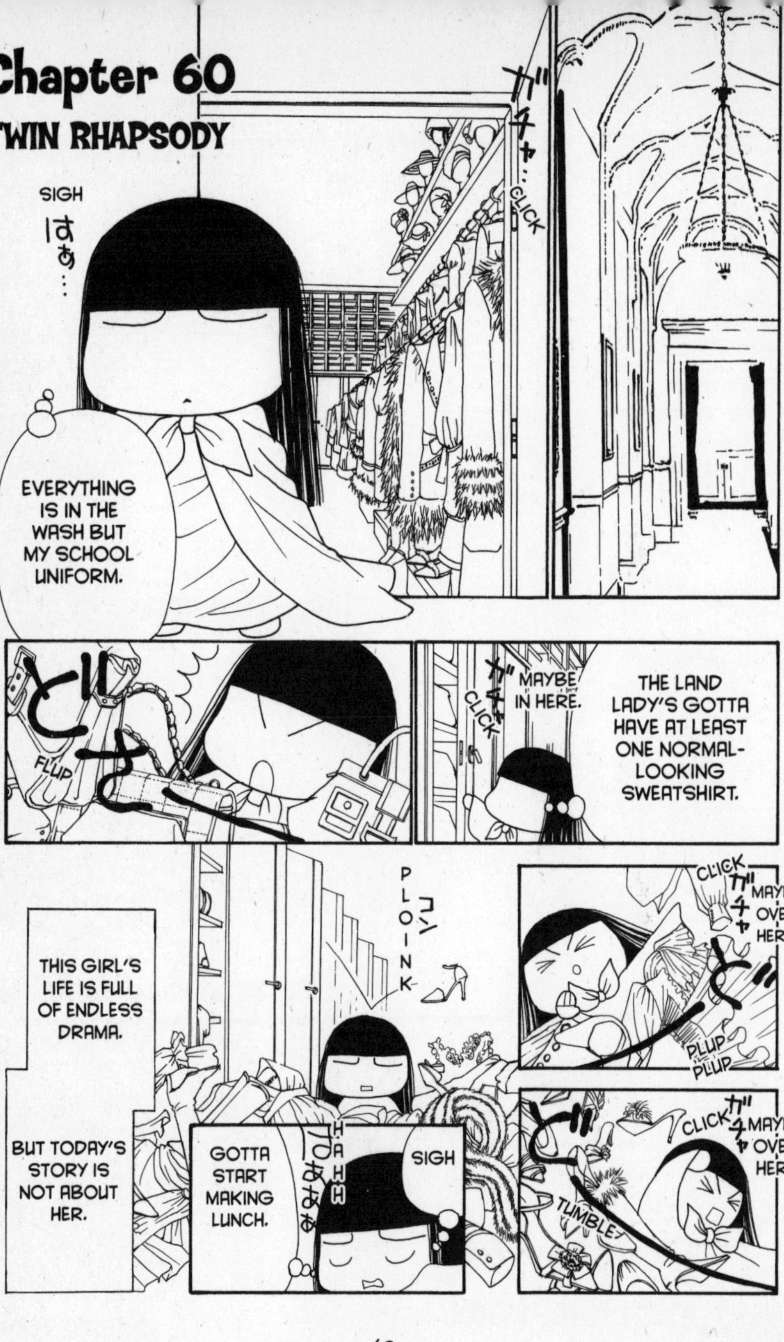

ガチャ…
CLICK
SIGH
すぁ…
EVERYTHING IS IN THE WASH BUT MY SCHOOL UNIFORM.
THE LAND LADY'S GOTTA HAVE AT LEAST ONE NORMAL-LOOKING SWEATSHIRT.
MAYBE IN HERE.
ガチャ
CLICK
とさ
FLUP
CLICK
ガチャ
MAYBE OVER HERE.
どさ
PLUP PLUP
CLICK
ガチャ
MAYBE OVER HERE
どさ
TUMBLE
PLOINK
コン
THIS GIRL'S LIFE IS FULL OF ENDLESS DRAMA.
SIGH
HAHH
はあぁ
GOTTA START MAKING LUNCH.
BUT TODAY'S STORY IS NOT ABOUT HER.

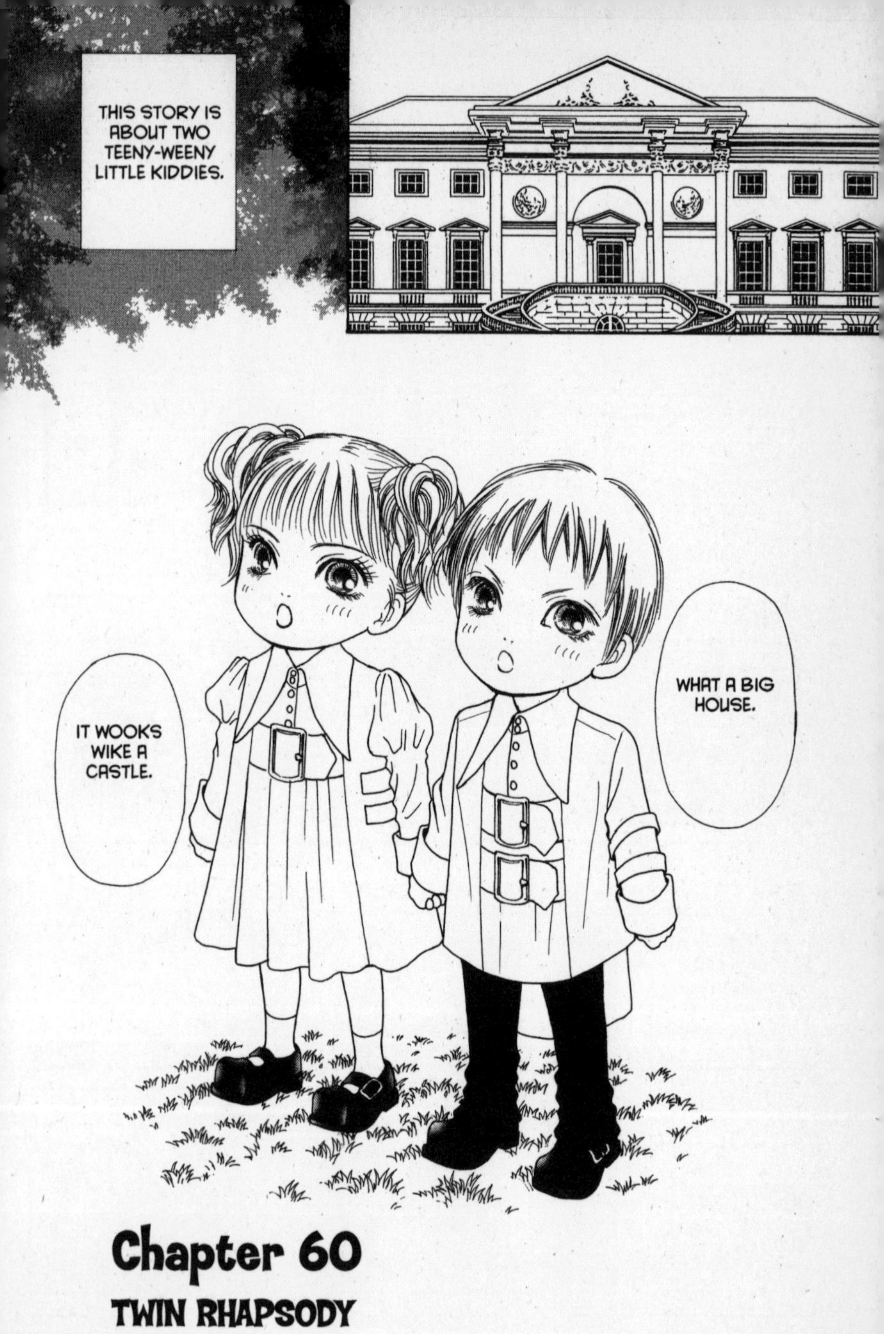
THIS STORY IS ABOUT TWO TEENY-WEENY LITTLE KIDDIES.
WHAT A BIG HOUSE.
IT WOOKS WIKE A CASTLE.

Chapter 60

TWIN RHAPSODY

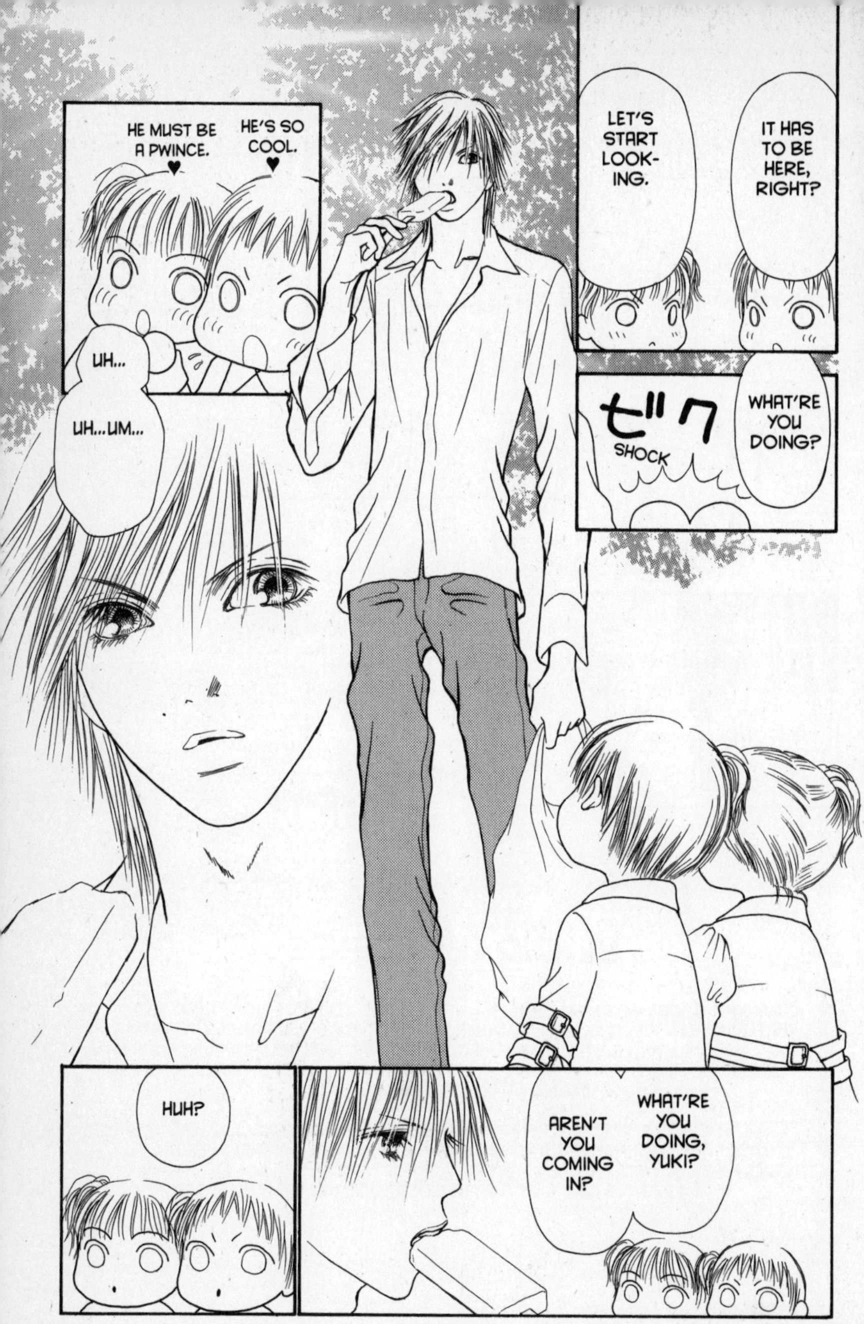
IT HAS TO BE HERE, RIGHT?
LET'S START LOOKING.
WHAT'RE YOU DOING?
ビク
SHOCK
HE'S SO COOL. ♥
HE MUST BE A PWINCE. ♥
UH...
UH...UM...
WHAT'RE YOU DOING, YUKI?
AREN'T YOU COMING IN?
HUH?

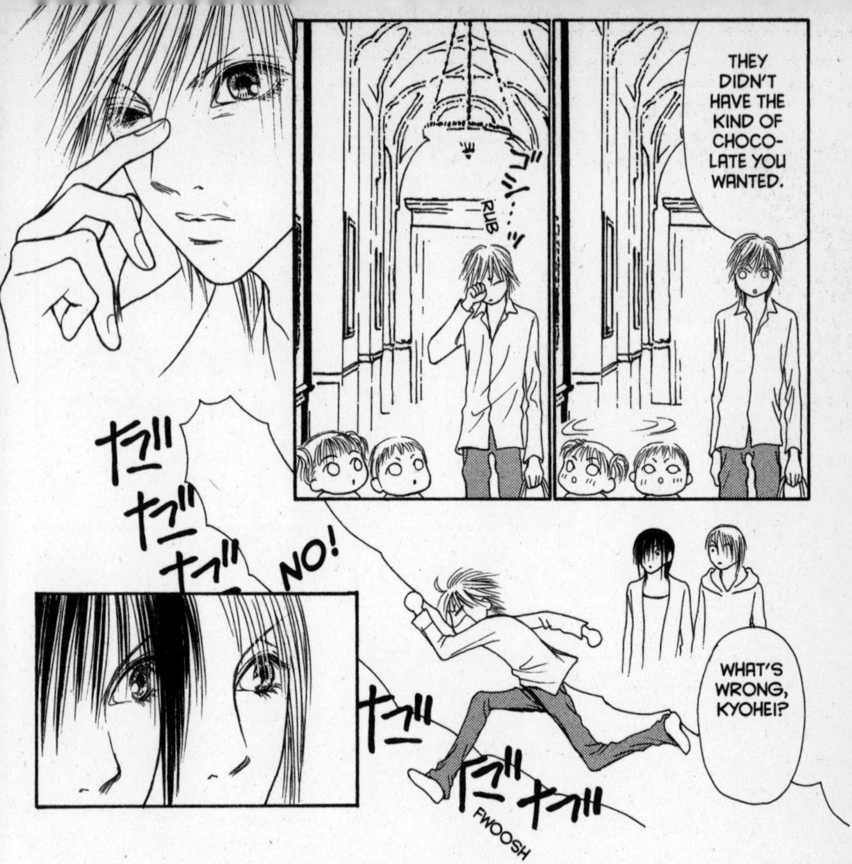

THEY DIDN'T HAVE THE KIND OF CHOCO-LATE YOU WANTED.
RUB
WHAT'S WRONG, KYOHEI?
NO!
FWOOSH

BEHIND THE SCENES

THE LAST STORY WAS KIND OF HEAVY, SO I WANTED TO WRITE SOMETHING CUTE AND LIGHTHEARTED. AND THEN I THOUGHT, OH YEAH, YUKI IS SUPPOSED TO HAVE A TWIN BROTHER AND SISTER (SUPPOSED TO?). IT'S SO FUN TO DRAW LITTLE KIDS. ♥ I GOT THE NAMES YUKI, GIN, AND YAE FROM "TOOYAMA NO KIN-SAN." (I LIKE THE HIROKI MATSUKATA VERSION. ♥)

KIN-SAN IS SOMETIMES CALLED BY THE NICKNAMES "SAEMONNOJOU" AND "KIN-SHIROU" (AND OCCASIONALLY KINJI). I WANTED TO CALL YAE "SAE" INSTEAD, BUT I THOUGHT SHE WOULD END UP PRONOUNCING IT "SHAE," SO I DECIDED AGAINST IT. I GUESS IT'S OBVIOUS THAT I SUCK AT COMING UP WITH NAMES.

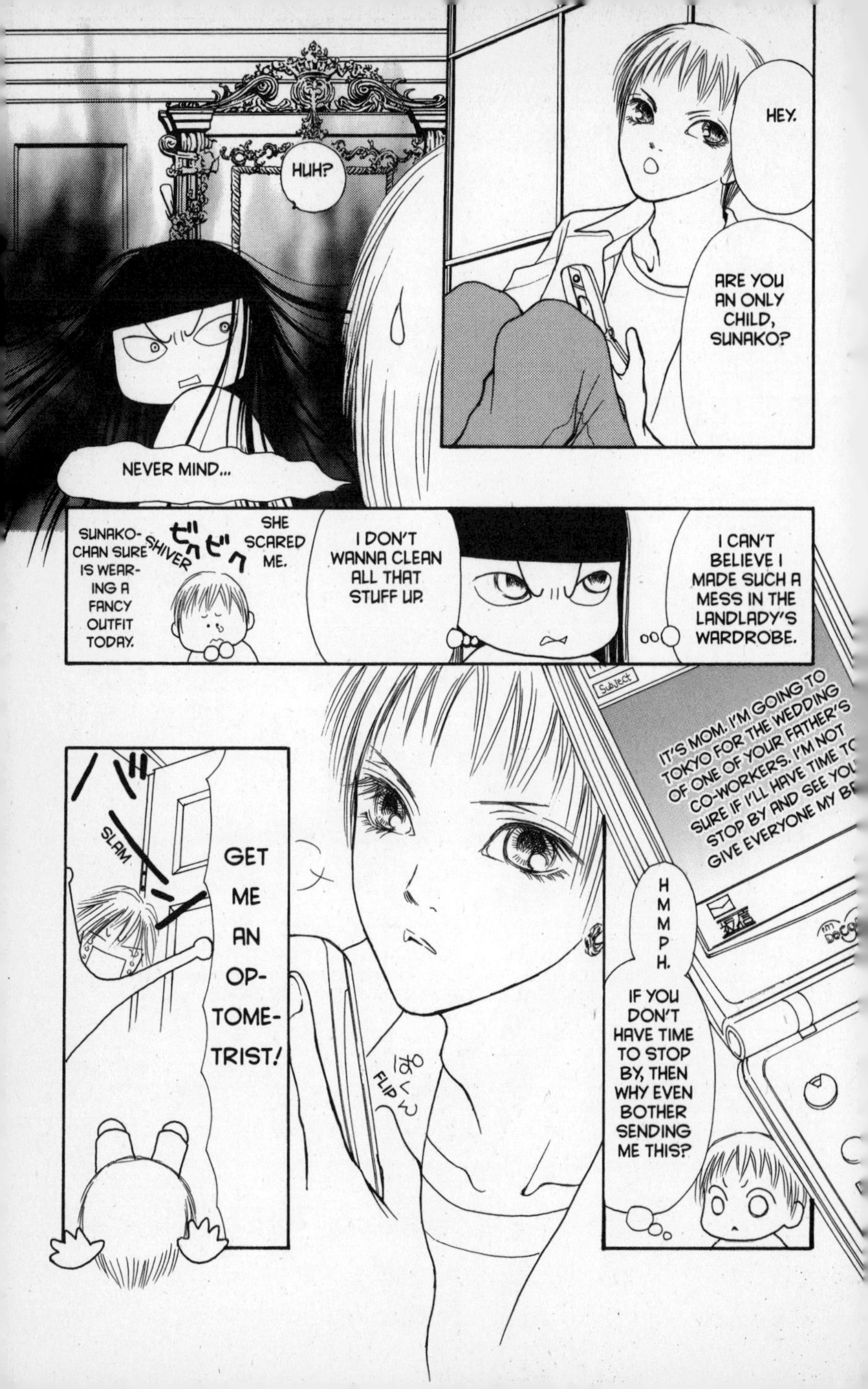
HEY.
ARE YOU AN ONLY CHILD, SUNAKO?
HUH?
NEVER MIND...
I CAN'T BELIEVE I MADE SUCH A MESS IN THE LANDLADY'S WARDROBE.
I DON'T WANNA CLEAN ALL THAT STUFF UP.
SHE SCARED ME.
ビクビク SHIVER
SUNAKO-CHAN SURE IS WEARING A FANCY OUTFIT TODAY.
Subject
IT'S MOM. I'M GOING TO TOKYO FOR THE WEDDING OF ONE OF YOUR FATHER'S CO-WORKERS. I'M NOT SURE IF I'LL HAVE TIME TO STOP BY AND SEE YO
GIVE EVERYONE MY BE
返信
HMMPH.
IF YOU DON'T HAVE TIME TO STOP BY, THEN WHY EVEN BOTHER SENDING ME THIS?
ぱく FLIP
バン SLAM
GET ME AN OPTOMETRIST!

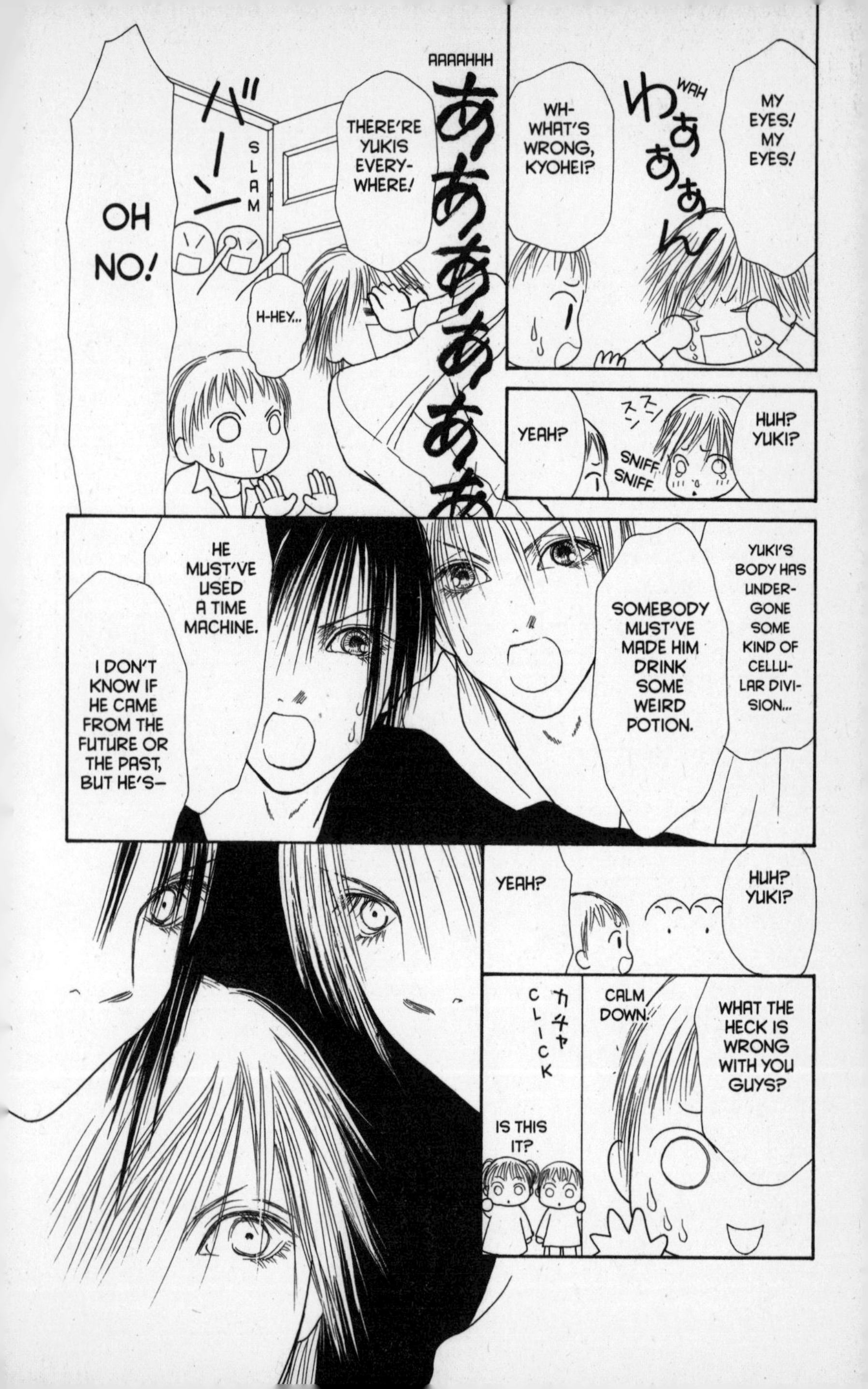
わぁあぁん
WAH
MY EYES! MY EYES!
WH- WHAT'S WRONG, KYOHEI?
HUH? YUKI?
スンスン
SNIFF SNIFF
YEAH?
ああああああ
AAAAAHHH
THERE'RE YUKIS EVERY-WHERE!
バーン
SLAM
H-HEY...
OH NO!
YUKI'S BODY HAS UNDER-GONE SOME KIND OF CELLU-LAR DIVI-SION...
SOMEBODY MUST'VE MADE HIM DRINK SOME WEIRD POTION.
HE MUST'VE USED A TIME MACHINE.
I DON'T KNOW IF HE CAME FROM THE FUTURE OR THE PAST, BUT HE'S—
HUH? YUKI?
YEAH?
WHAT THE HECK IS WRONG WITH YOU GUYS?
CALM DOWN.
カチャ
CLICK
IS THIS IT?

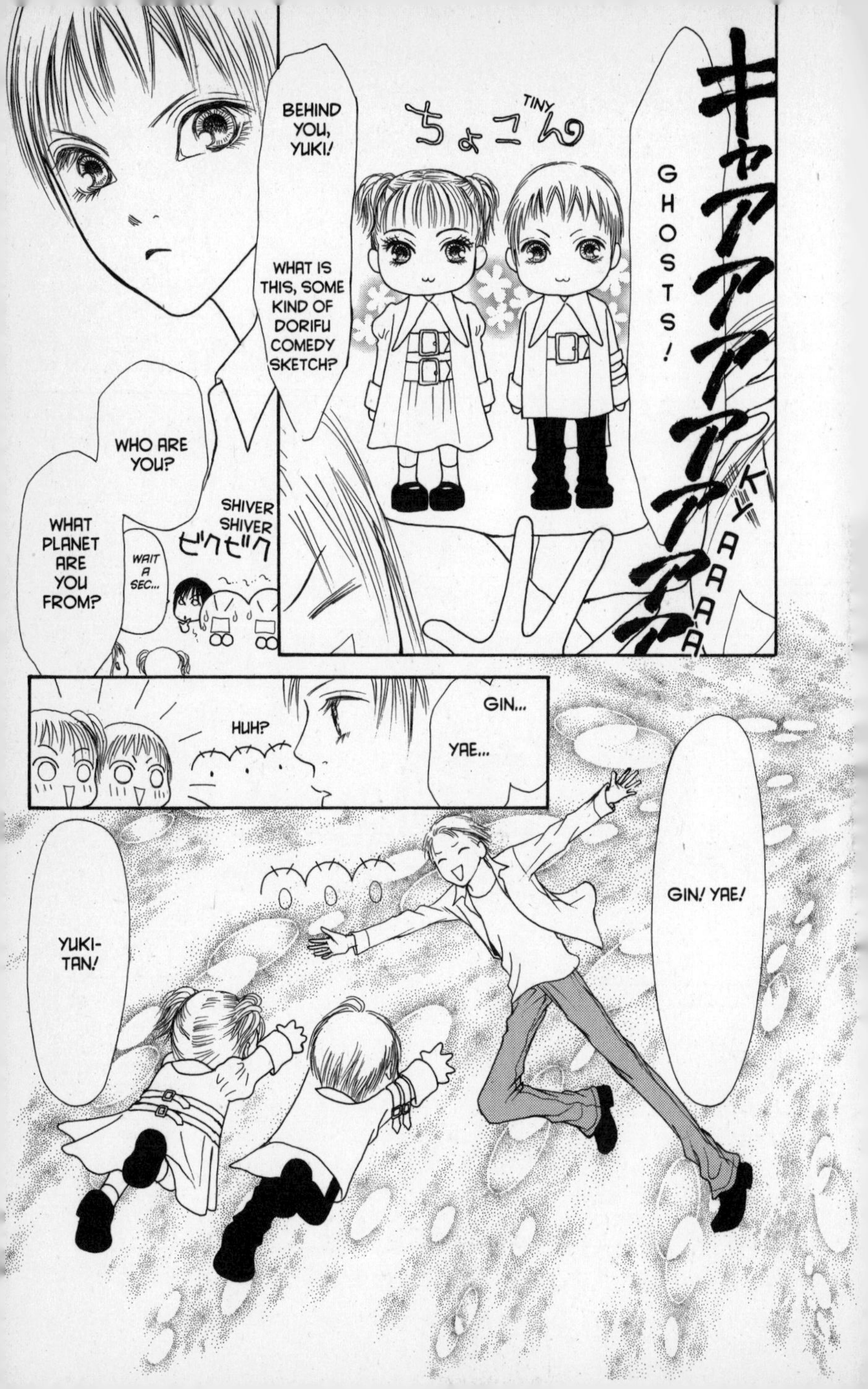
キャアアアアアア
GHOSTS!
KYAAAAA
TINY
ちょこん
BEHIND YOU, YUKI!
WHAT IS THIS, SOME KIND OF DORIFU COMEDY SKETCH?
WHO ARE YOU?
SHIVER SHIVER
ビクビク
WHAT PLANET ARE YOU FROM?
WAIT A SEC...
GIN...
YAE...
HUH?
GIN! YAE!
YUKI-TAN!

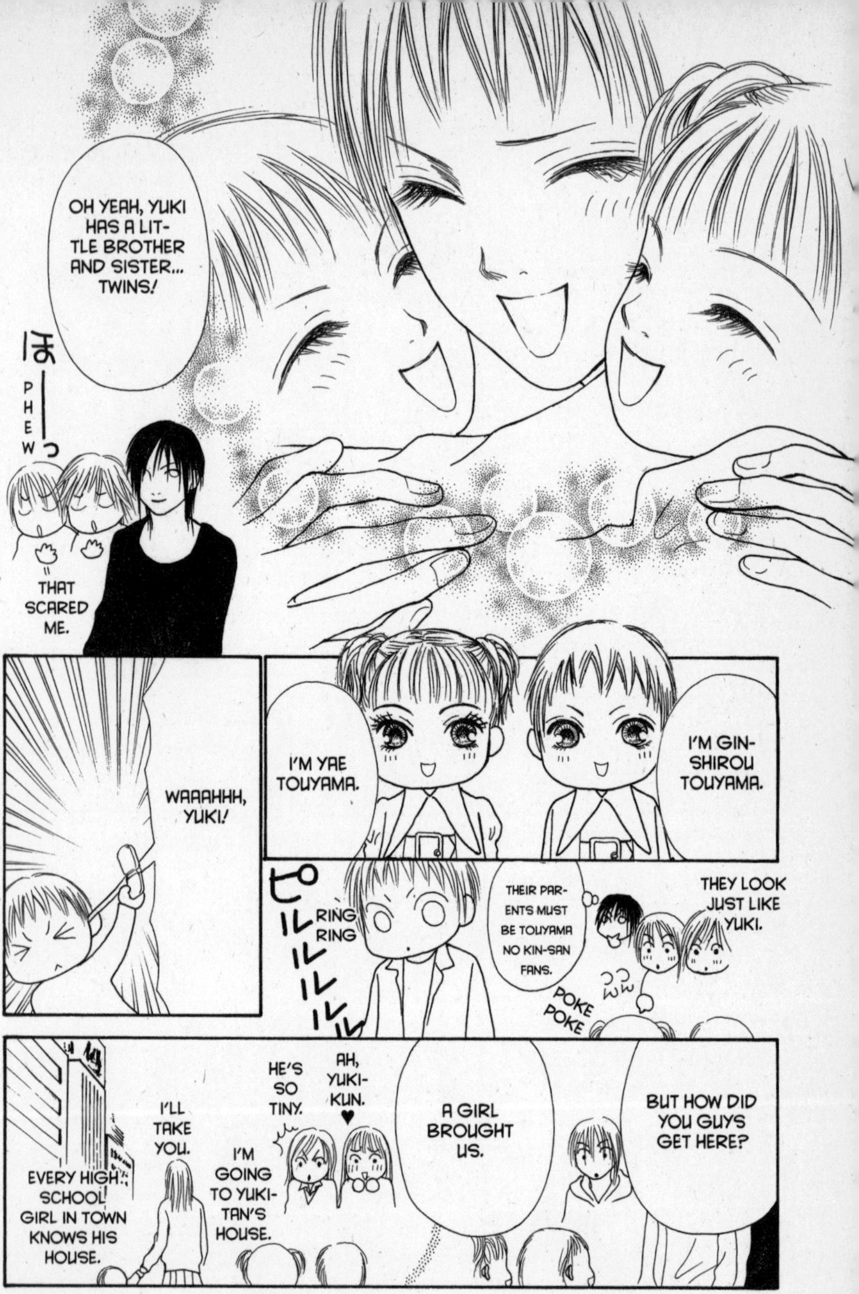
OH YEAH, YUKI HAS A LIT-TLE BROTHER AND SISTER... TWINS!
ほーっ
PHEW
THAT SCARED ME.
I'M GIN-SHIROU TOUYAMA.
I'M YAE TOUYAMA.
THEY LOOK JUST LIKE YUKI.
POKE POKE
THEIR PAR-ENTS MUST BE TOUYAMA NO KIN-SAN FANS.
ピルルルル
RING RING
WAAAHHH, YUKI!
BUT HOW DID YOU GUYS GET HERE?
A GIRL BROUGHT US.
AH, YUKI-KUN. ♥
HE'S SO TINY.
I'M GOING TO YUKI-TAN'S HOUSE.
I'LL TAKE YOU.
EVERY HIGH SCHOOL GIRL IN TOWN KNOWS HIS HOUSE.

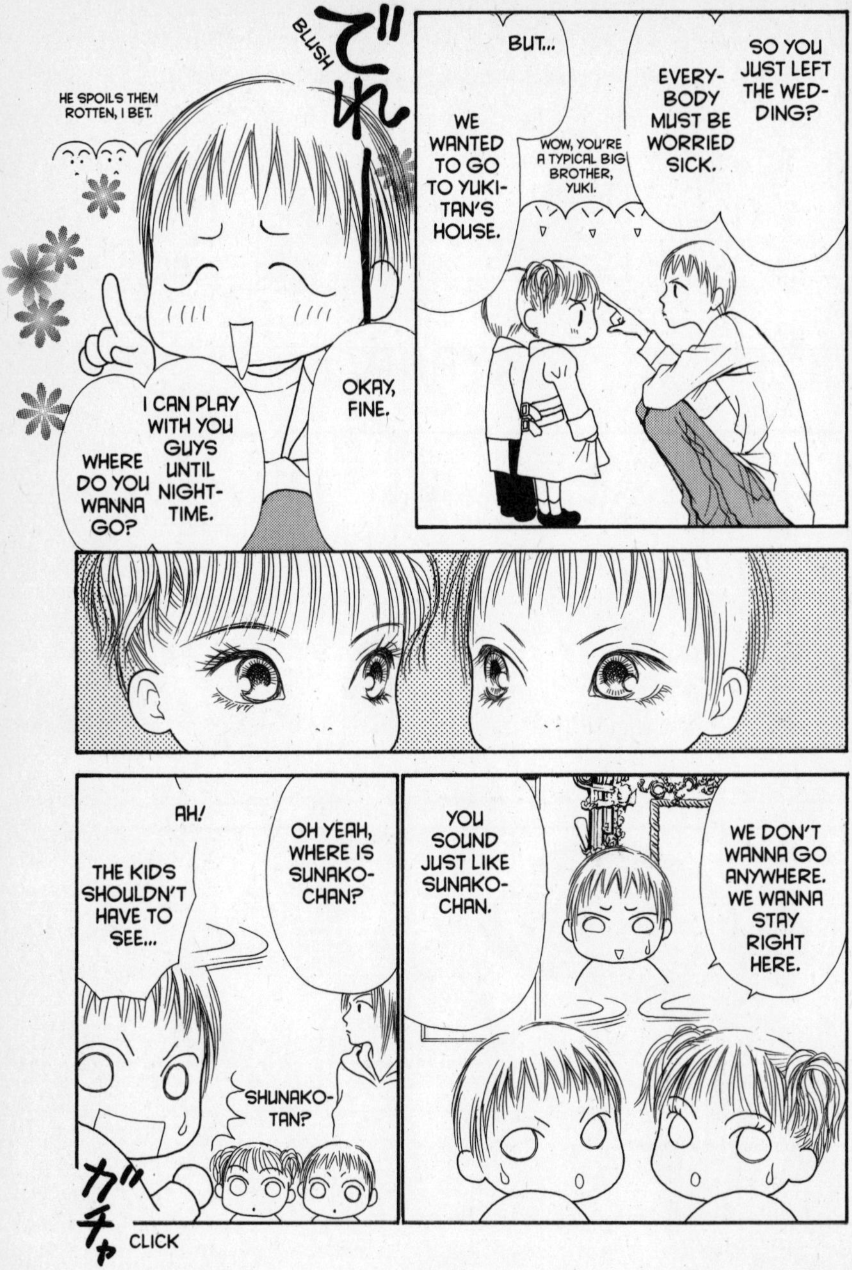
SO YOU JUST LEFT THE WEDDING?
EVERYBODY MUST BE WORRIED SICK.
WOW, YOU'RE A TYPICAL BIG BROTHER, YUKI.
BUT...
WE WANTED TO GO TO YUKI-TAN'S HOUSE.
でれー
BLUSH
OKAY, FINE.
I CAN PLAY WITH YOU GUYS UNTIL NIGHTTIME.
WHERE DO YOU WANNA GO?
HE SPOILS THEM ROTTEN, I BET.
WE DON'T WANNA GO ANYWHERE. WE WANNA STAY RIGHT HERE.
YOU SOUND JUST LIKE SUNAKO-CHAN.
OH YEAH, WHERE IS SUNAKO-CHAN?
AH!
THE KIDS SHOULDN'T HAVE TO SEE...
SHUNAKO-TAN?
ガチャ
CLICK

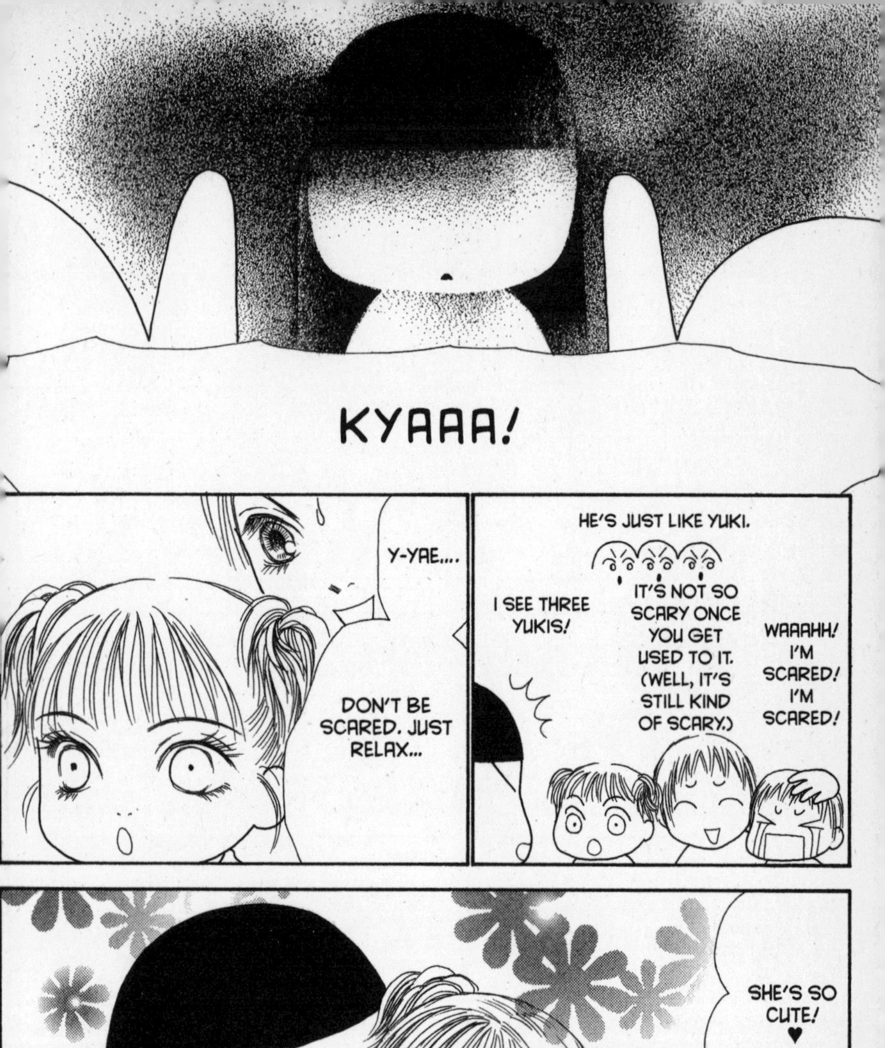
KYAAA!
HE'S JUST LIKE YUKI.
WAAAHH! I'M SCARED! I'M SCARED!
IT'S NOT SO SCARY ONCE YOU GET USED TO IT. (WELL, IT'S STILL KIND OF SCARY.)
I SEE THREE YUKIS!
Y-YAE....
DON'T BE SCARED. JUST RELAX...
SHE'S SO CUTE! ♥

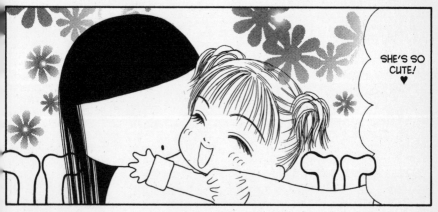

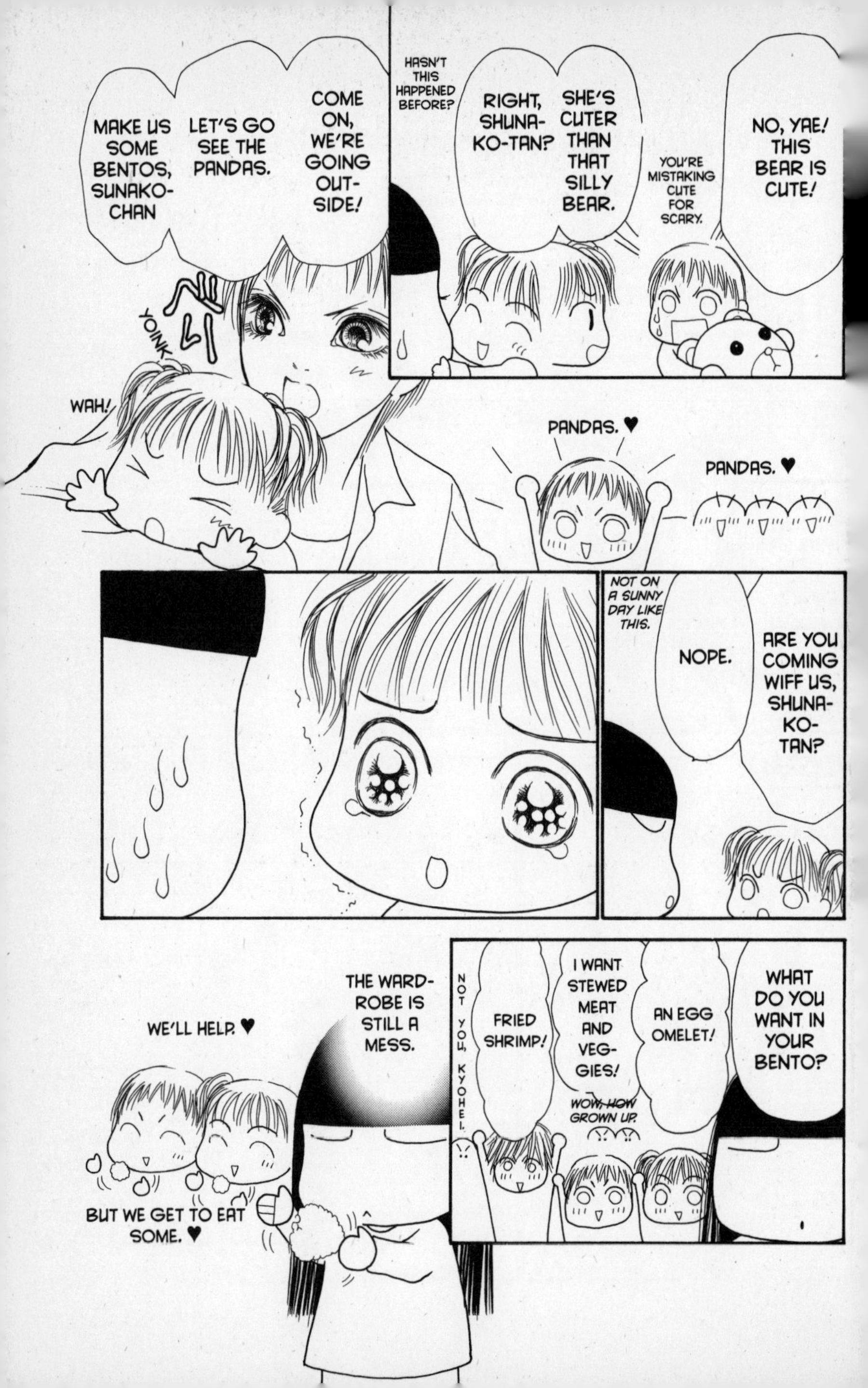
NO, YAE! THIS BEAR IS CUTE!
YOU'RE MISTAKING CUTE FOR SCARY.
SHE'S CUTER THAN THAT SILLY BEAR.
RIGHT, SHUNA-KO-TAN?
HASN'T THIS HAPPENED BEFORE?
COME ON, WE'RE GOING OUT-SIDE!
LET'S GO SEE THE PANDAS.
MAKE US SOME BENTOS, SUNAKO-CHAN
YOINK
WAH!
PANDAS. ♥
PANDAS. ♥
ARE YOU COMING WIFF US, SHUNA-KO-TAN?
NOPE.
NOT ON A SUNNY DAY LIKE THIS.
WHAT DO YOU WANT IN YOUR BENTO?
AN EGG OMELET!
I WANT STEWED MEAT AND VEG-GIES!
WOW, HOW GROWN UP.
FRIED SHRIMP!
NOT YOU, KYOHEI.
THE WARD-ROBE IS STILL A MESS.
WE'LL HELP. ♥
BUT WE GET TO EAT SOME. ♥

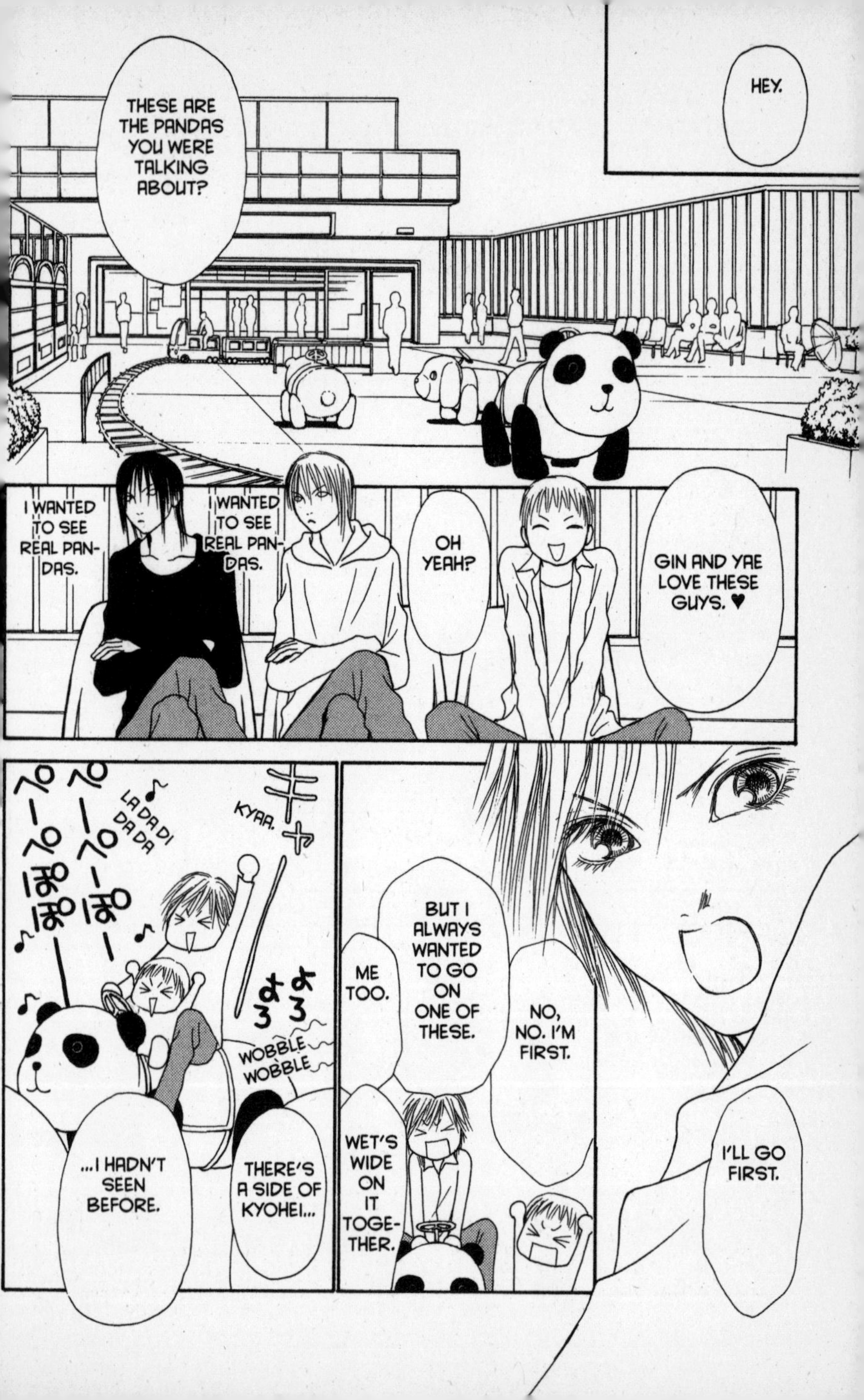
HEY.
THESE ARE THE PANDAS YOU WERE TALKING ABOUT?
GIN AND YAE LOVE THESE GUYS. ♥
OH YEAH?
I WANTED TO SEE REAL PANDAS.
I WANTED TO SEE REAL PANDAS.
I'LL GO FIRST.
NO, NO. I'M FIRST.
BUT I ALWAYS WANTED TO GO ON ONE OF THESE.
ME TOO.
WET'S WIDE ON IT TOGETHER.
キャ
KYAA.
LA DA DI DA DA
ぺーぺーぽー
ぺーぺーぽぽー
よろよろ
WOBBLE WOBBLE
THERE'S A SIDE OF KYOHEI...
...I HADN'T SEEN BEFORE.

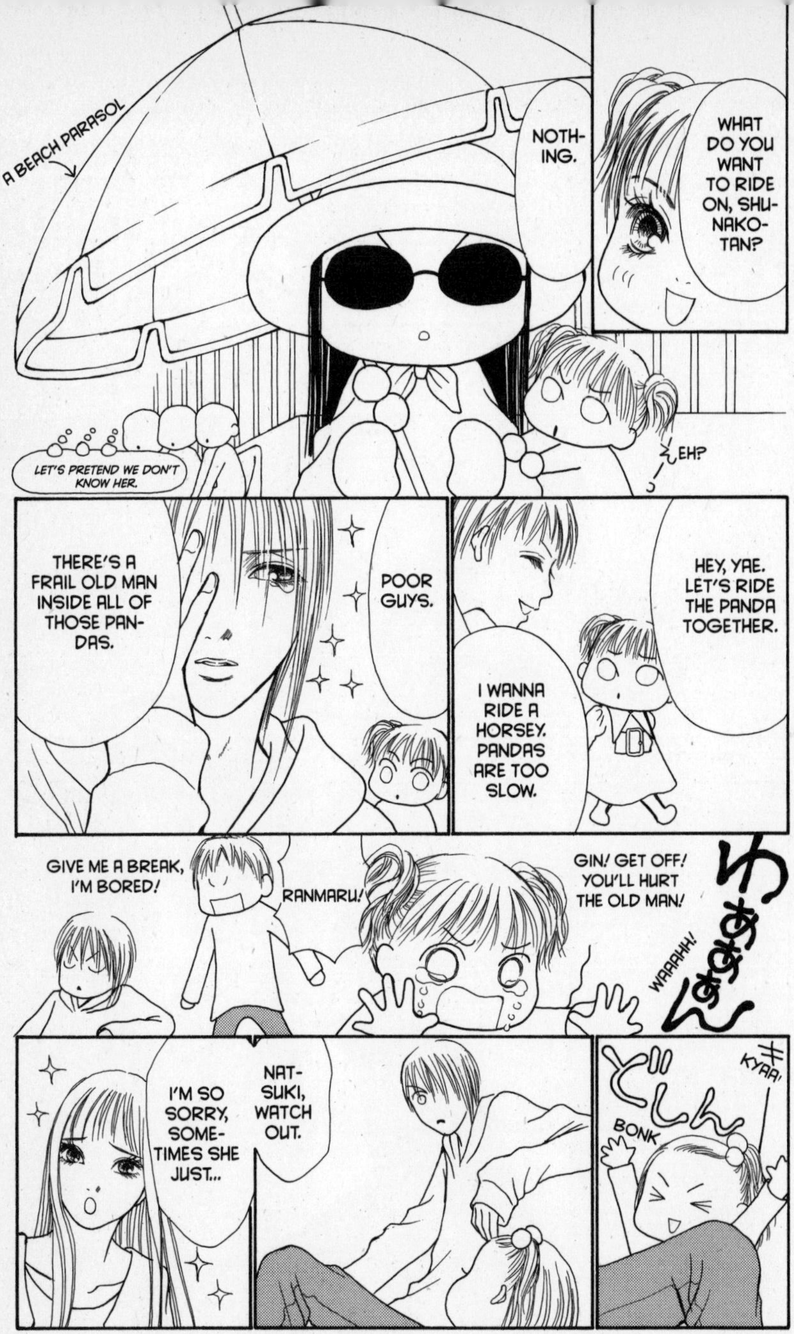
WHAT DO YOU WANT TO RIDE ON, SHUNAKO-TAN?
NOTHING.
A BEACH PARASOL
EH?
LET'S PRETEND WE DON'T KNOW HER.
HEY, YAE. LET'S RIDE THE PANDA TOGETHER.
I WANNA RIDE A HORSEY. PANDAS ARE TOO SLOW.
POOR GUYS.
THERE'S A FRAIL OLD MAN INSIDE ALL OF THOSE PANDAS.
わあああん
WAAAHH!
GIN! GET OFF! YOU'LL HURT THE OLD MAN!
RANMARU!
GIVE ME A BREAK, I'M BORED!
どしん
BONK
KYAA!
NATSUKI, WATCH OUT.
I'M SO SORRY, SOMETIMES SHE JUST...

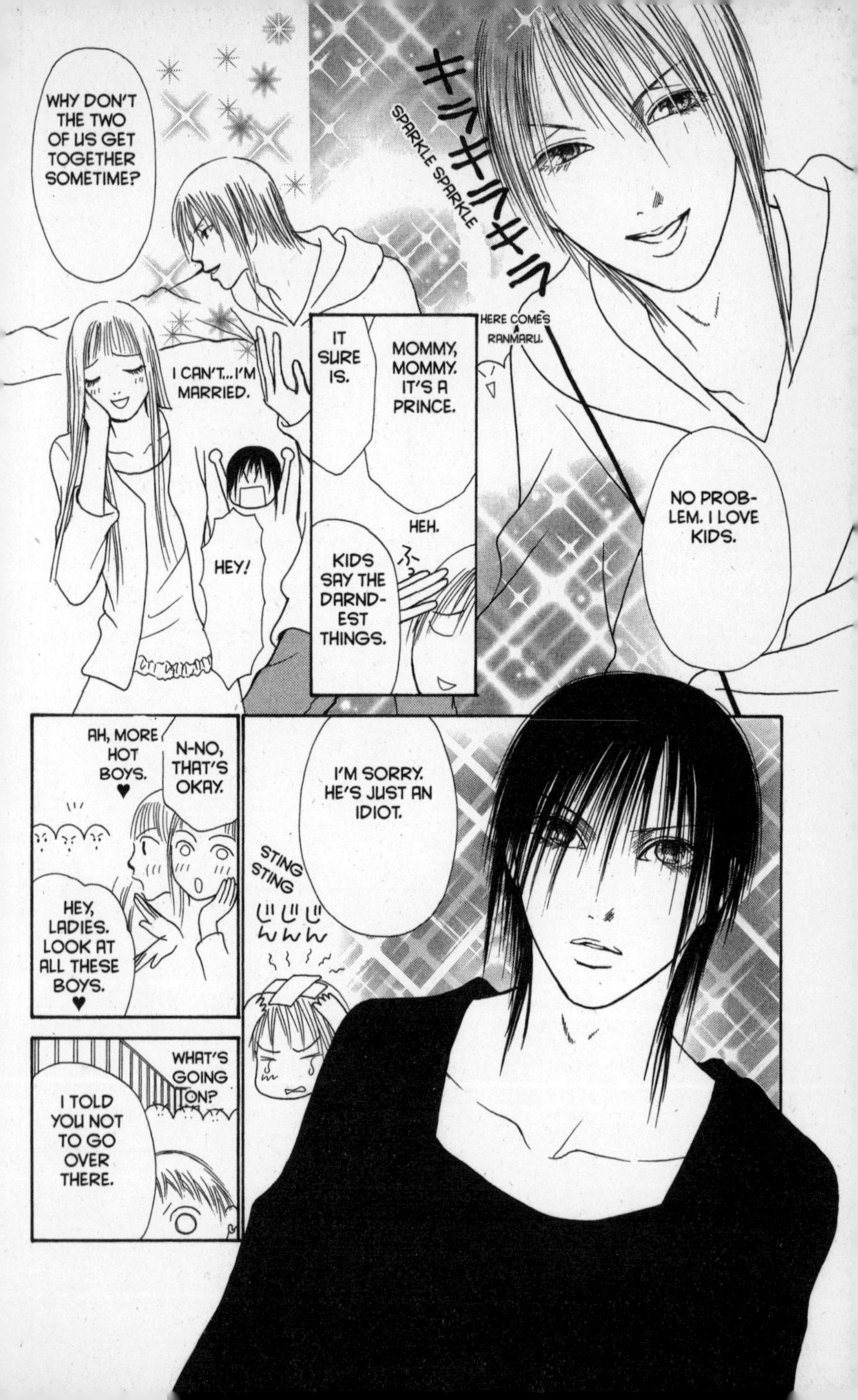
キラキラキラキラ
SPARKLE SPARKLE
HERE COMES RANMARU.
MOMMY, MOMMY. IT'S A PRINCE.
IT SURE IS.
HEH.
ふっ
KIDS SAY THE DARNDEST THINGS.
WHY DON'T THE TWO OF US GET TOGETHER SOMETIME?
I CAN'T...I'M MARRIED.
HEY!
NO PROBLEM. I LOVE KIDS.
I'M SORRY. HE'S JUST AN IDIOT.
STING STING
じんじんじん
N-NO, THAT'S OKAY.
AH, MORE HOT BOYS. ♥
HEY, LADIES. LOOK AT ALL THESE BOYS. ♥
WHAT'S GOING ON?
I TOLD YOU NOT TO GO OVER THERE.

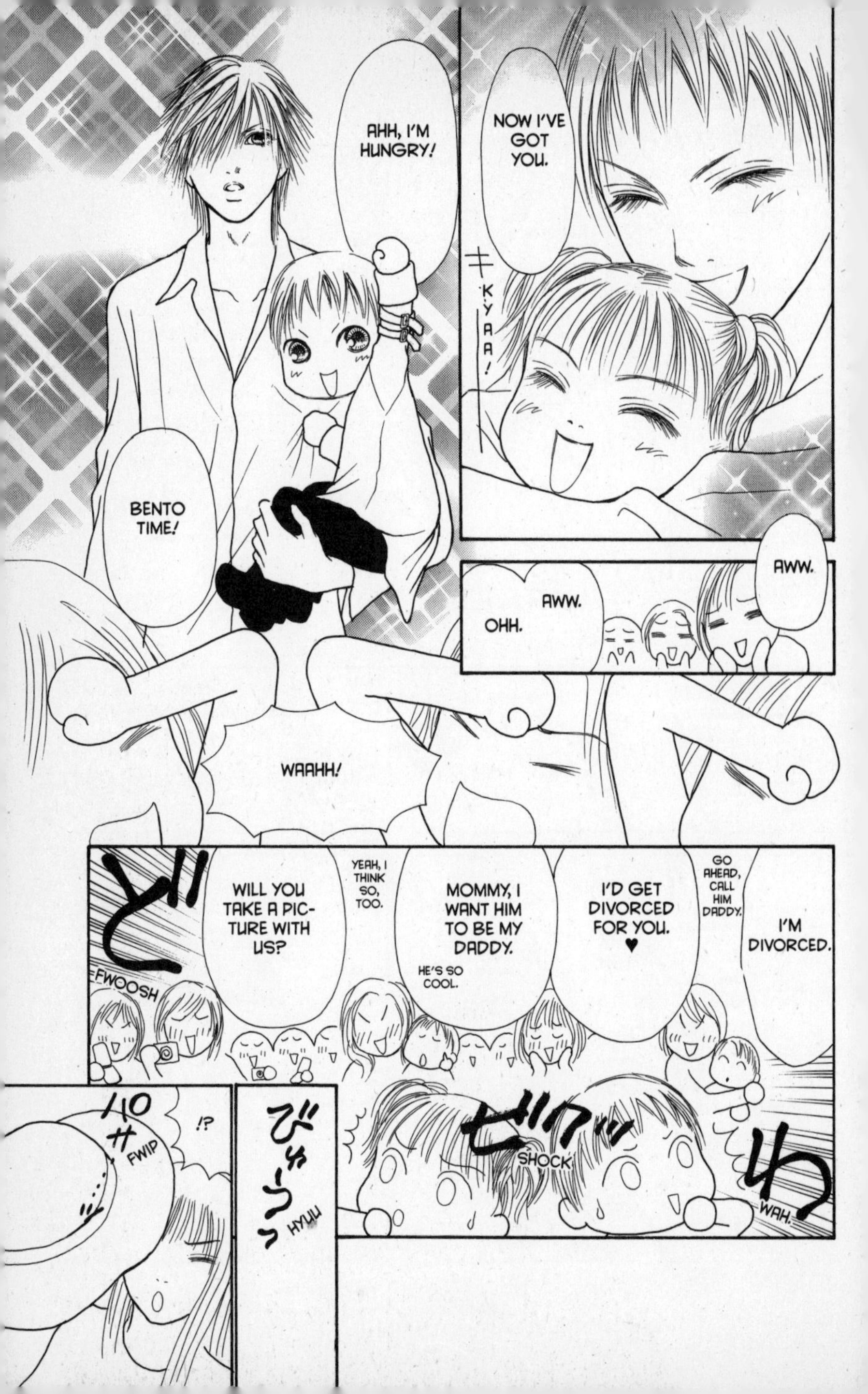
NOW I'VE GOT YOU.
KYAA!
AWW.
AWW.
OHH.
AHH, I'M HUNGRY!
BENTO TIME!
WAAHH!
I'M DIVORCED.
GO AHEAD, CALL HIM DADDY.
I'D GET DIVORCED FOR YOU. ♥
MOMMY, I WANT HIM TO BE MY DADDY.
HE'S SO COOL.
YEAH, I THINK SO, TOO.
WILL YOU TAKE A PICTURE WITH US?
FWOOSH
WAH.
SHOCK
HYUU
!?
FWIP

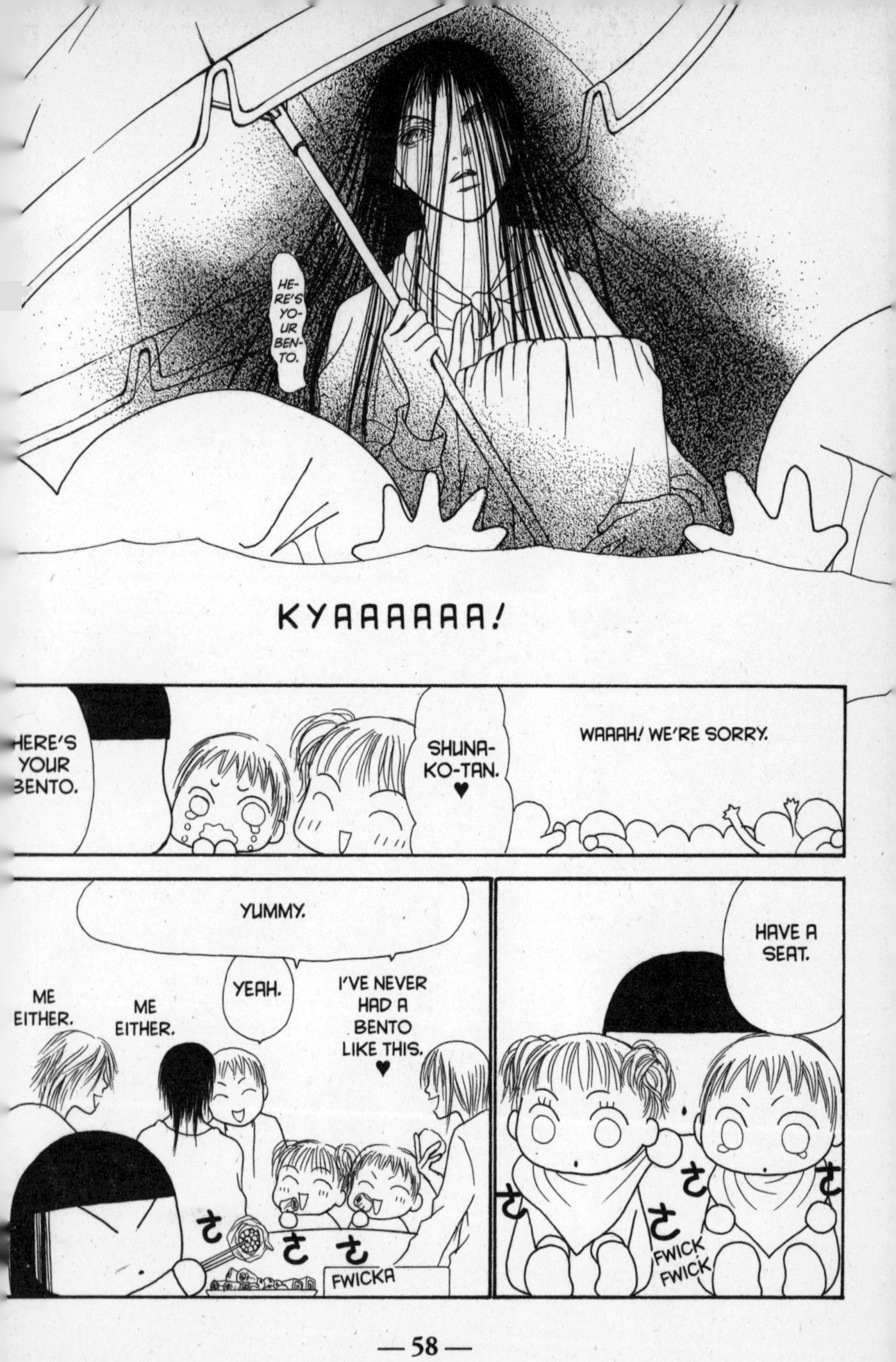
HERE'S YOUR BENTO.
KYAAAAAAA!
WAAAH! WE'RE SORRY.
SHUNA-KO-TAN. ♥
HERE'S YOUR BENTO.
HAVE A SEAT.
さ さ さ さ
FWICK FWICK
YUMMY.
I'VE NEVER HAD A BENTO LIKE THIS. ♥
YEAH.
ME EITHER.
ME EITHER.
さ さ さ
FWICKA

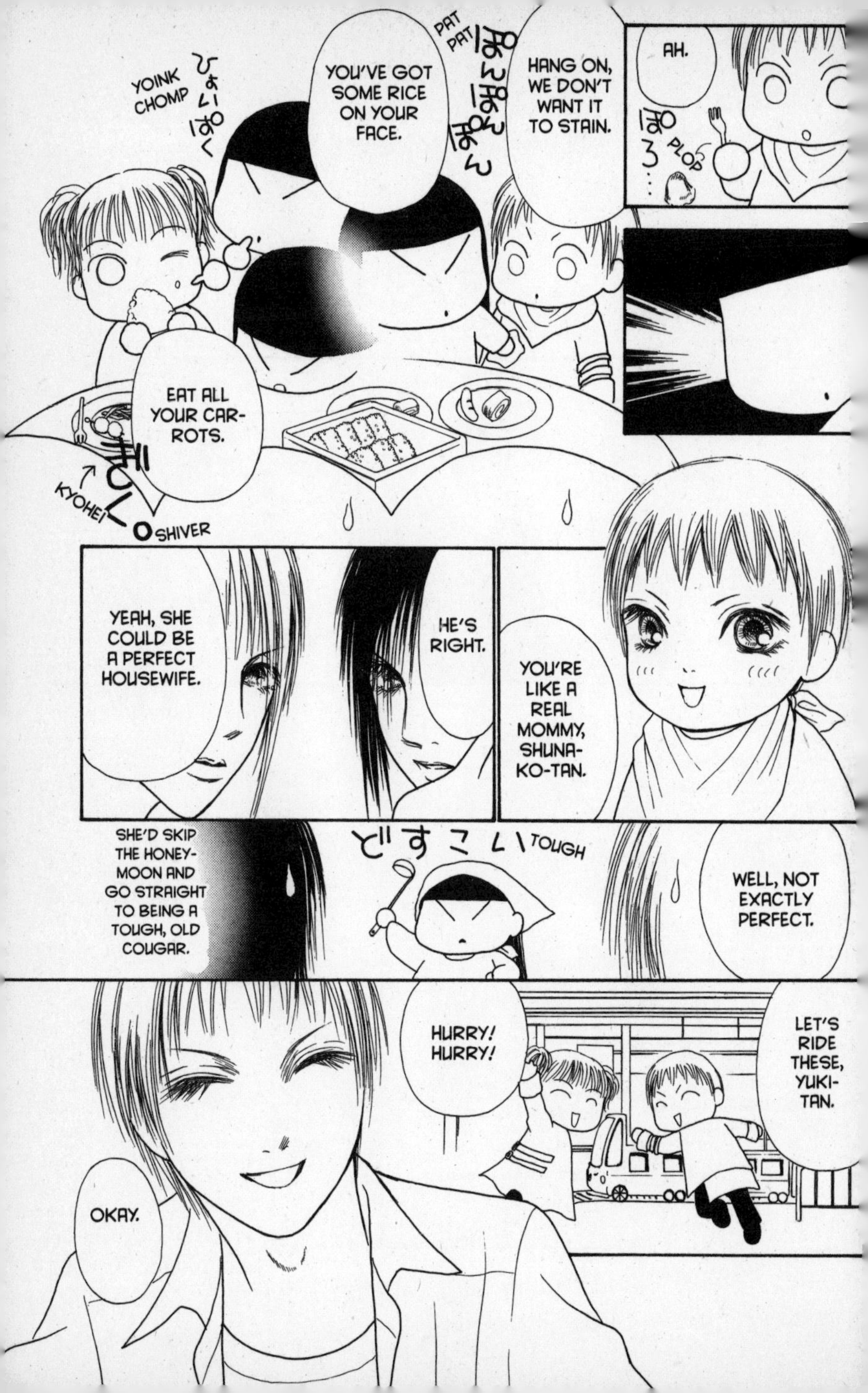
AH.
ぽろ…
PLOP
HANG ON, WE DON'T WANT IT TO STAIN.
ぽんぽんぽん
PAT PAT
YOU'VE GOT SOME RICE ON YOUR FACE.
ひょいぱく
YOINK CHOMP
EAT ALL YOUR CARROTS.
KYOHEI
SHIVER
YOU'RE LIKE A REAL MOMMY, SHUNAKO-TAN.
HE'S RIGHT.
YEAH, SHE COULD BE A PERFECT HOUSEWIFE.
WELL, NOT EXACTLY PERFECT.
どすこい
TOUGH
SHE'D SKIP THE HONEYMOON AND GO STRAIGHT TO BEING A TOUGH, OLD COUGAR.
LET'S RIDE THESE, YUKI-TAN.
HURRY! HURRY!
OKAY.

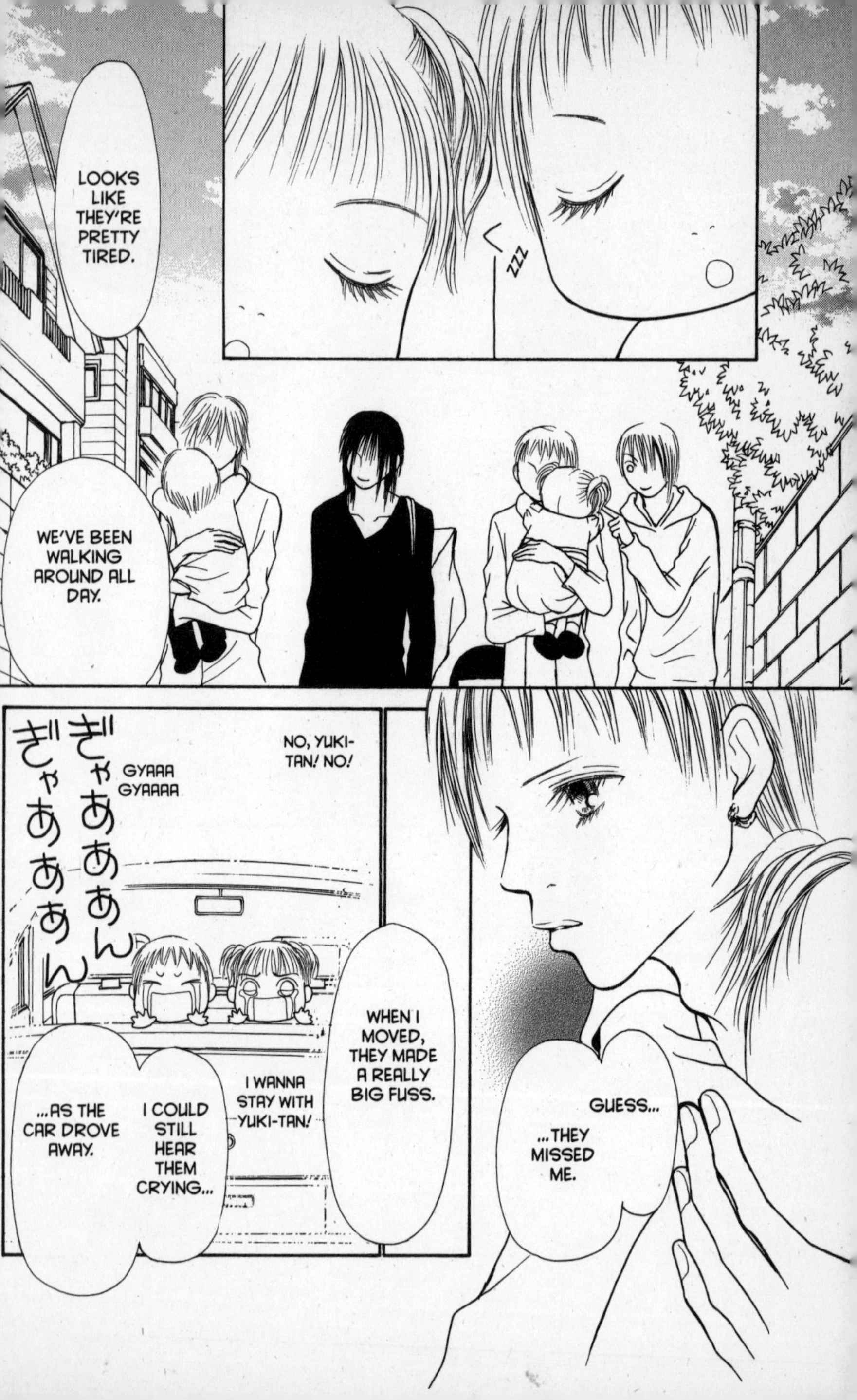
ZZZ
LOOKS LIKE THEY'RE PRETTY TIRED.
WE'VE BEEN WALKING AROUND ALL DAY.
WHEN I MOVED, THEY MADE A REALLY BIG FUSS.
NO, YUKI-TAN! NO!
ぎゃあああん ぎゃあああん
GYAAA GYAAAA
I WANNA STAY WITH YUKI-TAN!
I COULD STILL HEAR THEM CRYING...
...AS THE CAR DROVE AWAY.
GUESS...
...THEY MISSED ME.

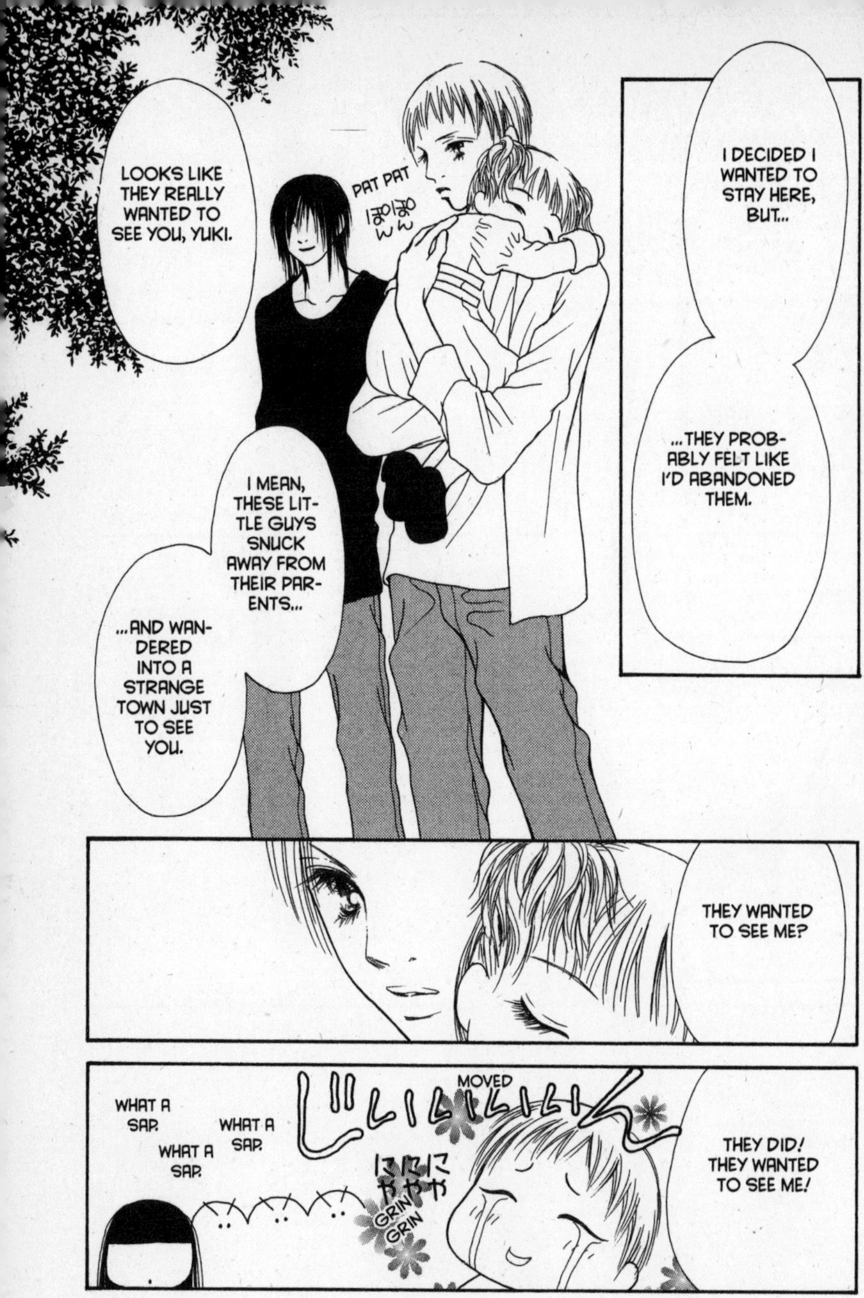
I DECIDED I WANTED TO STAY HERE, BUT...
...THEY PROBABLY FELT LIKE I'D ABANDONED THEM.
LOOKS LIKE THEY REALLY WANTED TO SEE YOU, YUKI.
PAT PAT
ぽんぽん
I MEAN, THESE LITTLE GUYS SNUCK AWAY FROM THEIR PARENTS...
...AND WANDERED INTO A STRANGE TOWN JUST TO SEE YOU.
THEY WANTED TO SEE ME?
THEY DID! THEY WANTED TO SEE ME!
じいいいいん
MOVED
にやにや
GRIN GRIN
WHAT A SAP.
WHAT A SAP.
WHAT A SAP.

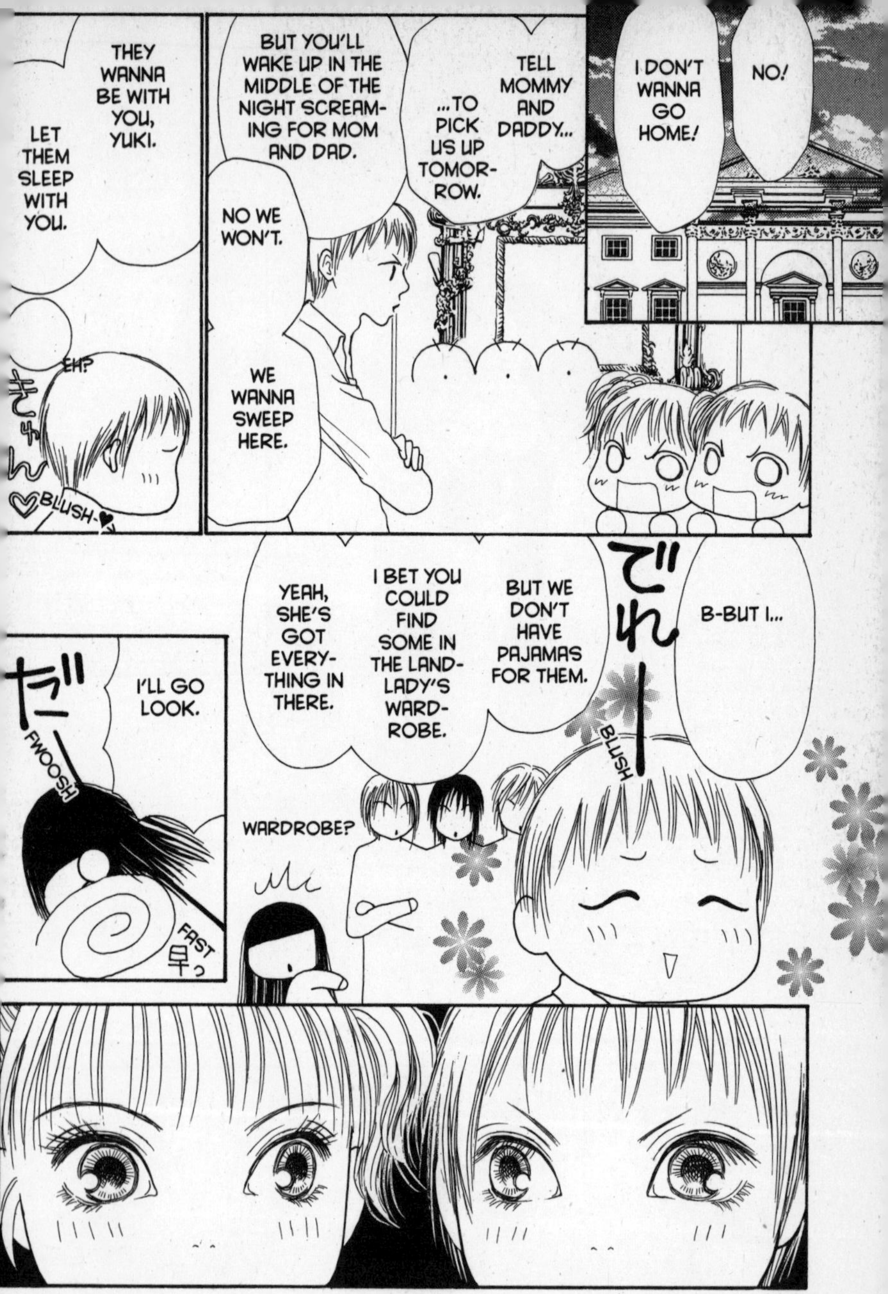
NO!
I DON'T WANNA GO HOME!
...
TELL MOMMY AND DADDY...
...TO PICK US UP TOMORROW.
BUT YOU'LL WAKE UP IN THE MIDDLE OF THE NIGHT SCREAMING FOR MOM AND DAD.
NO WE WON'T.
WE WANNA SWEEP HERE.
THEY WANNA BE WITH YOU, YUKI.
LET THEM SLEEP WITH YOU.
EH?
きゅん
BLUSH-
B-BUT I...
でれー
BLUSH
BUT WE DON'T HAVE PAJAMAS FOR THEM.
I BET YOU COULD FIND SOME IN THE LAND-LADY'S WARD-ROBE.
YEAH, SHE'S GOT EVERY-THING IN THERE.
WARDROBE?
I'LL GO LOOK.
だー
FWOOSH
FAST
早っ

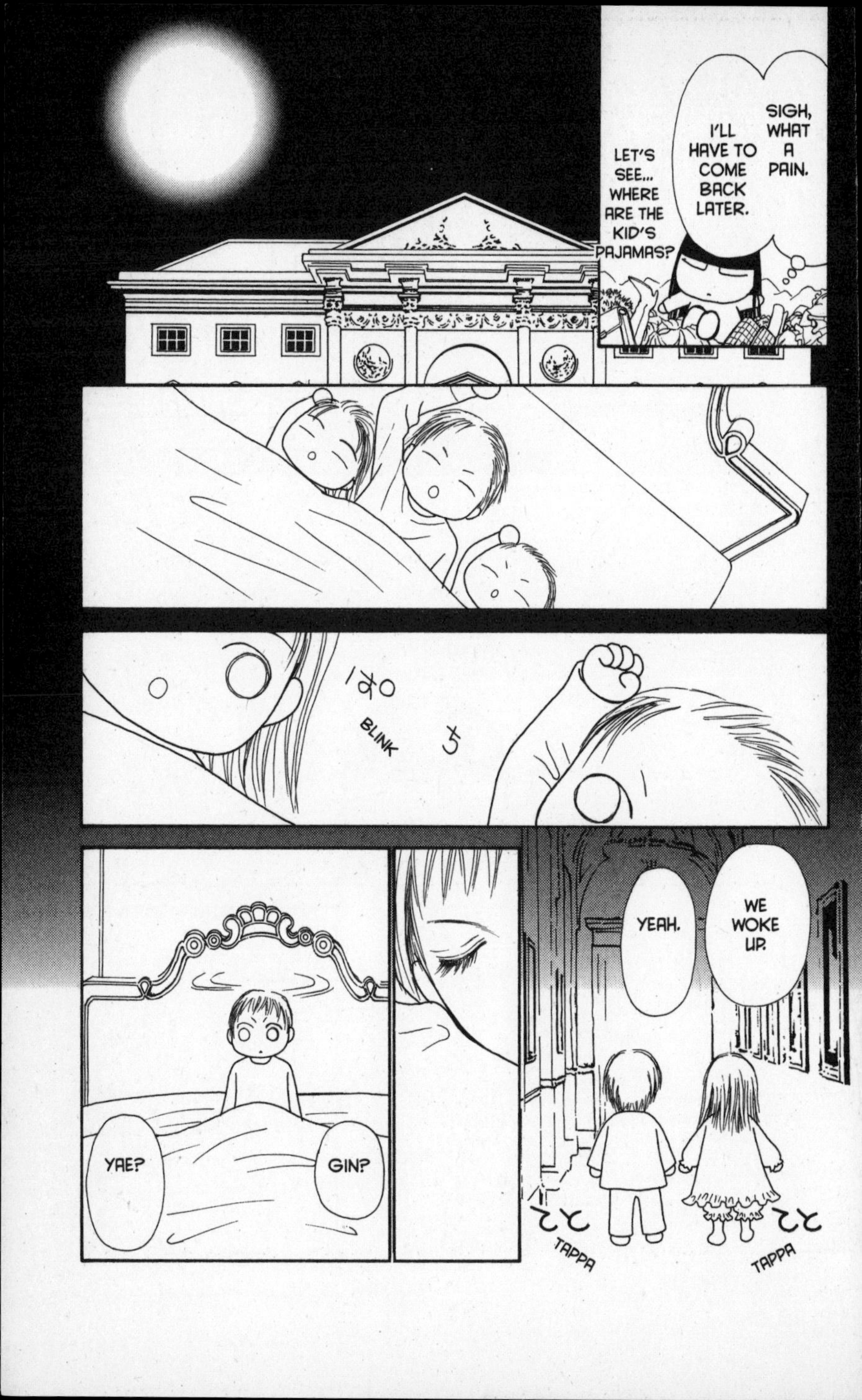
SIGH, WHAT A PAIN.
I'LL HAVE TO COME BACK LATER.
LET'S SEE... WHERE ARE THE KID'S PAJAMAS?
はっ
BLINK
ぱ
WE WOKE UP.
YEAH.
とと
TAPPA
とと
TAPPA
GIN?
YAE?

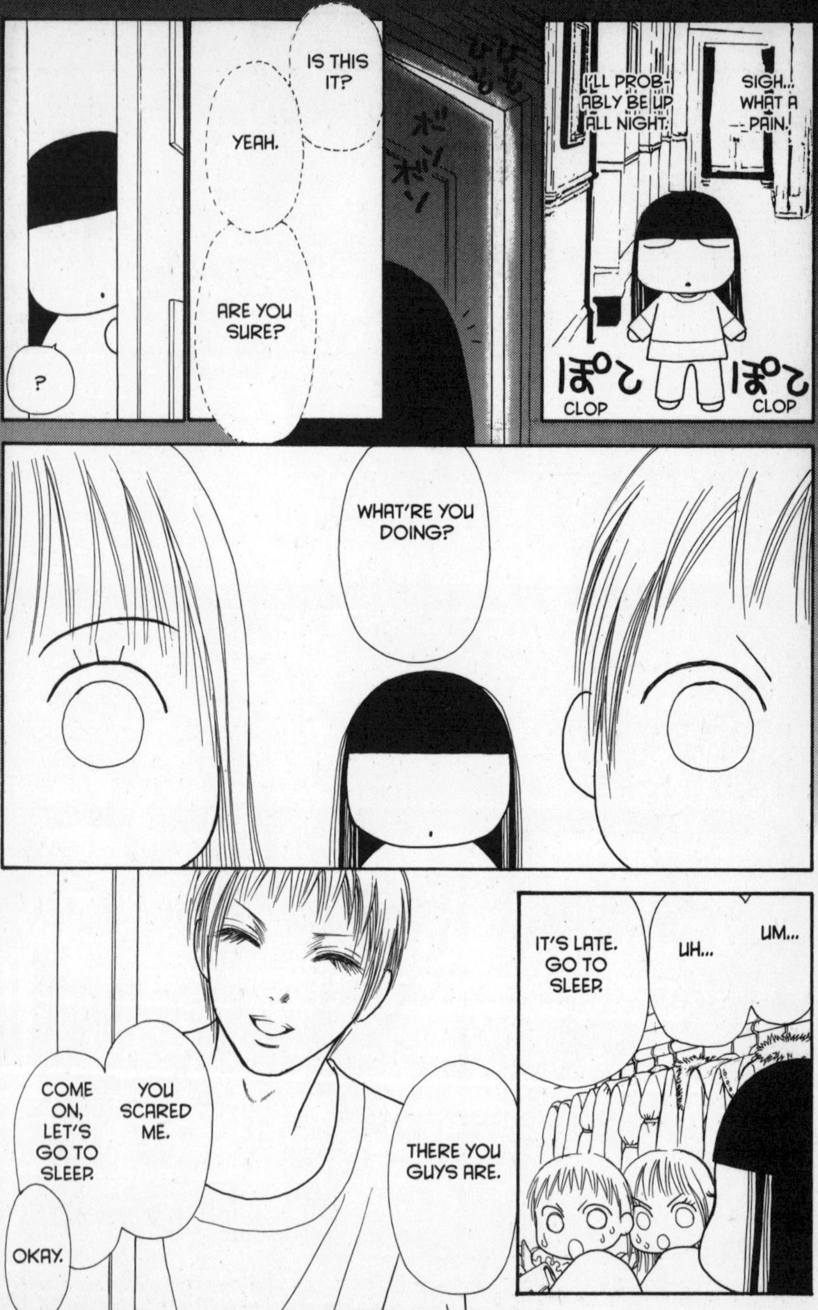
SIGH... WHAT A PAIN.
I'LL PROB-ABLY BE UP ALL NIGHT.
ぽて
CLOP
ぽて
CLOP
ひそひそ
ボソボソ
IS THIS IT?
YEAH.
ARE YOU SURE?
?
WHAT'RE YOU DOING?
UM...
UH...
IT'S LATE. GO TO SLEEP.
THERE YOU GUYS ARE.
YOU SCARED ME.
COME ON, LET'S GO TO SLEEP.
OKAY.

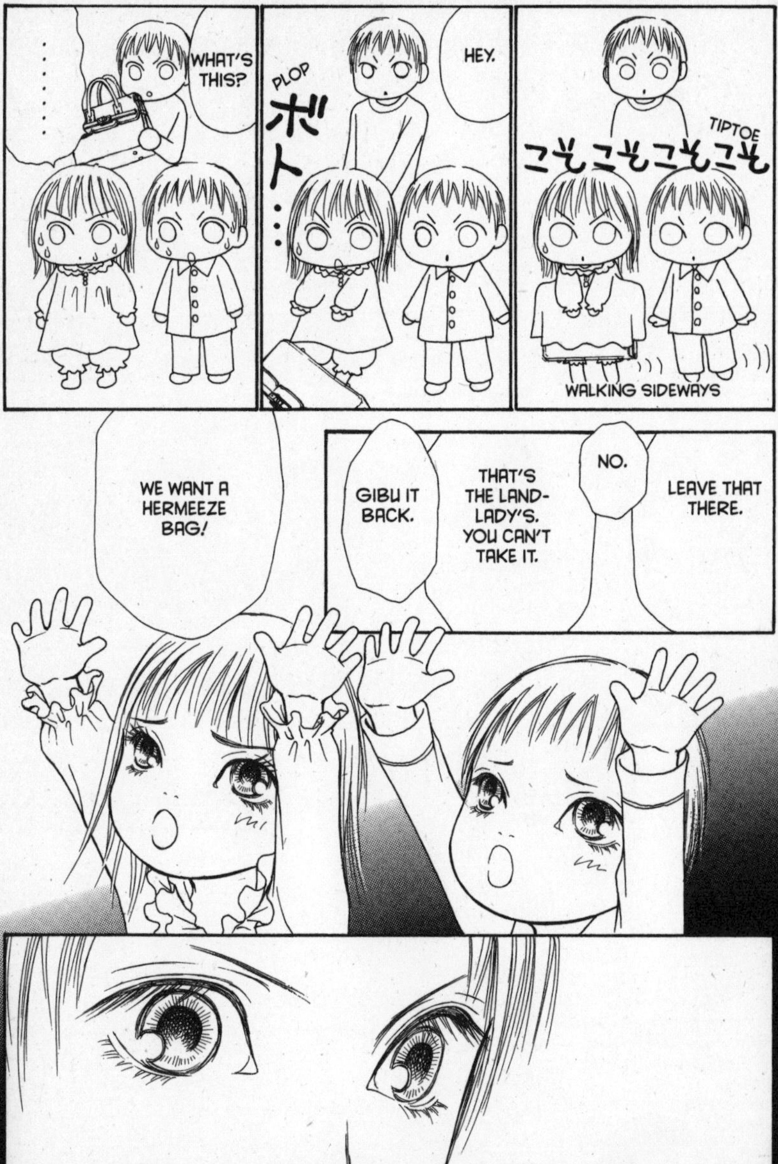
TIPTOE
こそこそこそこそ
WALKING SIDEWAYS
HEY.
PLOP
ボト…
WHAT'S THIS?
……
LEAVE THAT THERE.
NO.
THAT'S THE LAND-LADY'S. YOU CAN'T TAKE IT.
GIBU IT BACK.
WE WANT A HERMEEZE BAG!

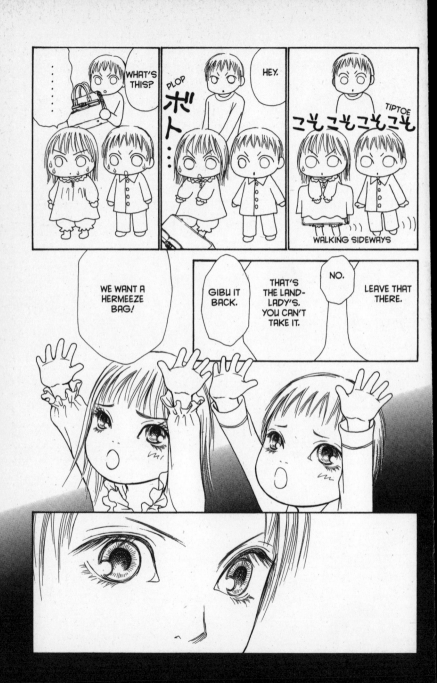

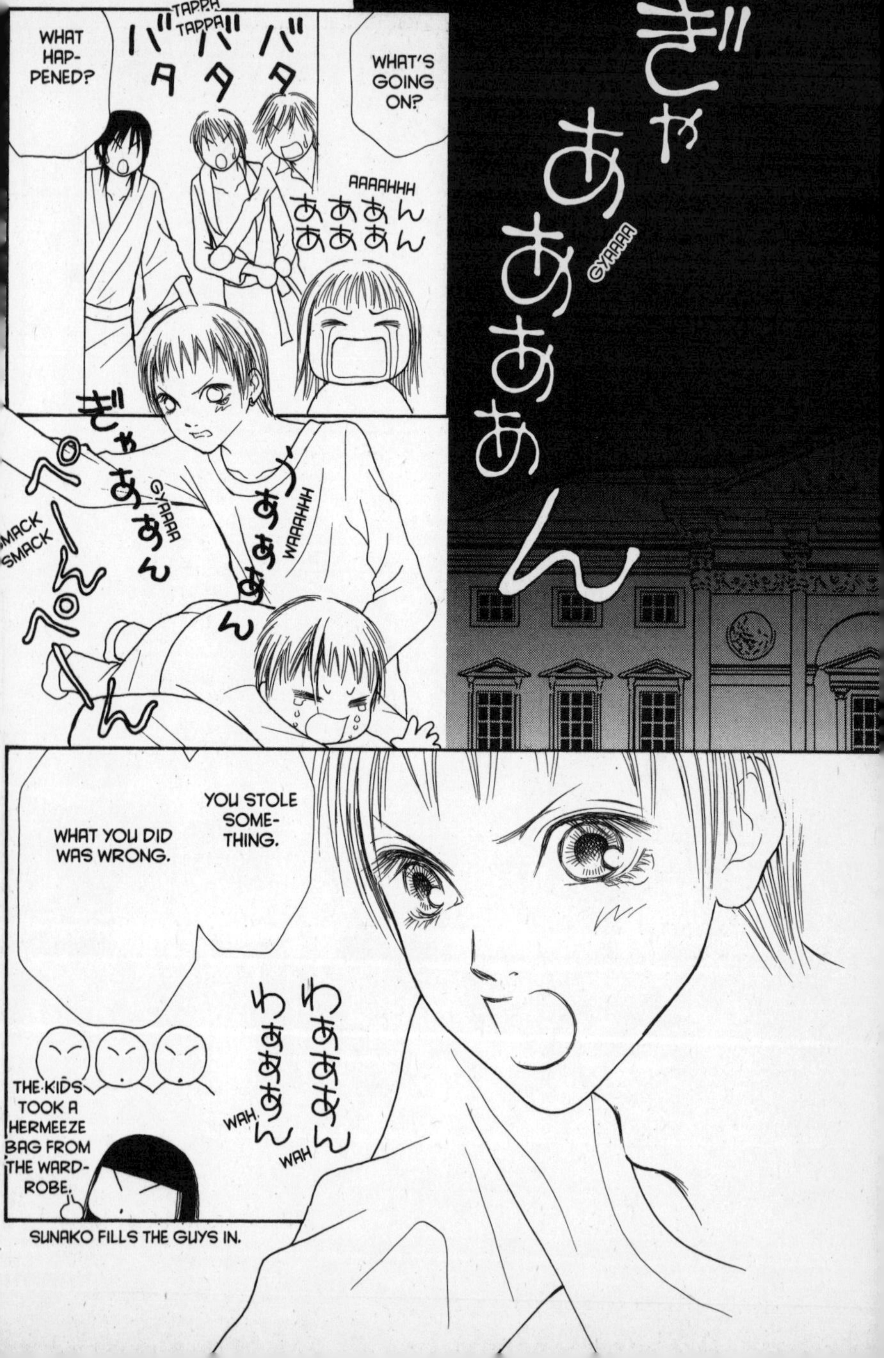
ぎゃああああん
GYAAAA
WHAT'S GOING ON?
バタバタバタ
TAPPA TAPPA
WHAT HAPPENED?
あああん あああん
AAAAHHH
うあああん
WAAAHHH
ぎゃああん
GYAAAA
ぺーんぺーん
SMACK SMACK
YOU STOLE SOMETHING.
WHAT YOU DID WAS WRONG.
わあああん わあああん
WAH WAH
THE KIDS TOOK A HERMEEZE BAG FROM THE WARDROBE.
SUNAKO FILLS THE GUYS IN.

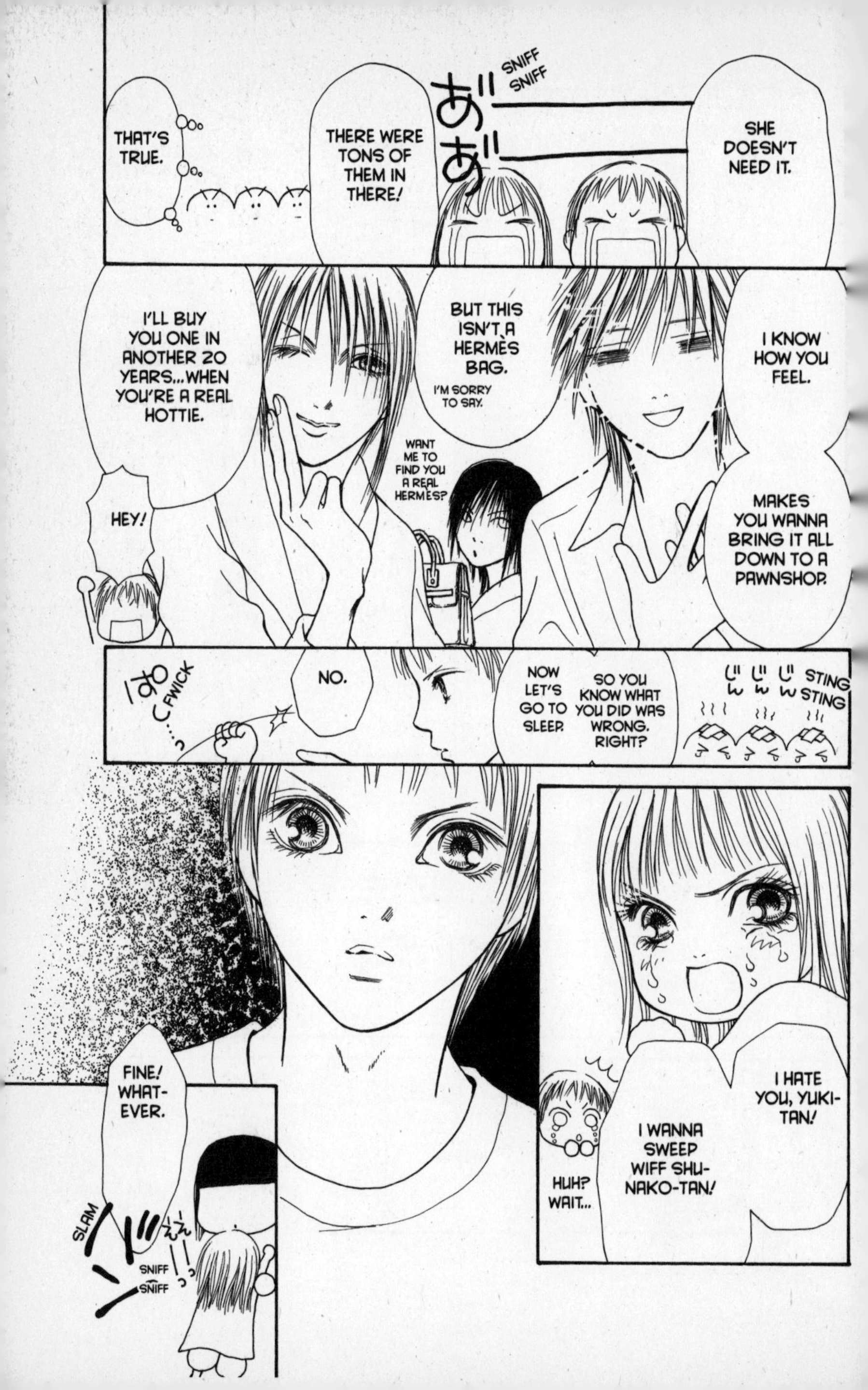
SHE DOESN'T NEED IT.
あ゛あ゛
SNIFF SNIFF
THERE WERE TONS OF THEM IN THERE!
THAT'S TRUE.
I KNOW HOW YOU FEEL.
MAKES YOU WANNA BRING IT ALL DOWN TO A PAWNSHOP.
BUT THIS ISN'T A HERMÈS BAG.
I'M SORRY TO SAY.
WANT ME TO FIND YOU A REAL HERMÈS?
I'LL BUY YOU ONE IN ANOTHER 20 YEARS...WHEN YOU'RE A REAL HOTTIE.
HEY!
じんじんじん
STING STING
SO YOU KNOW WHAT YOU DID WAS WRONG. RIGHT?
NOW LET'S GO TO SLEEP.
NO.
ぽし…っ
FWICK
I HATE YOU, YUKI-TAN!
I WANNA SWEEP WIFF SHU-NAKO-TAN!
HUH? WAIT...
FINE! WHAT-EVER.
SLAM
SNIFF SNIFF

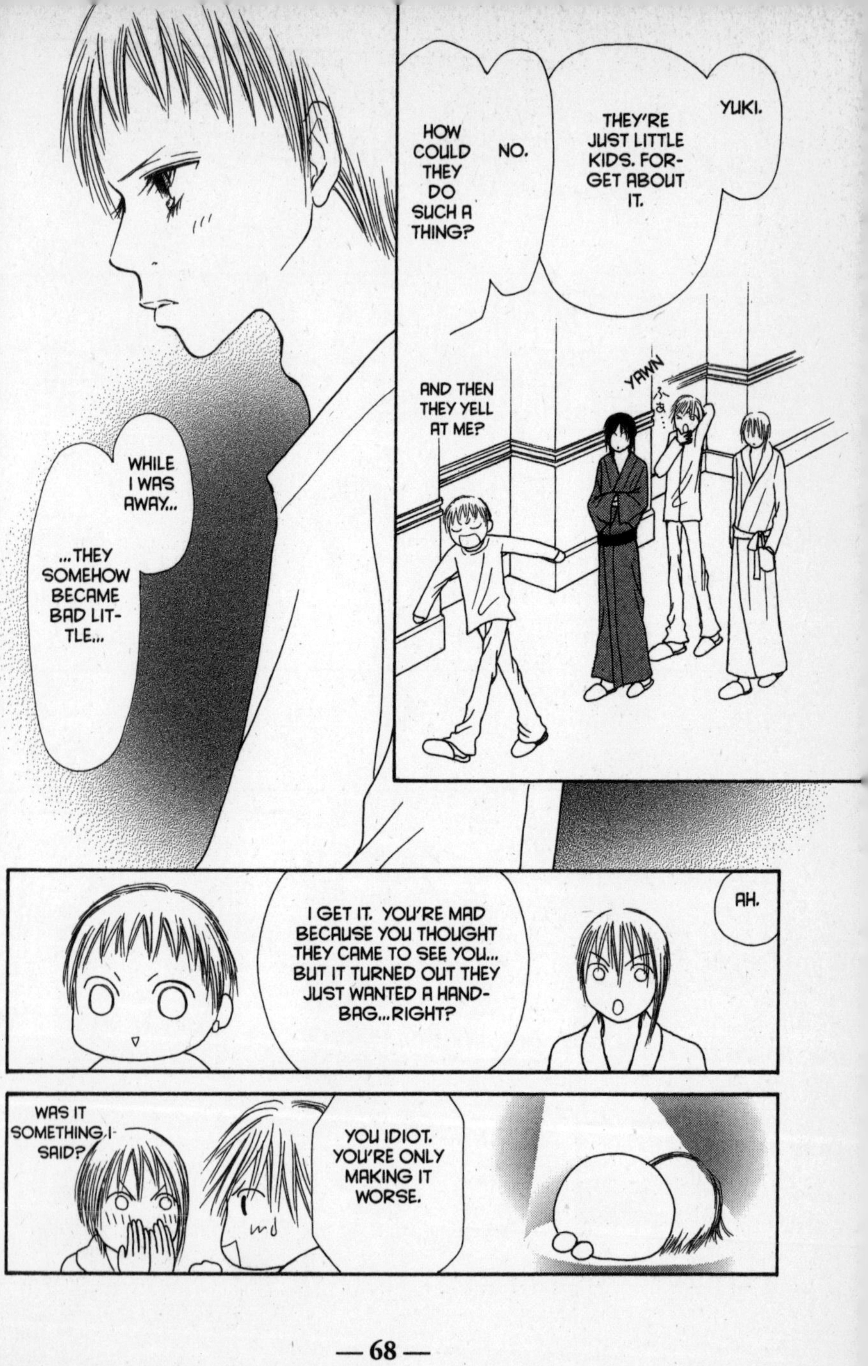
YUKI.
THEY'RE JUST LITTLE KIDS. FOR-GET ABOUT IT.
NO.
HOW COULD THEY DO SUCH A THING?
AND THEN THEY YELL AT ME?
YAWN
ふぁ…
WHILE I WAS AWAY...
...THEY SOMEHOW BECAME BAD LIT-TLE...
AH.
I GET IT. YOU'RE MAD BECAUSE YOU THOUGHT THEY CAME TO SEE YOU... BUT IT TURNED OUT THEY JUST WANTED A HAND-BAG...RIGHT?
YOU IDIOT. YOU'RE ONLY MAKING IT WORSE.
WAS IT SOMETHING I SAID?

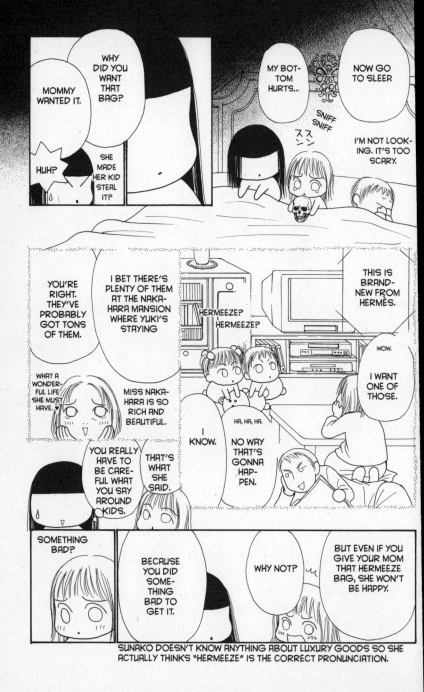

NOW GO TO SLEEP.
MY BOTTOM HURTS...
SNIFF SNIFF
I'M NOT LOOKING. IT'S TOO SCARY.
WHY DID YOU WANT THAT BAG?
MOMMY WANTED IT.
SHE MADE HER KID STEAL IT?
HUH?
THIS IS BRAND-NEW FROM HERMÈS.
WOW.
I WANT ONE OF THOSE.
HERMEEZE? HERMEEZE?
HA, HA, HA.
NO WAY THAT'S GONNA HAPPEN.
I KNOW.
I BET THERE'S PLENTY OF THEM AT THE NAKAHARA MANSION WHERE YUKI'S STAYING
YOU'RE RIGHT. THEY'VE PROBABLY GOT TONS OF THEM.
MISS NAKAHARA IS SO RICH AND BEAUTIFUL.
WHAT A WONDERFUL LIFE SHE MUST HAVE. ♥
THAT'S WHAT SHE SAID.
YOU REALLY HAVE TO BE CAREFUL WHAT YOU SAY AROUND KIDS.
BUT EVEN IF YOU GIVE YOUR MOM THAT HERMEEZE BAG, SHE WON'T BE HAPPY.
WHY NOT?
BECAUSE YOU DID SOMETHING BAD TO GET IT.
SOMETHING BAD?

SUNAKO DOESN'T KNOW ANYTHING ABOUT LUXURY GOODS SO SHE ACTUALLY THINKS "HERMEEZE" IS THE CORRECT PRONUNCIATION.

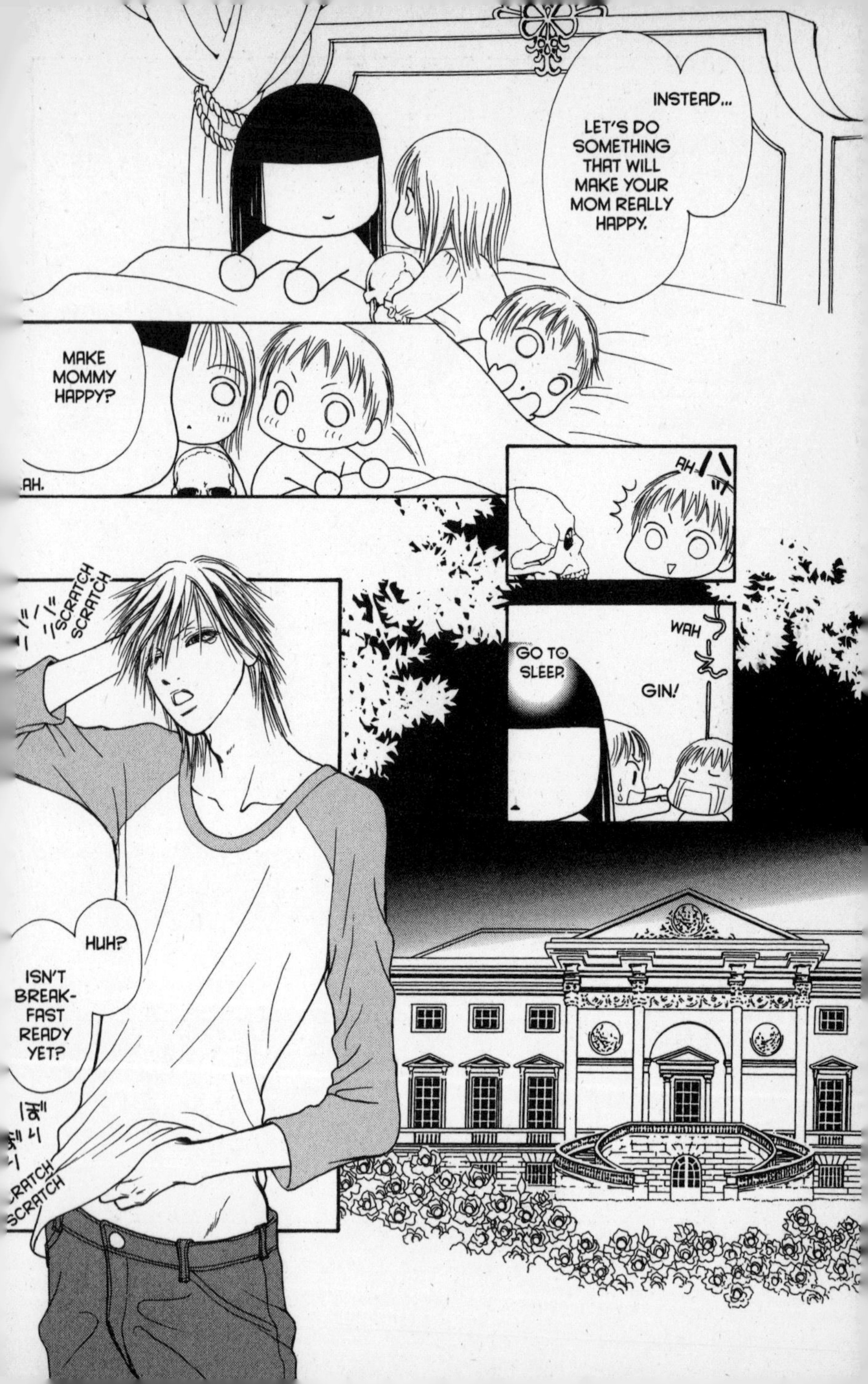
INSTEAD...
LET'S DO SOMETHING THAT WILL MAKE YOUR MOM REALLY HAPPY.
MAKE MOMMY HAPPY?
AH.
AH
WAH
GIN!
GO TO SLEEP.
SCRATCH SCRATCH
HUH?
ISN'T BREAK-FAST READY YET?
SCRATCH SCRATCH

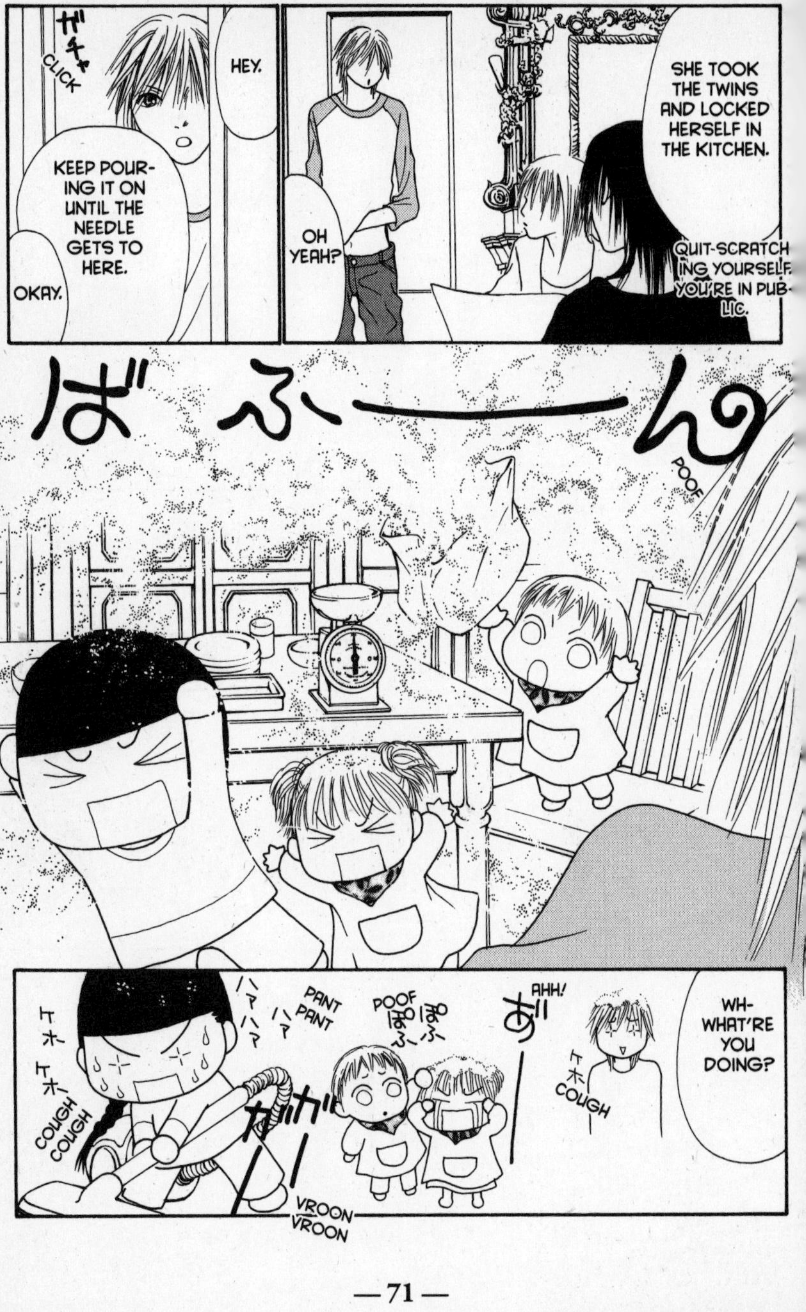
SHE TOOK THE TWINS AND LOCKED HERSELF IN THE KITCHEN.
QUIT-SCRATCHING YOURSELF. YOU'RE IN PUBLIC.
OH YEAH?
ガチャ CLICK
HEY.
KEEP POURING IT ON UNTIL THE NEEDLE GETS TO HERE.
OKAY.
ばふーーん
POOF
WH-WHAT'RE YOU DOING?
ケホ COUGH
あ AHH!
ぽふぽふ POOF
ハァハァ PANT PANT
VROON VROON
ケホケホ COUGH COUGH

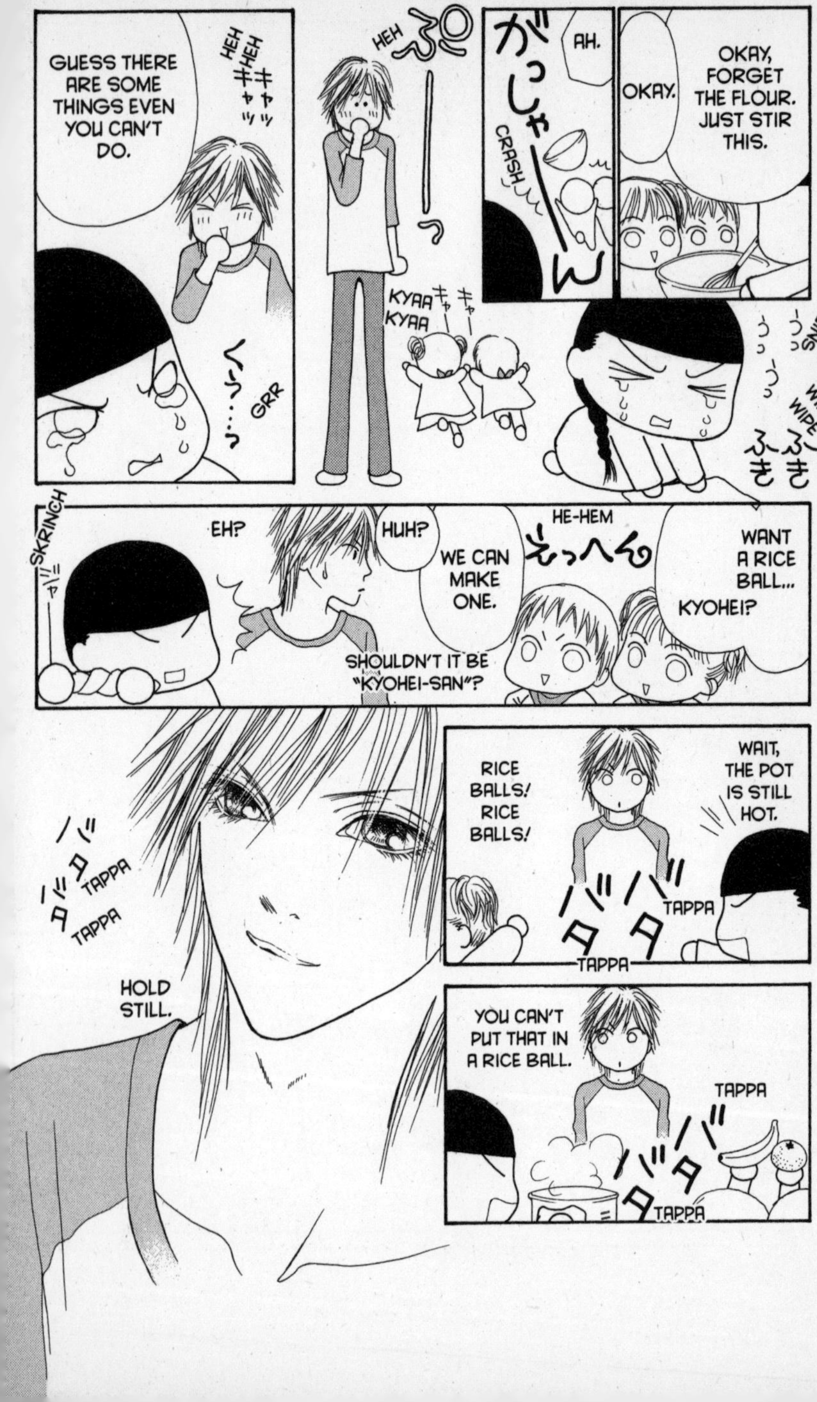
OKAY, FORGET THE FLOUR. JUST STIR THIS.
OKAY.
AH.
がっしゃーん
CRASH
うっうっ
SNIFF SNIFF
ふきふき
WIPE WIPE
HEH
ぷーっ
キャ キャー
KYAA KYAA
HEH HEH
キャッキャッ
GUESS THERE ARE SOME THINGS EVEN YOU CAN'T DO.
くぅ…っ
GRR
WANT A RICE BALL... KYOHEI?
HE-HEM
えっへん
WE CAN MAKE ONE.
HUH?
SHOULDN'T IT BE "KYOHEI-SAN"?
EH?
ジャー
SKRINCH
WAIT, THE POT IS STILL HOT.
RICE BALLS! RICE BALLS!
バタバタ
TAPPA
TAPPA
YOU CAN'T PUT THAT IN A RICE BALL.
バタバタ
TAPPA
TAPPA
HOLD STILL.
バタバタ
TAPPA
TAPPA

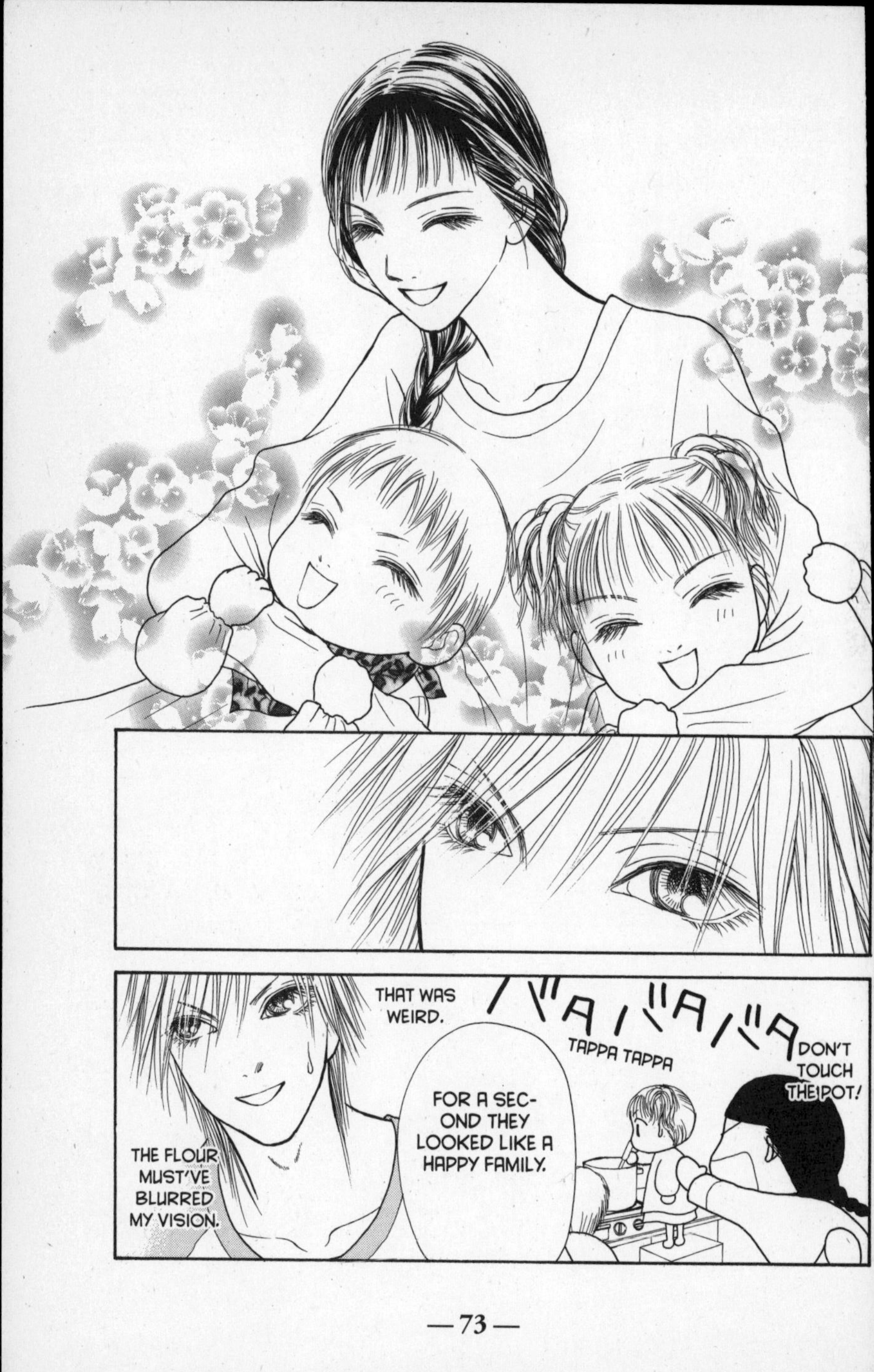
DON'T TOUCH THE POT!
TAPPA TAPPA
THAT WAS WEIRD.
FOR A SEC- OND THEY LOOKED LIKE A HAPPY FAMILY.
THE FLOUR MUST'VE BLURRED MY VISION.

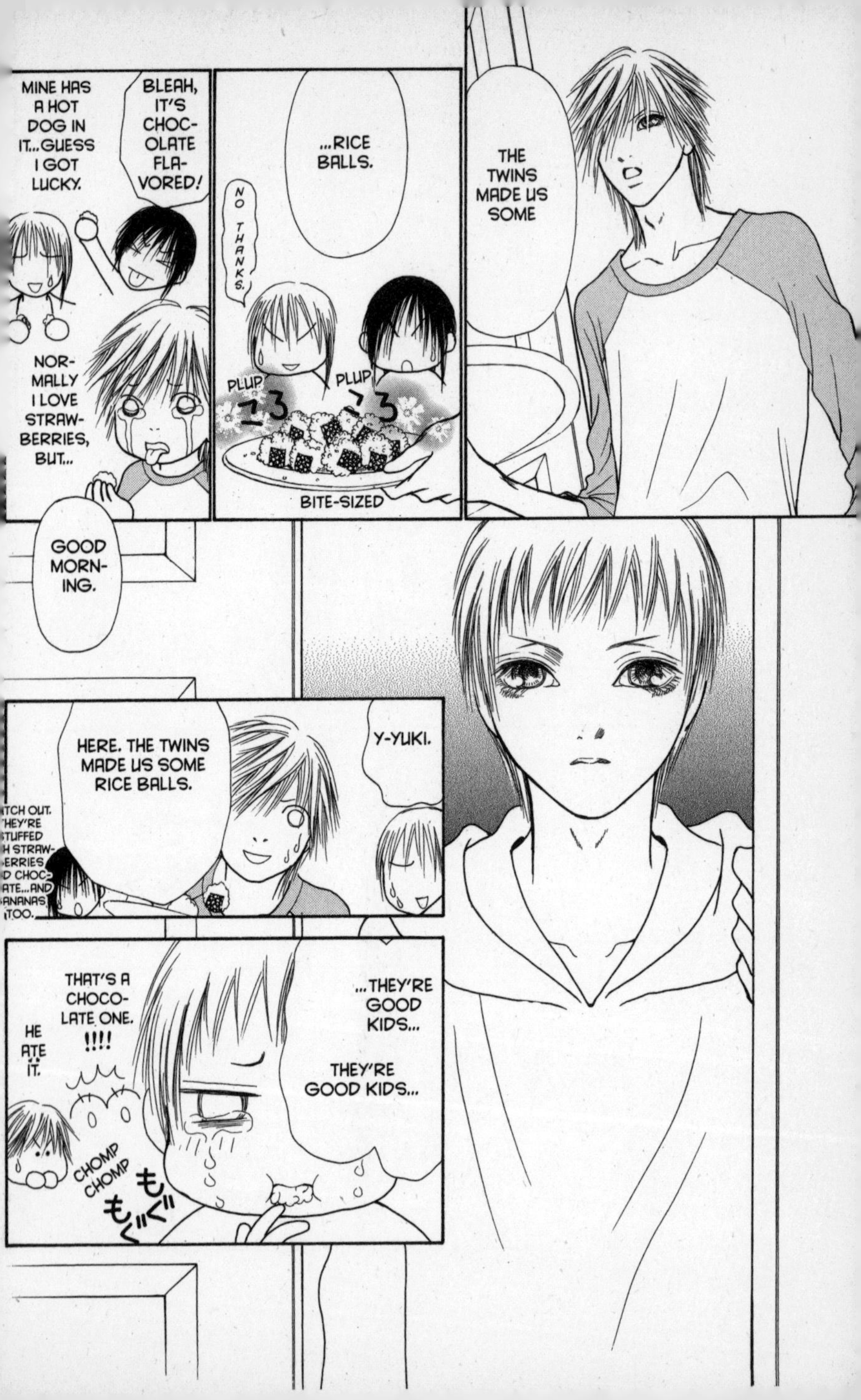
THE TWINS MADE US SOME
...RICE BALLS.
NO THANKS.
PLUP
PLUP
BITE-SIZED
BLEAH, IT'S CHOCOLATE FLAVORED!
MINE HAS A HOT DOG IN IT...GUESS I GOT LUCKY.
NORMALLY I LOVE STRAWBERRIES, BUT...
GOOD MORNING.
Y-YUKI.
HERE. THE TWINS MADE US SOME RICE BALLS.
TCH OUT. THEY'RE STUFFED H STRAWBERRIES D CHOCOLATE...AND ANANAS TOO.
...THEY'RE GOOD KIDS...
THEY'RE GOOD KIDS...
THAT'S A CHOCOLATE ONE.
!!!!
HE ATE IT.
CHOMP CHOMP
もぐもぐ

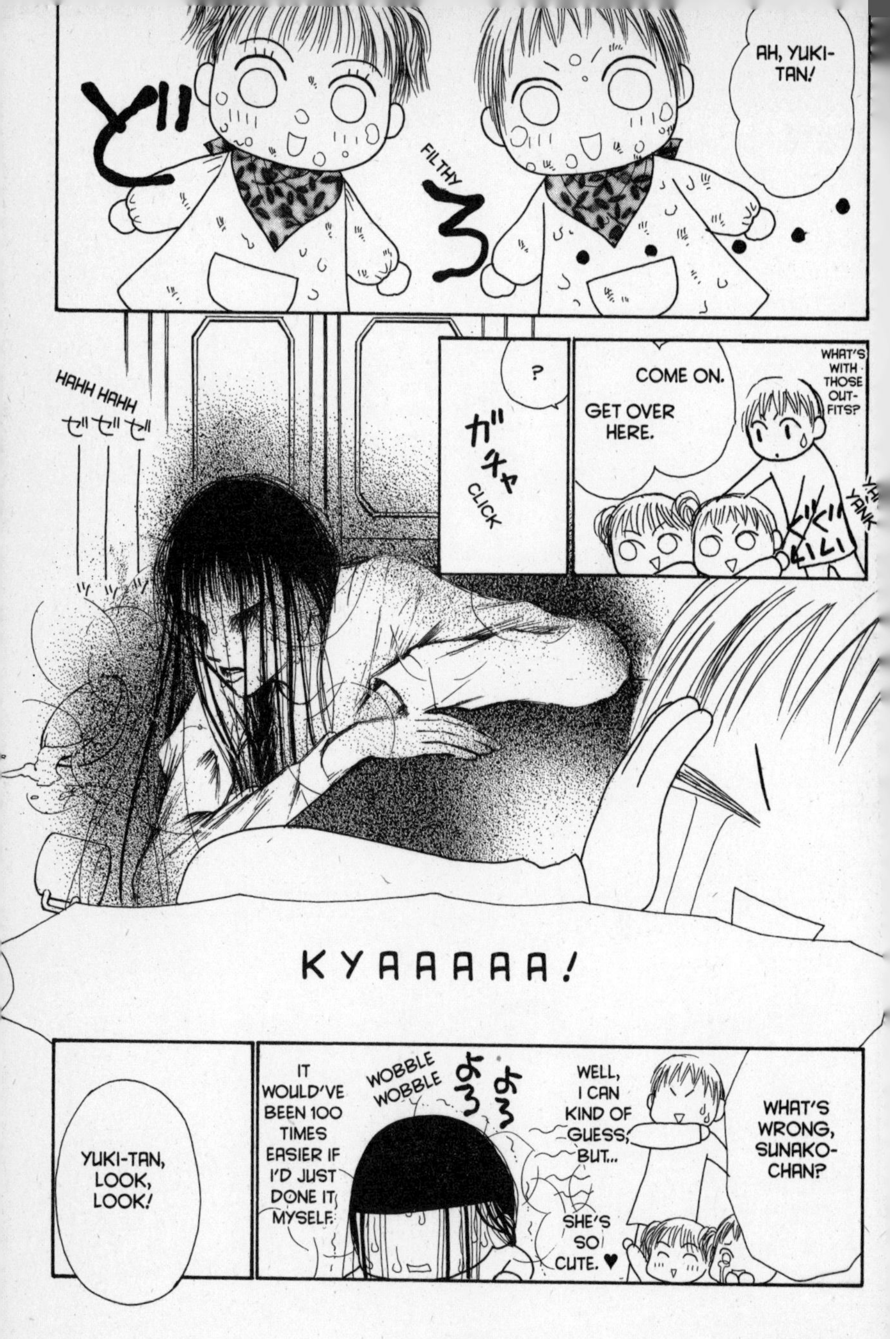
AH, YUKI-TAN!
FILTHY
どろ
WHAT'S WITH THOSE OUT-FITS?
YANK
ぐいぐい
COME ON.
GET OVER HERE.
?
ガチャ
CLICK
HAHH HAHH
ぜぜぜ
KYAAAAAA!
WHAT'S WRONG, SUNAKO-CHAN?
WELL, I CAN KIND OF GUESS, BUT...
SHE'S SO CUTE. ♥
WOBBLE WOBBLE
よろよろ
IT WOULD'VE BEEN 100 TIMES EASIER IF I'D JUST DONE IT MYSELF.
YUKI-TAN, LOOK, LOOK!

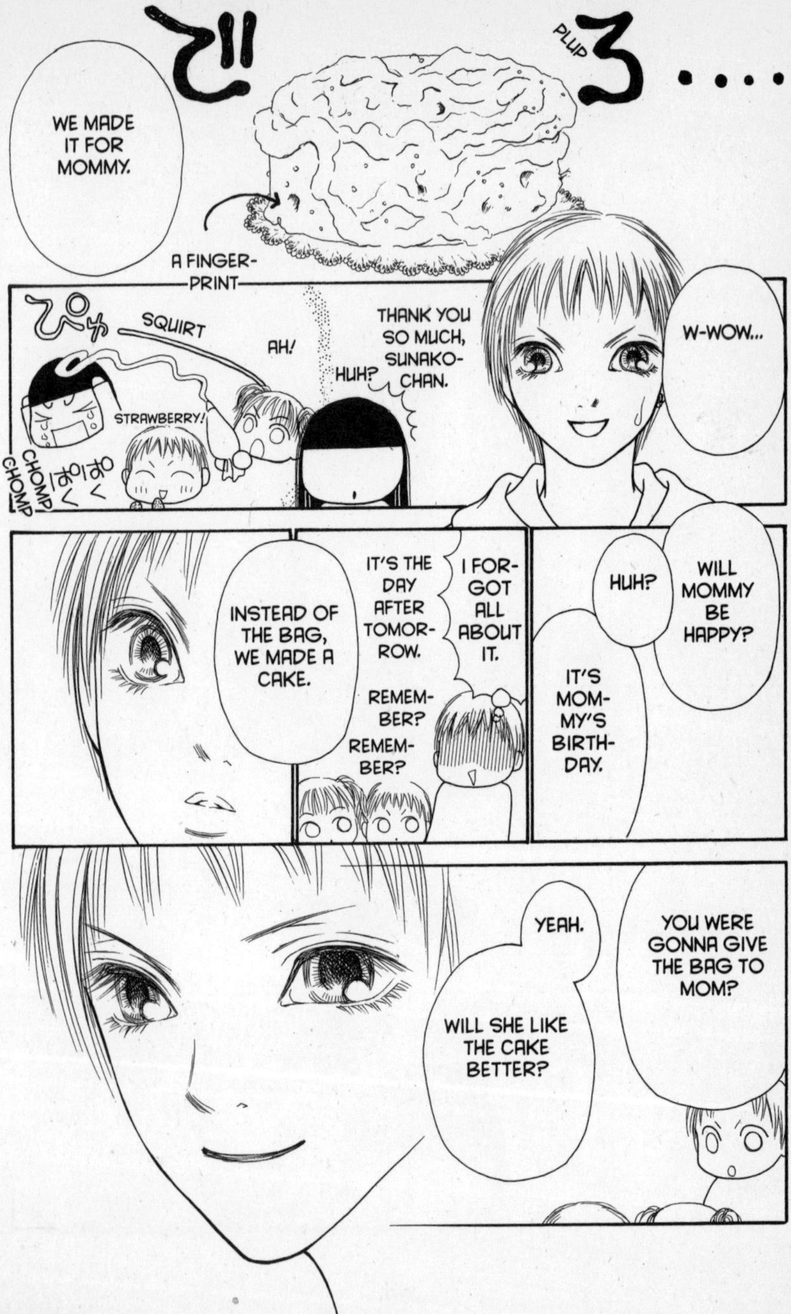

PLUP
でろ…
A FINGER-PRINT
WE MADE IT FOR MOMMY.
W-WOW...
THANK YOU SO MUCH, SUNAKO-CHAN.
HUH?
AH!
ぴゅ
SQUIRT
STRAWBERRY!
ぱくぱく
CHOMP CHOMP
WILL MOMMY BE HAPPY?
HUH?
IT'S MOMMY'S BIRTHDAY.
I FORGOT ALL ABOUT IT.
IT'S THE DAY AFTER TOMORROW.
REMEMBER?
REMEMBER?
INSTEAD OF THE BAG, WE MADE A CAKE.
YOU WERE GONNA GIVE THE BAG TO MOM?
YEAH.
WILL SHE LIKE THE CAKE BETTER?

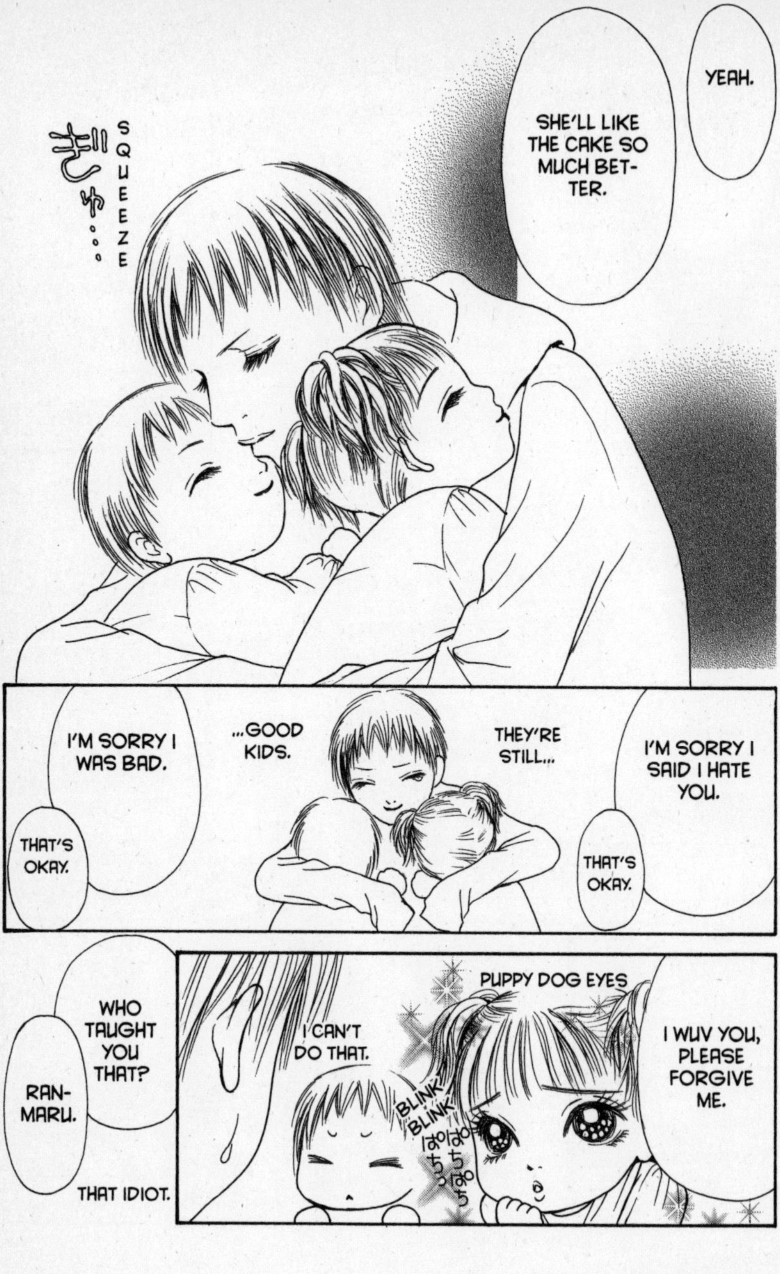
YEAH.
SHE'LL LIKE THE CAKE SO MUCH BET-TER.
SQUEEZE
ぎゅ…
I'M SORRY I SAID I HATE YOU.
THAT'S OKAY.
THEY'RE STILL...
...GOOD KIDS.
I'M SORRY I WAS BAD.
THAT'S OKAY.
PUPPY DOG EYES
I WUV YOU, PLEASE FORGIVE ME.
BLINK BLINK
I CAN'T DO THAT.
WHO TAUGHT YOU THAT?
RAN-MARU.
THAT IDIOT.

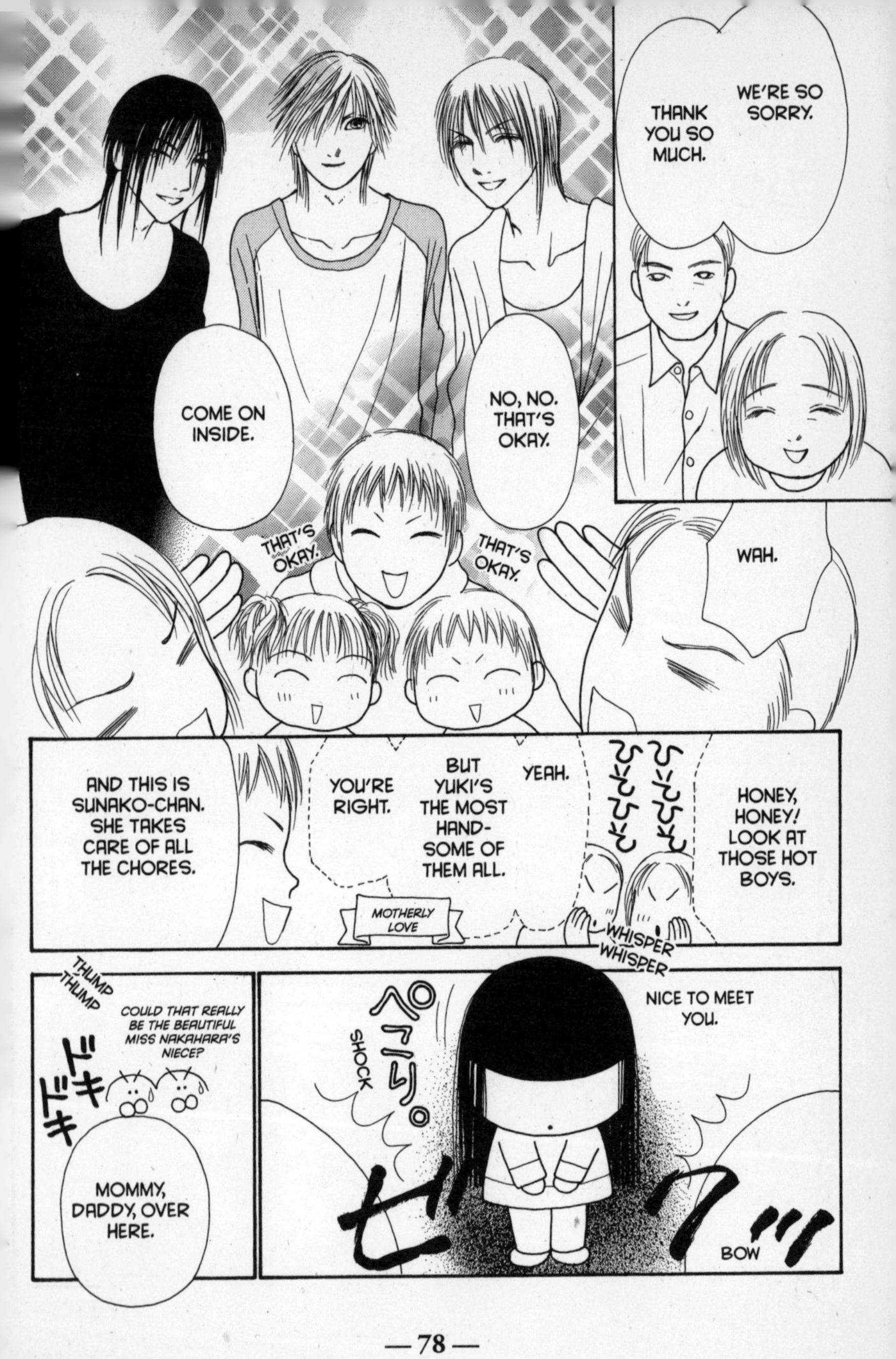
WE'RE SO SORRY.
THANK YOU SO MUCH.
NO, NO. THAT'S OKAY.
COME ON INSIDE.
WAH.
THAT'S OKAY.
THAT'S OKAY.
HONEY, HONEY! LOOK AT THOSE HOT BOYS.
ひそひそ
ひそひそ
WHISPER WHISPER
YEAH.
BUT YUKI'S THE MOST HAND-SOME OF THEM ALL.
YOU'RE RIGHT.
MOTHERLY LOVE
AND THIS IS SUNAKO-CHAN. SHE TAKES CARE OF ALL THE CHORES.
NICE TO MEET YOU.
ペこり。
BOW
SHOCK
THUMP THUMP
ドキドキ
COULD THAT REALLY BE THE BEAUTIFUL MISS NAKAHARA'S NIECE?
MOMMY, DADDY, OVER HERE.

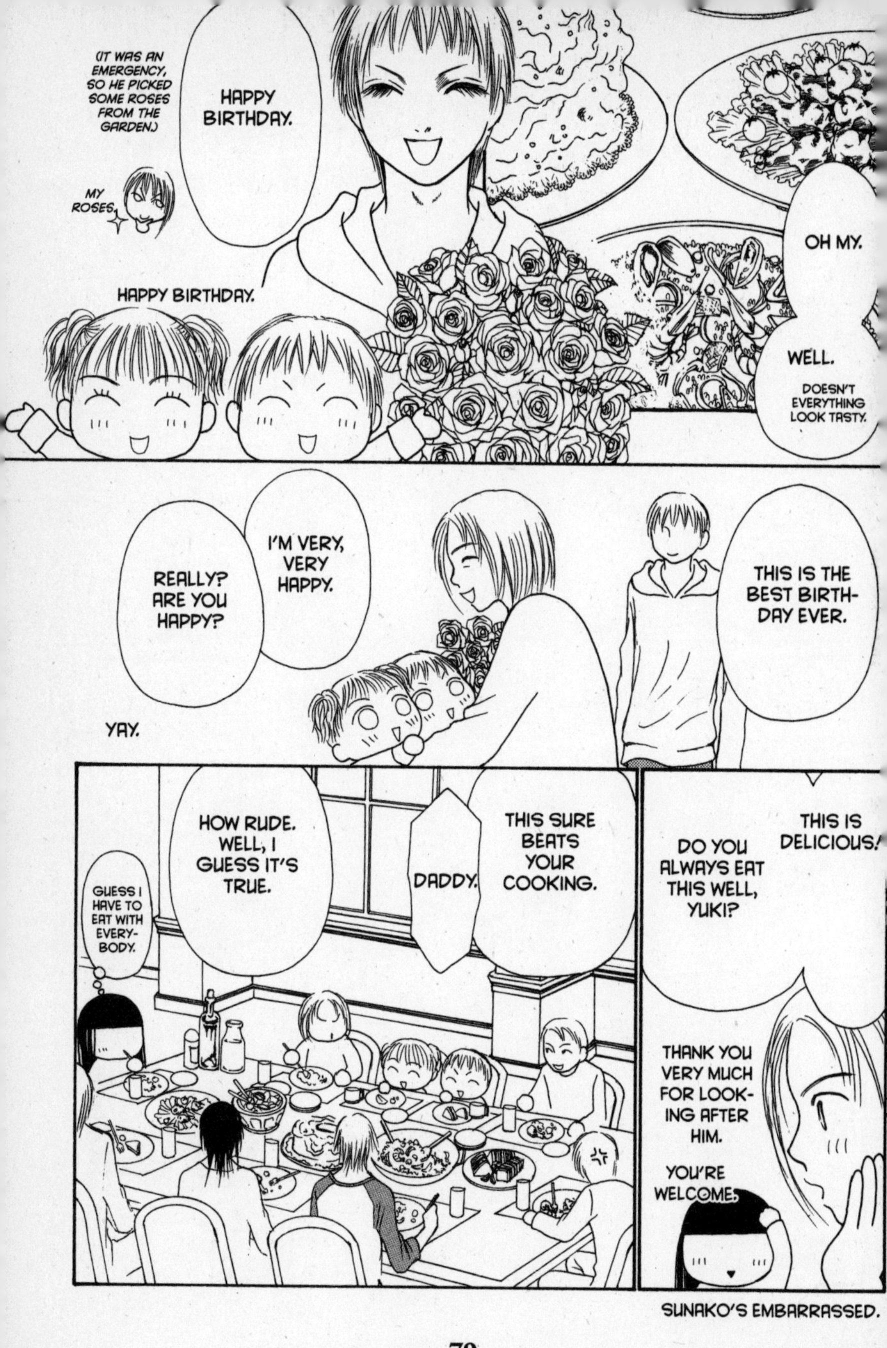
OH MY.
WELL.
DOESN'T EVERYTHING LOOK TASTY.
HAPPY BIRTHDAY.
(IT WAS AN EMERGENCY, SO HE PICKED SOME ROSES FROM THE GARDEN.)
MY ROSES.
HAPPY BIRTHDAY.
THIS IS THE BEST BIRTHDAY EVER.
I'M VERY, VERY HAPPY.
REALLY? ARE YOU HAPPY?
YAY.
THIS IS DELICIOUS!
DO YOU ALWAYS EAT THIS WELL, YUKI?
THANK YOU VERY MUCH FOR LOOKING AFTER HIM.
YOU'RE WELCOME.
SUNAKO'S EMBARRASSED.
THIS SURE BEATS YOUR COOKING.
DADDY.
HOW RUDE. WELL, I GUESS IT'S TRUE.
GUESS I HAVE TO EAT WITH EVERYBODY.

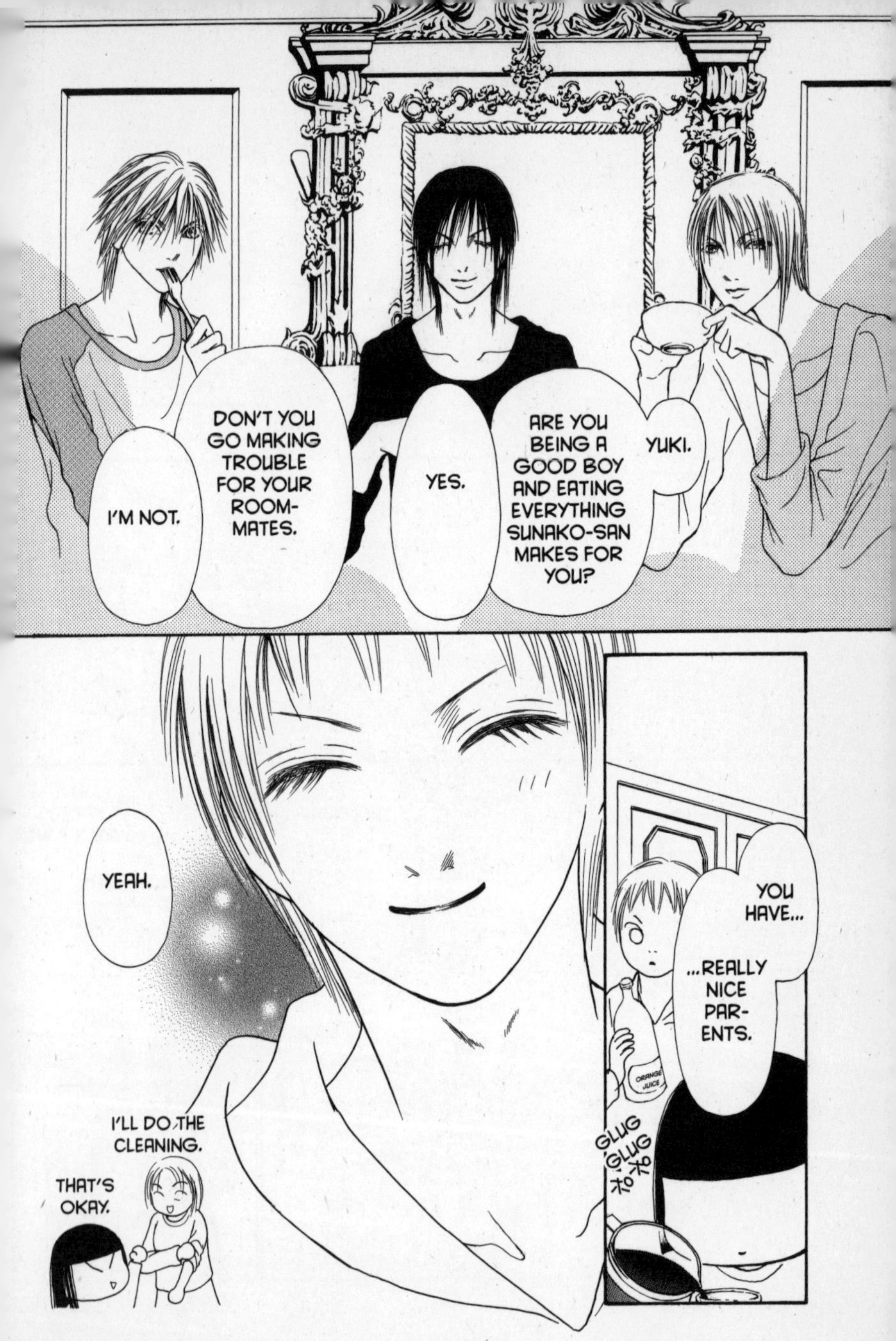
YUKI.
ARE YOU BEING A GOOD BOY AND EATING EVERYTHING SUNAKO-SAN MAKES FOR YOU?
YES.
DON'T YOU GO MAKING TROUBLE FOR YOUR ROOM-MATES.
I'M NOT.
YOU HAVE...
...REALLY NICE PAR-ENTS.
ORANGE JUICE
GLUG GLUG
YEAH.
I'LL DO THE CLEANING.
THAT'S OKAY.

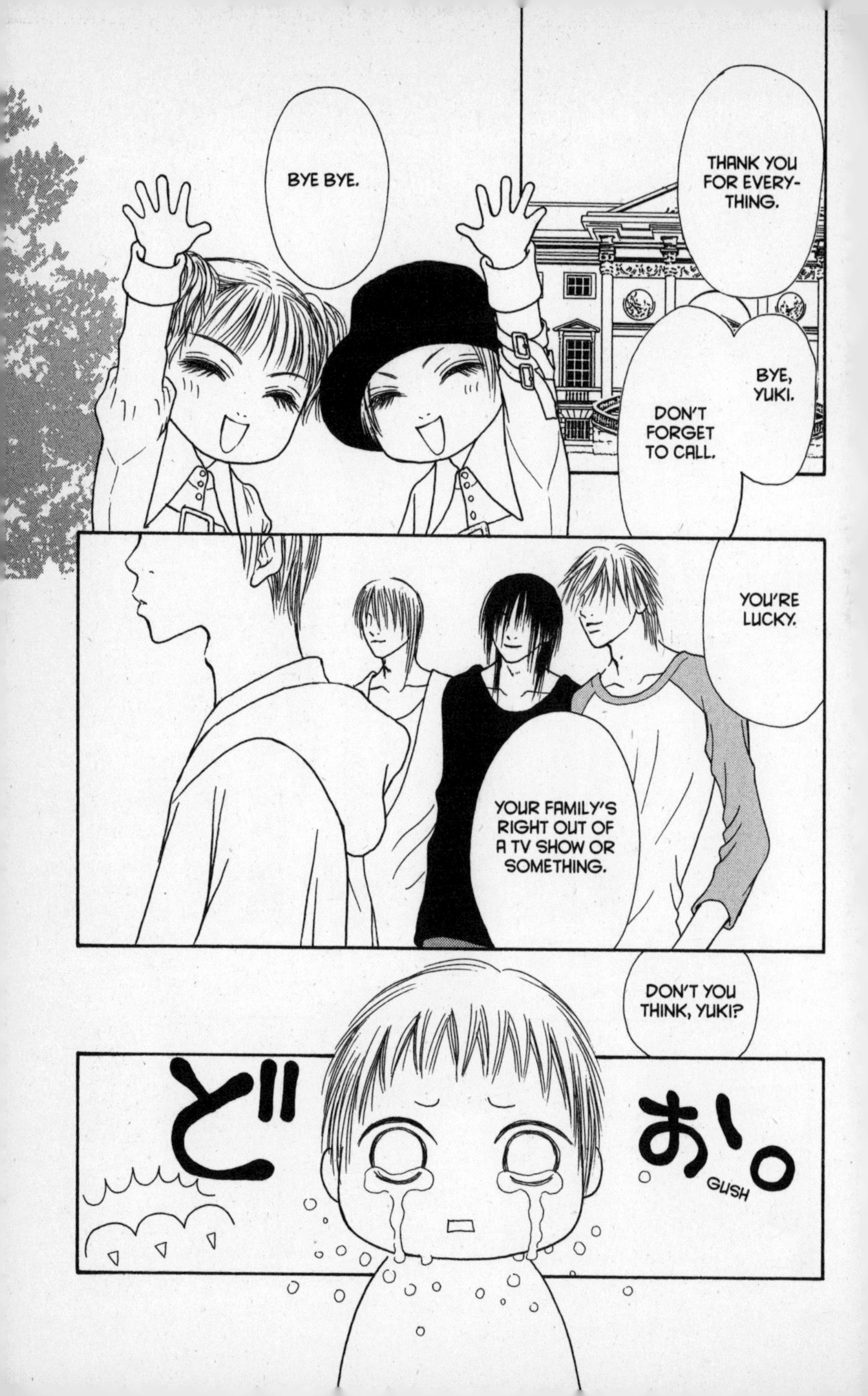
THANK YOU FOR EVERY-THING.
BYE, YUKI.
DON'T FORGET TO CALL.
BYE BYE.
YOU'RE LUCKY.
YOUR FAMILY'S RIGHT OUT OF A TV SHOW OR SOMETHING.
DON'T YOU THINK, YUKI?
どお。
GUSH

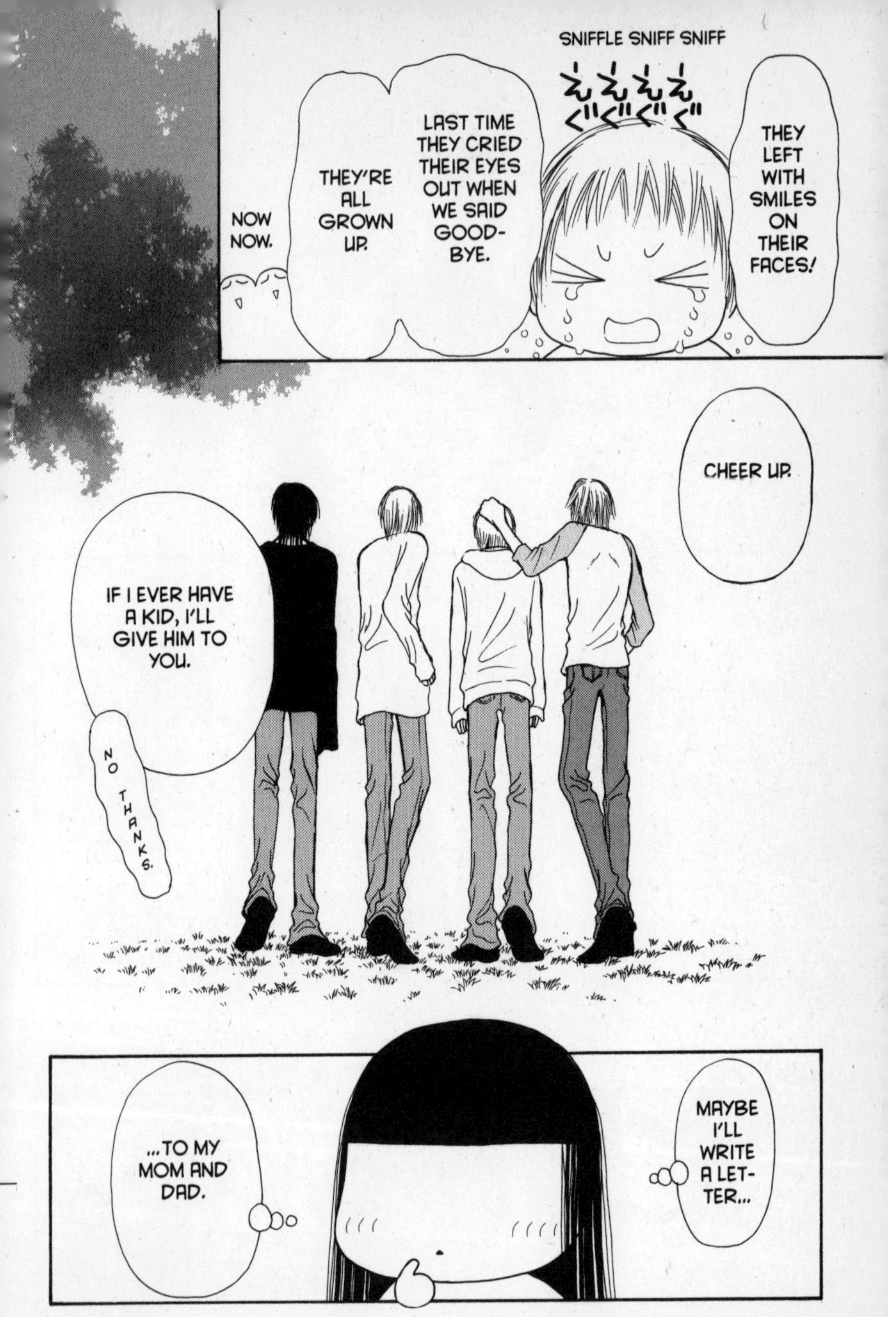
SNIFFLE SNIFF SNIFF
ええええ ぐぐぐぐ
THEY LEFT WITH SMILES ON THEIR FACES!
LAST TIME THEY CRIED THEIR EYES OUT WHEN WE SAID GOOD-BYE.
THEY'RE ALL GROWN UP.
NOW NOW.
CHEER UP.
IF I EVER HAVE A KID, I'LL GIVE HIM TO YOU.
NO THANKS.
MAYBE I'LL WRITE A LETTER...
...TO MY MOM AND DAD.

Chapter 61
MISSED LOVE

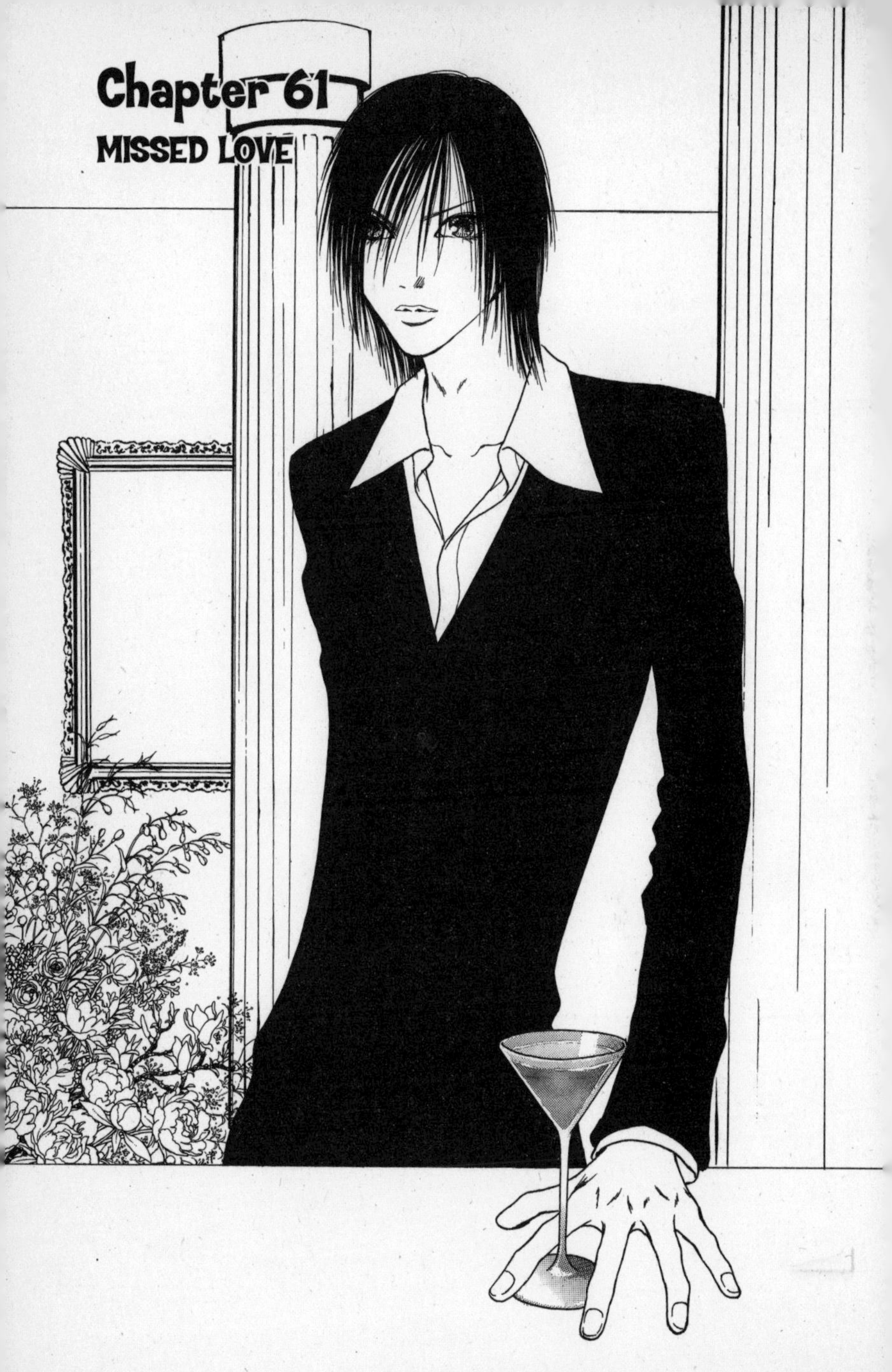

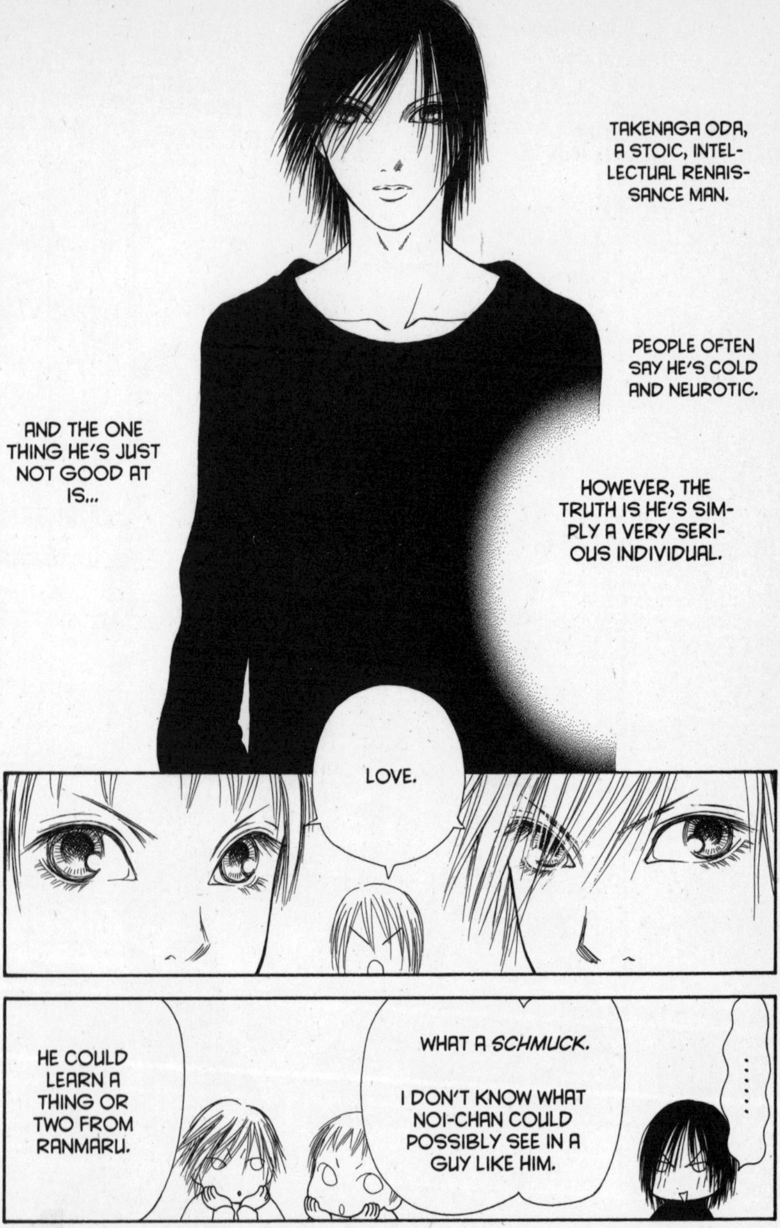
TAKENAGA ODA, A STOIC, INTELLECTUAL RENAISSANCE MAN.
PEOPLE OFTEN SAY HE'S COLD AND NEUROTIC.
HOWEVER, THE TRUTH IS HE'S SIMPLY A VERY SERIOUS INDIVIDUAL.
AND THE ONE THING HE'S JUST NOT GOOD AT IS...
LOVE.
......
WHAT A *SCHMUCK.*
I DON'T KNOW WHAT NOI-CHAN COULD POSSIBLY SEE IN A GUY LIKE HIM.
HE COULD LEARN A THING OR TWO FROM RANMARU.

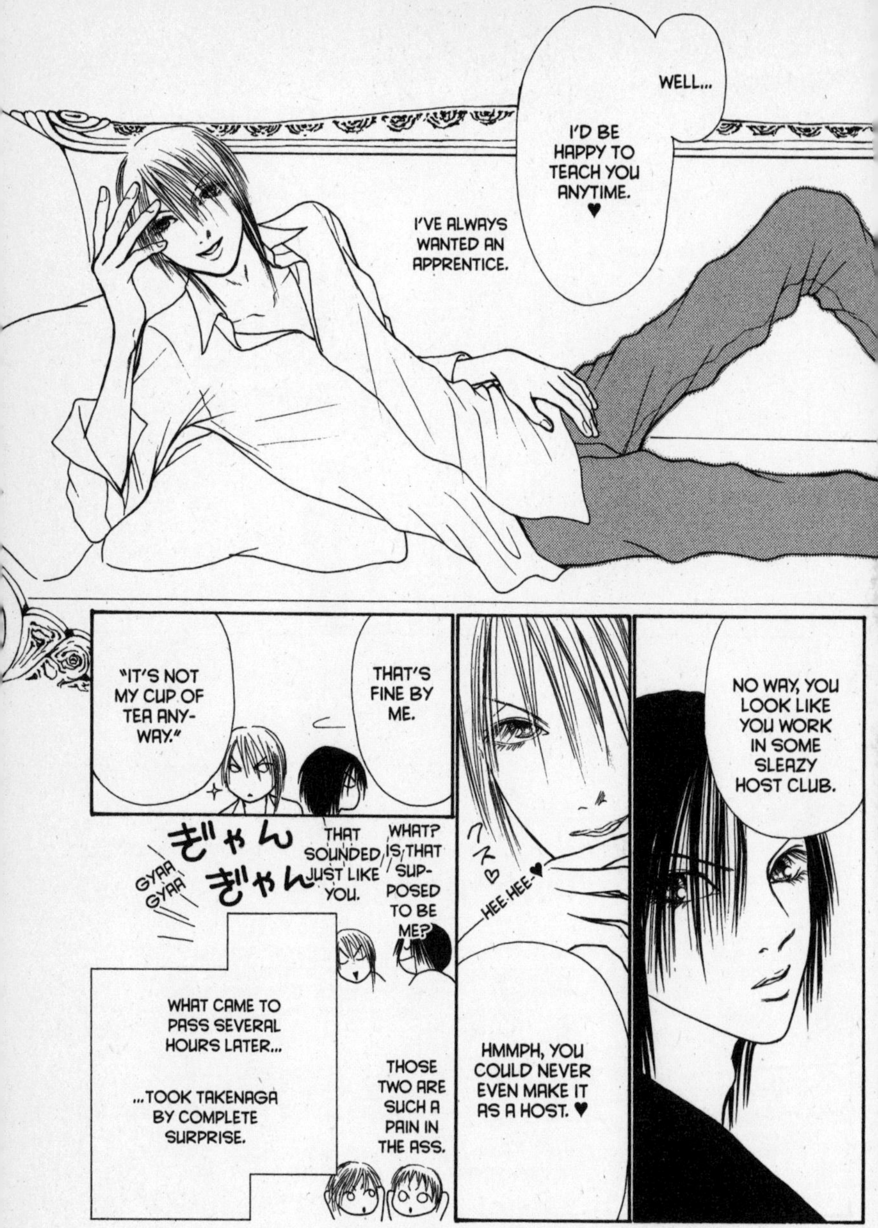
WELL...
I'D BE HAPPY TO TEACH YOU ANYTIME. ♥
I'VE ALWAYS WANTED AN APPRENTICE.
NO WAY, YOU LOOK LIKE YOU WORK IN SOME SLEAZY HOST CLUB.
クス♡
HEE-HEE-♥
HMMPH, YOU COULD NEVER EVEN MAKE IT AS A HOST. ♥
THAT'S FINE BY ME.
"IT'S NOT MY CUP OF TEA ANY-WAY."
WHAT? IS THAT SUP-POSED TO BE ME?
THAT SOUNDED JUST LIKE YOU.
ぎゃん ぎゃん
GYAA GYAA
THOSE TWO ARE SUCH A PAIN IN THE ASS.
WHAT CAME TO PASS SEVERAL HOURS LATER...
...TOOK TAKENAGA BY COMPLETE SURPRISE.

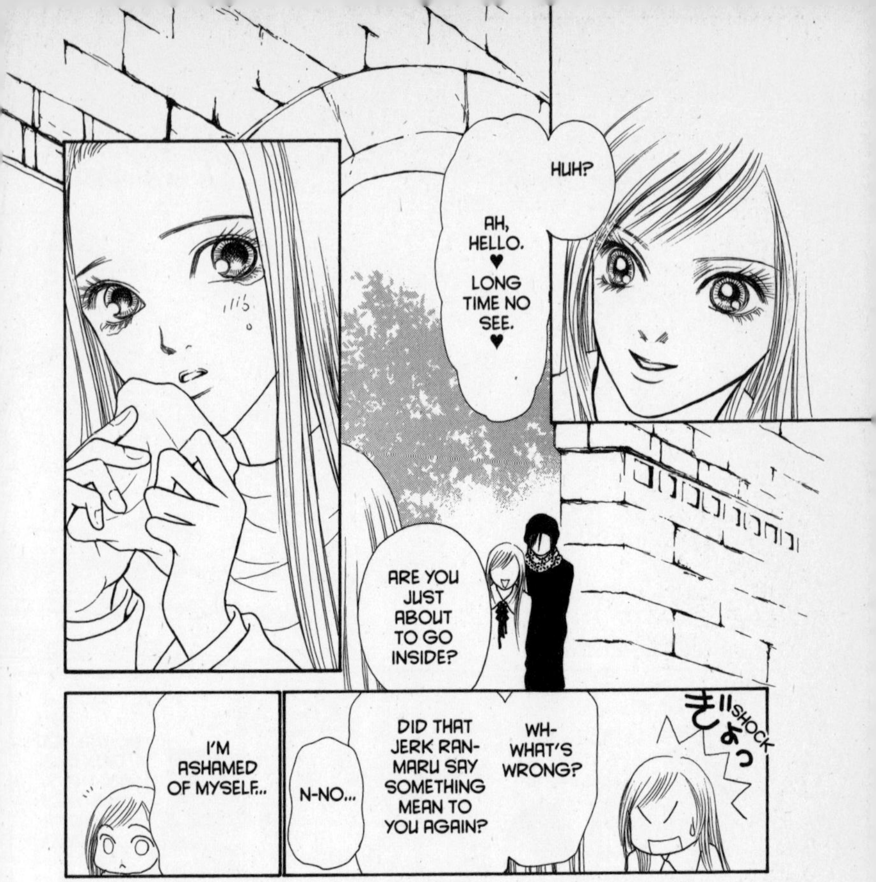
HUH?
AH, HELLO. ♥ LONG TIME NO SEE. ♥
ARE YOU JUST ABOUT TO GO INSIDE?
ぎょっ
SHOCK
WH- WHAT'S WRONG?
DID THAT JERK RANMARU SAY SOMETHING MEAN TO YOU AGAIN?
N-NO...
I'M ASHAMED OF MYSELF...

BEHIND THE SCENES

THE STORY THAT COMES AFTER THIS ONE IN THE TANKOUBON ACTUALLY CAME FIRST IN THE MAGAZINE, BUT I HAD THE ORDER CHANGED.

WHILE I WAS WORKING ON THIS STORY, YUKIO IKEDA-SAMA AND YUU YOSHII-SAMA FROM *BESSATSU FRIEND* CAME BY TO HELP ME. THANKS, GUYS. ♥♥♥♥

YUU YOSHII'S HOST CHARACTER FROM "DEEP LOVE HOST" MADE A LITTLE CAMEO. SHE'S ACTUALLY GONE TO HOST CLUBS TO DO RESEARCH, SO THIS CHARACTER IS JUST LIKE A REAL HOST. ♥(YUU YOSHII DRAWS REALLY HOT GUYS.)

I THINK THE HOST CHARACTERS I DRAW ARE SORT OF OLD SCHOOL. I DIDN'T GO TO ANY CLUBS FOR RESEARCH, AND I THINK I MADE THE RIGHT CHOICE.

YOU'LL GET THE MOST OUT OF THIS STORY IF YOU TAKE A MOMENT TO READ THE RANMARU BONUS MANGA "RANMARU'S DEPRESSING DAY" AT THE BEGINNING OF WALLFLOWER VOLUME 14.

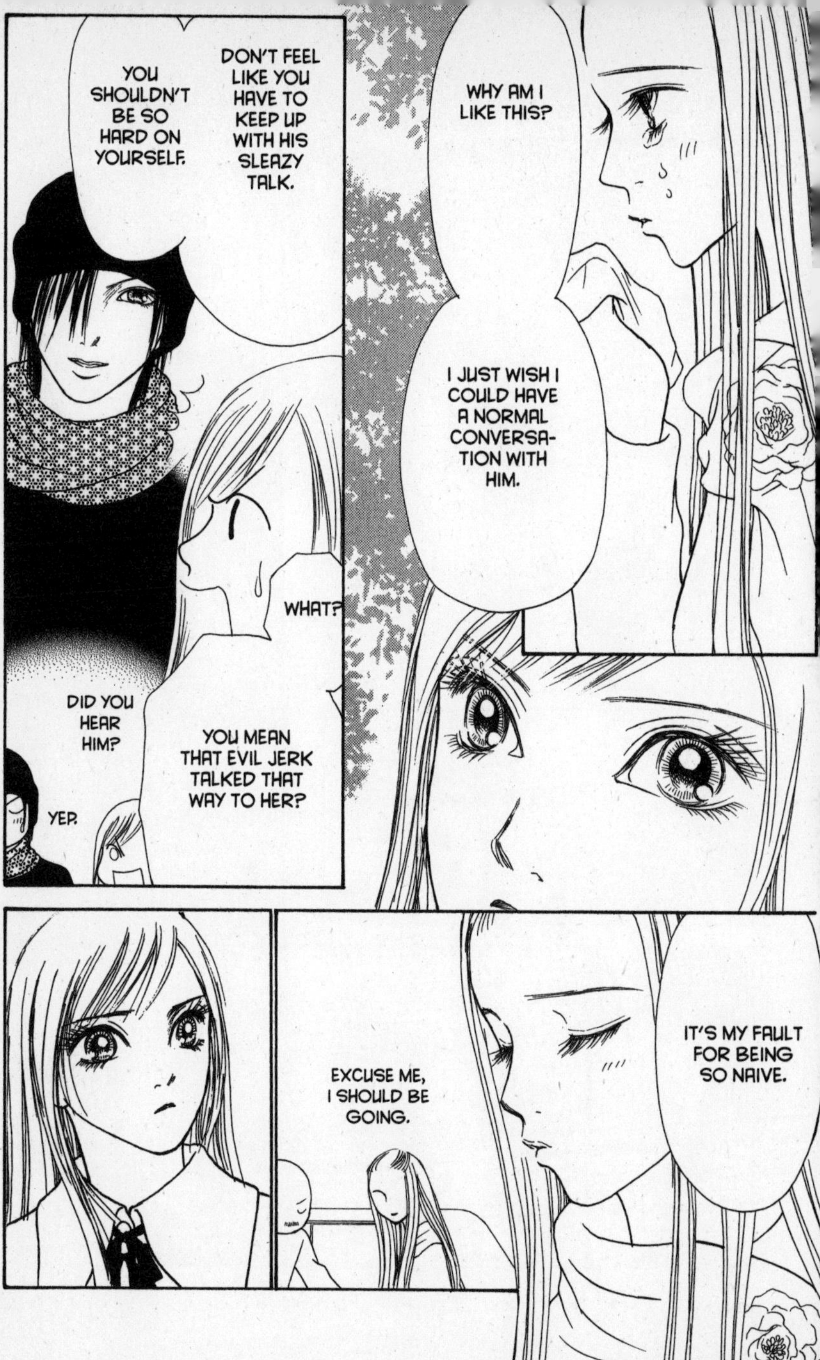
WHY AM I LIKE THIS?
I JUST WISH I COULD HAVE A NORMAL CONVERSATION WITH HIM.
DON'T FEEL LIKE YOU HAVE TO KEEP UP WITH HIS SLEAZY TALK.
YOU SHOULDN'T BE SO HARD ON YOURSELF.
WHAT?
YOU MEAN THAT EVIL JERK TALKED THAT WAY TO HER?
DID YOU HEAR HIM?
YEP.
IT'S MY FAULT FOR BEING SO NAIVE.
EXCUSE ME, I SHOULD BE GOING.

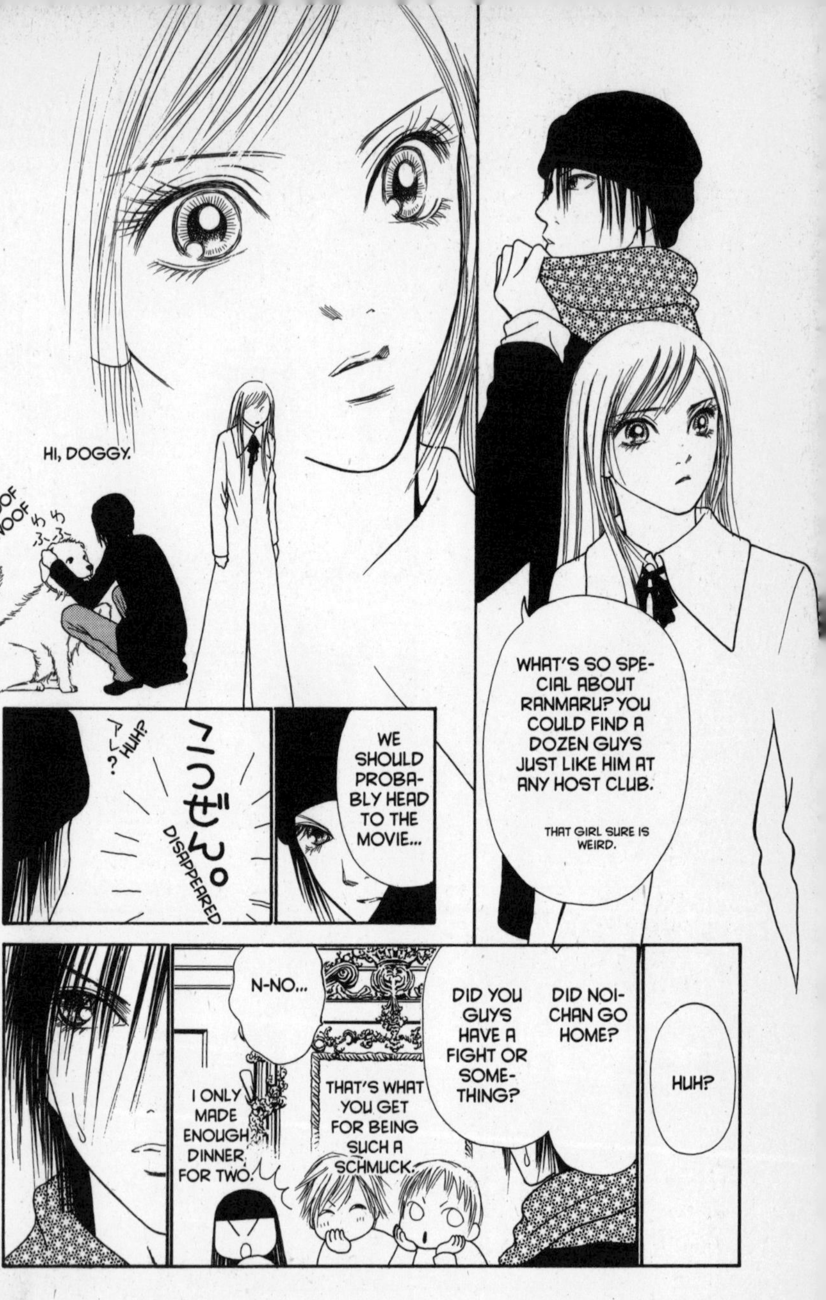
WHAT'S SO SPECIAL ABOUT RANMARU? YOU COULD FIND A DOZEN GUYS JUST LIKE HIM AT ANY HOST CLUB.
THAT GIRL SURE IS WEIRD.
HI, DOGGY.
WOOF WOOF
WE SHOULD PROBABLY HEAD TO THE MOVIE...
こつぜん。
DISAPPEARED
アレ？
HUH?
HUH?
DID NOI-CHAN GO HOME?
DID YOU GUYS HAVE A FIGHT OR SOMETHING?
N-NO...
THAT'S WHAT YOU GET FOR BEING SUCH A SCHMUCK.
I ONLY MADE ENOUGH DINNER FOR TWO.

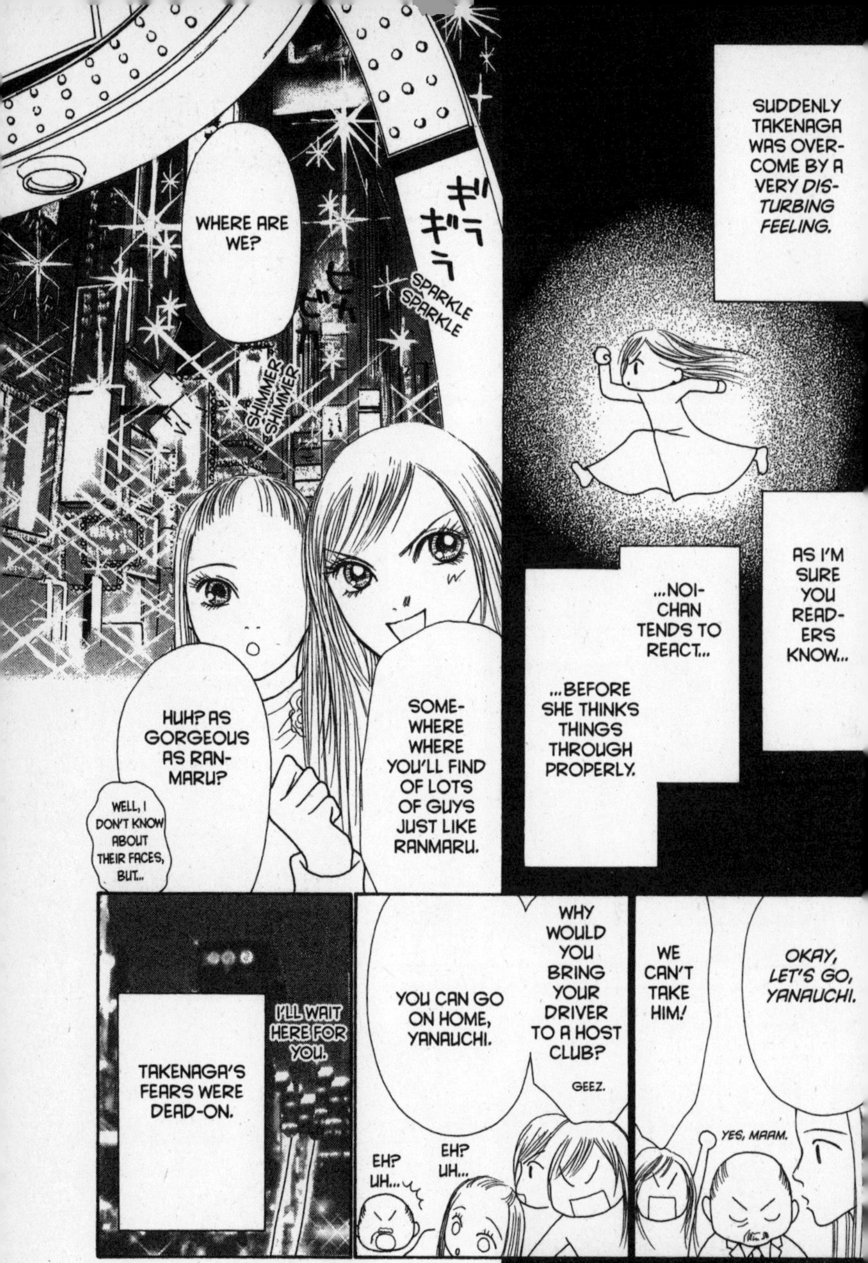
SUDDENLY TAKENAGA WAS OVER-COME BY A VERY *DIS-TURBING* *FEELING.*
AS I'M SURE YOU READ-ERS KNOW...
...NOI-CHAN TENDS TO REACT...
...BEFORE SHE THINKS THINGS THROUGH PROPERLY.
WHERE ARE WE?
ギラギラ
SPARKLE SPARKLE
SHIMMER SHIMMER
SOME-WHERE WHERE YOU'LL FIND OF LOTS OF GUYS JUST LIKE RANMARU.
HUH? AS GORGEOUS AS RAN-MARU?
WELL, I DON'T KNOW ABOUT THEIR FACES, BUT...
OKAY, LET'S GO, YANAUCHI.
YES, MAAM.
WE CAN'T TAKE HIM!
WHY WOULD YOU BRING YOUR DRIVER TO A HOST CLUB?
GEEZ.
YOU CAN GO ON HOME, YANAUCHI.
EH? UH...
EH? UH...
I'LL WAIT HERE FOR YOU.
TAKENAGA'S FEARS WERE DEAD-ON.

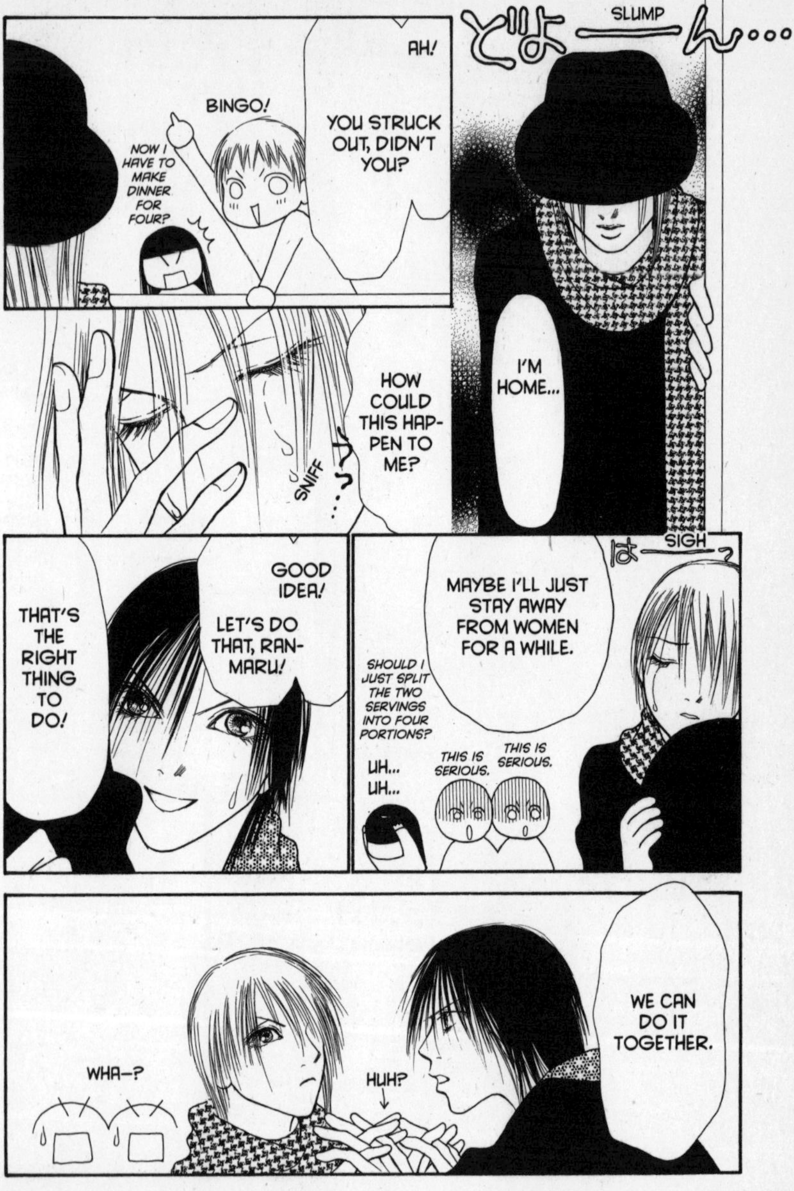
どよーーん…
SLUMP
I'M HOME...
AH!
YOU STRUCK OUT, DIDN'T YOU?
BINGO!
NOW I HAVE TO MAKE DINNER FOR FOUR?
HOW COULD THIS HAPPEN TO ME?
SNIFF
はーーっ
SIGH
MAYBE I'LL JUST STAY AWAY FROM WOMEN FOR A WHILE.
SHOULD I JUST SPLIT THE TWO SERVINGS INTO FOUR PORTIONS?
THIS IS SERIOUS.
THIS IS SERIOUS.
UH... UH...
GOOD IDEA!
LET'S DO THAT, RANMARU!
THAT'S THE RIGHT THING TO DO!
WE CAN DO IT TOGETHER.
HUH?
WHA-?

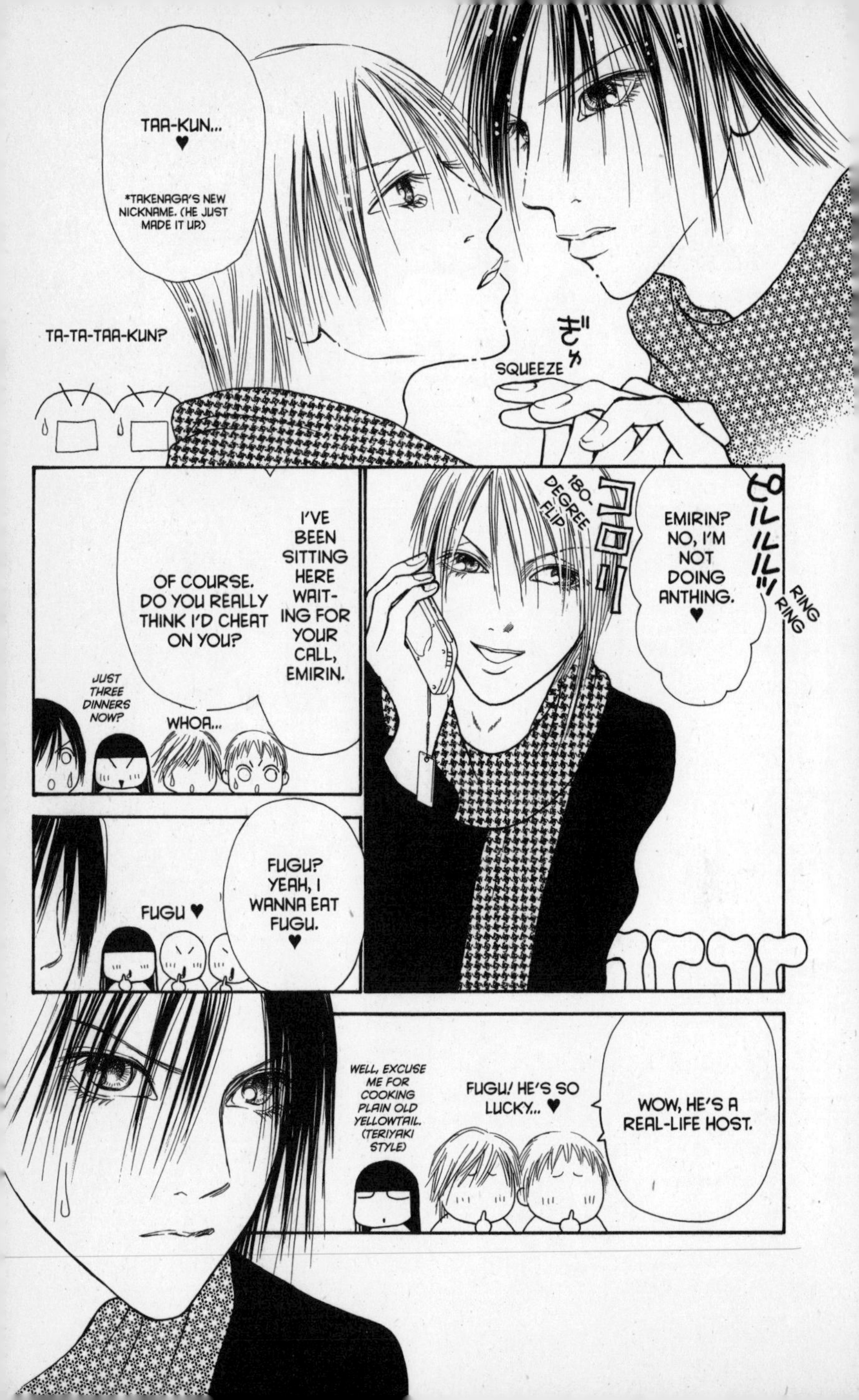
ぎゅ
SQUEEZE
TAA-KUN... ♥
*TAKENAGA'S NEW NICKNAME. (HE JUST MADE IT UP)
TA-TA-TAA-KUN?
ピルルルッ
RING RING
EMIRIN? NO, I'M NOT DOING ANTHING. ♥
コロッ
180-DEGREE FLIP
I'VE BEEN SITTING HERE WAITING FOR YOUR CALL, EMIRIN.
OF COURSE. DO YOU REALLY THINK I'D CHEAT ON YOU?
WHOA...
JUST THREE DINNERS NOW?
FUGU? YEAH, I WANNA EAT FUGU. ♥
FUGU ♥
WOW, HE'S A REAL-LIFE HOST.
FUGU! HE'S SO LUCKY... ♥
WELL, EXCUSE ME FOR COOKING PLAIN OLD YELLOWTAIL. (TERIYAKI STYLE)

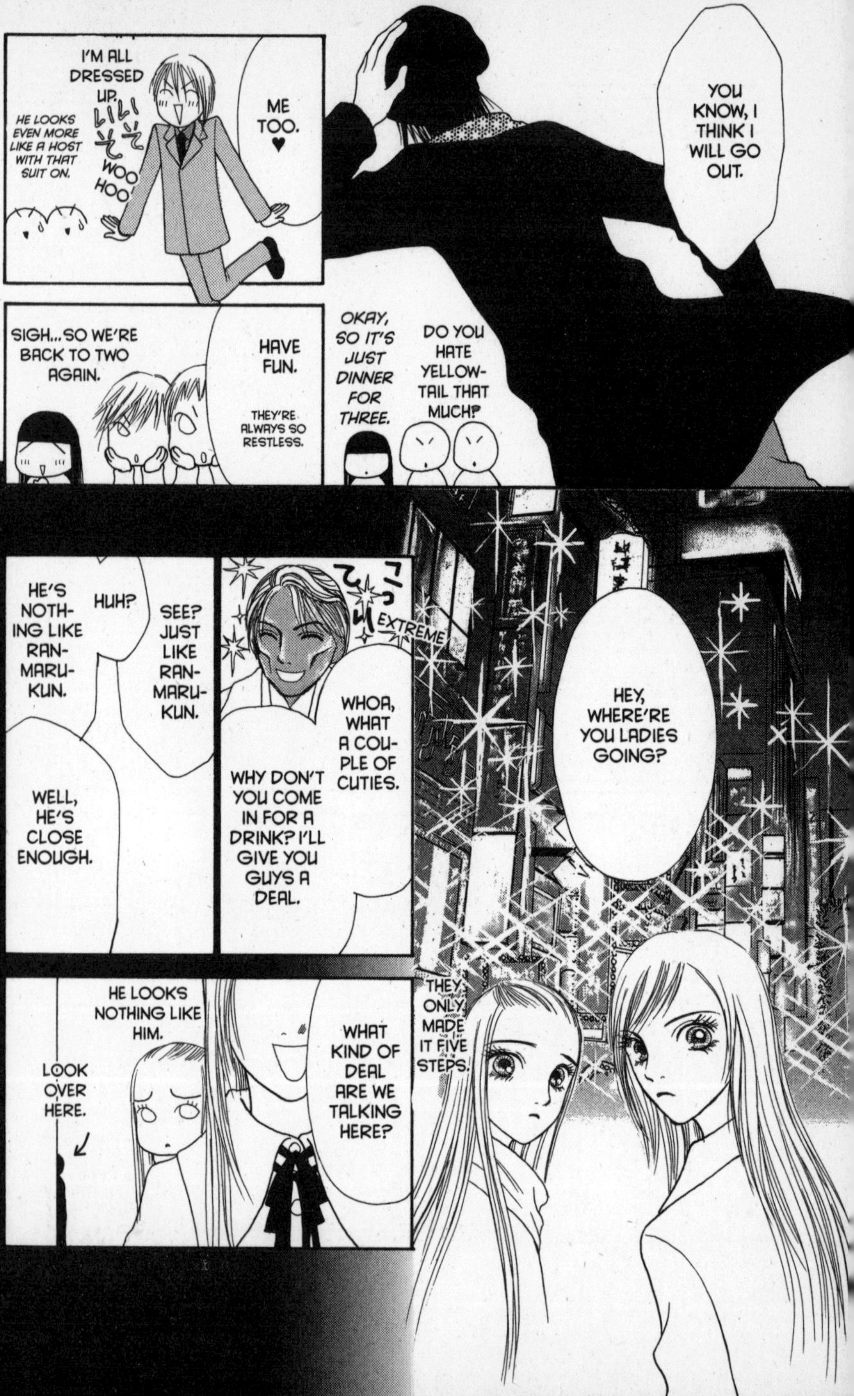
YOU KNOW, I THINK I WILL GO OUT.
ME TOO. ♥
I'M ALL DRESSED UP.
WOO HOO!
HE LOOKS EVEN MORE LIKE A HOST WITH THAT SUIT ON.
DO YOU HATE YELLOWTAIL THAT MUCH?
OKAY, SO IT'S JUST DINNER FOR THREE.
HAVE FUN.
THEY'RE ALWAYS SO RESTLESS.
SIGH... SO WE'RE BACK TO TWO AGAIN.
HEY, WHERE'RE YOU LADIES GOING?
THEY ONLY MADE IT FIVE STEPS.
EXTREME
WHOA, WHAT A COUPLE OF CUTIES.
WHY DON'T YOU COME IN FOR A DRINK? I'LL GIVE YOU GUYS A DEAL.
SEE? JUST LIKE RAN-MARU-KUN.
HUH?
HE'S NOTHING LIKE RAN-MARU-KUN.
WELL, HE'S CLOSE ENOUGH.
WHAT KIND OF DEAL ARE WE TALKING HERE?
HE LOOKS NOTHING LIKE HIM.
LOOK OVER HERE.

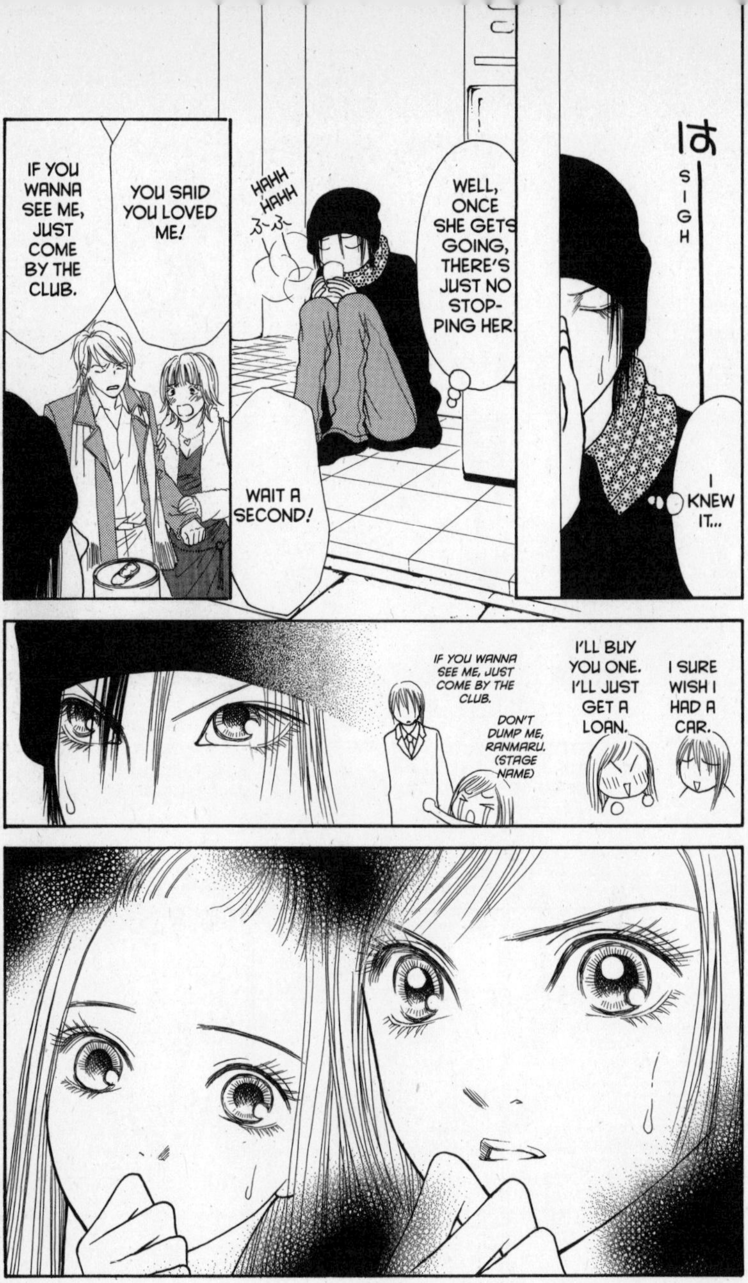
は
SIGH
I KNEW IT...
WELL, ONCE SHE GETS GOING, THERE'S JUST NO STOP-PING HER.
HAHH HAHH
ふーふー
WAIT A SECOND!
YOU SAID YOU LOVED ME!
IF YOU WANNA SEE ME, JUST COME BY THE CLUB.
I SURE WISH I HAD A CAR.
I'LL BUY YOU ONE. I'LL JUST GET A LOAN.
IF YOU WANNA SEE ME, JUST COME BY THE CLUB.
DON'T DUMP ME, RANMARU. (STAGE NAME)

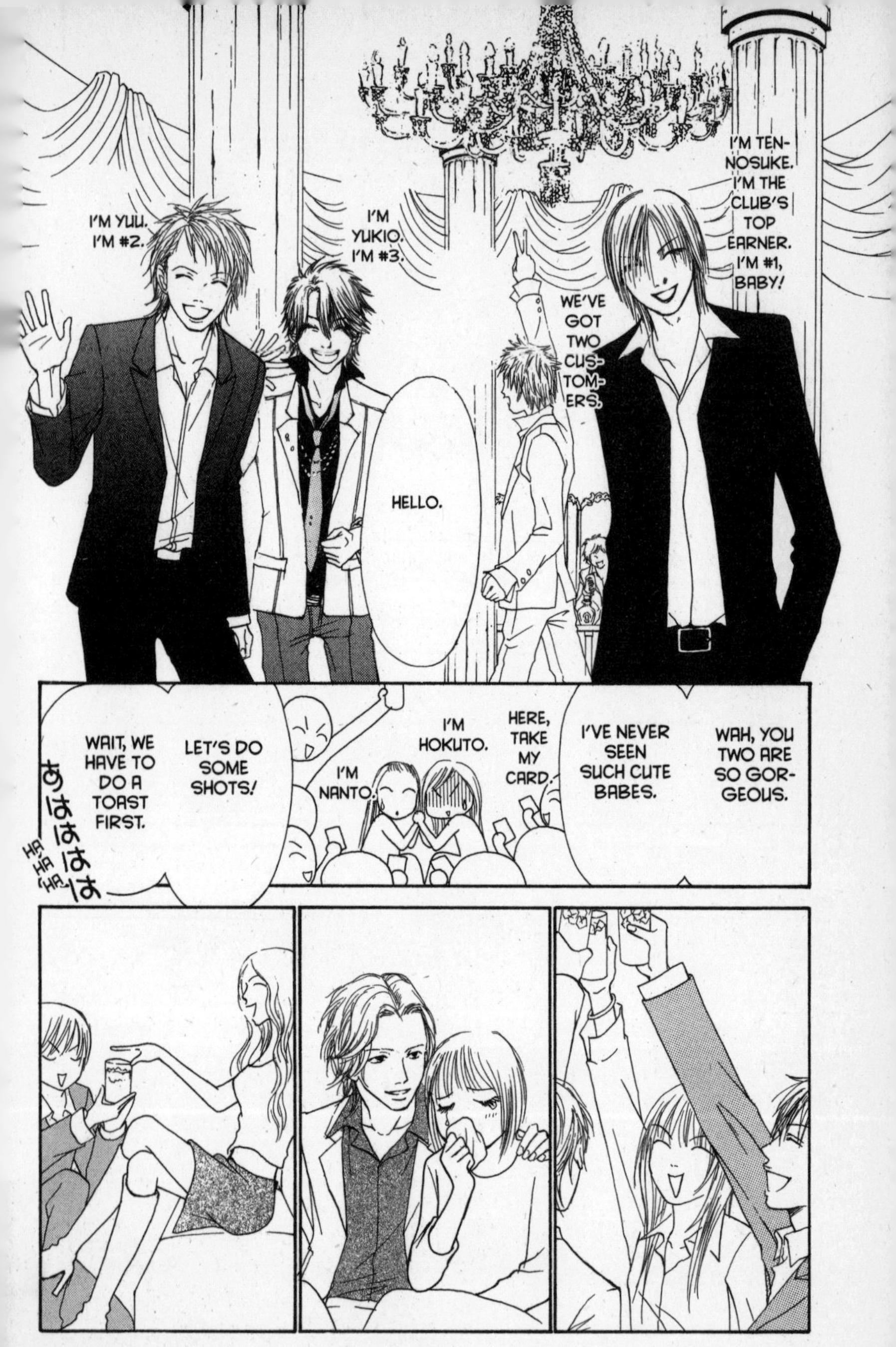
I'M TEN-NOSUKE. I'M THE CLUB'S TOP EARNER. I'M #1, BABY!
WE'VE GOT TWO CUSTOMERS.
HELLO.
I'M YUKIO. I'M #3.
I'M YUU. I'M #2.
WAH, YOU TWO ARE SO GORGEOUS.
I'VE NEVER SEEN SUCH CUTE BABES.
HERE, TAKE MY CARD.
I'M HOKUTO.
I'M NANTO.
LET'S DO SOME SHOTS!
WAIT, WE HAVE TO DO A TOAST FIRST.
あははは
HA HA HA

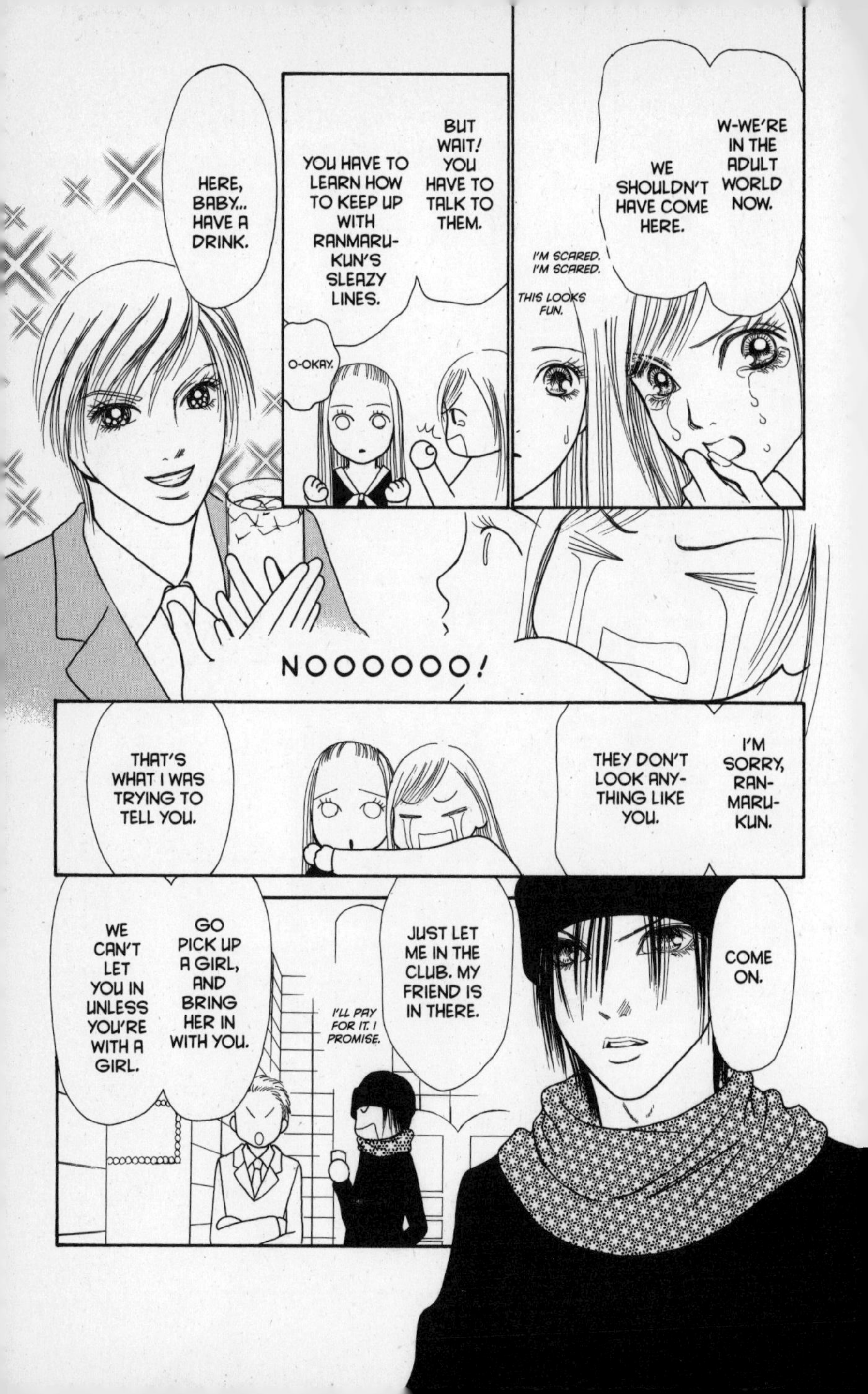
W-WE'RE IN THE ADULT WORLD NOW.
WE SHOULDN'T HAVE COME HERE.
I'M SCARED. I'M SCARED.
THIS LOOKS FUN.
BUT WAIT! YOU HAVE TO TALK TO THEM.
YOU HAVE TO LEARN HOW TO KEEP UP WITH RANMARU-KUN'S SLEAZY LINES.
O-OKAY.
HERE, BABY... HAVE A DRINK.
NOOOOOO!
I'M SORRY, RAN-MARU-KUN.
THEY DON'T LOOK ANY-THING LIKE YOU.
THAT'S WHAT I WAS TRYING TO TELL YOU.
COME ON.
JUST LET ME IN THE CLUB. MY FRIEND IS IN THERE.
I'LL PAY FOR IT. I PROMISE.
GO PICK UP A GIRL, AND BRING HER IN WITH YOU.
WE CAN'T LET YOU IN UNLESS YOU'RE WITH A GIRL.

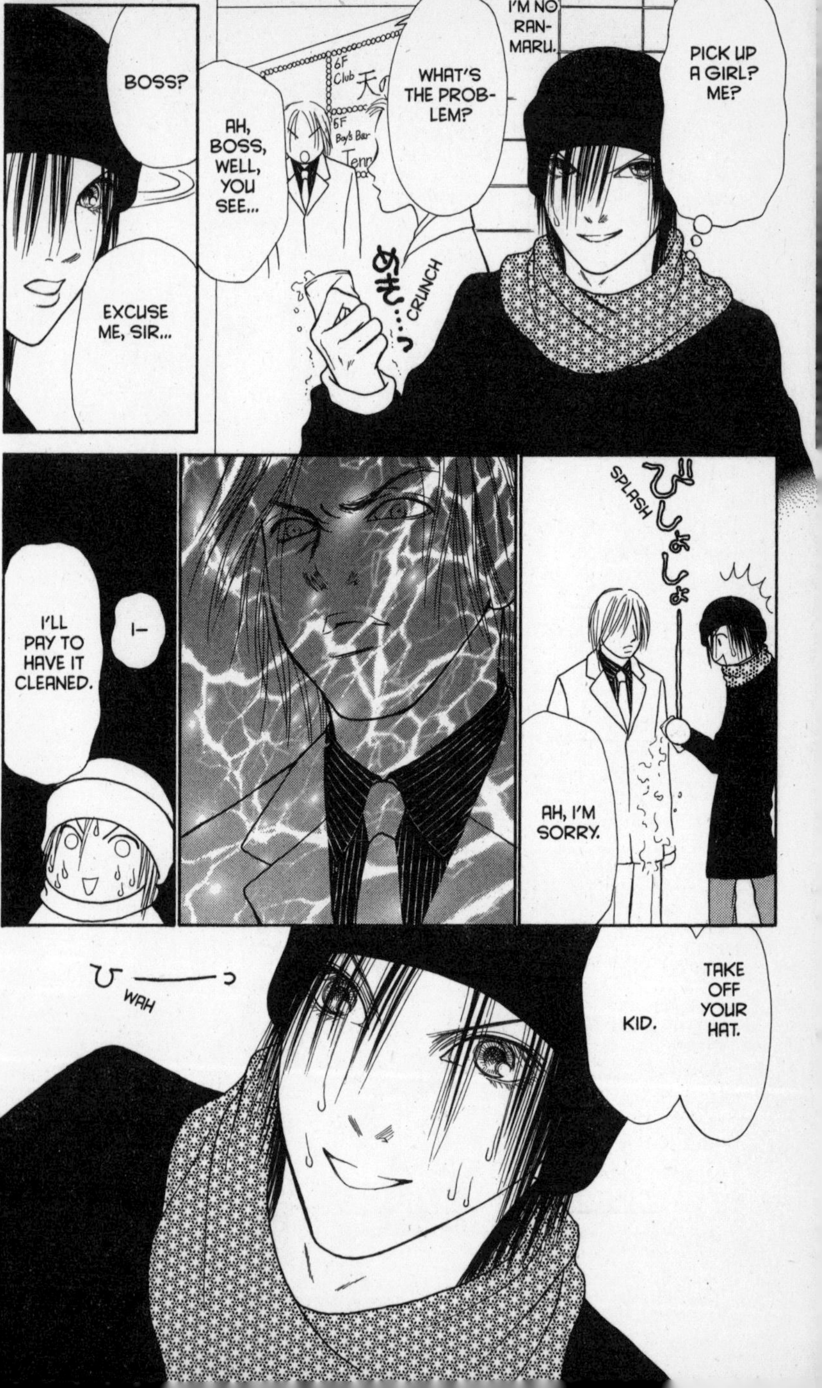
PICK UP A GIRL? ME?
I'M NO RAN-MARU.
WHAT'S THE PROB-LEM?
6F Club 天の
5F Boy's Bar Tenn
AH, BOSS, WELL, YOU SEE...
めき…っ
CRUNCH
BOSS?
EXCUSE ME, SIR...
びしょしょ
SPLASH
AH, I'M SORRY.
I—
I'LL PAY TO HAVE IT CLEANED.
TAKE OFF YOUR HAT.
KID.
ひーっ
WAH

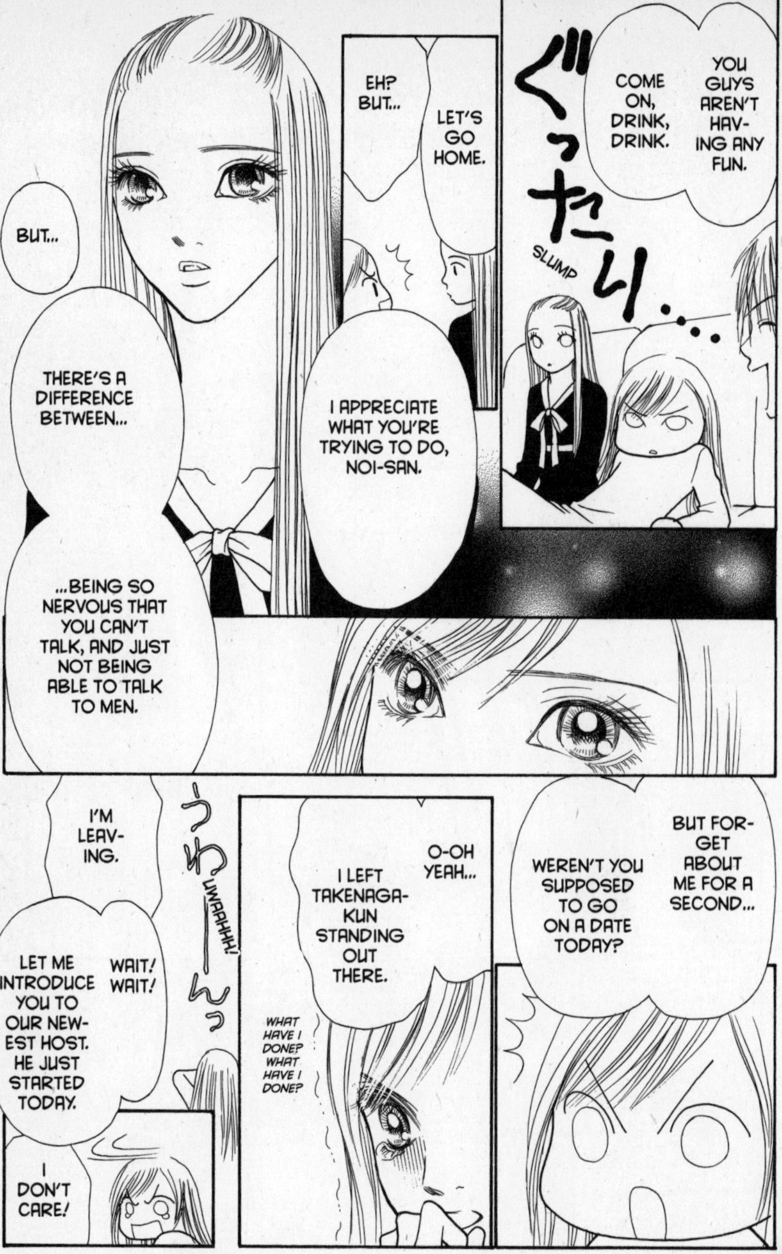
YOU GUYS AREN'T HAV-ING ANY FUN.
COME ON, DRINK, DRINK.
ぐったり…
SLUMP
LET'S GO HOME.
EH? BUT...
I APPRECIATE WHAT YOU'RE TRYING TO DO, NOI-SAN.
BUT...
THERE'S A DIFFERENCE BETWEEN...
...BEING SO NERVOUS THAT YOU CAN'T TALK, AND JUST NOT BEING ABLE TO TALK TO MEN.
BUT FOR-GET ABOUT ME FOR A SECOND...
WEREN'T YOU SUPPOSED TO GO ON A DATE TODAY?
O-OH YEAH...
I LEFT TAKENAGA-KUN STANDING OUT THERE.
WHAT HAVE I DONE? WHAT HAVE I DONE?
I'M LEAV-ING.
うわーんっ
UWAAHH!
WAIT! WAIT!
LET ME INTRODUCE YOU TO OUR NEW-EST HOST. HE JUST STARTED TODAY.
I DON'T CARE!

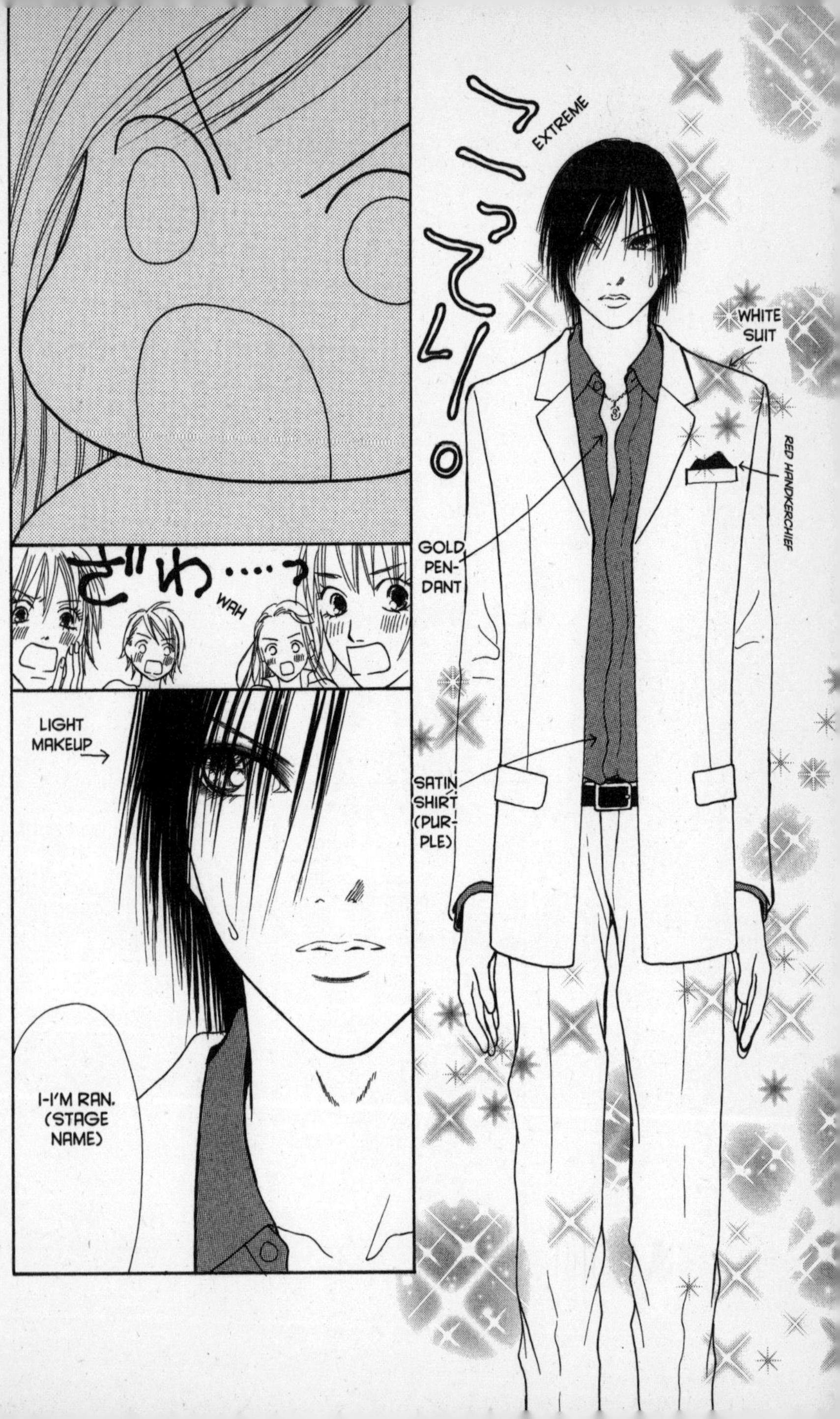
EXTREME
WHITE SUIT
RED HANDKERCHIEF
GOLD PENDANT
SATIN SHIRT (PURPLE)
ざわ…っ
WAH
LIGHT MAKEUP
I-I'M RAN. (STAGE NAME)

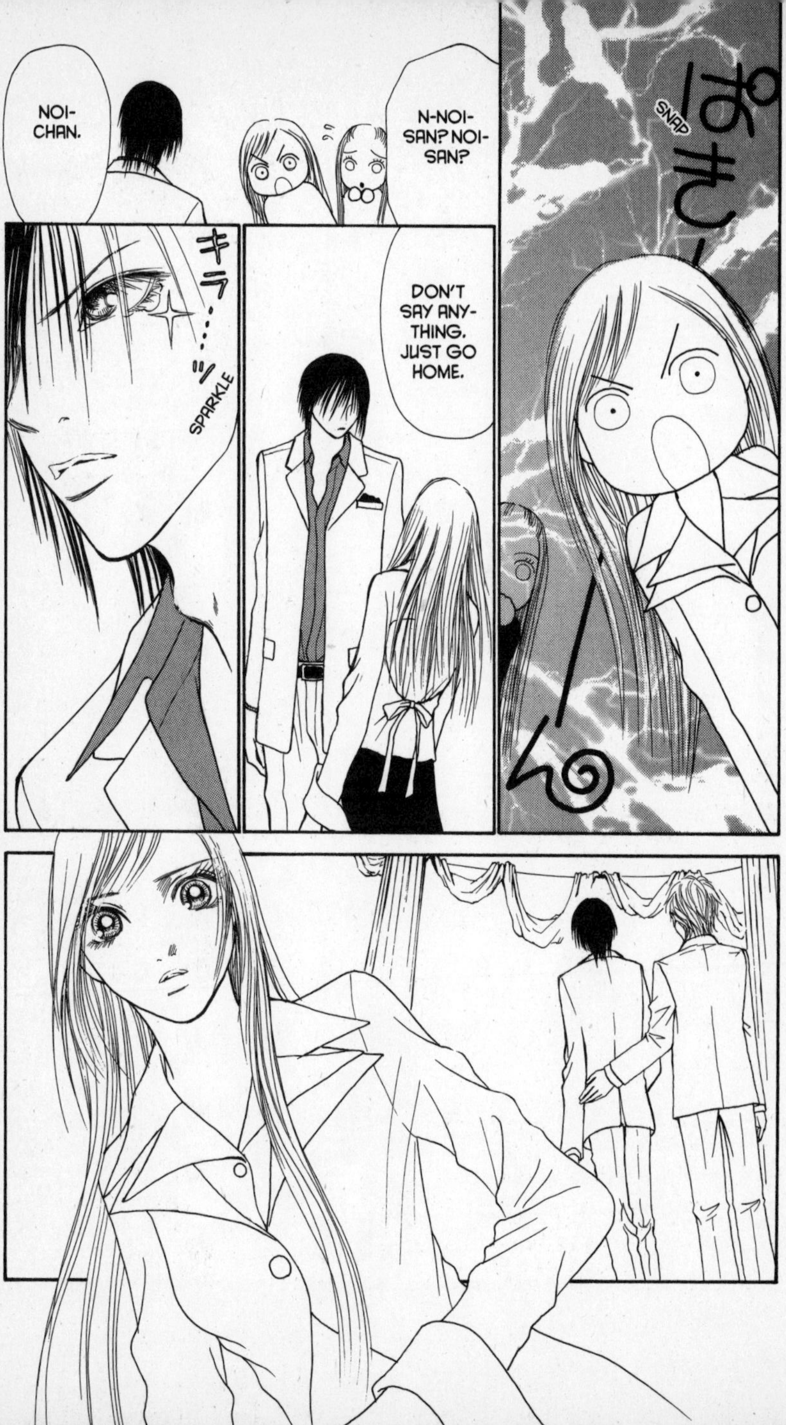

ぽきーん
SNAP
N-NOI-SAN? NOI-SAN?
NOI-CHAN.
DON'T SAY ANYTHING. JUST GO HOME.
キラ…ッ
SPARKLE

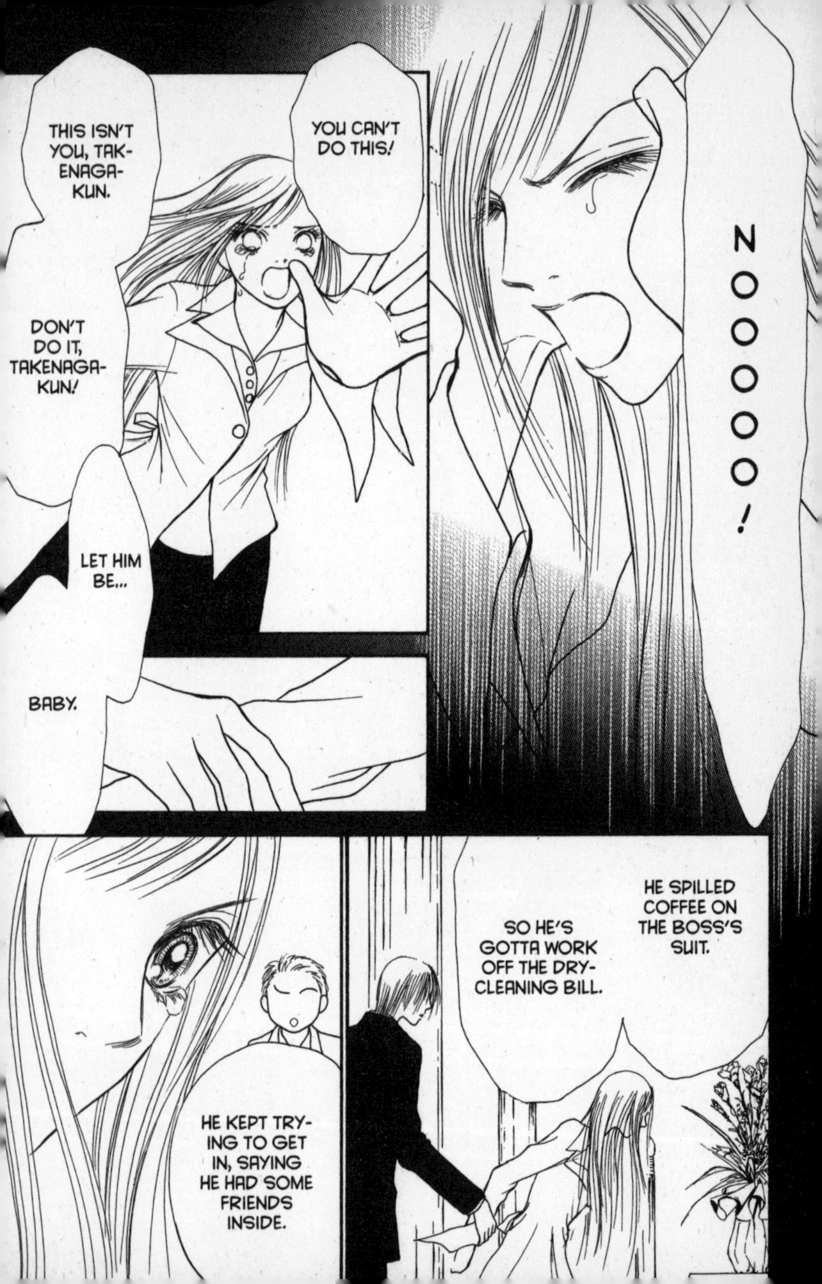
NOOOOO!
YOU CAN'T DO THIS!
THIS ISN'T YOU, TAKENAGA-KUN.
DON'T DO IT, TAKENAGA-KUN!
LET HIM BE...
BABY.
HE SPILLED COFFEE ON THE BOSS'S SUIT.
SO HE'S GOTTA WORK OFF THE DRY-CLEANING BILL.
HE KEPT TRYING TO GET IN, SAYING HE HAD SOME FRIENDS INSIDE.

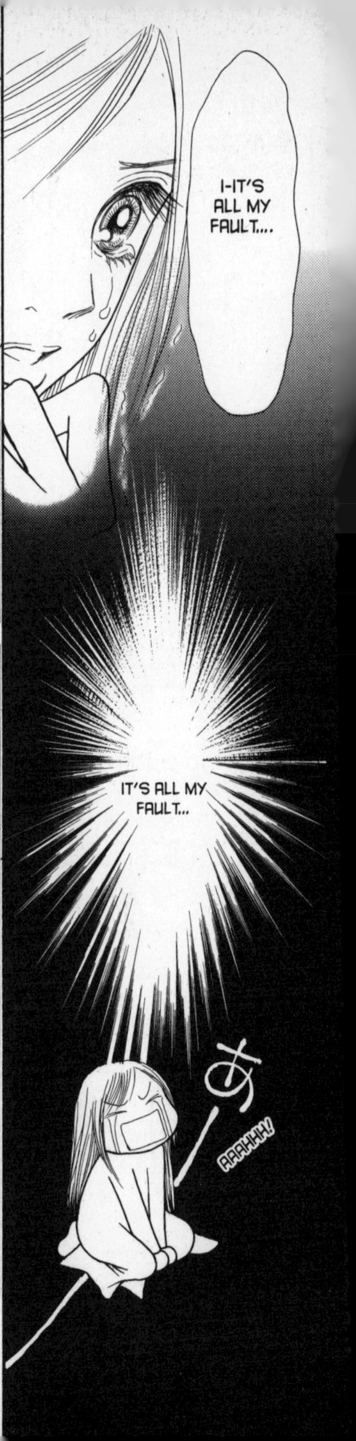
I-IT'S ALL MY FAULT....
IT'S ALL MY FAULT...
AAAHHH!

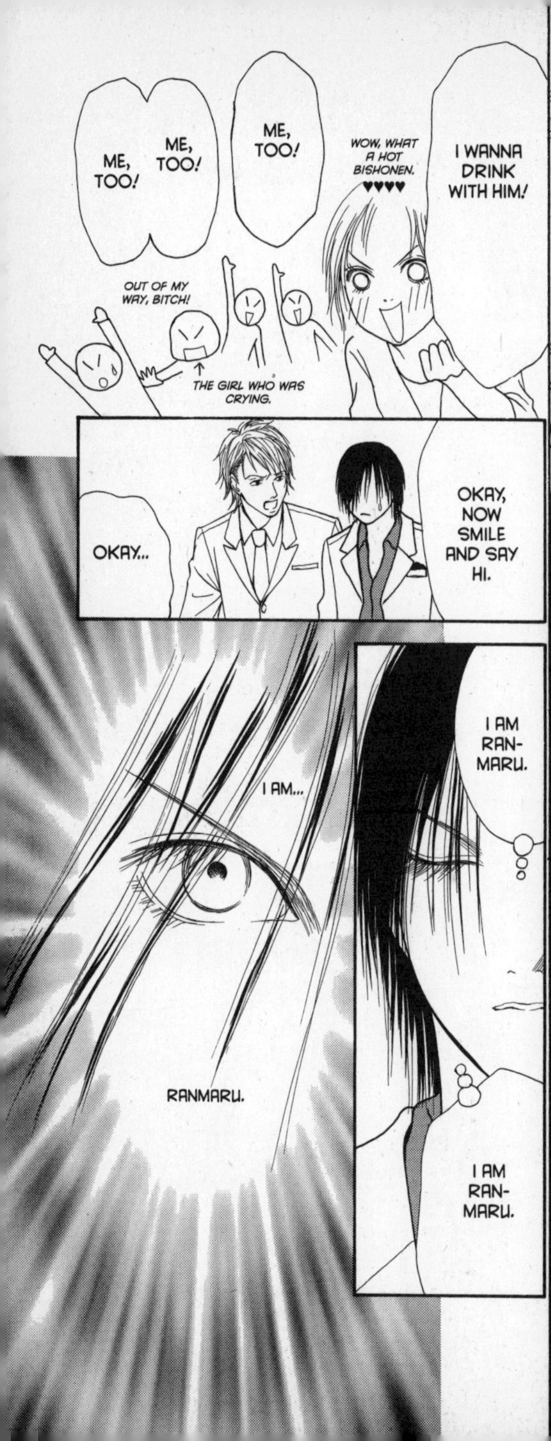
I WANNA DRINK WITH HIM!
WOW, WHAT A HOT BISHONEN. ♥♥♥♥
ME, TOO!
ME, TOO!
ME, TOO!
OUT OF MY WAY, BITCH!
THE GIRL WHO WAS CRYING.
OKAY, NOW SMILE AND SAY HI.
OKAY...
I AM RAN-MARU.
I AM RAN-MARU.
I AM...
RANMARU.

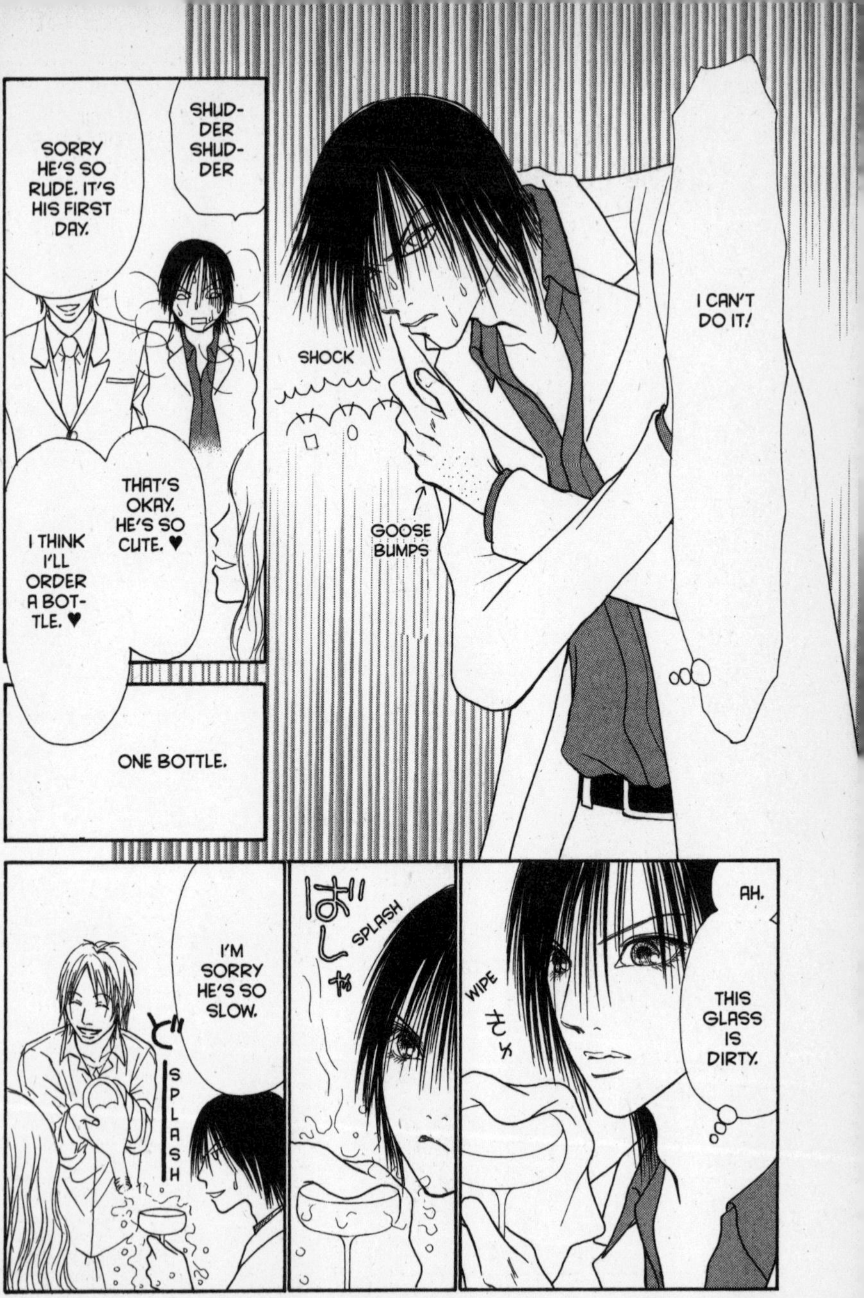
I CAN'T DO IT!
SHOCK
GOOSE BUMPS
SHUDDER SHUDDER
SORRY HE'S SO RUDE. IT'S HIS FIRST DAY.
THAT'S OKAY. HE'S SO CUTE. ♥
I THINK I'LL ORDER A BOTTLE. ♥
ONE BOTTLE.
AH.
THIS GLASS IS DIRTY.
WIPE
SPLASH
I'M SORRY HE'S SO SLOW.
SPLASH

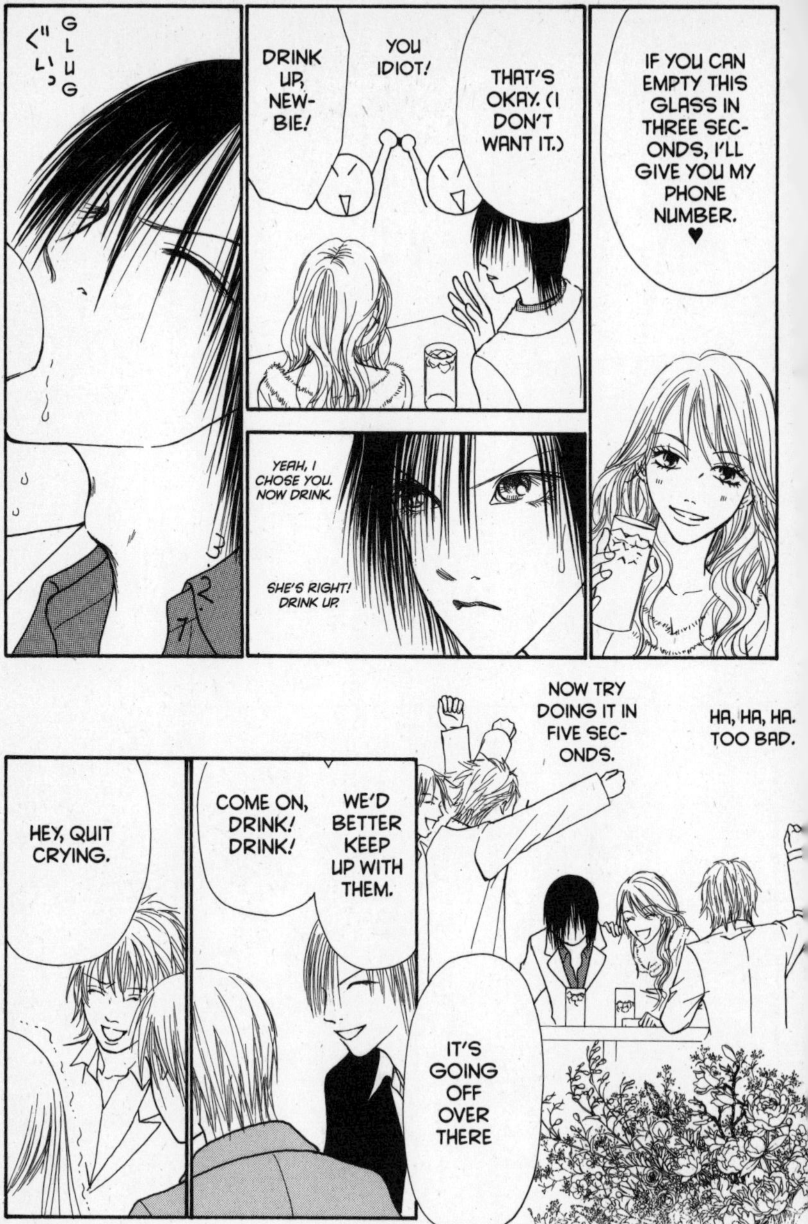
IF YOU CAN EMPTY THIS GLASS IN THREE SECONDS, I'LL GIVE YOU MY PHONE NUMBER. ♥
THAT'S OKAY. (I DON'T WANT IT.)
YOU IDIOT!
DRINK UP, NEWBIE!
YEAH, I CHOSE YOU. NOW DRINK.
SHE'S RIGHT! DRINK UP.
GLUG
ぐいっ
HA, HA, HA. TOO BAD.
NOW TRY DOING IT IN FIVE SECONDS.
IT'S GOING OFF OVER THERE
WE'D BETTER KEEP UP WITH THEM.
COME ON, DRINK! DRINK!
HEY, QUIT CRYING.

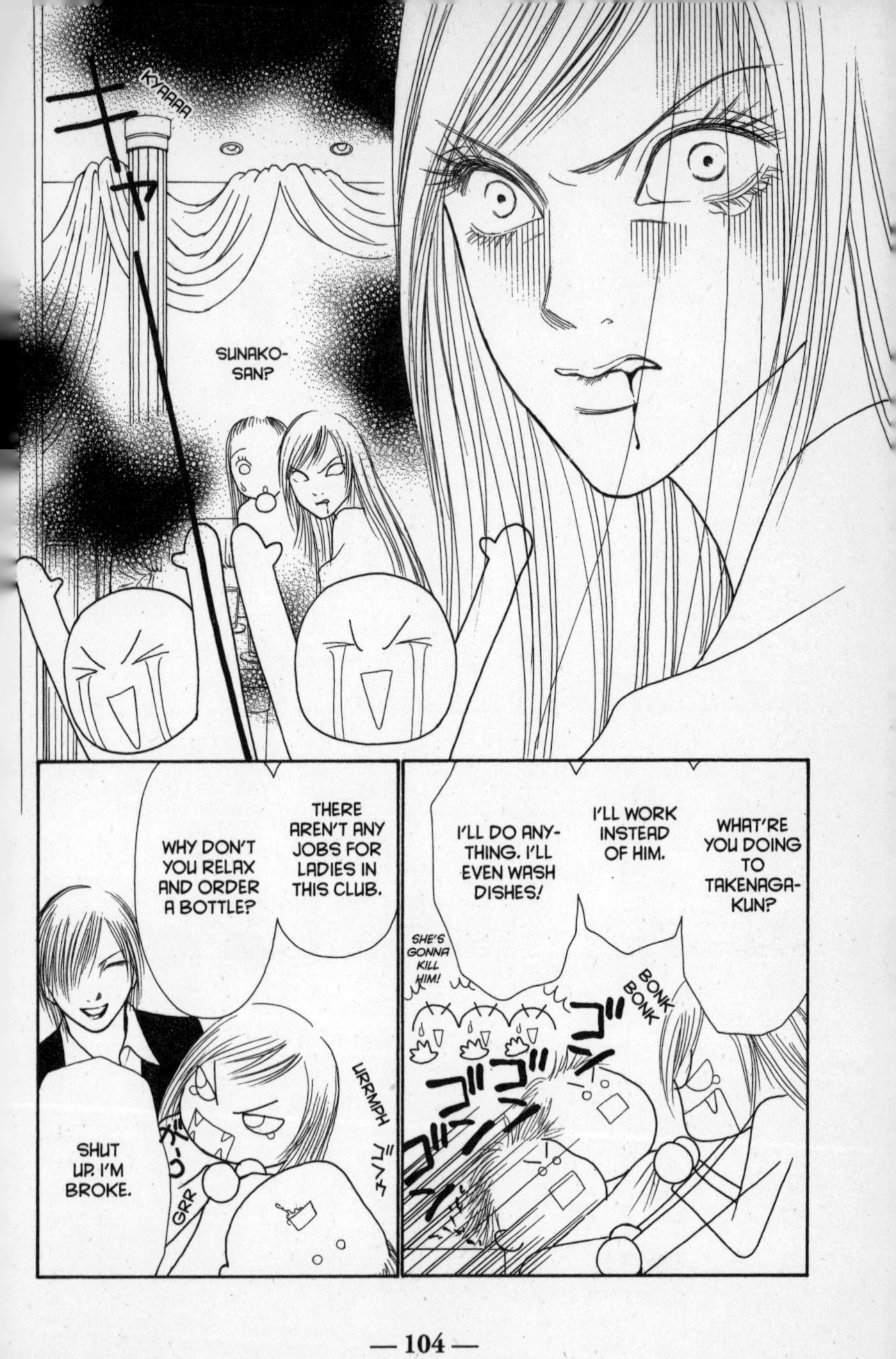
KYAAAA
SUNAKO-SAN?
WHAT'RE YOU DOING TO TAKENAGA-KUN?
I'LL WORK INSTEAD OF HIM.
I'LL DO ANY-THING. I'LL EVEN WASH DISHES!
BONK BONK
SHE'S GONNA KILL HIM!
THERE AREN'T ANY JOBS FOR LADIES IN THIS CLUB.
WHY DON'T YOU RELAX AND ORDER A BOTTLE?
URRMPH
GRR
SHUT UP. I'M BROKE.

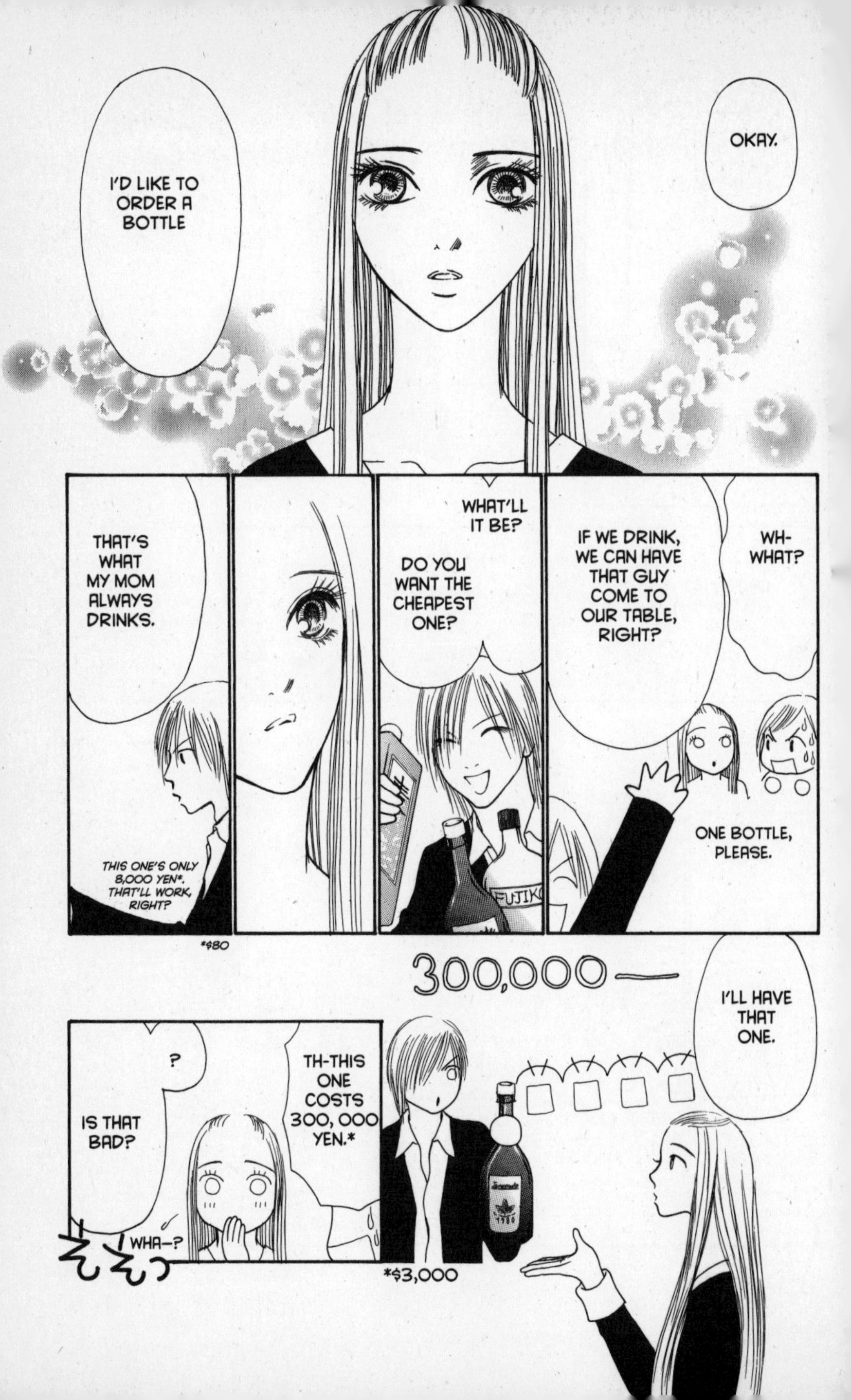
OKAY.
I'D LIKE TO ORDER A BOTTLE
WH-WHAT?
IF WE DRINK, WE CAN HAVE THAT GUY COME TO OUR TABLE, RIGHT?
ONE BOTTLE, PLEASE.
WHAT'LL IT BE?
DO YOU WANT THE CHEAPEST ONE?
FUJIKO
THAT'S WHAT MY MOM ALWAYS DRINKS.
THIS ONE'S ONLY 8,000 YEN*. THAT'LL WORK, RIGHT?
*$80
I'LL HAVE THAT ONE.
300,000—
TH-THIS ONE COSTS 300, 000 YEN.*
*$3,000
?
IS THAT BAD?
WHA-?

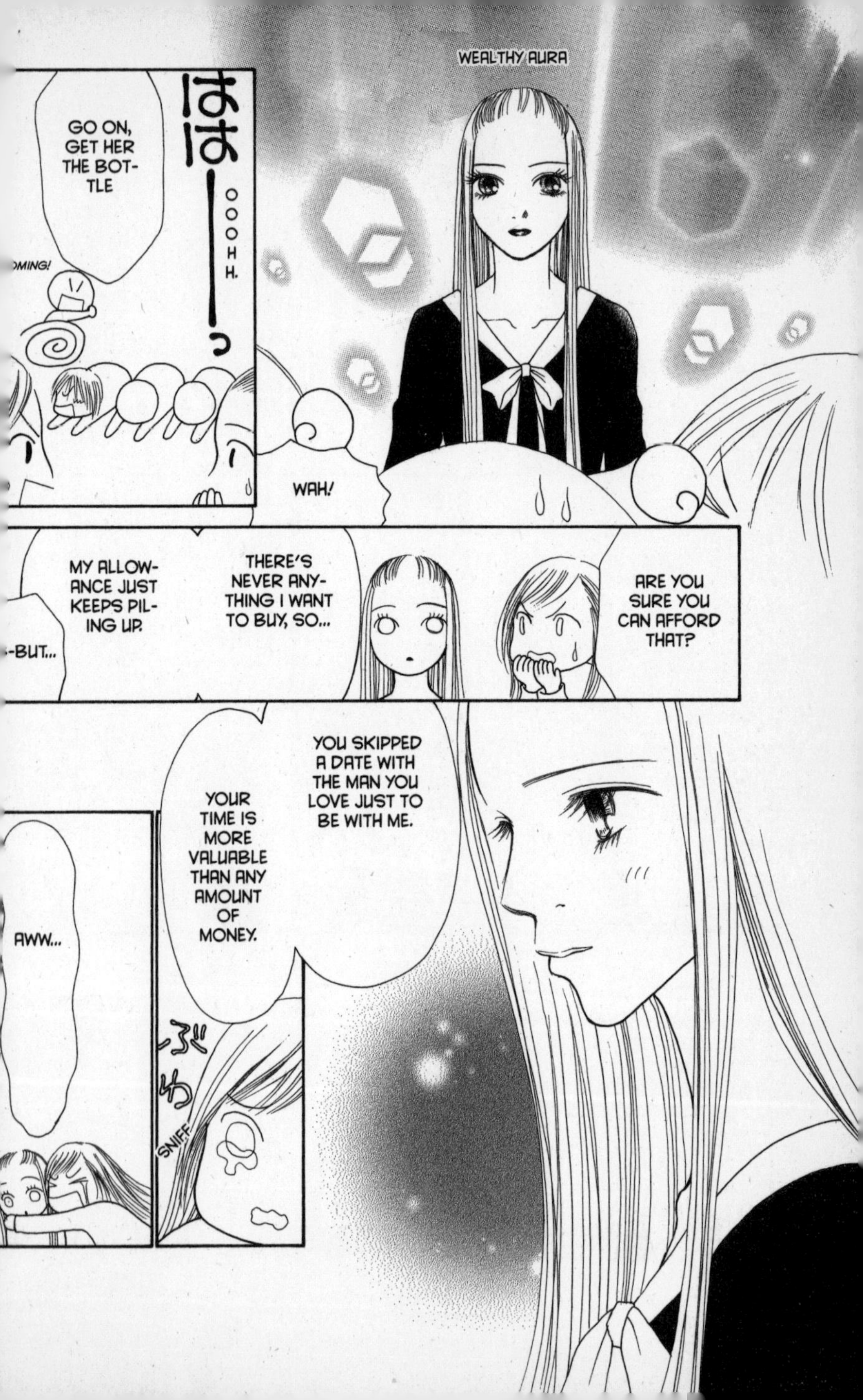
WEALTHY AURA
WAH!
ははーっ
OOOOHH.
GO ON, GET HER THE BOTTLE
OMING!
ARE YOU SURE YOU CAN AFFORD THAT?
THERE'S NEVER ANYTHING I WANT TO BUY, SO...
MY ALLOWANCE JUST KEEPS PILING UP.
-BUT...
YOU SKIPPED A DATE WITH THE MAN YOU LOVE JUST TO BE WITH ME.
YOUR TIME IS MORE VALUABLE THAN ANY AMOUNT OF MONEY.
ぶわ
SNIFF
AWW...

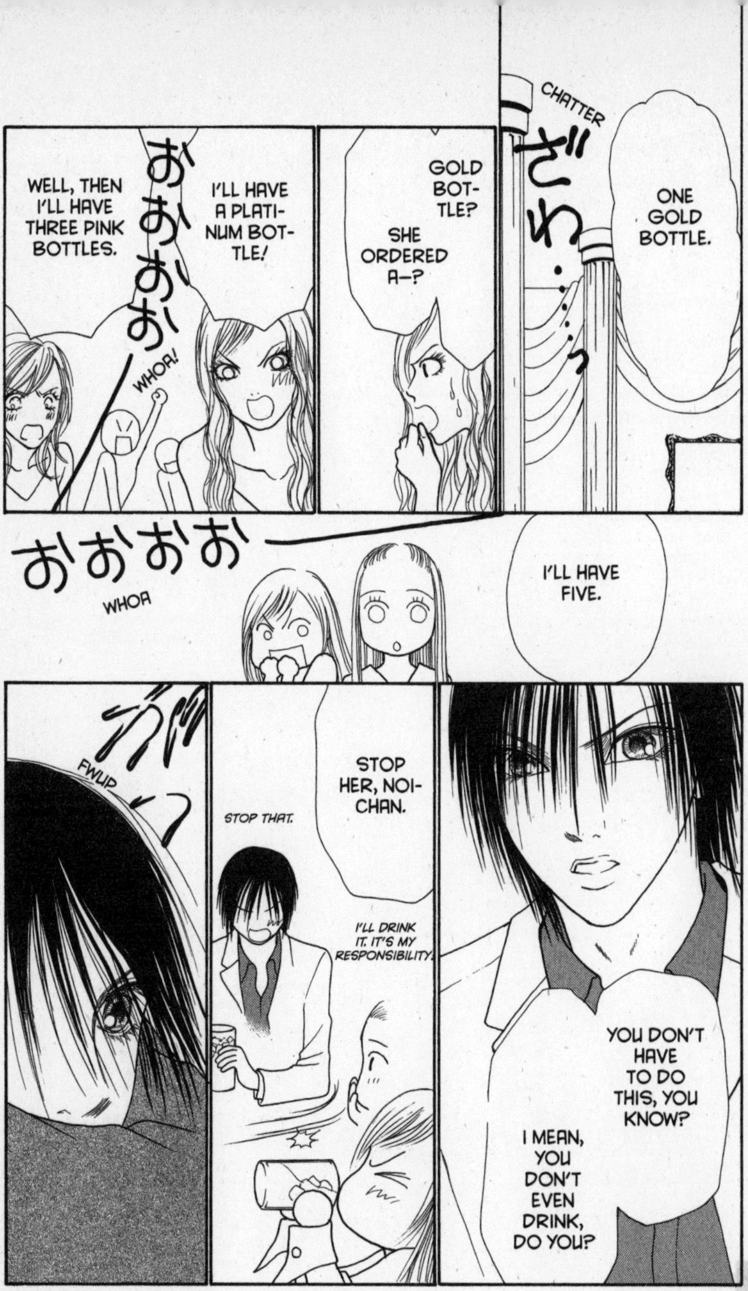
CHATTER
ざわ…っ
ONE GOLD BOTTLE.
GOLD BOT-TLE?
SHE ORDERED A—?
I'LL HAVE A PLATI-NUM BOT-TLE!
おおおお
WELL, THEN I'LL HAVE THREE PINK BOTTLES.
WHOA!
I'LL HAVE FIVE.
おおおお
WHOA
YOU DON'T HAVE TO DO THIS, YOU KNOW?
I MEAN, YOU DON'T EVEN DRINK, DO YOU?
STOP HER, NOI-CHAN.
STOP THAT.
I'LL DRINK IT. IT'S MY RESPONSIBILITY.
FWUP

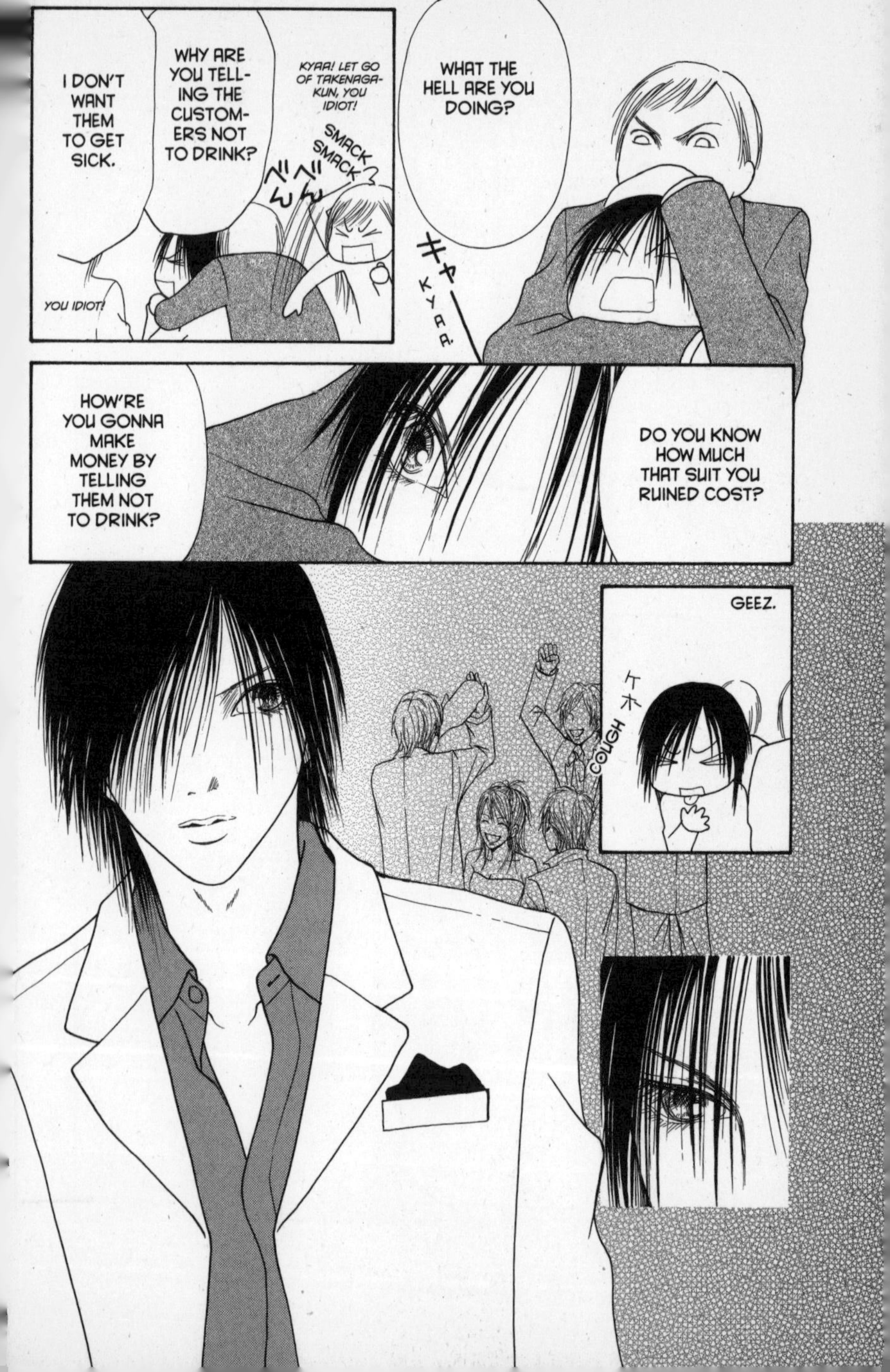
WHAT THE HELL ARE YOU DOING?
キャ
KYAA.
KYAA! LET GO OF TAKENAGA-KUN, YOU IDIOT!
SMACK SMACK
WHY ARE YOU TELLING THE CUSTOMERS NOT TO DRINK?
I DON'T WANT THEM TO GET SICK.
YOU IDIOT!
DO YOU KNOW HOW MUCH THAT SUIT YOU RUINED COST?
HOW'RE YOU GONNA MAKE MONEY BY TELLING THEM NOT TO DRINK?
GEEZ.
ケホ
COUGH

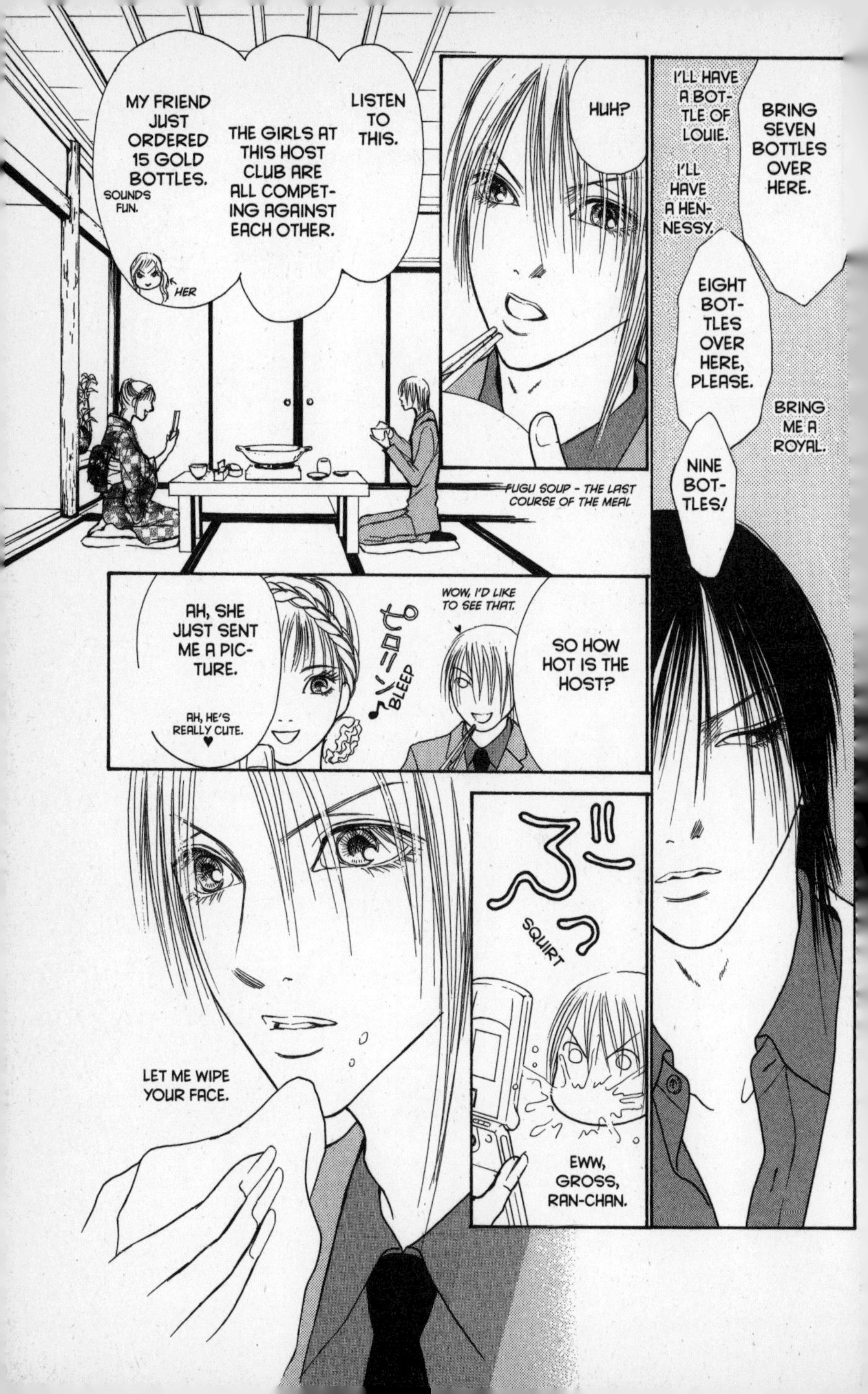
BRING SEVEN BOTTLES OVER HERE.
I'LL HAVE A BOTTLE OF LOUIE.
I'LL HAVE A HENNESSY.
EIGHT BOTTLES OVER HERE, PLEASE.
BRING ME A ROYAL.
NINE BOTTLES!
HUH?
LISTEN TO THIS.
THE GIRLS AT THIS HOST CLUB ARE ALL COMPETING AGAINST EACH OTHER.
MY FRIEND JUST ORDERED 15 GOLD BOTTLES.
SOUNDS FUN.
HER
FUGU SOUP - THE LAST COURSE OF THE MEAL
WOW, I'D LIKE TO SEE THAT.
SO HOW HOT IS THE HOST?
BLEEP
AH, SHE JUST SENT ME A PICTURE.
AH, HE'S REALLY CUTE.
SQUIRT
EWW, GROSS, RAN-CHAN.
LET ME WIPE YOUR FACE.

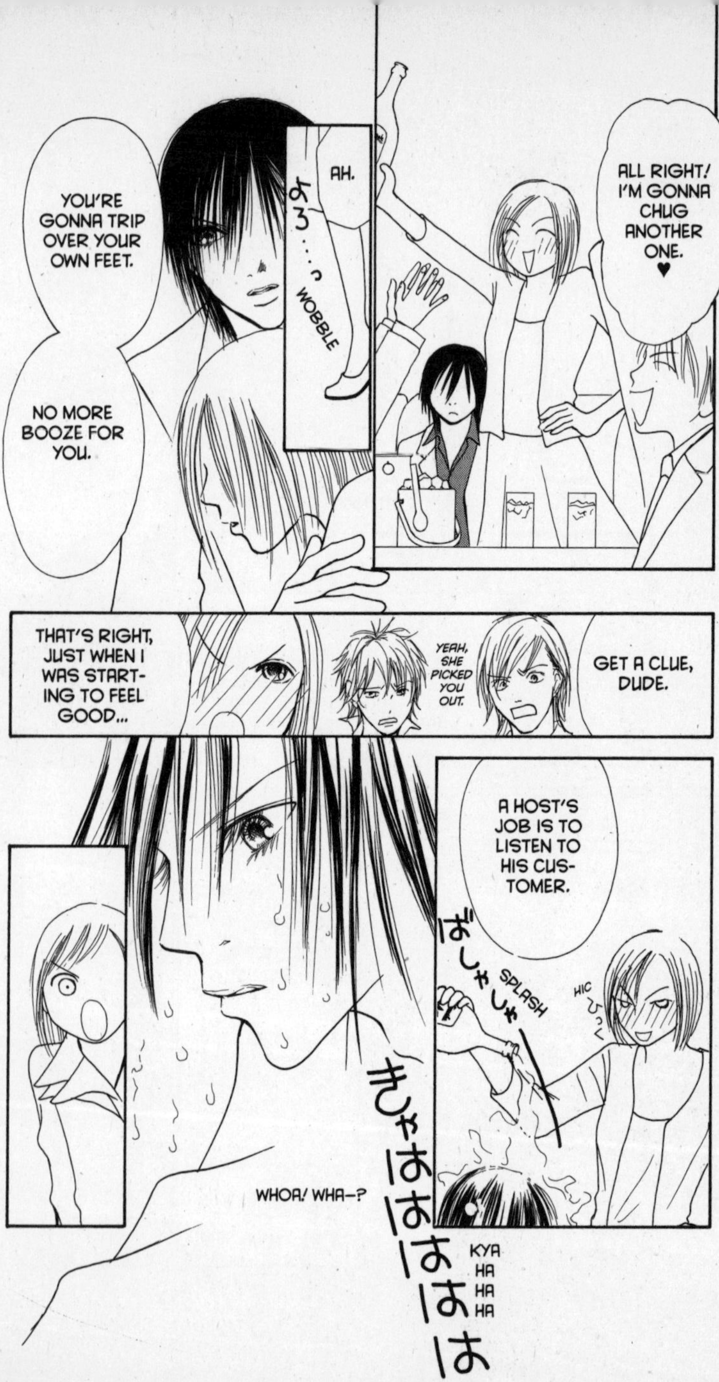
ALL RIGHT! I'M GONNA CHUG ANOTHER ONE. ♥
AH.
よろ…っ
WOBBLE
YOU'RE GONNA TRIP OVER YOUR OWN FEET.
NO MORE BOOZE FOR YOU.
GET A CLUE, DUDE.
YEAH, SHE PICKED YOU OUT.
THAT'S RIGHT, JUST WHEN I WAS START-ING TO FEEL GOOD...
A HOST'S JOB IS TO LISTEN TO HIS CUS-TOMER.
ばしゃしゃ
SPLASH
ひっく
HIC
きゃははははは
KYA HA HA HA
WHOA! WHA-?

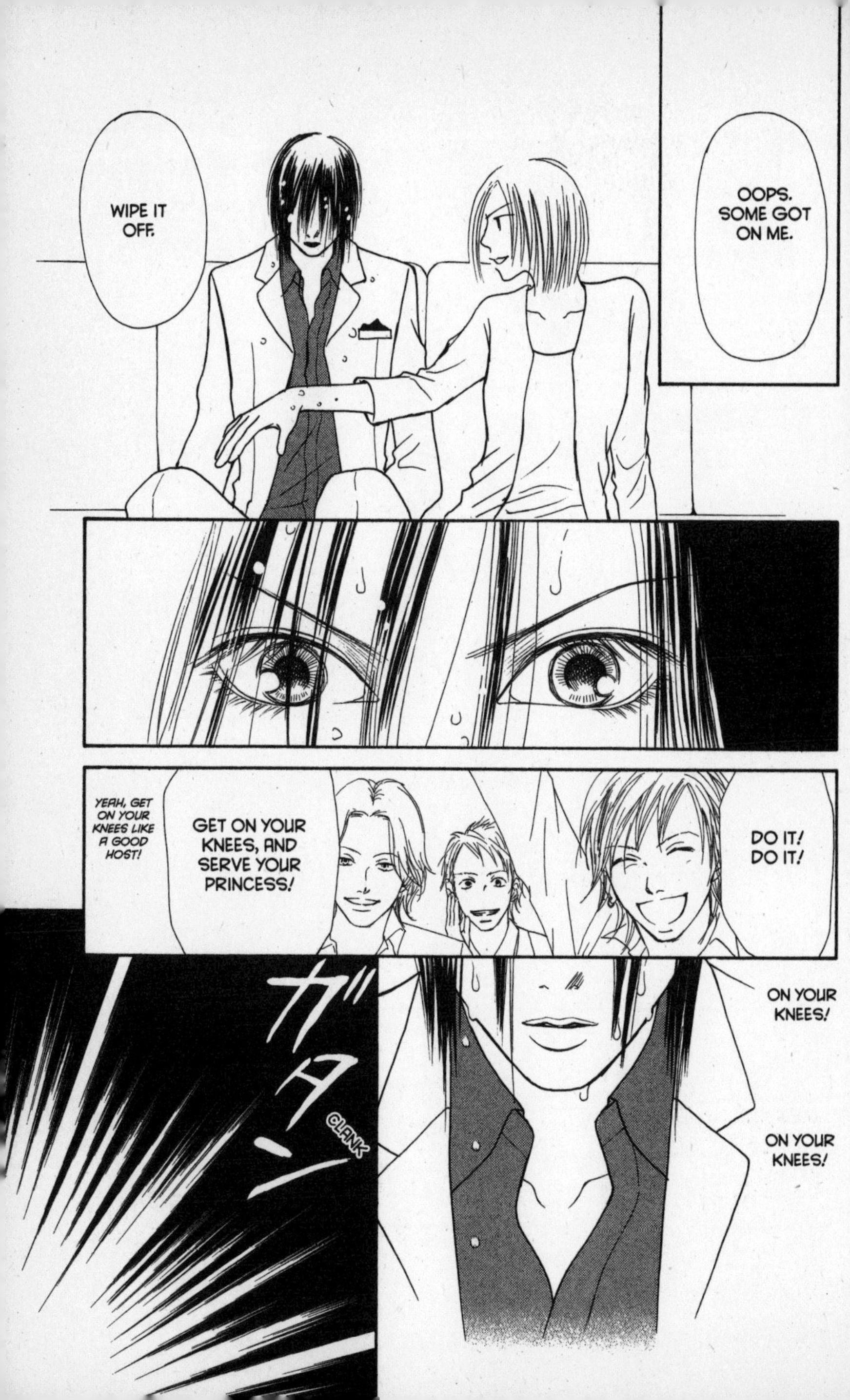
OOPS. SOME GOT ON ME.
WIPE IT OFF.
DO IT! DO IT!
GET ON YOUR KNEES, AND SERVE YOUR PRINCESS!
YEAH, GET ON YOUR KNEES LIKE A GOOD HOST!
ON YOUR KNEES!
ON YOUR KNEES!
CLANK

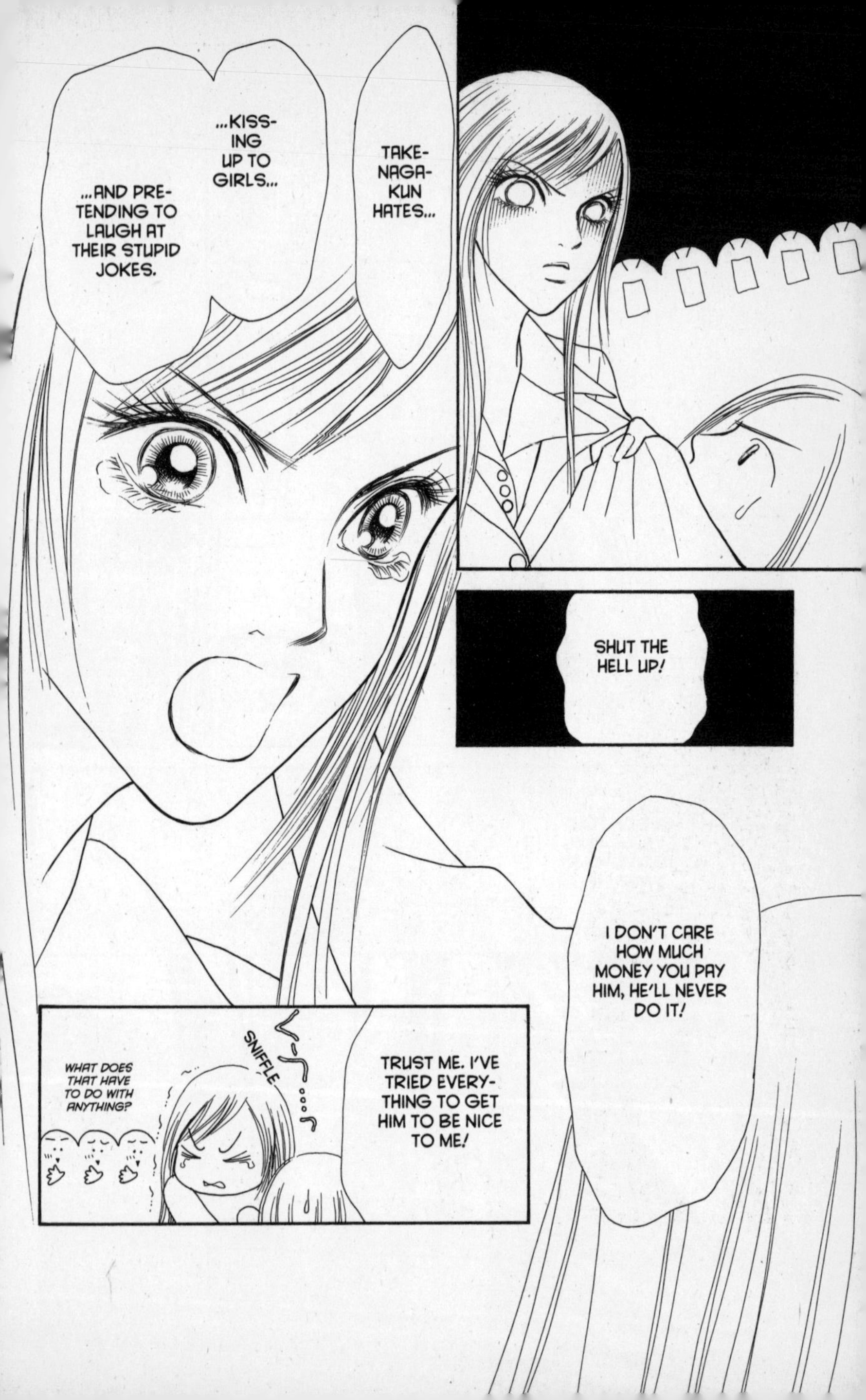
TAKE-NAGA-KUN HATES...
...KISS-ING UP TO GIRLS...
...AND PRE-TENDING TO LAUGH AT THEIR STUPID JOKES.
SHUT THE HELL UP!
I DON'T CARE HOW MUCH MONEY YOU PAY HIM, HE'LL NEVER DO IT!
TRUST ME. I'VE TRIED EVERY-THING TO GET HIM TO BE NICE TO ME!
SNIFFLE
WHAT DOES THAT HAVE TO DO WITH ANYTHING?

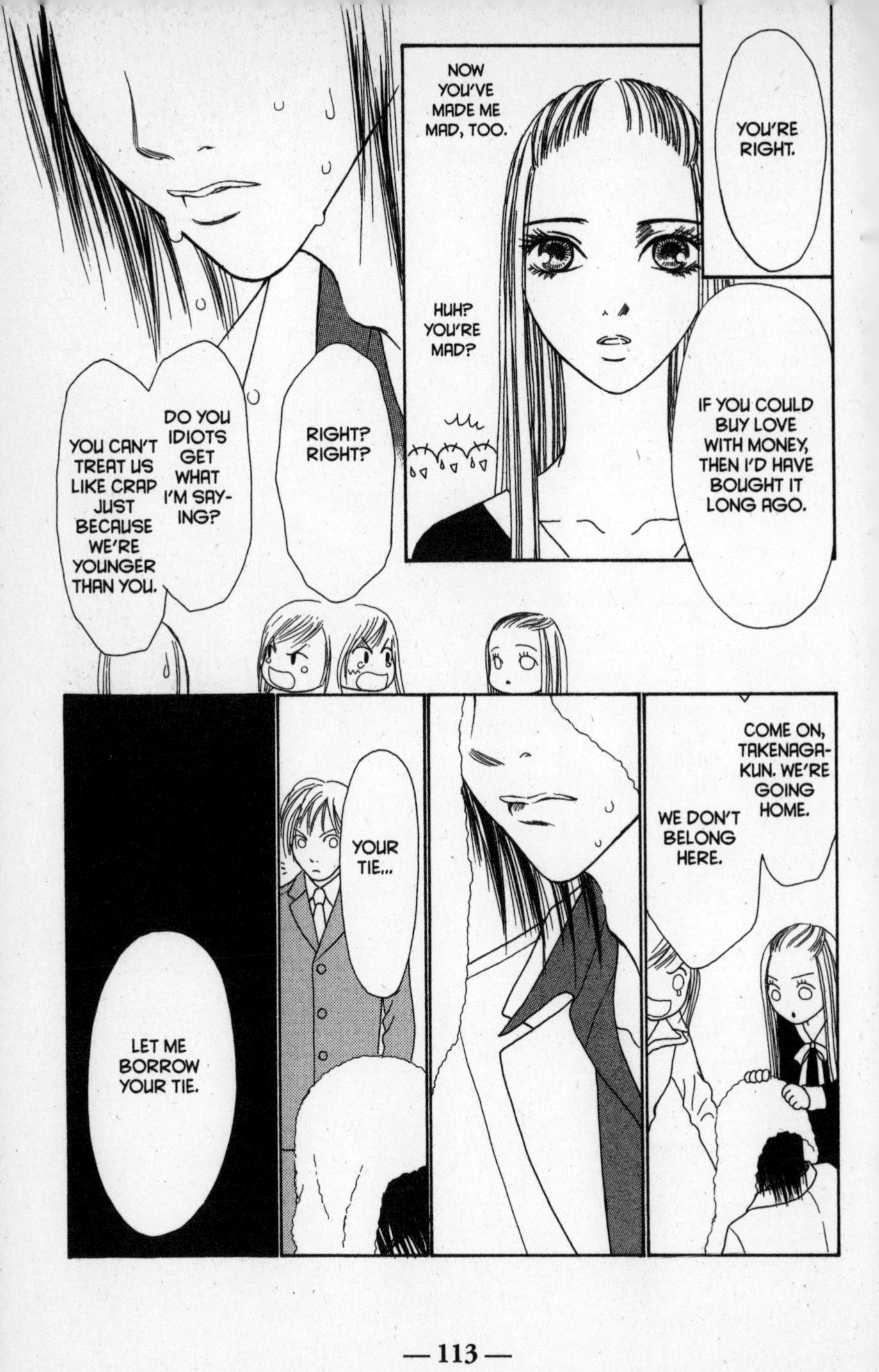
YOU'RE RIGHT.
IF YOU COULD BUY LOVE WITH MONEY, THEN I'D HAVE BOUGHT IT LONG AGO.
NOW YOU'VE MADE ME MAD, TOO.
HUH? YOU'RE MAD?
RIGHT? RIGHT?
DO YOU IDIOTS GET WHAT I'M SAYING?
YOU CAN'T TREAT US LIKE CRAP JUST BECAUSE WE'RE YOUNGER THAN YOU.
COME ON, TAKENAGA-KUN. WE'RE GOING HOME.
WE DON'T BELONG HERE.
YOUR TIE...
LET ME BORROW YOUR TIE.

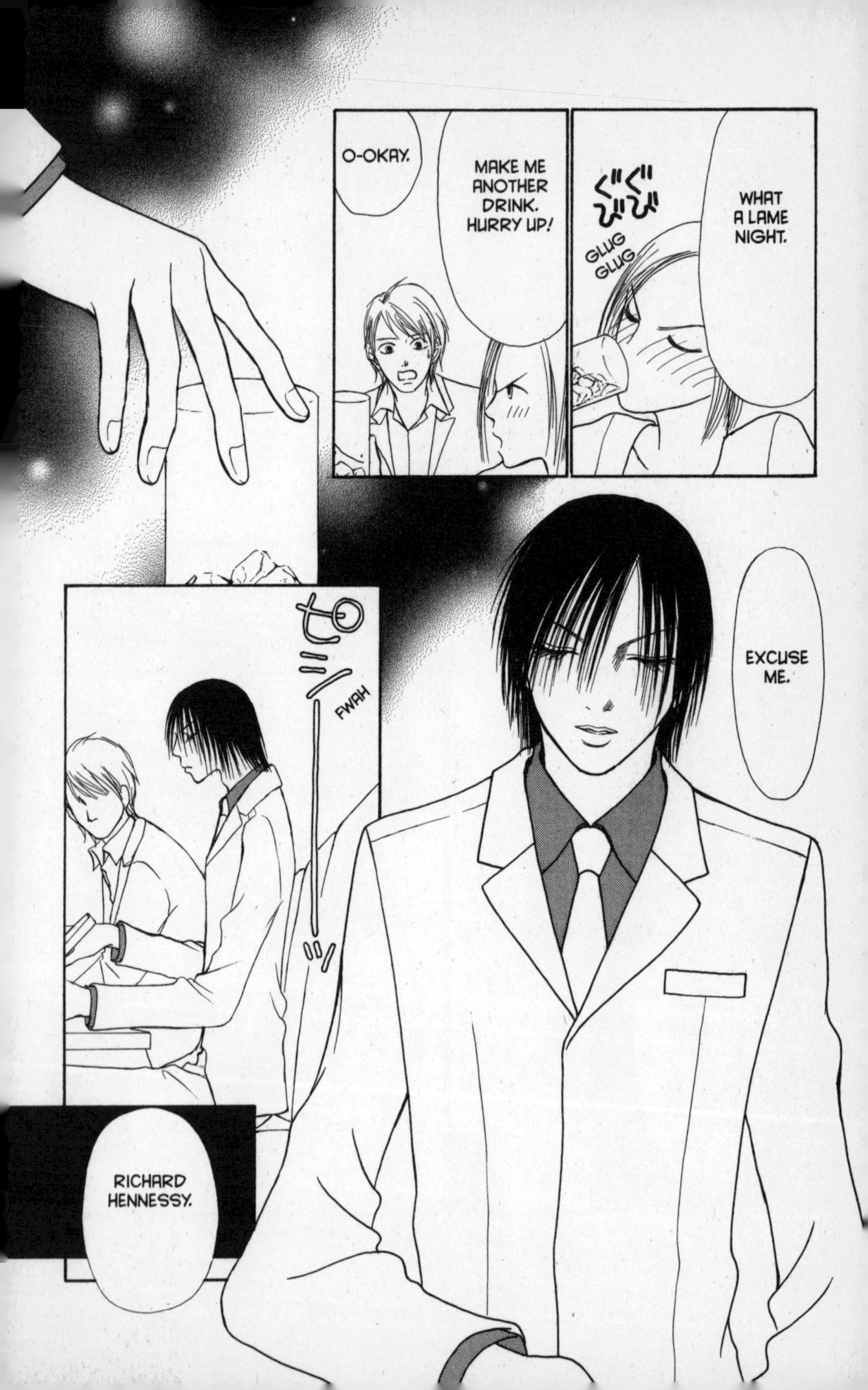
WHAT A LAME NIGHT.
ぐびぐび
GLUG GLUG
MAKE ME ANOTHER DRINK. HURRY UP!
O-OKAY.
EXCUSE ME.
FWAH
RICHARD HENNESSY.

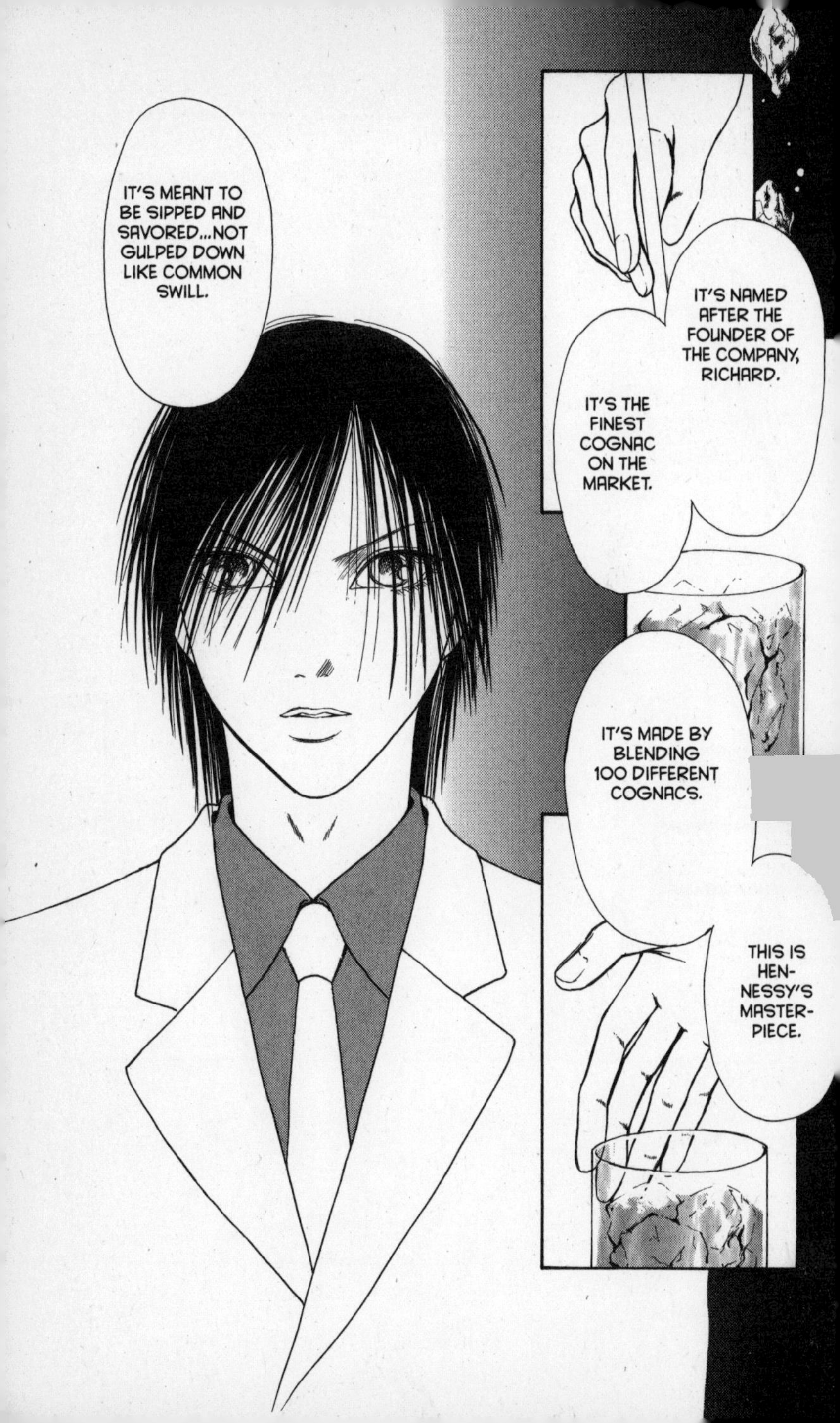
IT'S NAMED AFTER THE FOUNDER OF THE COMPANY, RICHARD.
IT'S THE FINEST COGNAC ON THE MARKET.
IT'S MADE BY BLENDING 100 DIFFERENT COGNACS.
THIS IS HEN-NESSY'S MASTER-PIECE.
IT'S MEANT TO BE SIPPED AND SAVORED...NOT GULPED DOWN LIKE COMMON SWILL.

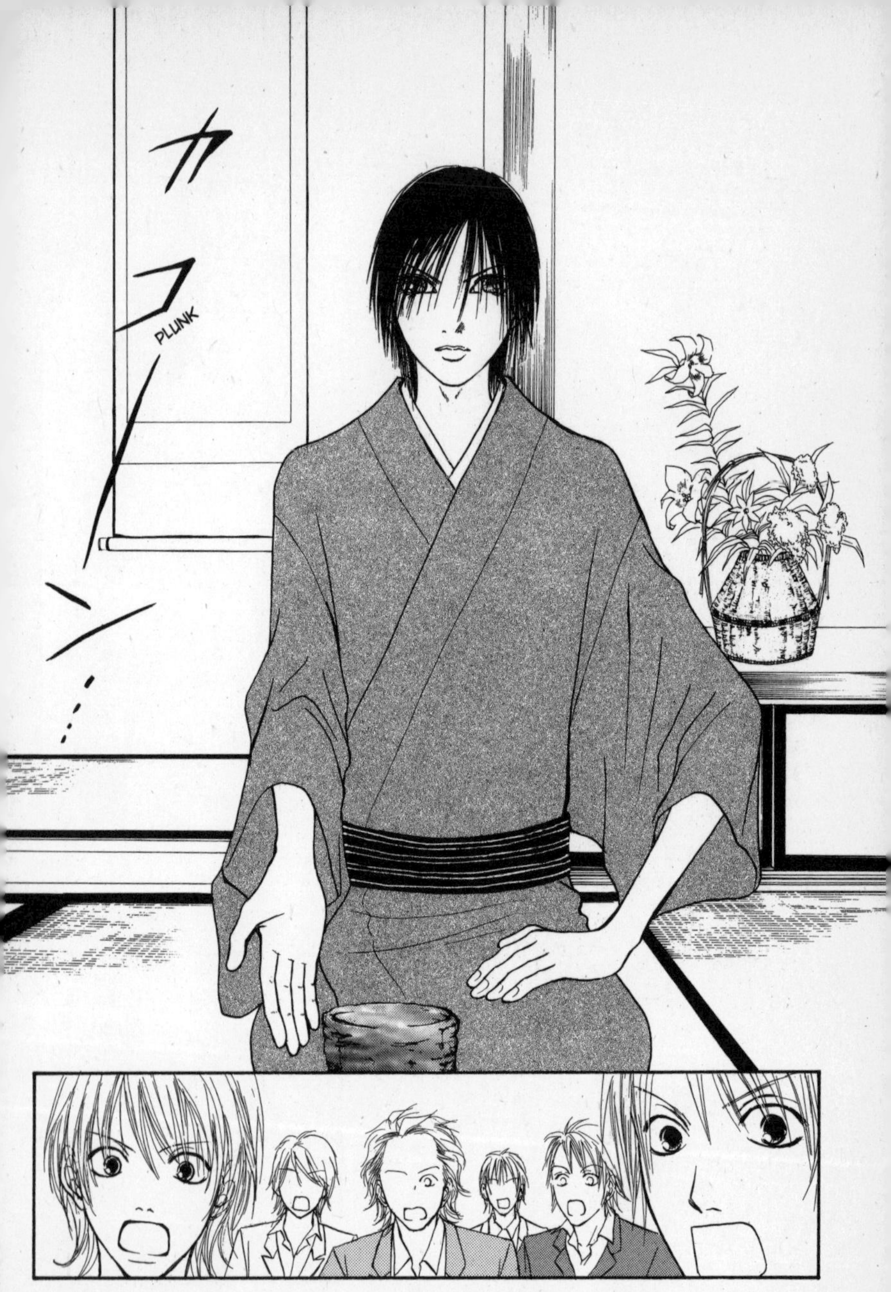
カコーン…
PLUNK

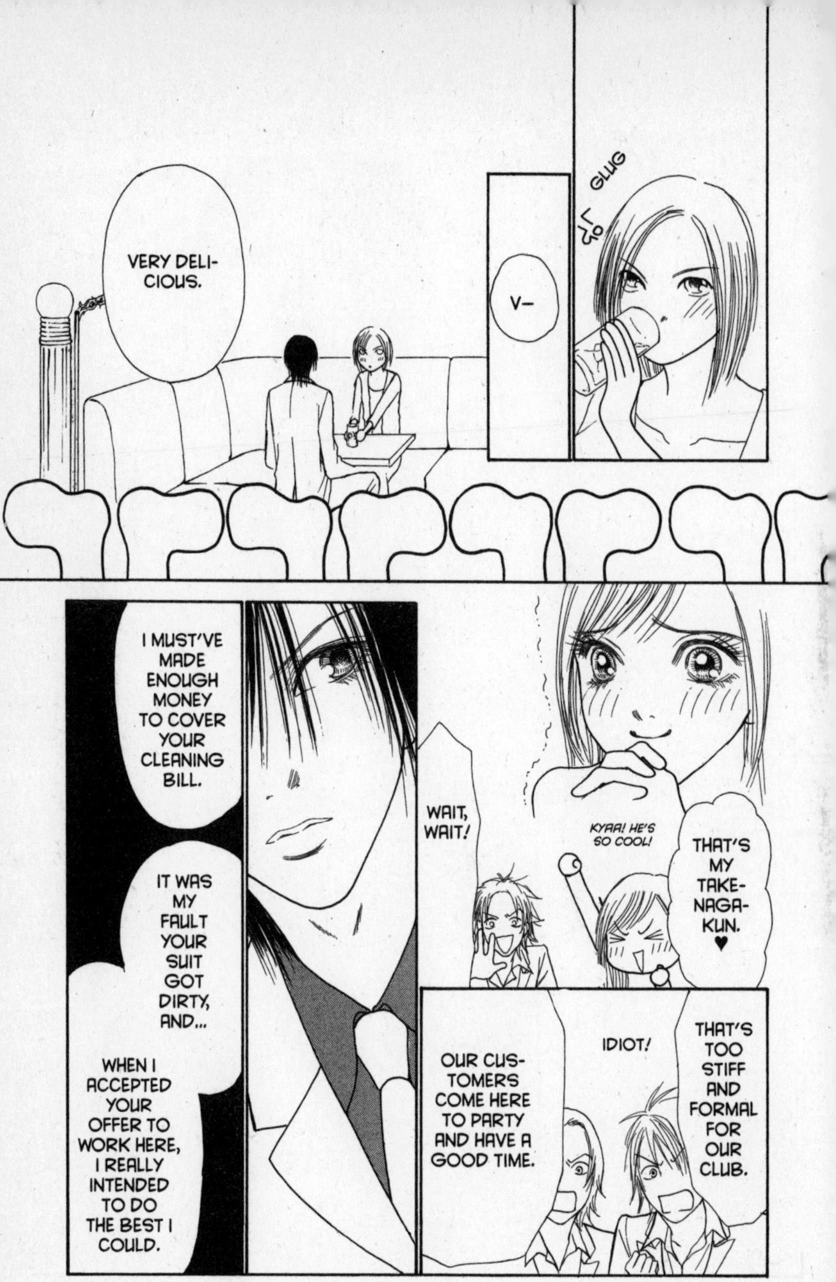
GLUG
V–
VERY DELICIOUS.
THAT'S MY TAKENAGA-KUN. ♥
KYAA! HE'S SO COOL!
WAIT, WAIT!
THAT'S TOO STIFF AND FORMAL FOR OUR CLUB.
IDIOT!
OUR CUSTOMERS COME HERE TO PARTY AND HAVE A GOOD TIME.
I MUST'VE MADE ENOUGH MONEY TO COVER YOUR CLEANING BILL.
IT WAS MY FAULT YOUR SUIT GOT DIRTY, AND...
WHEN I ACCEPTED YOUR OFFER TO WORK HERE, I REALLY INTENDED TO DO THE BEST I COULD.

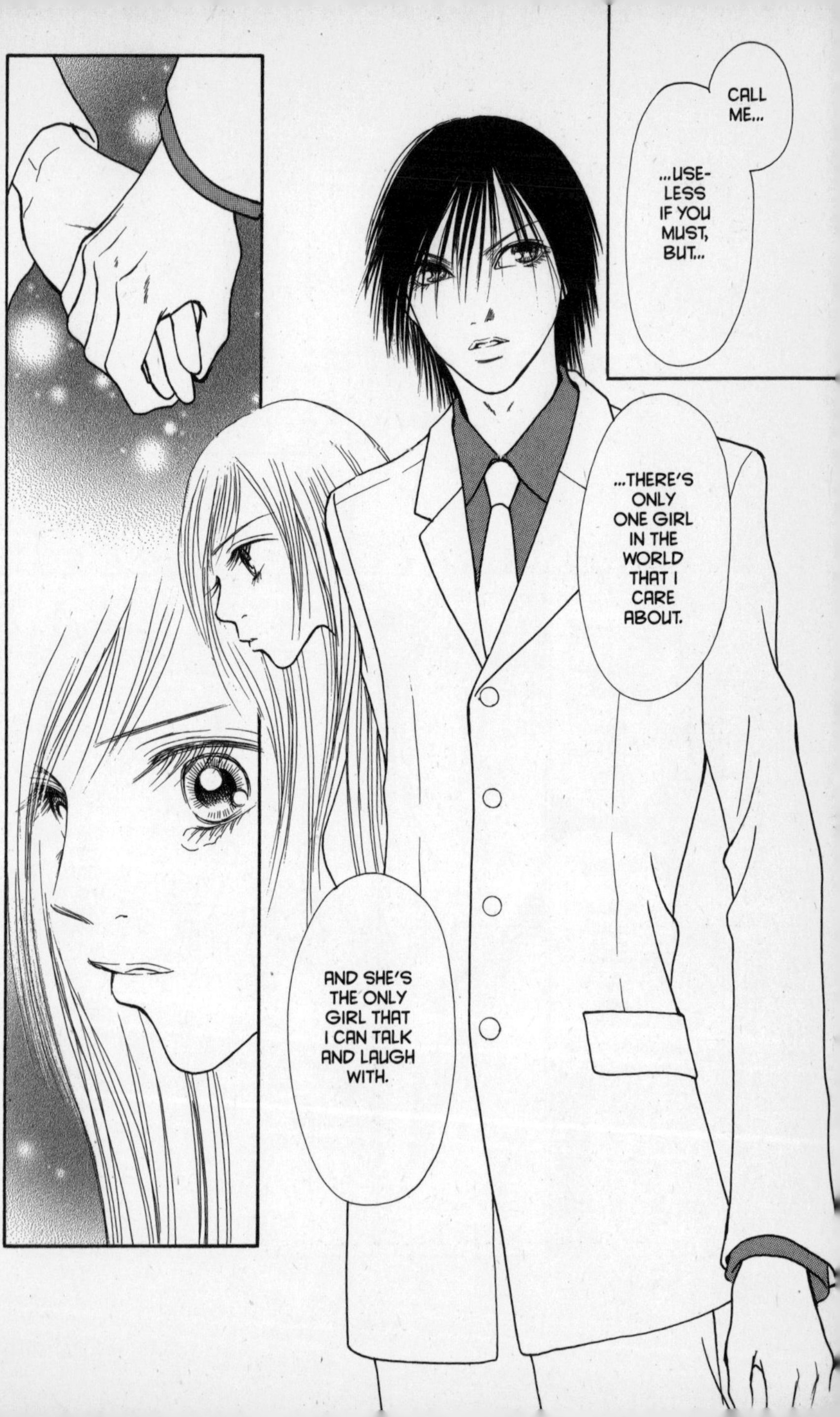
CALL ME...
...USE-LESS IF YOU MUST, BUT...
...THERE'S ONLY ONE GIRL IN THE WORLD THAT I CARE ABOUT.
AND SHE'S THE ONLY GIRL THAT I CAN TALK AND LAUGH WITH.

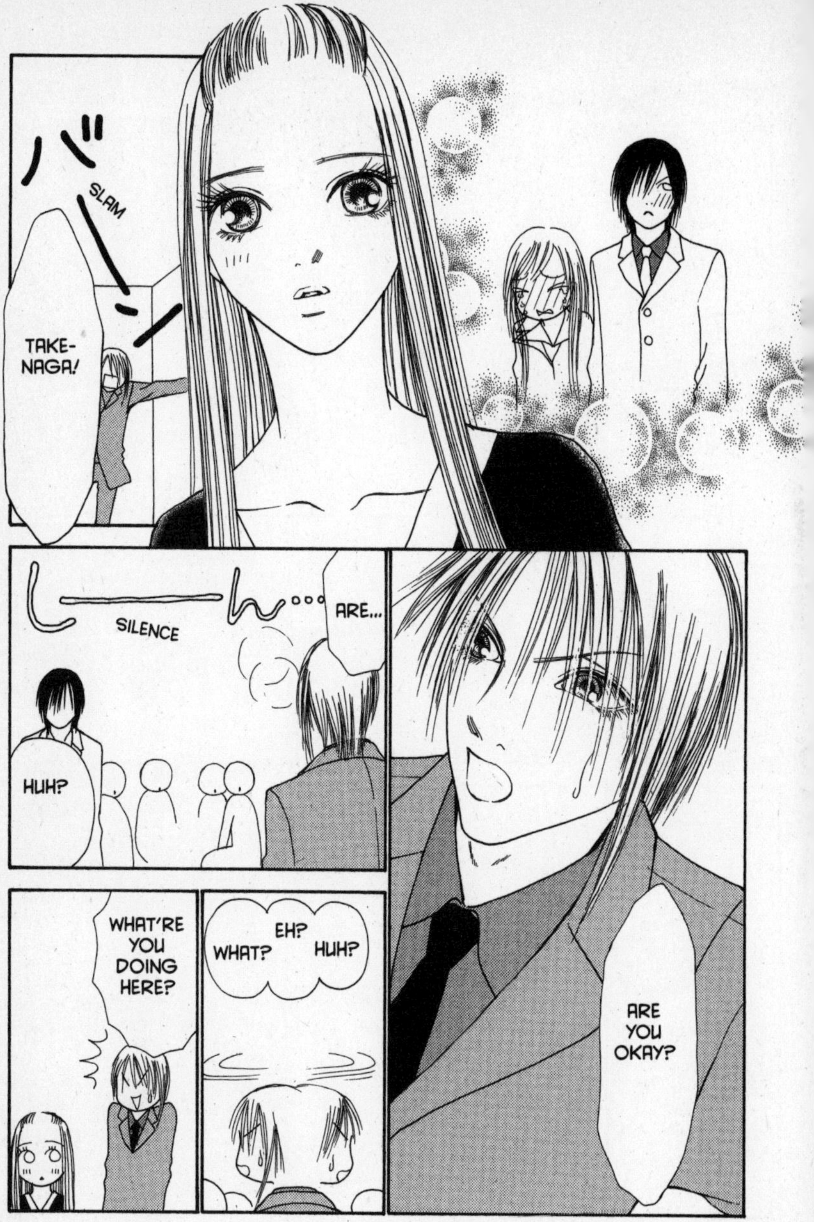

バーン
SLAM
TAKE-NAGA!
ARE YOU OKAY?
しーん…
SILENCE
ARE...
HUH?
EH? WHAT? HUH?
WHAT'RE YOU DOING HERE?

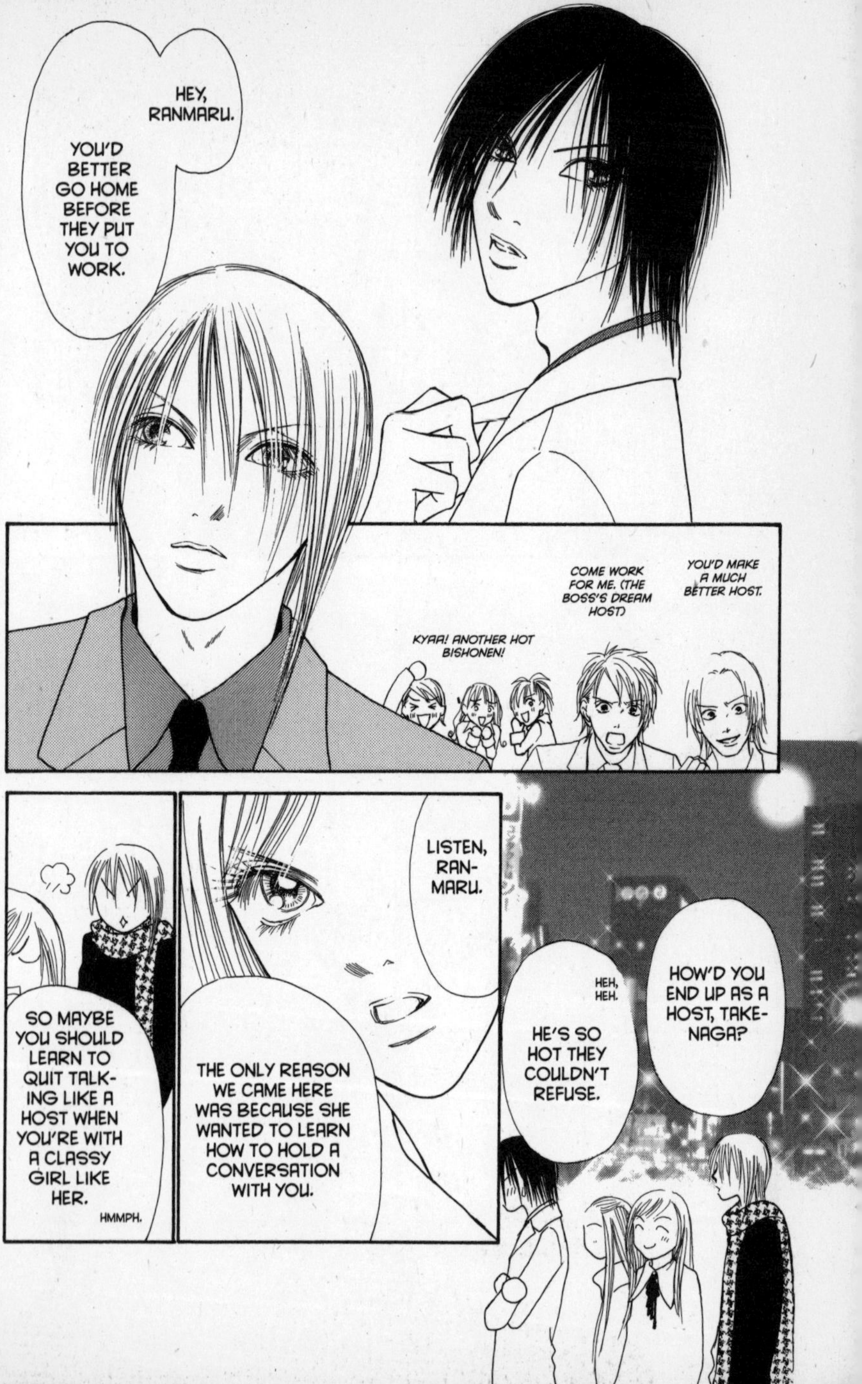
HEY, RANMARU.
YOU'D BETTER GO HOME BEFORE THEY PUT YOU TO WORK.
YOU'D MAKE A MUCH BETTER HOST.
COME WORK FOR ME. (THE BOSS'S DREAM HOST)
KYAA! ANOTHER HOT BISHONEN!
HOW'D YOU END UP AS A HOST, TAKE-NAGA?
HEH, HEH.
HE'S SO HOT THEY COULDN'T REFUSE.
LISTEN, RAN-MARU.
THE ONLY REASON WE CAME HERE WAS BECAUSE SHE WANTED TO LEARN HOW TO HOLD A CONVERSATION WITH YOU.
SO MAYBE YOU SHOULD LEARN TO QUIT TALK-ING LIKE A HOST WHEN YOU'RE WITH A CLASSY GIRL LIKE HER.
HMMPH.

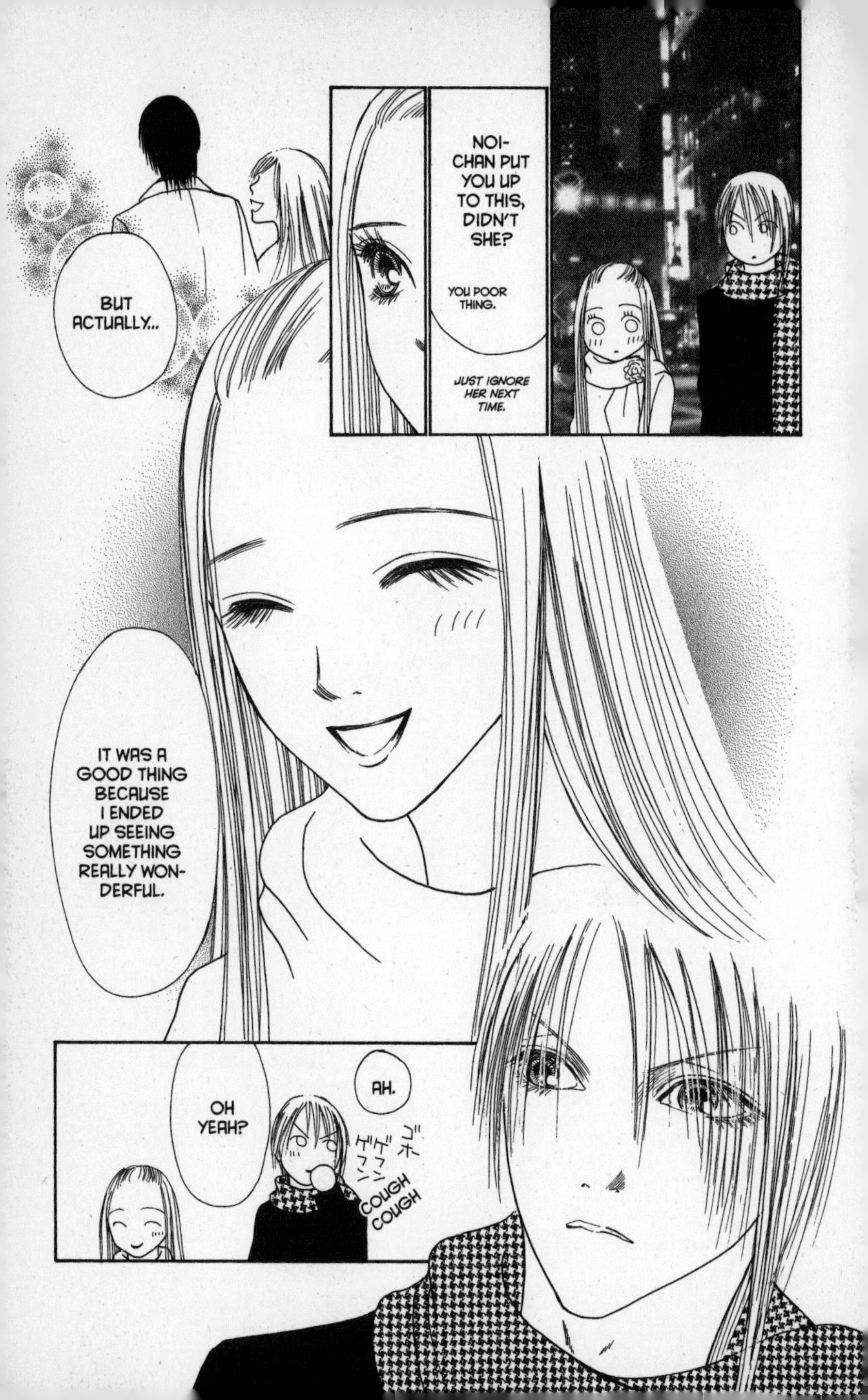
NOI-CHAN PUT YOU UP TO THIS, DIDN'T SHE?
YOU POOR THING.
JUST IGNORE HER NEXT TIME.
BUT ACTUALLY...
IT WAS A GOOD THING BECAUSE I ENDED UP SEEING SOMETHING REALLY WON-DERFUL.
AH.
COUGH COUGH
OH YEAH?

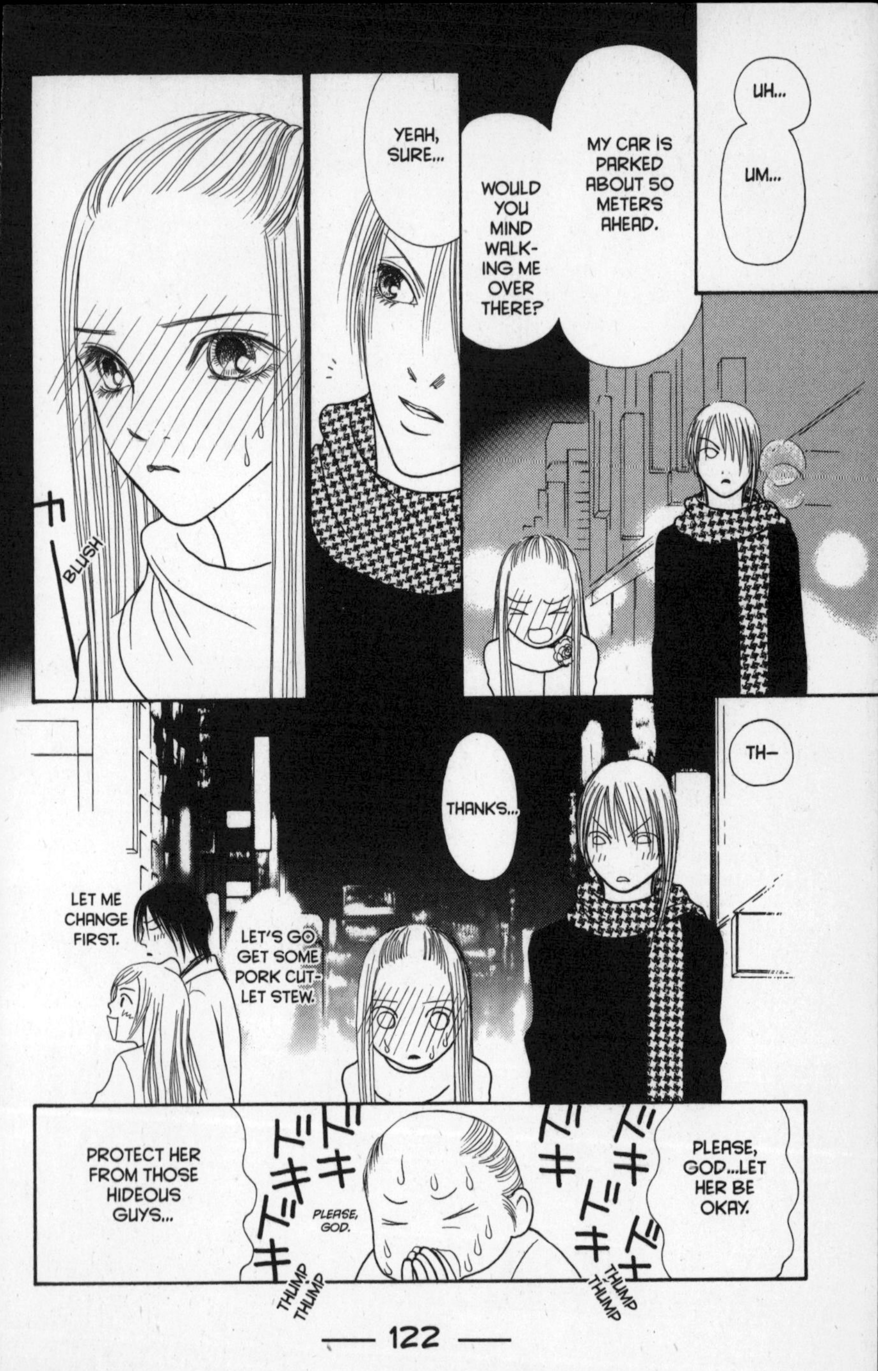
UH...
UM...
MY CAR IS PARKED ABOUT 50 METERS AHEAD.
WOULD YOU MIND WALKING ME OVER THERE?
YEAH, SURE...
BLUSH
TH-
THANKS...
LET'S GO GET SOME PORK CUTLET STEW.
LET ME CHANGE FIRST.
PLEASE, GOD...LET HER BE OKAY.
THUMP THUMP
PLEASE, GOD.
PROTECT HER FROM THOSE HIDEOUS GUYS...
THUMP THUMP

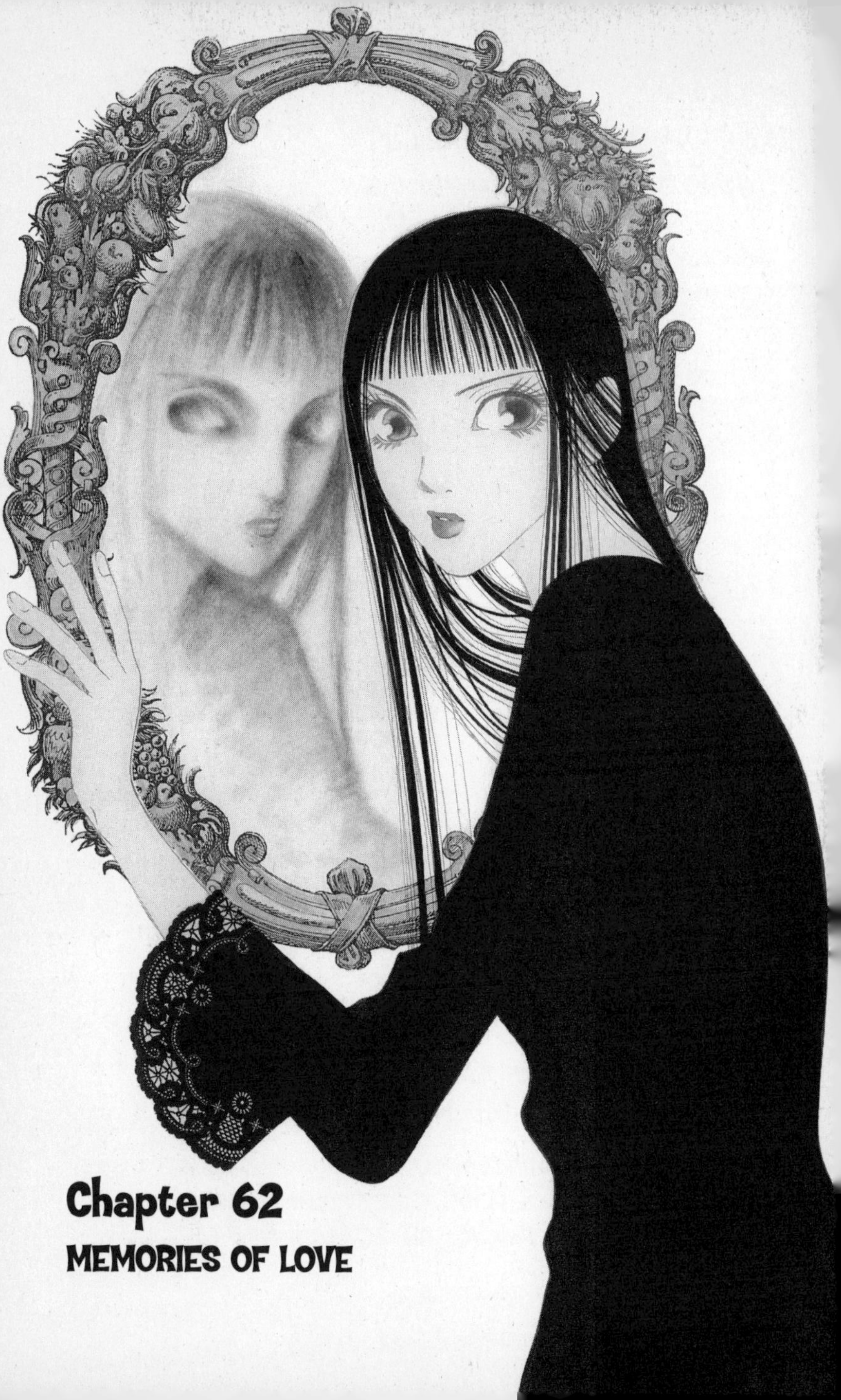

Chapter 62

MEMORIES OF LOVE

THANK YOU FOR BUYING DEL REY MANGA BOOKS. ♥♥♥♥

I DON'T GET ANY BONUS PAGES THIS VOLUME. MAYBE I'LL HAVE TO GO ALL OUT IN VOLUME 16. ♥

SPECIAL THANKS

TO ALL OF YOU WHO SENT IN LETTERS.
♥♥♥♥

KIYOHARU-SAMA, MERRY-SAMA, KAGEROU-SAMA, D'ESPAIRS RAY-SAMA, DIR EN GRAY-SAMA, MITSUHIRO OIKAWA-SAMA

EVERYBODY FROM FULL FACE, YUKI-CHAN-SAMA ♥, UEDA-SAMA, KATO-SAMA, ETOU-SAMA, TOSHI-YA-SHI, EVERYBODY FROM FREE-WILL, DYNAMITE TOMMY-SAMA, EMIKO KAKECHI-SAMA ♥, EVERYBODY FROM PS COM-PANY, OZAKI-SAMA, TANAKA-SAMA, SHINADA-SAMA, PSY-TO-SAMA, SATAROU-SAMA, N-SAMA THE GORGEOUS WRITER ♥

CHOBI-SAMA, NABEKO-SAMA, TOMMY-SAMA, NAKAMURA-KUN-SAMA, YOSHII-SAMA

YUKIO IKEDA-SAMA, YUU YOSHII-SAMA, MACHIKO SAKU-RAI-SAMA

MINE-SAMA, INO-SAMA, EVERYBODY FROM THE EDITING DEPARTMENT

EVERYBODY WHO'S READING THIS BOOK RIGHT NOW. ♥♥♥♥

THIS BOOK IS MADE POSSIBLE BY YOUR GENEROUS SUP-PORT. THANK YOU ALL SO MUCH. ♥♥♥♥

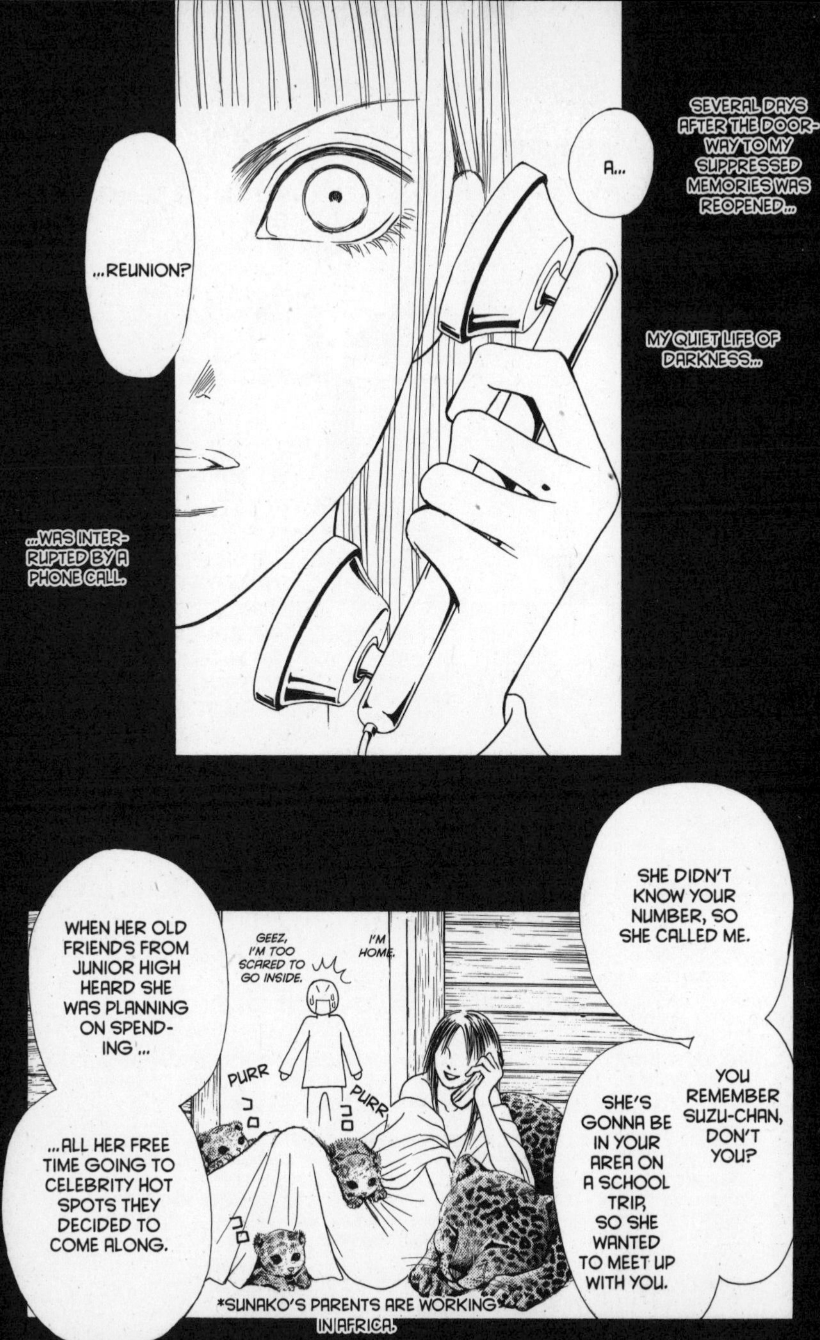
SEVERAL DAYS AFTER THE DOOR-WAY TO MY SUPPRESSED MEMORIES WAS REOPENED...
A...
MY QUIET LIFE OF DARKNESS...
...REUNION?
...WAS INTER-RUPTED BY A PHONE CALL.
SHE DIDN'T KNOW YOUR NUMBER, SO SHE CALLED ME.
YOU REMEMBER SUZU-CHAN, DON'T YOU?
SHE'S GONNA BE IN YOUR AREA ON A SCHOOL TRIP, SO SHE WANTED TO MEET UP WITH YOU.
I'M HOME.
GEEZ, I'M TOO SCARED TO GO INSIDE.
PURR
PURR
WHEN HER OLD FRIENDS FROM JUNIOR HIGH HEARD SHE WAS PLANNING ON SPEND-ING...
...ALL HER FREE TIME GOING TO CELEBRITY HOT SPOTS THEY DECIDED TO COME ALONG.
*SUNAKO'S PARENTS ARE WORKING IN AFRICA.

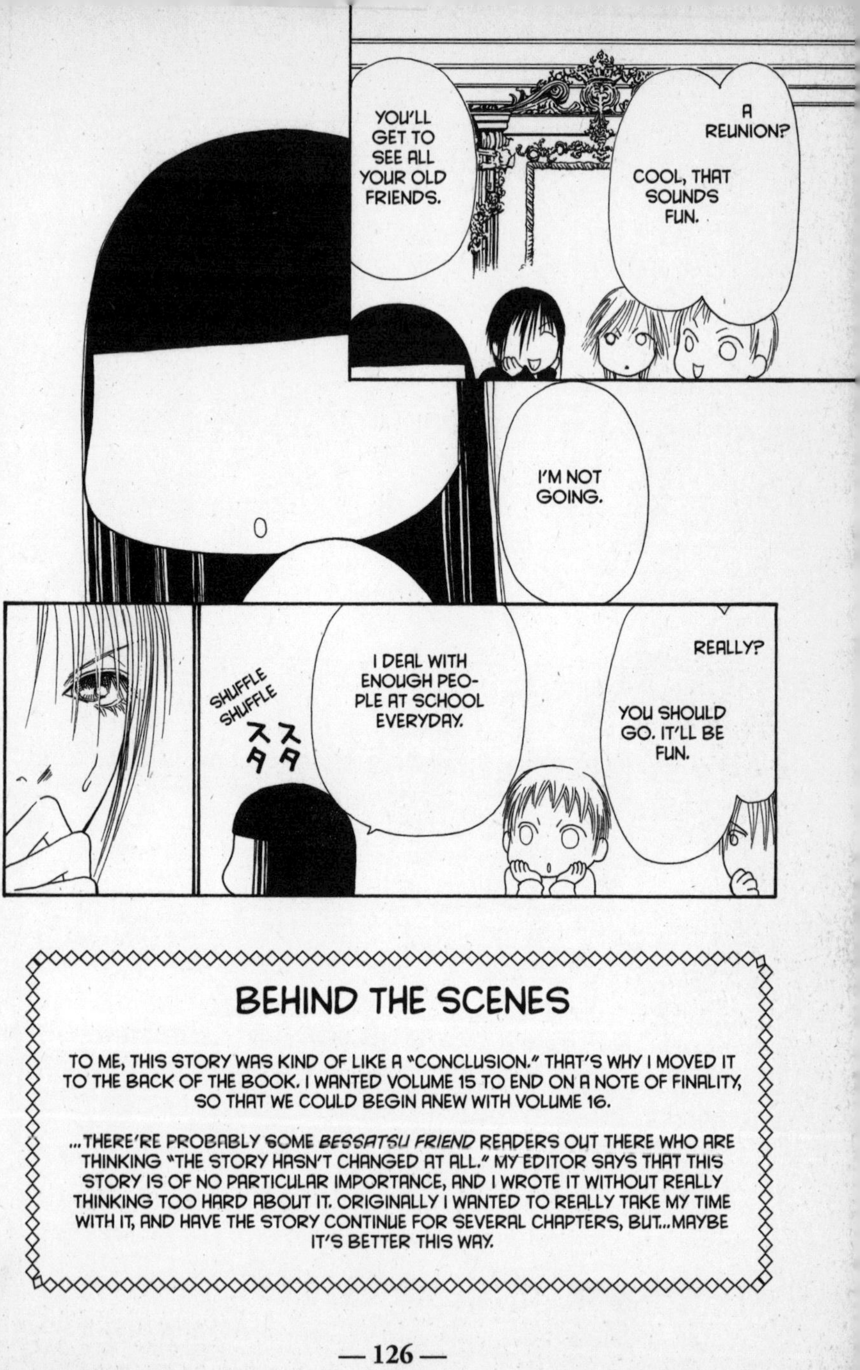
A REUNION?
COOL, THAT SOUNDS FUN.
YOU'LL GET TO SEE ALL YOUR OLD FRIENDS.
I'M NOT GOING.
REALLY?
YOU SHOULD GO. IT'LL BE FUN.
I DEAL WITH ENOUGH PEO-PLE AT SCHOOL EVERYDAY.
SHUFFLE SHUFFLE
スタスタ

BEHIND THE SCENES

TO ME, THIS STORY WAS KIND OF LIKE A "CONCLUSION." THAT'S WHY I MOVED IT TO THE BACK OF THE BOOK. I WANTED VOLUME 15 TO END ON A NOTE OF FINALITY, SO THAT WE COULD BEGIN ANEW WITH VOLUME 16.

...THERE'RE PROBABLY SOME *BESSATSU FRIEND* READERS OUT THERE WHO ARE THINKING "THE STORY HASN'T CHANGED AT ALL." MY EDITOR SAYS THAT THIS STORY IS OF NO PARTICULAR IMPORTANCE, AND I WROTE IT WITHOUT REALLY THINKING TOO HARD ABOUT IT. ORIGINALLY I WANTED TO REALLY TAKE MY TIME WITH IT, AND HAVE THE STORY CONTINUE FOR SEVERAL CHAPTERS, BUT...MAYBE IT'S BETTER THIS WAY.

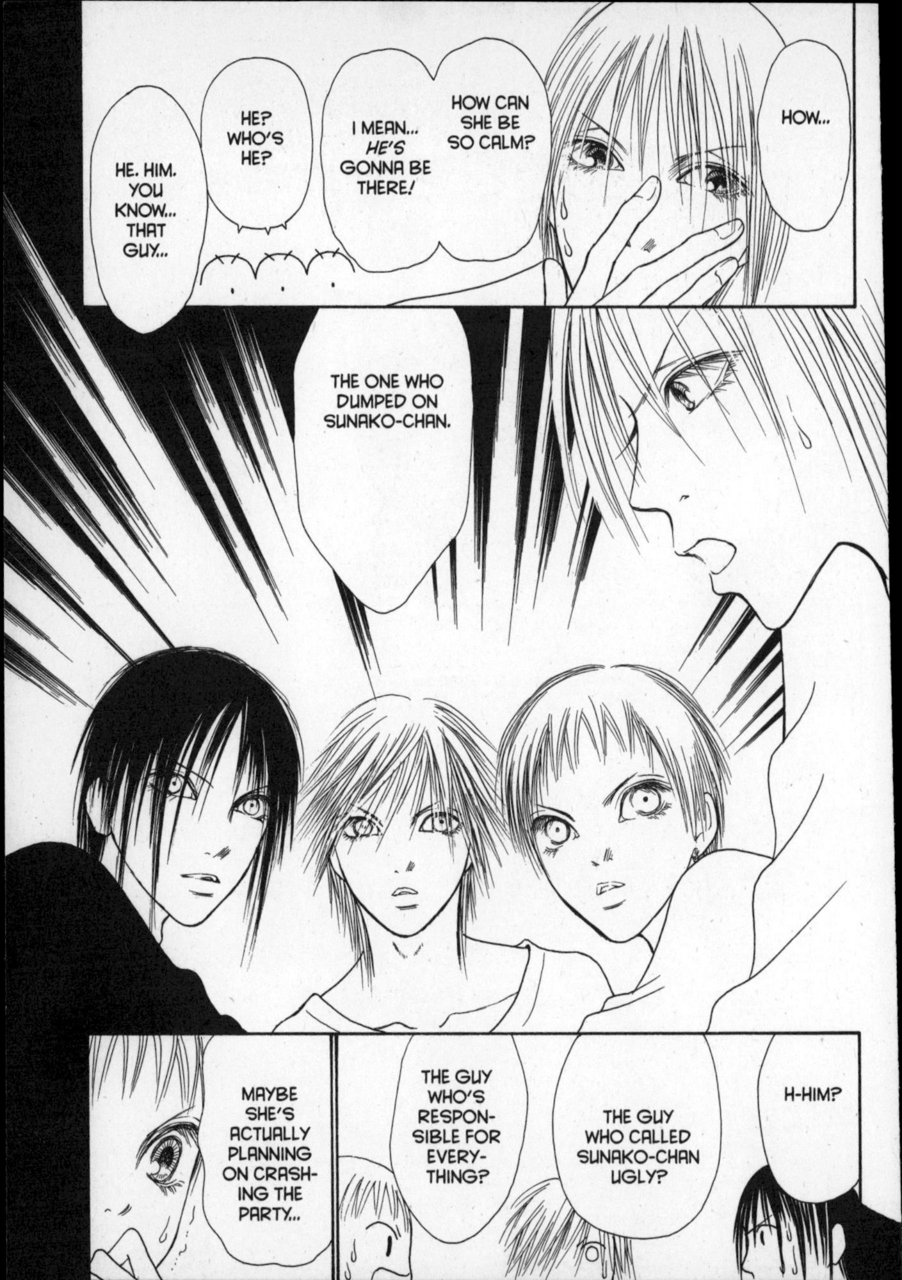
HOW...
HOW CAN SHE BE SO CALM?
I MEAN... *HE'S* GONNA BE THERE!
HE? WHO'S HE?
HE. HIM. YOU KNOW... THAT GUY...
THE ONE WHO DUMPED ON SUNAKO-CHAN.
H-HIM?
THE GUY WHO CALLED SUNAKO-CHAN UGLY?
THE GUY WHO'S RESPON-SIBLE FOR EVERY-THING?
MAYBE SHE'S ACTUALLY PLANNING ON CRASH-ING THE PARTY...

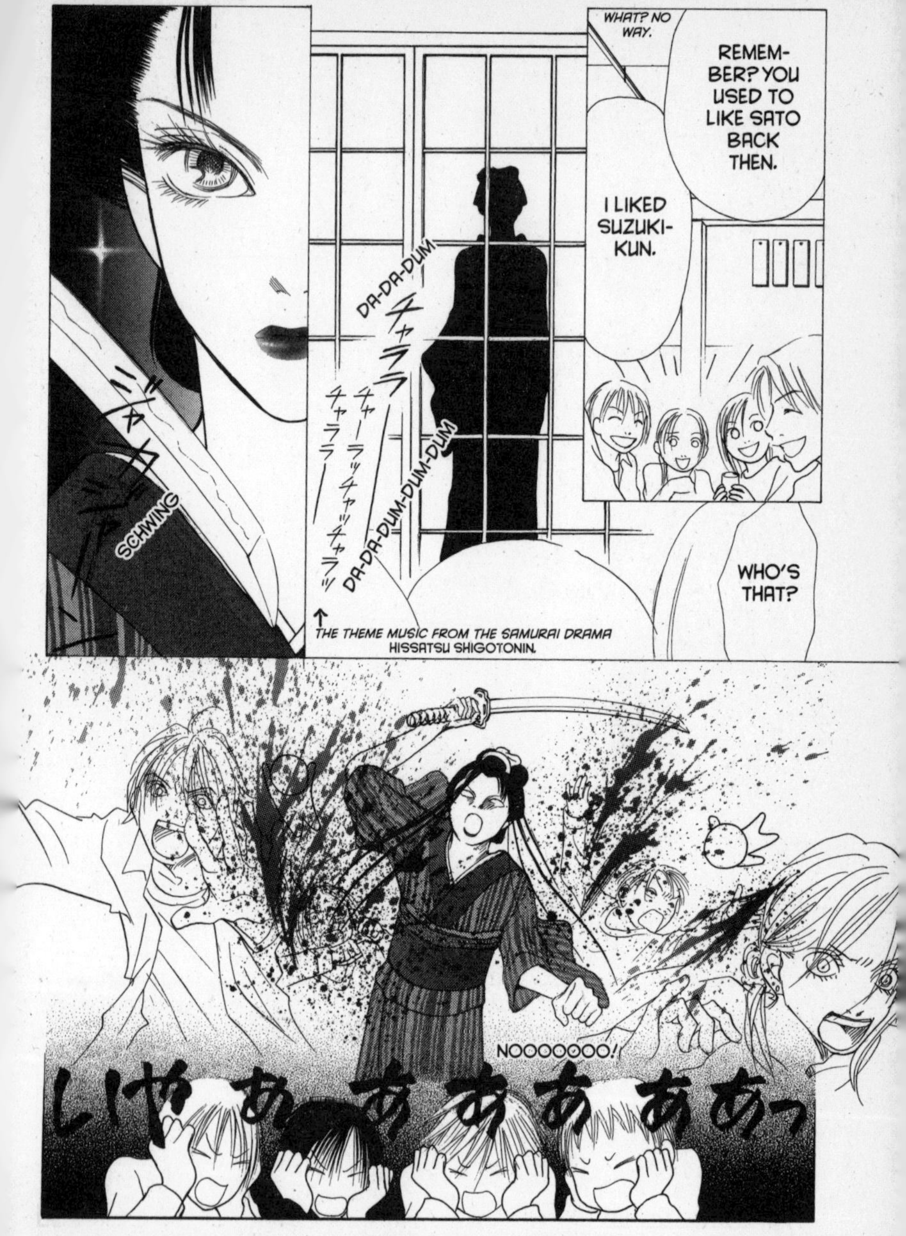
REMEMBER? YOU USED TO LIKE SATO BACK THEN.
WHAT? NO WAY.
I LIKED SUZUKI-KUN.
WHO'S THAT?
DA-DA-DUM
チャララ
チャーラッチャッチャラッ
チャララ
DA-DA-DUM-DUM-DUM
↑ THE THEME MUSIC FROM THE SAMURAI DRAMA HISSATSU SHIGOTONIN.
SCHWING
NOOOOOOO!
いやあああああっ

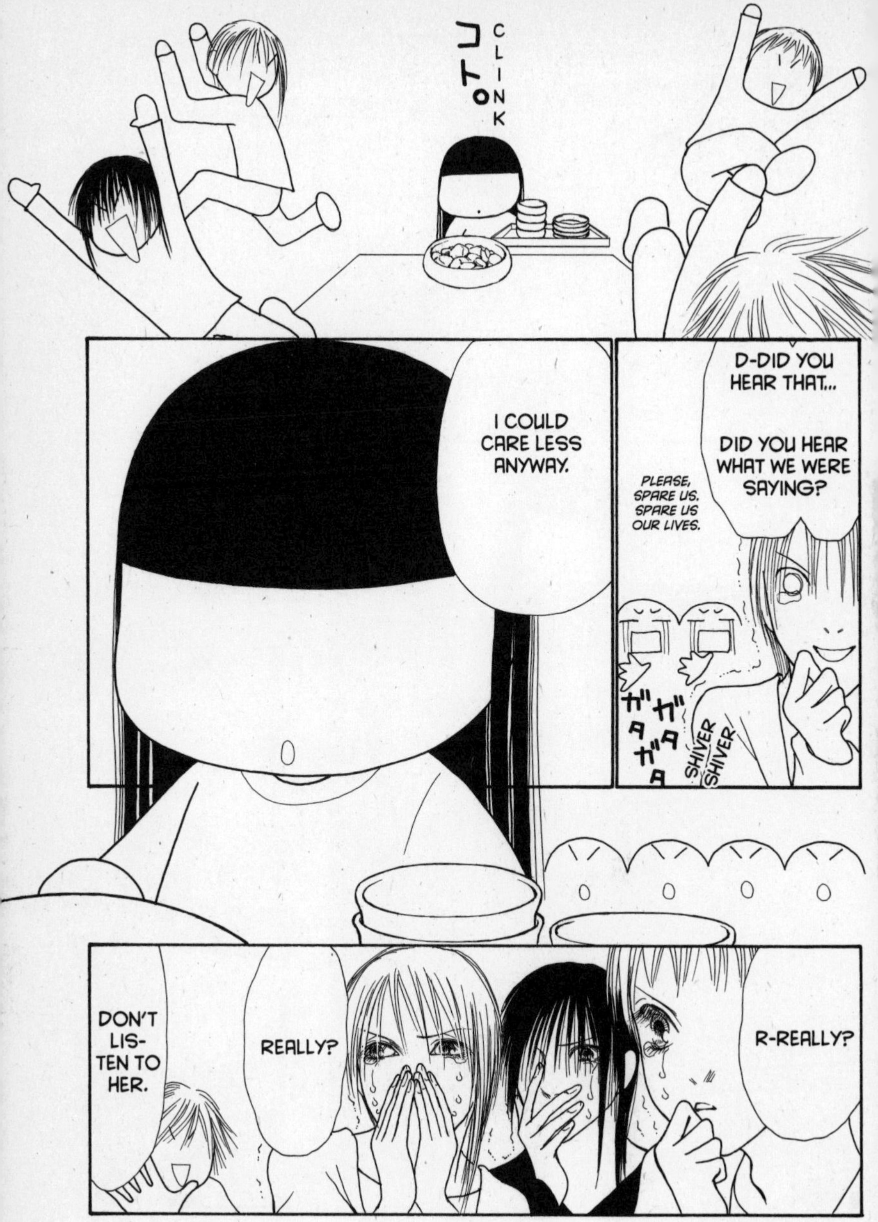
CLINK
D-DID YOU HEAR THAT...
DID YOU HEAR WHAT WE WERE SAYING?
PLEASE, SPARE US. SPARE US OUR LIVES.
SHIVER SHIVER
I COULD CARE LESS ANYWAY.
R-REALLY?
REALLY?
DON'T LIS- TEN TO HER.

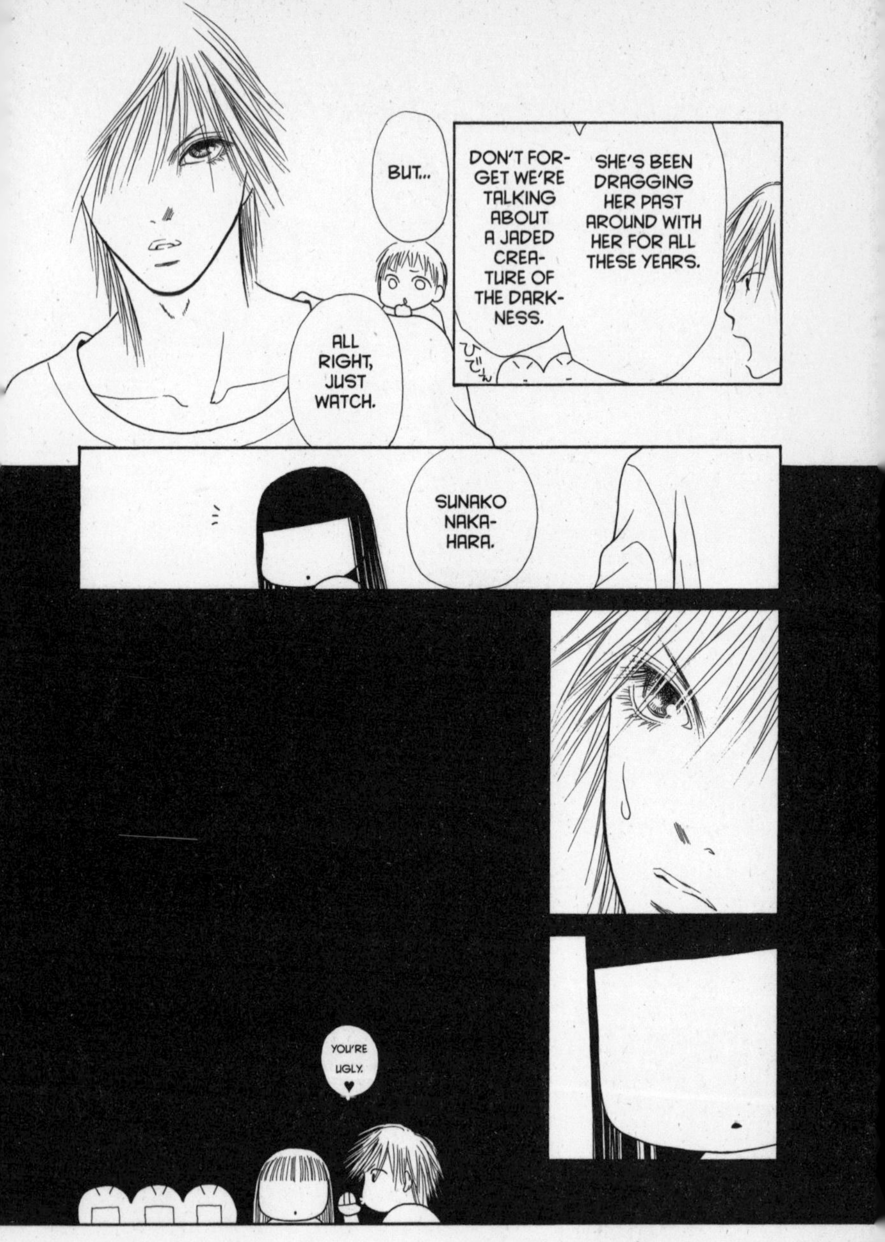
SHE'S BEEN DRAGGING HER PAST AROUND WITH HER FOR ALL THESE YEARS.
DON'T FORGET WE'RE TALKING ABOUT A JADED CREATURE OF THE DARKNESS.
BUT...
ALL RIGHT, JUST WATCH.
SUNAKO NAKAHARA.
YOU'RE UGLY. ♥

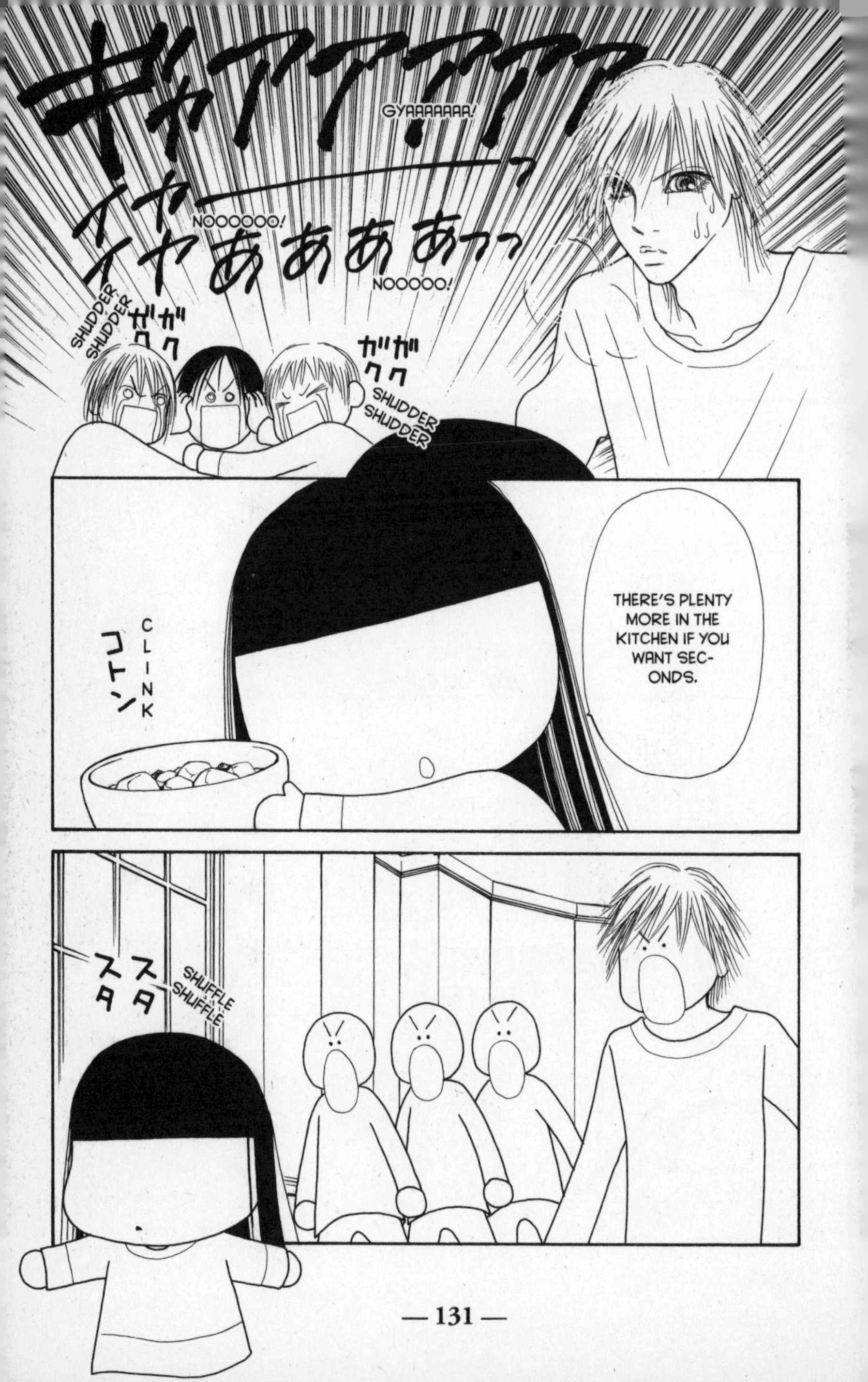

ギャアアアア
GYAAAAAAA!
イヤ———っ
NOOOOOO!
イヤあああああっっ
NOOOOO!
ガガクク
SHUDDER SHUDDER
ガガクク
SHUDDER SHUDDER
THERE'S PLENTY MORE IN THE KITCHEN IF YOU WANT SEC-ONDS.
コトン
CLINK
スタスタ
SHUFFLE SHUFFLE

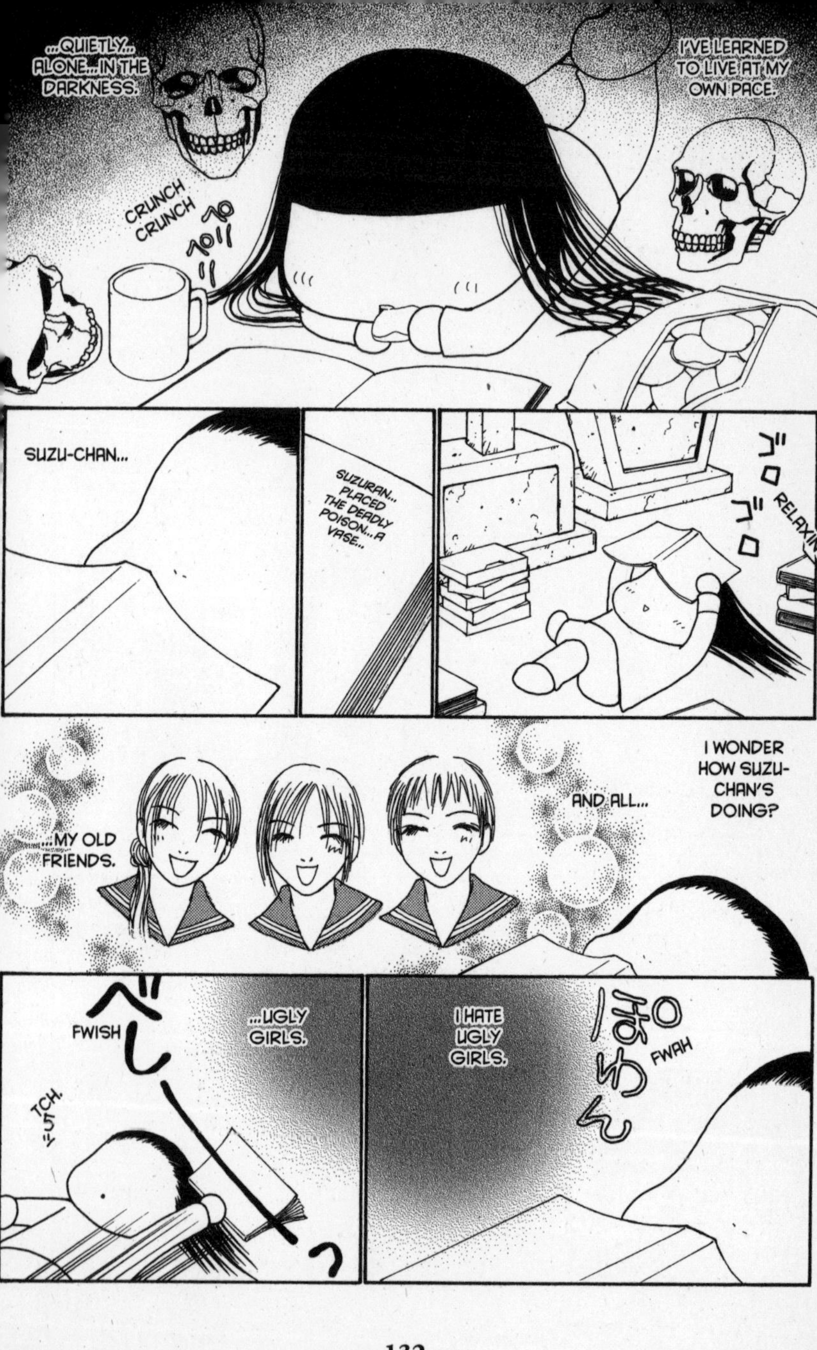
I'VE LEARNED TO LIVE AT MY OWN PACE.
...QUIETLY... ALONE...IN THE DARKNESS.
CRUNCH CRUNCH
ゴロ ゴロ
RELAXING
SUZURAN... PLACED THE DEADLY POISON...A VASE...
SUZU-CHAN...
I WONDER HOW SUZU-CHAN'S DOING?
AND ALL...
...MY OLD FRIENDS.
ほわん
FWAH
I HATE UGLY GIRLS.
...UGLY GIRLS.
べしー
FWISH
TCH.

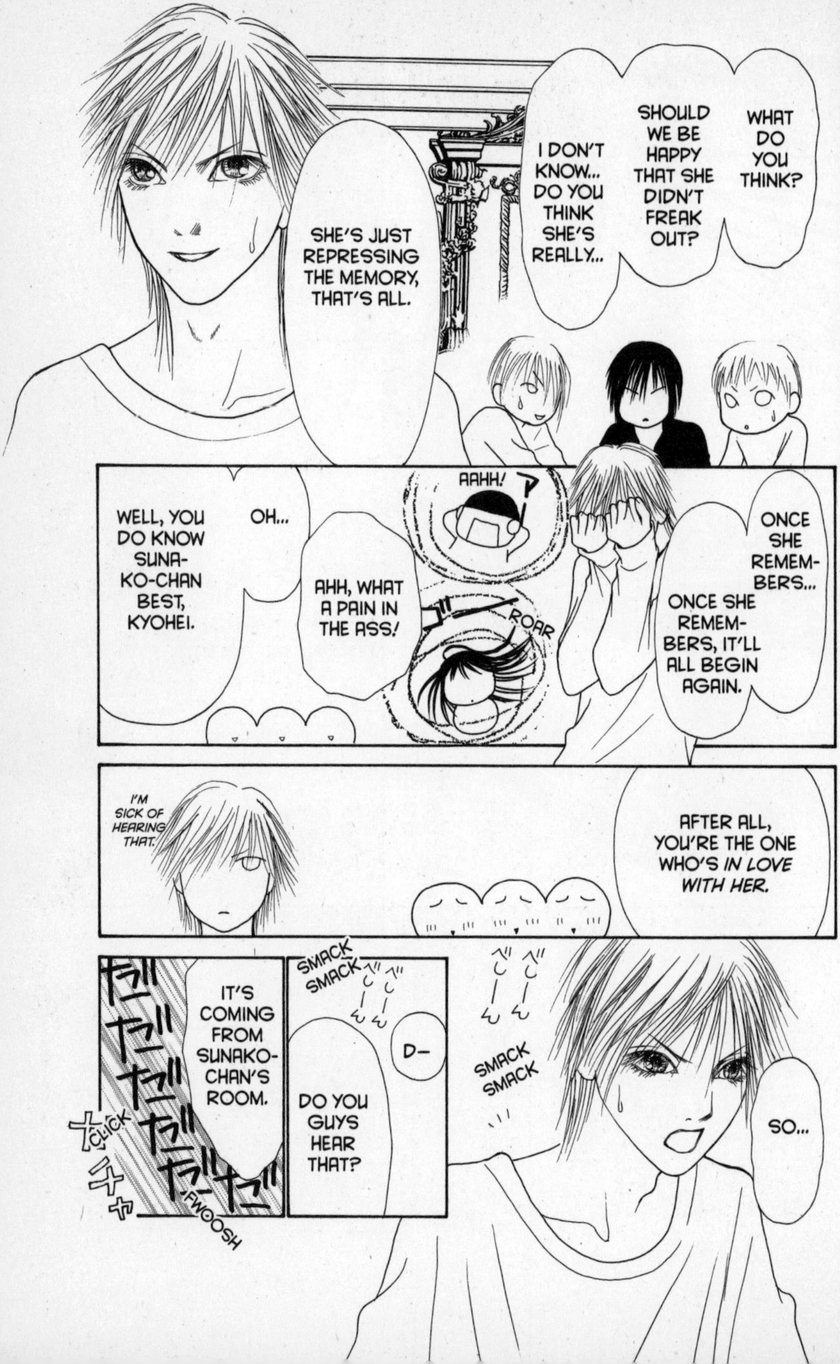
WHAT DO YOU THINK?
SHOULD WE BE HAPPY THAT SHE DIDN'T FREAK OUT?
I DON'T KNOW... DO YOU THINK SHE'S REALLY...
SHE'S JUST REPRESSING THE MEMORY, THAT'S ALL.
ONCE SHE REMEMBERS...
ONCE SHE REMEMBERS, IT'LL ALL BEGIN AGAIN.
AAHH!
ROAR
AHH, WHAT A PAIN IN THE ASS!
OH...
WELL, YOU DO KNOW SUNAKO-CHAN BEST, KYOHEI.
AFTER ALL, YOU'RE THE ONE WHO'S *IN LOVE WITH HER.*
I'M SICK OF HEARING THAT.
SO...
SMACK SMACK
D-
DO YOU GUYS HEAR THAT?
SMACK SMACK
IT'S COMING FROM SUNAKO-CHAN'S ROOM.
CLICK
FWOOSH

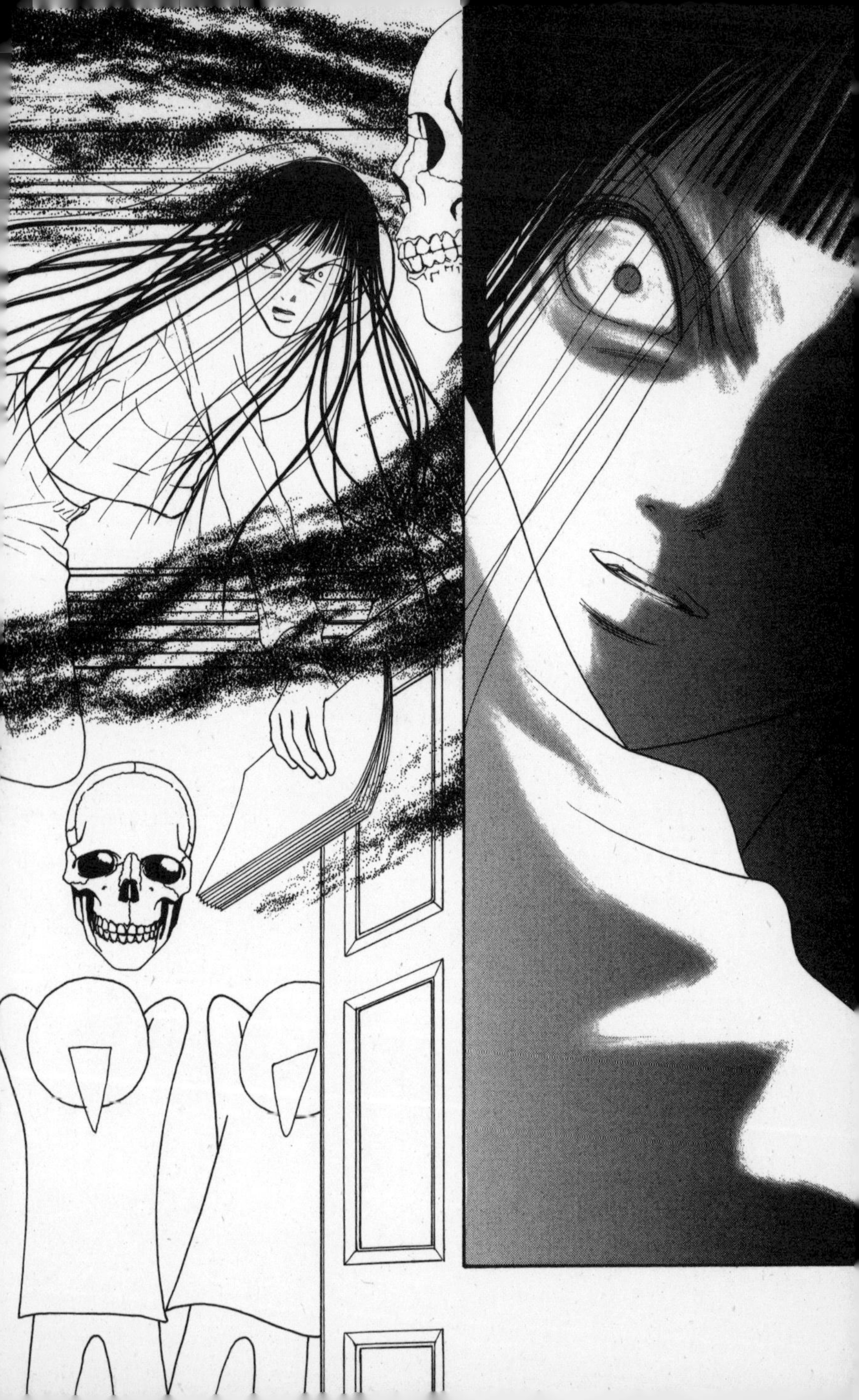

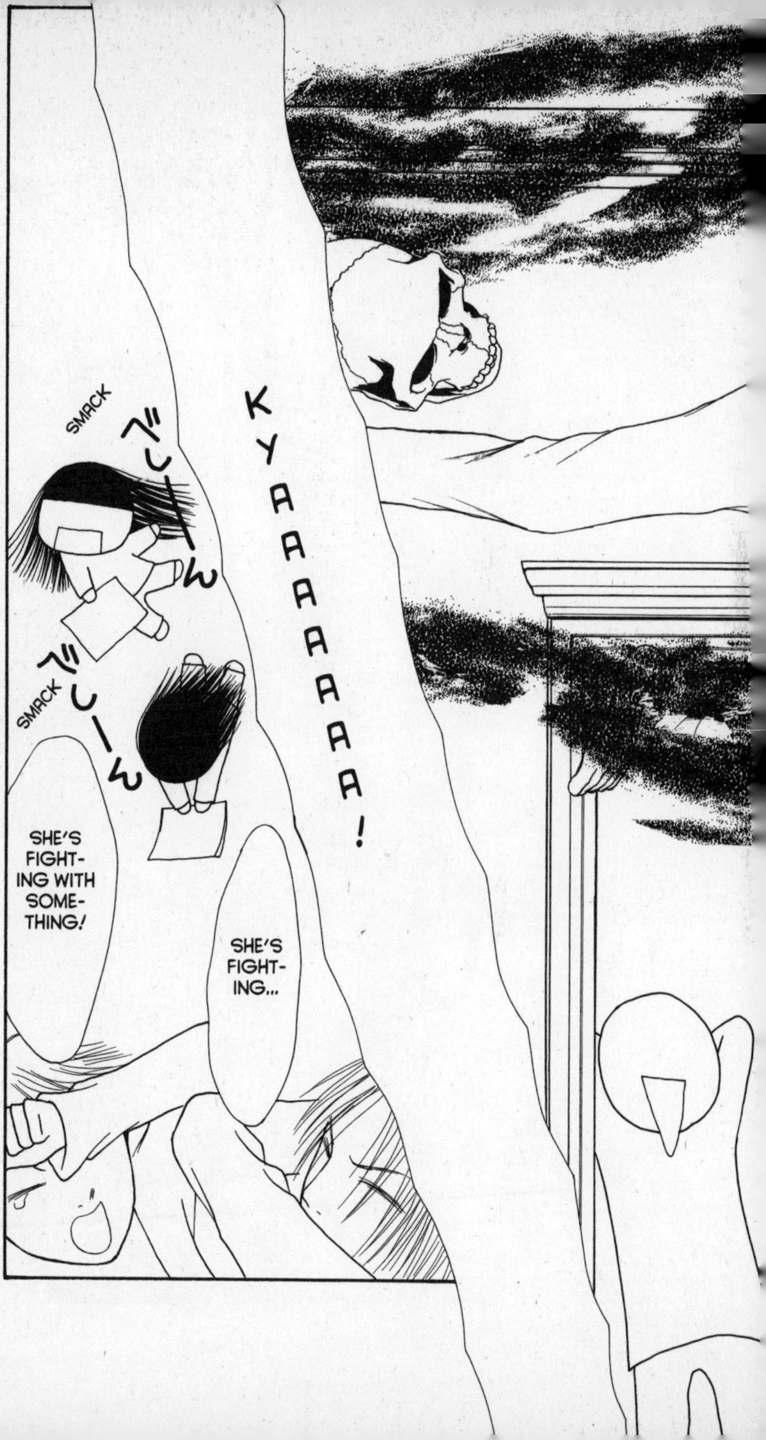
KYAAAAAAA!
べしーん
SMACK
べしーん
SMACK
SHE'S FIGHTING...
SHE'S FIGHTING WITH SOMETHING!

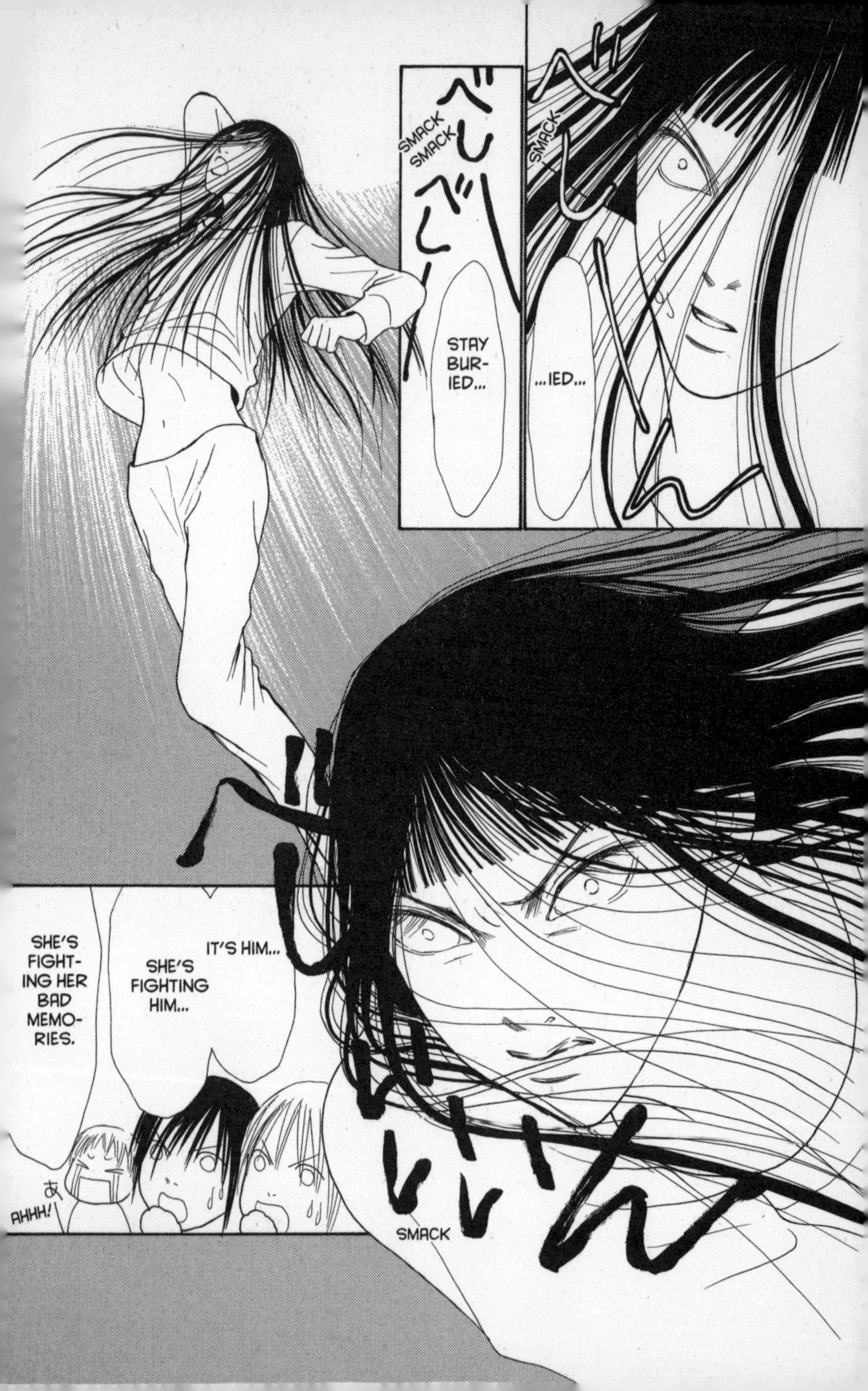
SMACK
...IED...
べしべし
SMACK SMACK
STAY BUR-IED...
SMACK
IT'S HIM...
SHE'S FIGHTING HIM...
SHE'S FIGHT-ING HER BAD MEMO-RIES.
あ
AHHH!

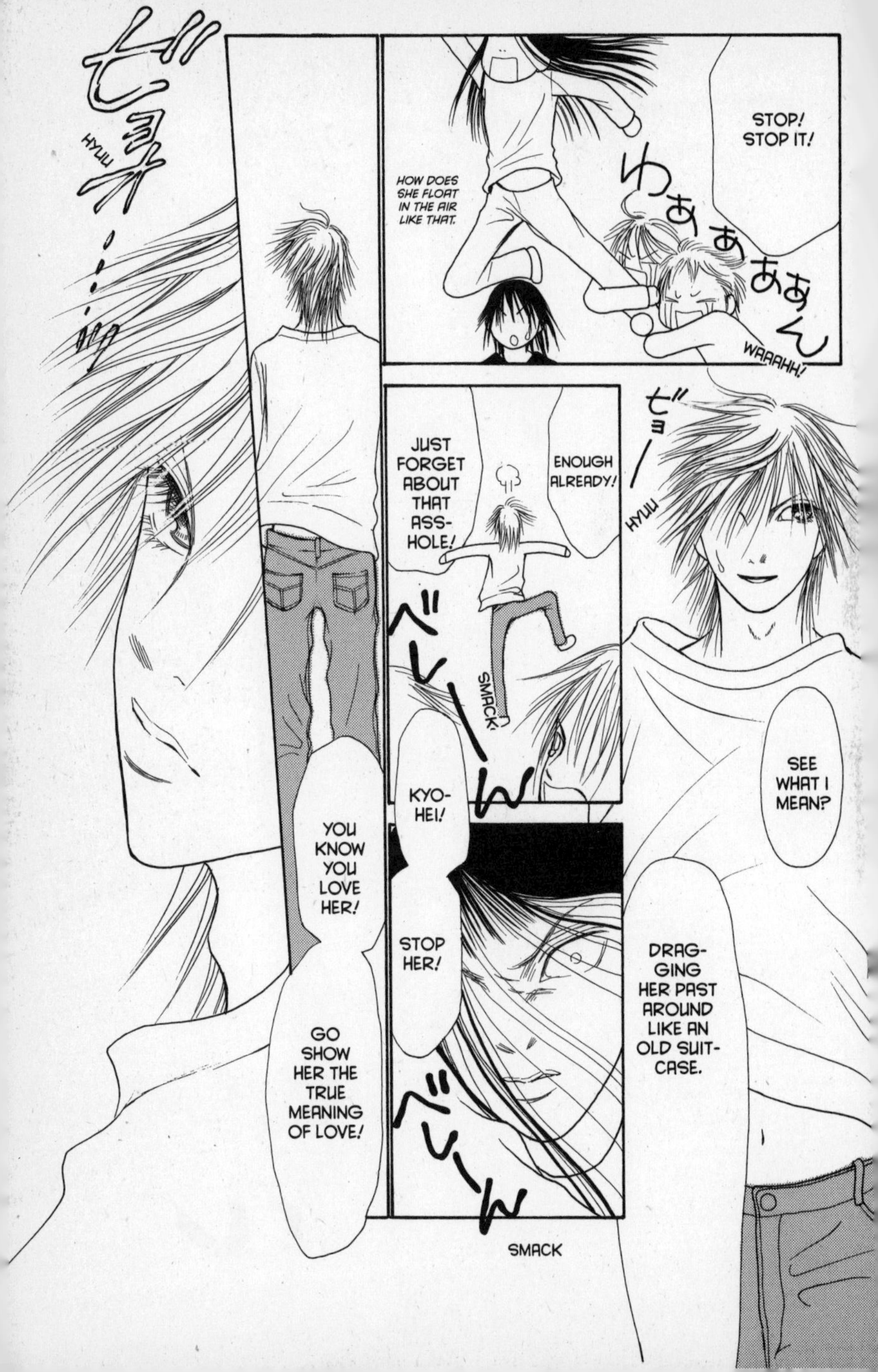

STOP! STOP IT!
わぁあああん
WAAAHH!
HOW DOES SHE FLOAT IN THE AIR LIKE THAT.
HYUU
SEE WHAT I MEAN?
DRAGGING HER PAST AROUND LIKE AN OLD SUITCASE.
ENOUGH ALREADY!
JUST FORGET ABOUT THAT ASSHOLE!
べしーん
SMACK
KYO-HEI!
STOP HER!
べしーん
SMACK
YOU KNOW YOU LOVE HER!
GO SHOW HER THE TRUE MEANING OF LOVE!
HYUU

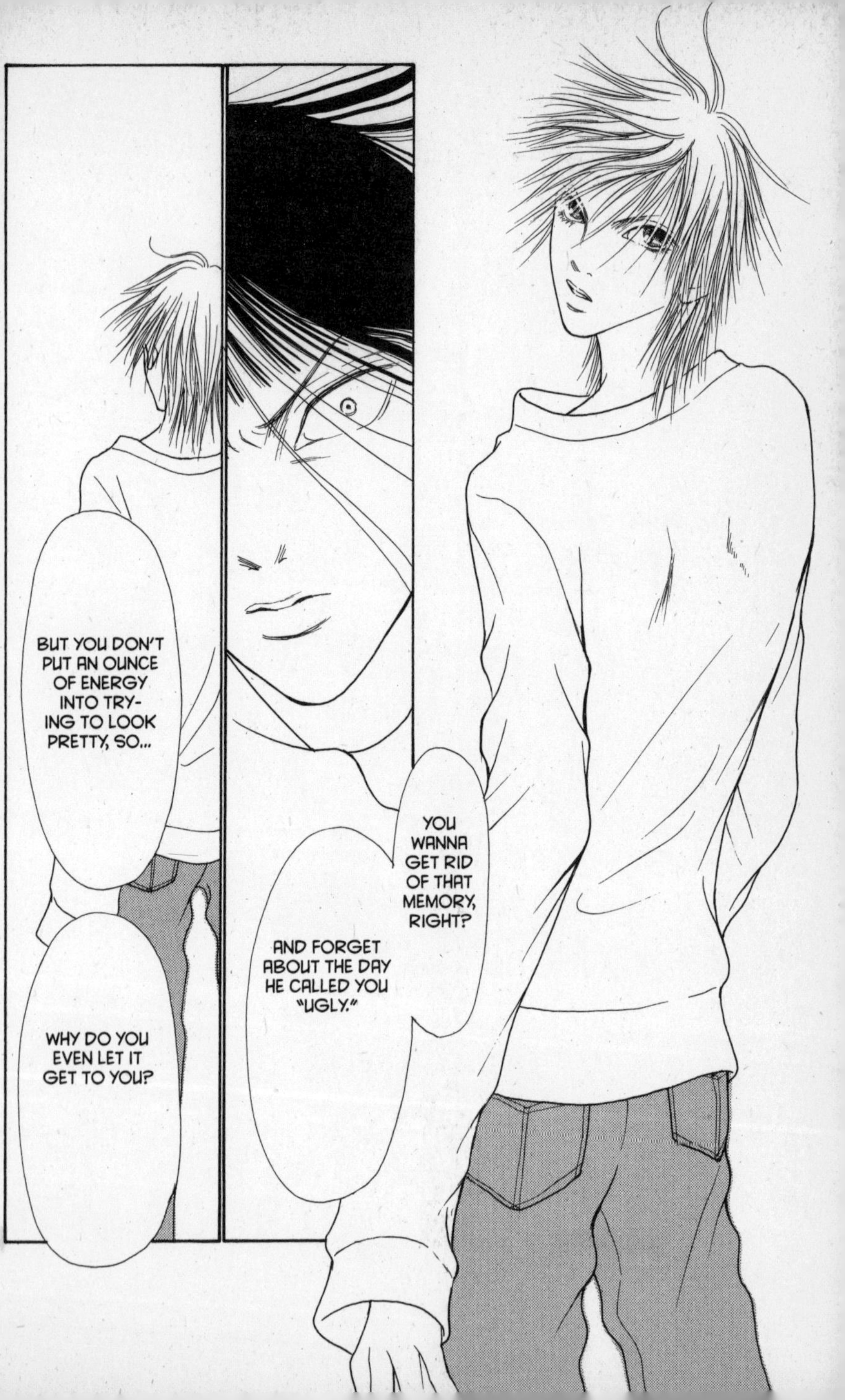
YOU WANNA GET RID OF THAT MEMORY, RIGHT?
AND FORGET ABOUT THE DAY HE CALLED YOU "UGLY."
BUT YOU DON'T PUT AN OUNCE OF ENERGY INTO TRY-ING TO LOOK PRETTY, SO...
WHY DO YOU EVEN LET IT GET TO YOU?

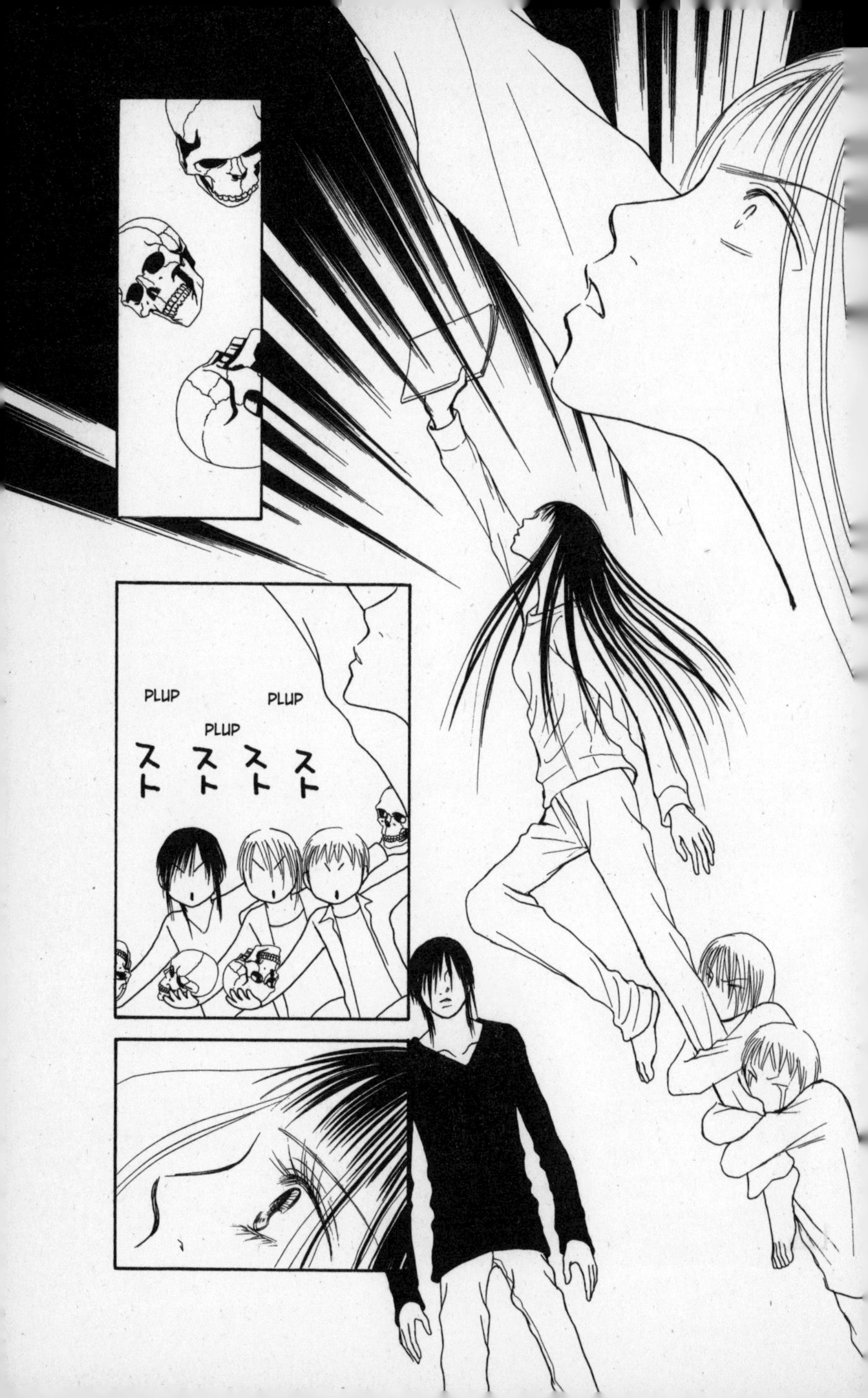
PLUP
PLUP
PLUP
スト
スト
スト
スト

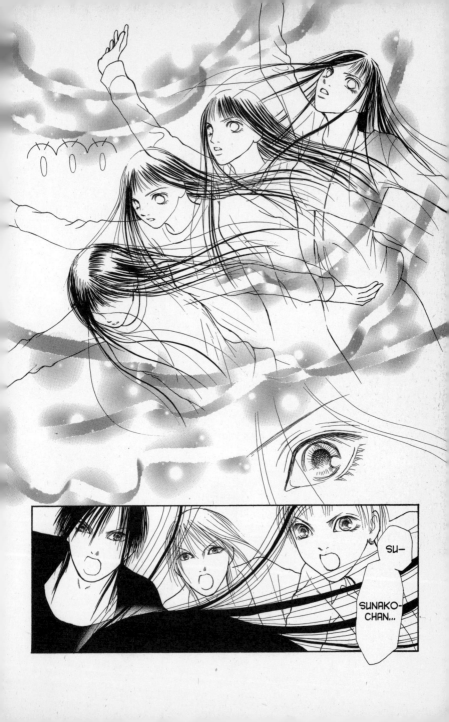

SU—

SUNAKO-
CHAN...

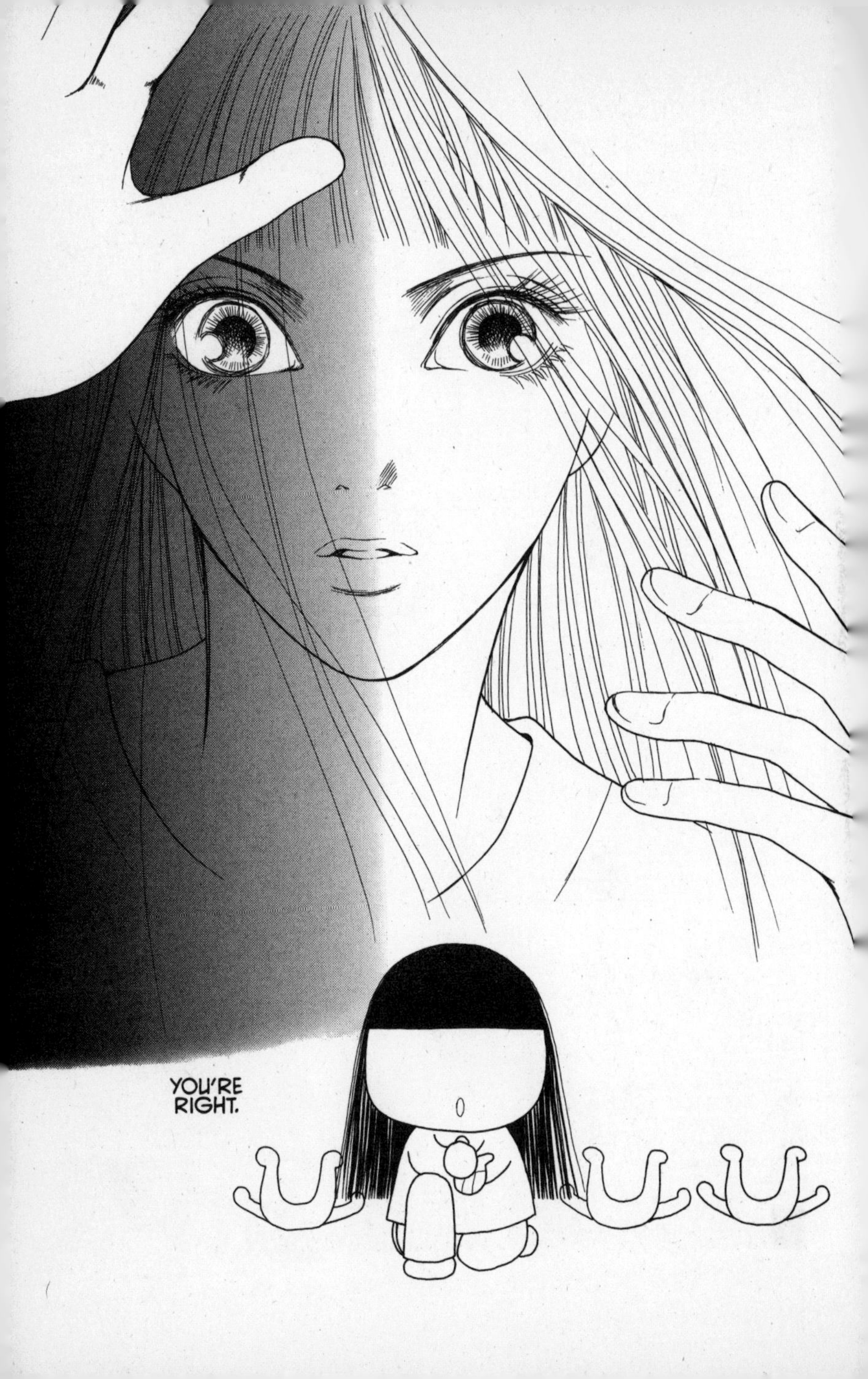
YOU'RE RIGHT.

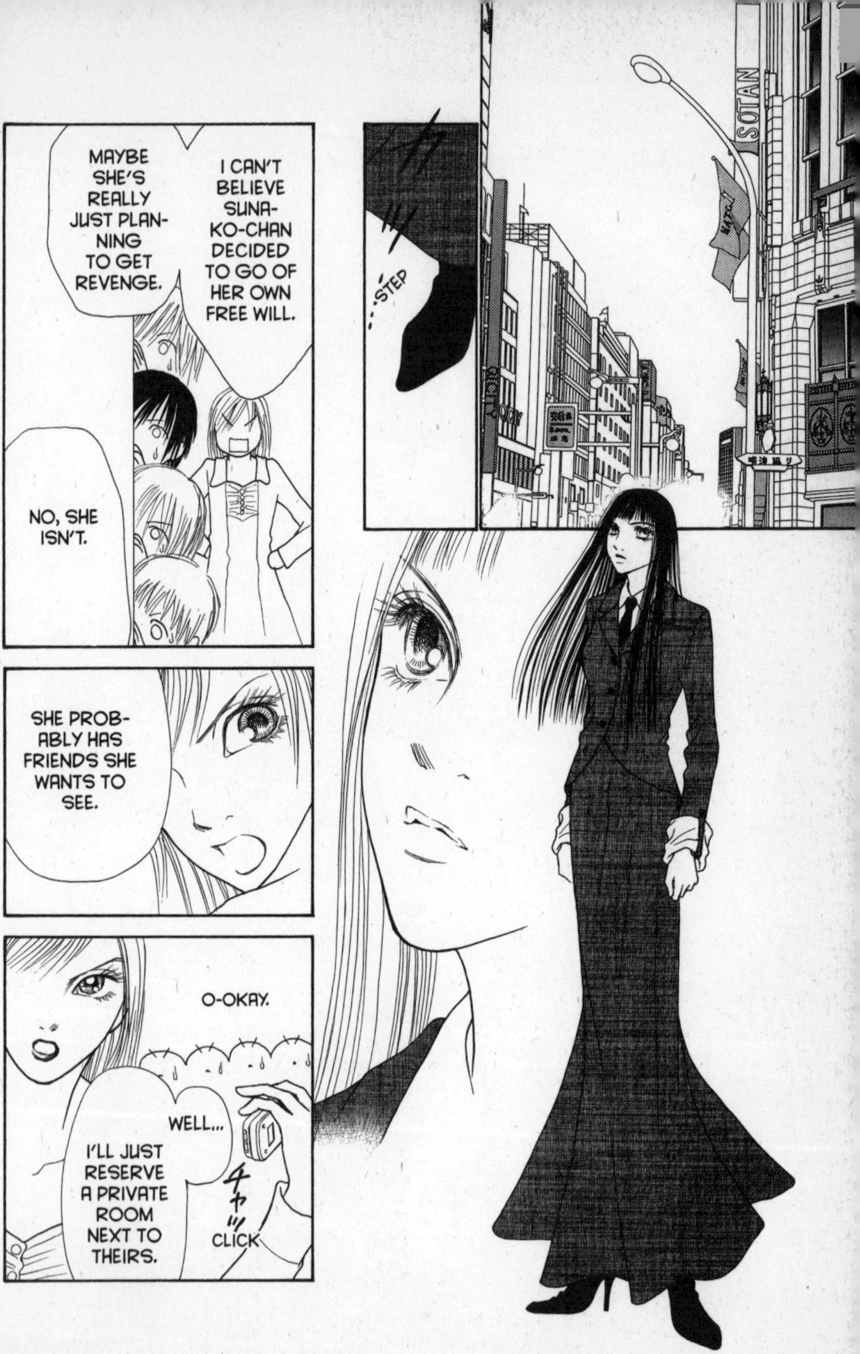
SOTAN
...STEP
I CAN'T BELIEVE SUNA-KO-CHAN DECIDED TO GO OF HER OWN FREE WILL.
MAYBE SHE'S REALLY JUST PLAN-NING TO GET REVENGE.
NO, SHE ISN'T.
SHE PROB-ABLY HAS FRIENDS SHE WANTS TO SEE.
O-OKAY.
WELL...
I'LL JUST RESERVE A PRIVATE ROOM NEXT TO THEIRS.
CLICK

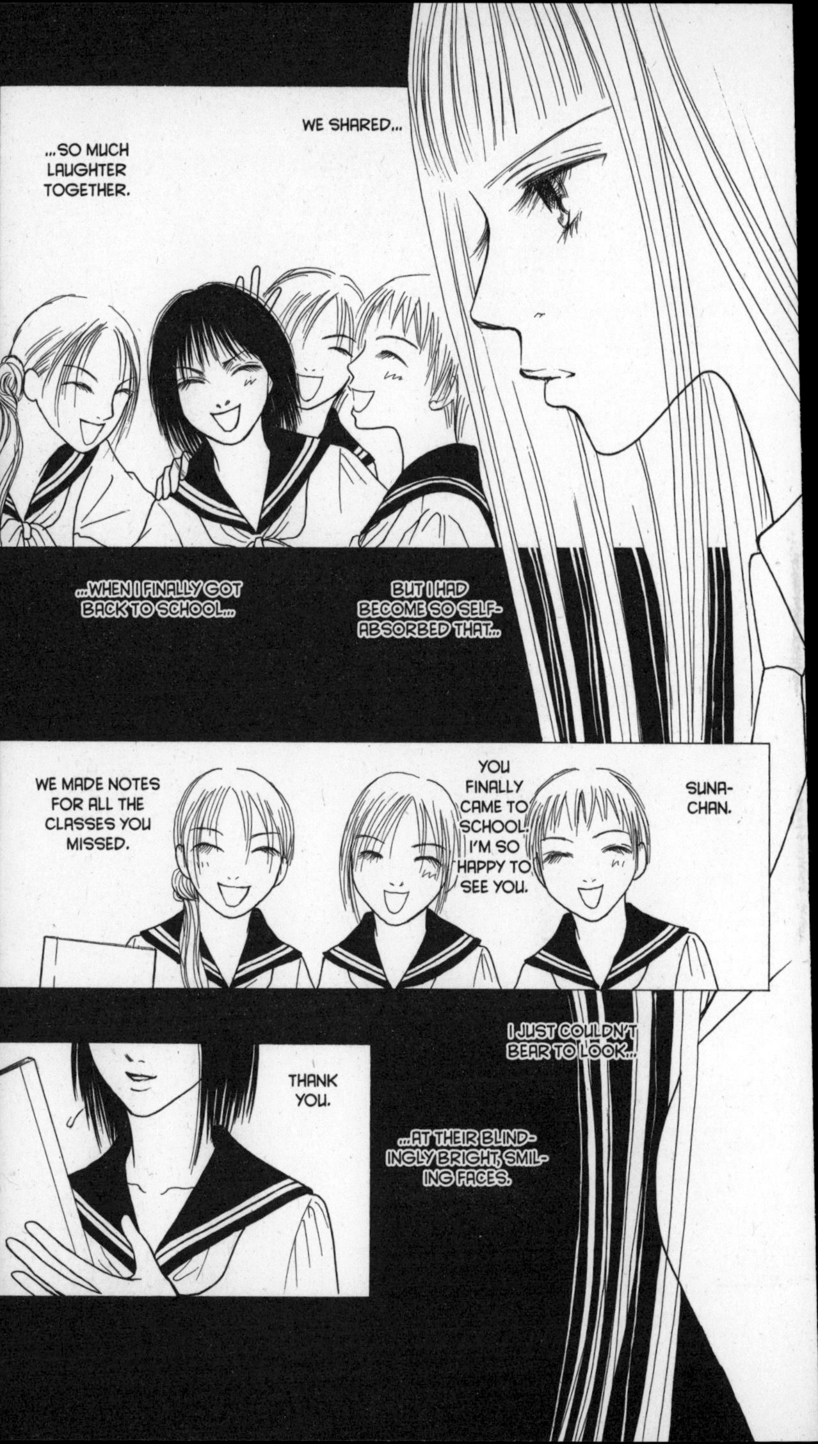
WE SHARED...
...SO MUCH LAUGHTER TOGETHER.
BUT I HAD BECOME SO SELF-ABSORBED THAT...
...WHEN I FINALLY GOT BACK TO SCHOOL...
SUNA-CHAN.
YOU FINALLY CAME TO SCHOOL. I'M SO HAPPY TO SEE YOU.
WE MADE NOTES FOR ALL THE CLASSES YOU MISSED.
I JUST COULDN'T BEAR TO LOOK...
...AT THEIR BLINDINGLY BRIGHT, SMILING FACES.
THANK YOU.

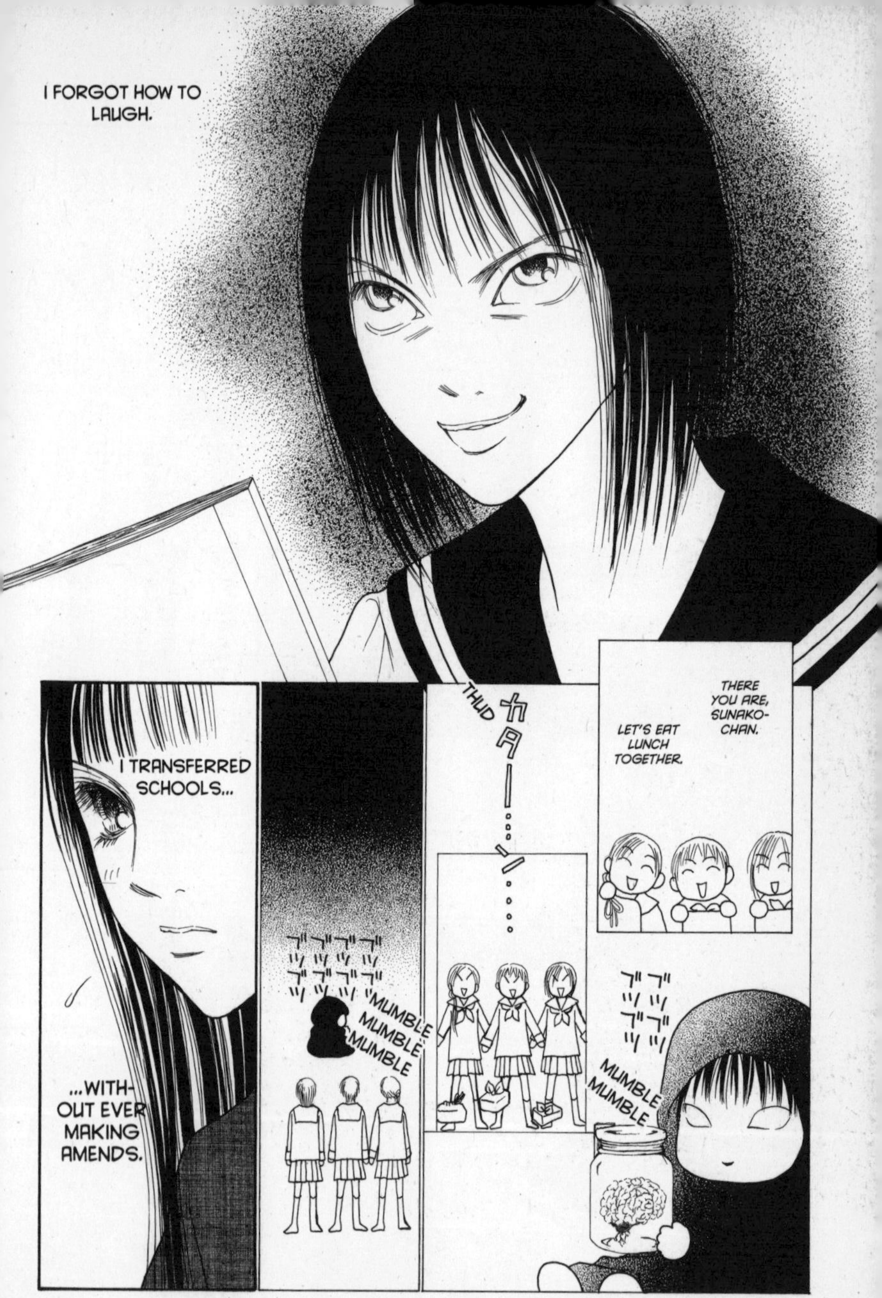

I FORGOT HOW TO LAUGH.
THERE YOU ARE, SUNAKO-CHAN.
LET'S EAT LUNCH TOGETHER.
カターン…
THUD
ブツブツ
ブツブツ
MUMBLE MUMBLE
ブツブツブツブツ
ブツブツブツブツ
MUMBLE MUMBLE MUMBLE
I TRANSFERRED SCHOOLS...
...WITHOUT EVER MAKING AMENDS.

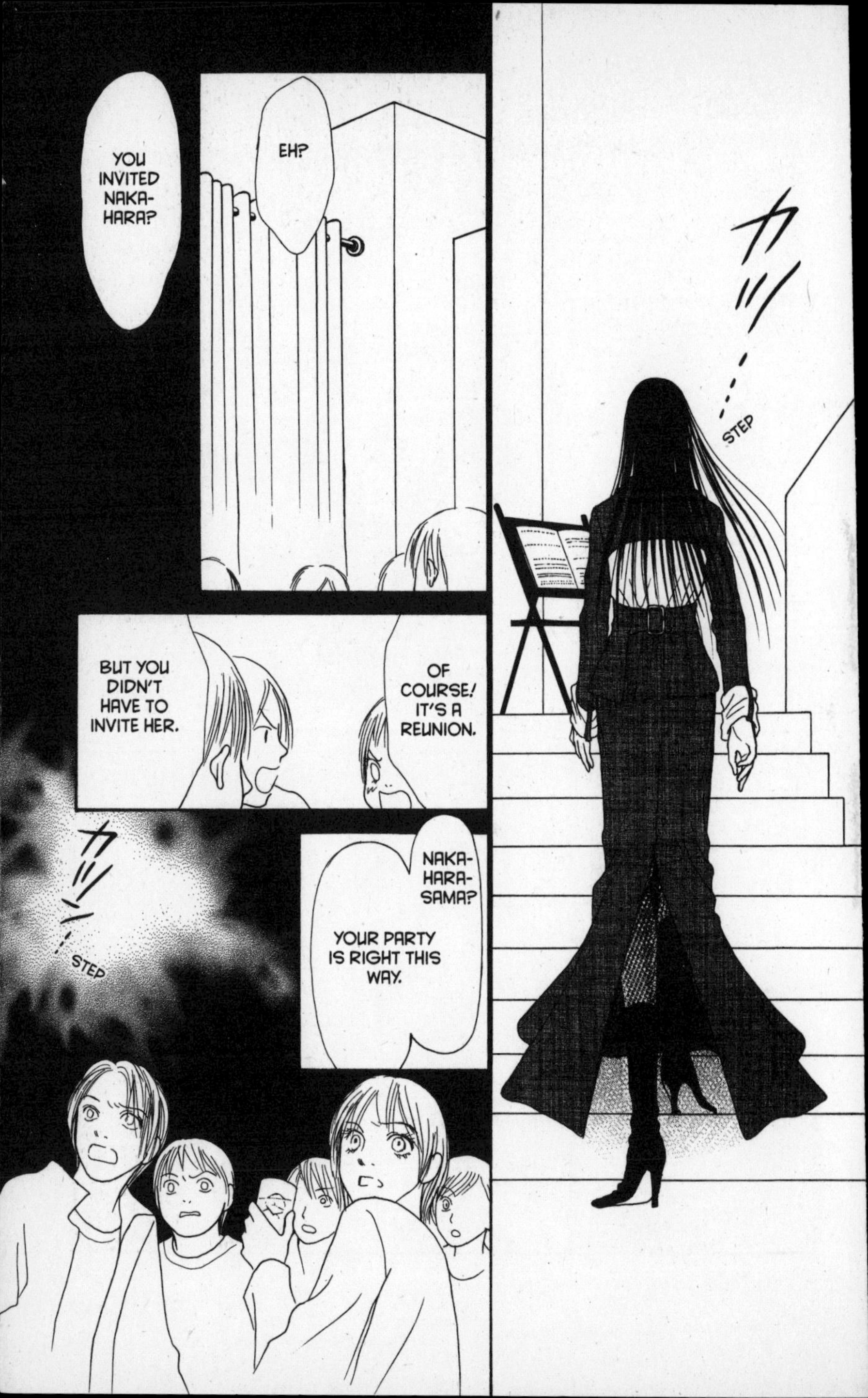
カッ
STEP
EH?
YOU INVITED NAKA-HARA?
OF COURSE! IT'S A REUNION.
BUT YOU DIDN'T HAVE TO INVITE HER.
NAKA-HARA-SAMA?
YOUR PARTY IS RIGHT THIS WAY.
カッ
STEP

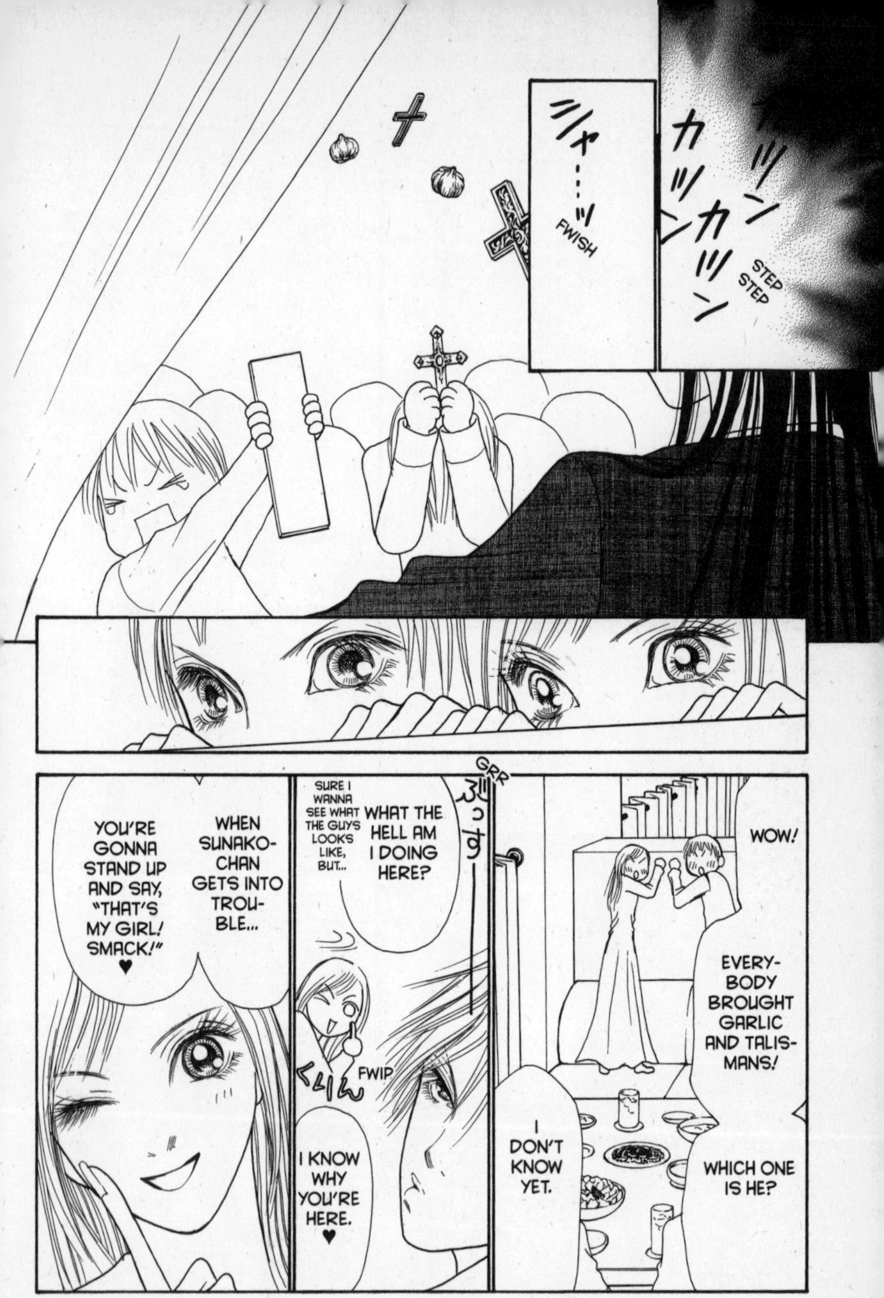
カツンカツンカツン
STEP STEP
シャーーッ
FWISH
WOW!
EVERY-BODY BROUGHT GARLIC AND TALIS-MANS!
WHICH ONE IS HE?
I DON'T KNOW YET.
ぶっすー
GRR
WHAT THE HELL AM I DOING HERE?
SURE I WANNA SEE WHAT THE GUYS LOOKS LIKE, BUT...
くいん
FWIP
I KNOW WHY YOU'RE HERE. ♥
WHEN SUNAKO-CHAN GETS INTO TROU-BLE...
YOU'RE GONNA STAND UP AND SAY, "THAT'S MY GIRL! SMACK!" ♥

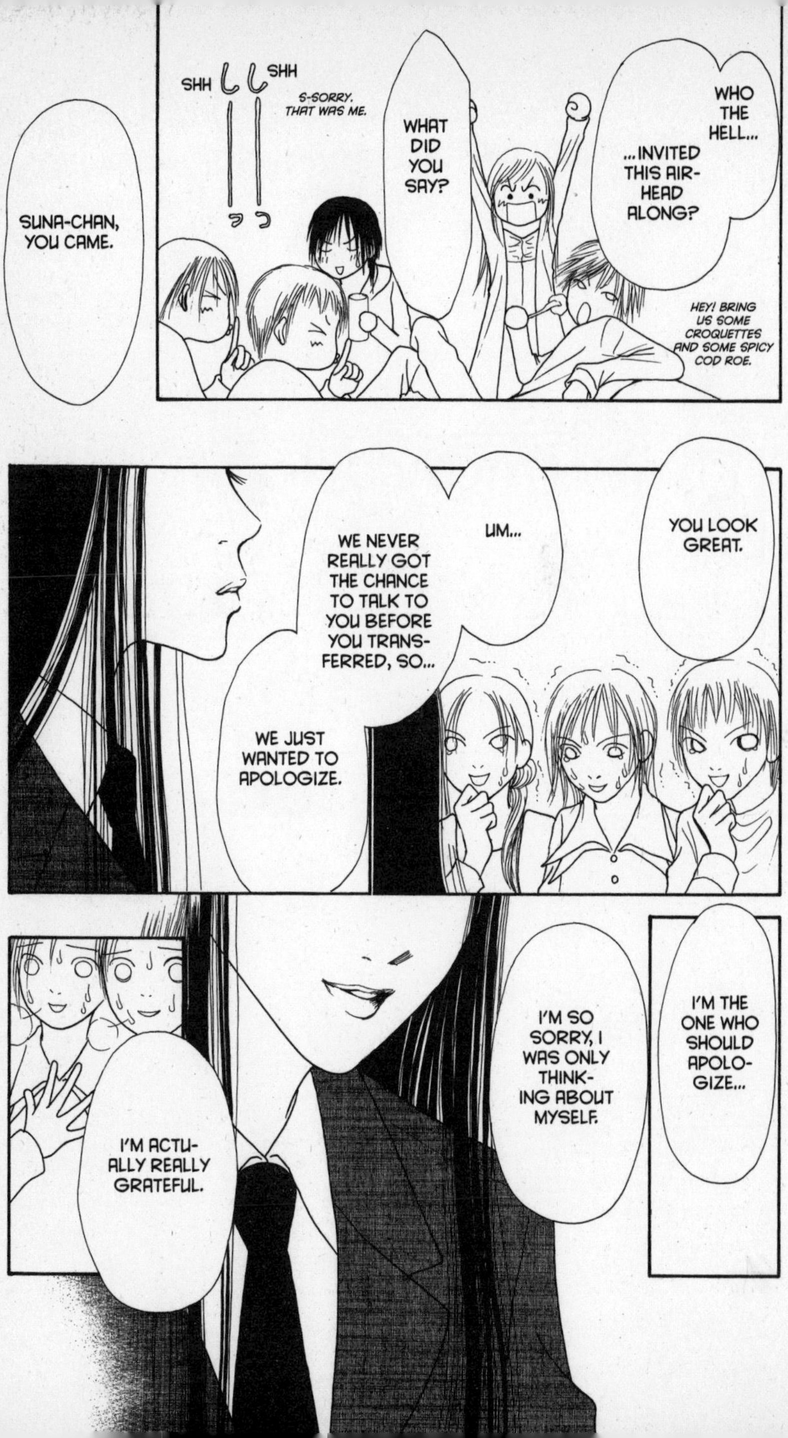
WHO THE HELL...
...INVITED THIS AIR-HEAD ALONG?
HEY! BRING US SOME CROQUETTES AND SOME SPICY COD ROE.
WHAT DID YOU SAY?
S-SORRY. THAT WAS ME.
SHH SHH
SUNA-CHAN, YOU CAME.
YOU LOOK GREAT.
UM...
WE NEVER REALLY GOT THE CHANCE TO TALK TO YOU BEFORE YOU TRANS-FERRED, SO...
WE JUST WANTED TO APOLOGIZE.
I'M THE ONE WHO SHOULD APOLO-GIZE...
I'M SO SORRY, I WAS ONLY THINK-ING ABOUT MYSELF.
I'M ACTU-ALLY REALLY GRATEFUL.

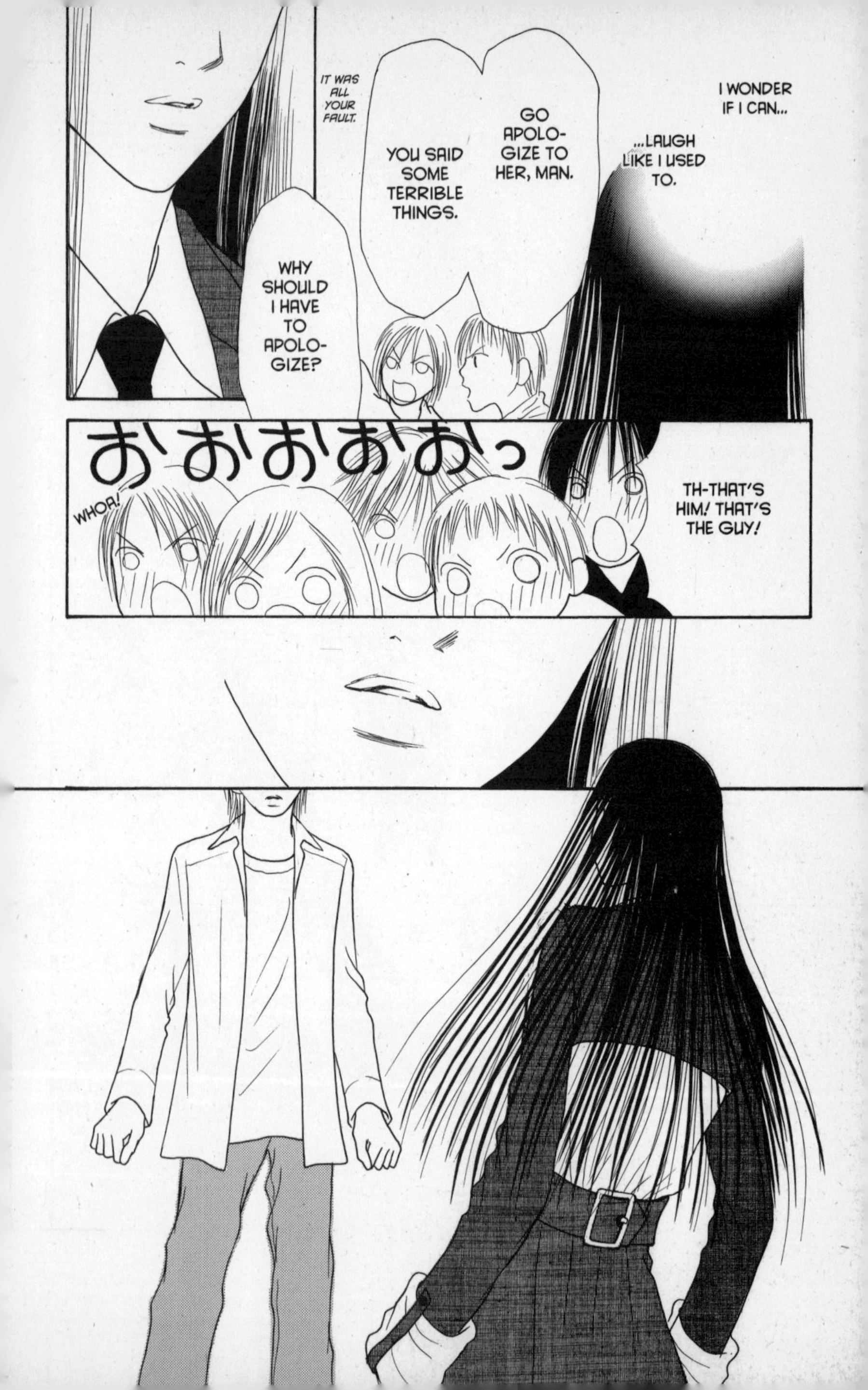
I WONDER IF I CAN...
...LAUGH LIKE I USED TO.
GO APOLO-GIZE TO HER, MAN.
YOU SAID SOME TERRIBLE THINGS.
IT WAS ALL YOUR FAULT.
WHY SHOULD I HAVE TO APOLO-GIZE?
おおおおおっ
TH-THAT'S HIM! THAT'S THE GUY!
WHOA!

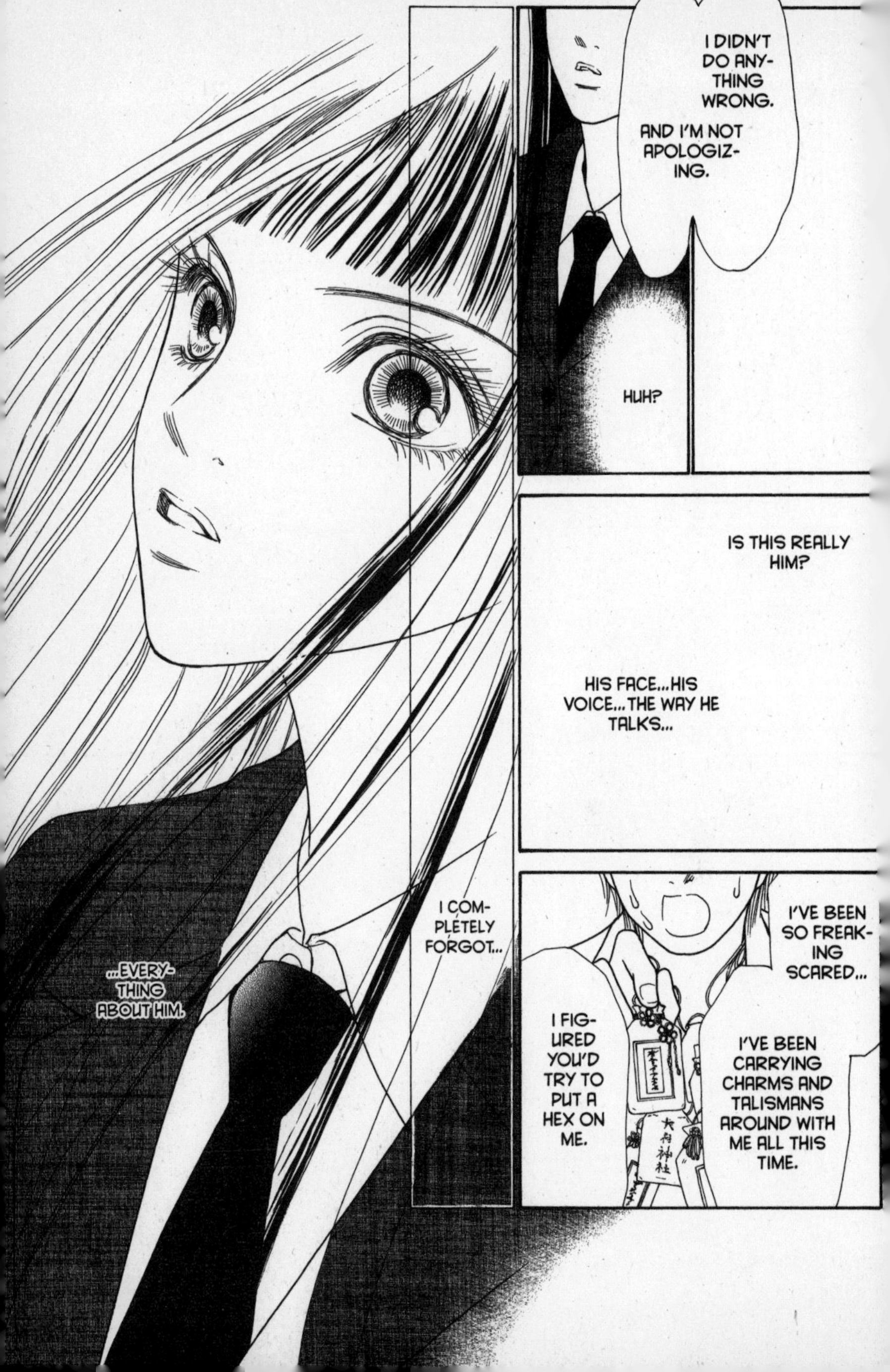
I DIDN'T DO ANY-THING WRONG.
AND I'M NOT APOLOGIZ-ING.
HUH?
IS THIS REALLY HIM?
HIS FACE...HIS VOICE...THE WAY HE TALKS...
I'VE BEEN SO FREAK-ING SCARED...
I'VE BEEN CARRYING CHARMS AND TALISMANS AROUND WITH ME ALL THIS TIME.
I FIG-URED YOU'D TRY TO PUT A HEX ON ME.
I COM-PLETELY FORGOT...
...EVERY-THING ABOUT HIM.

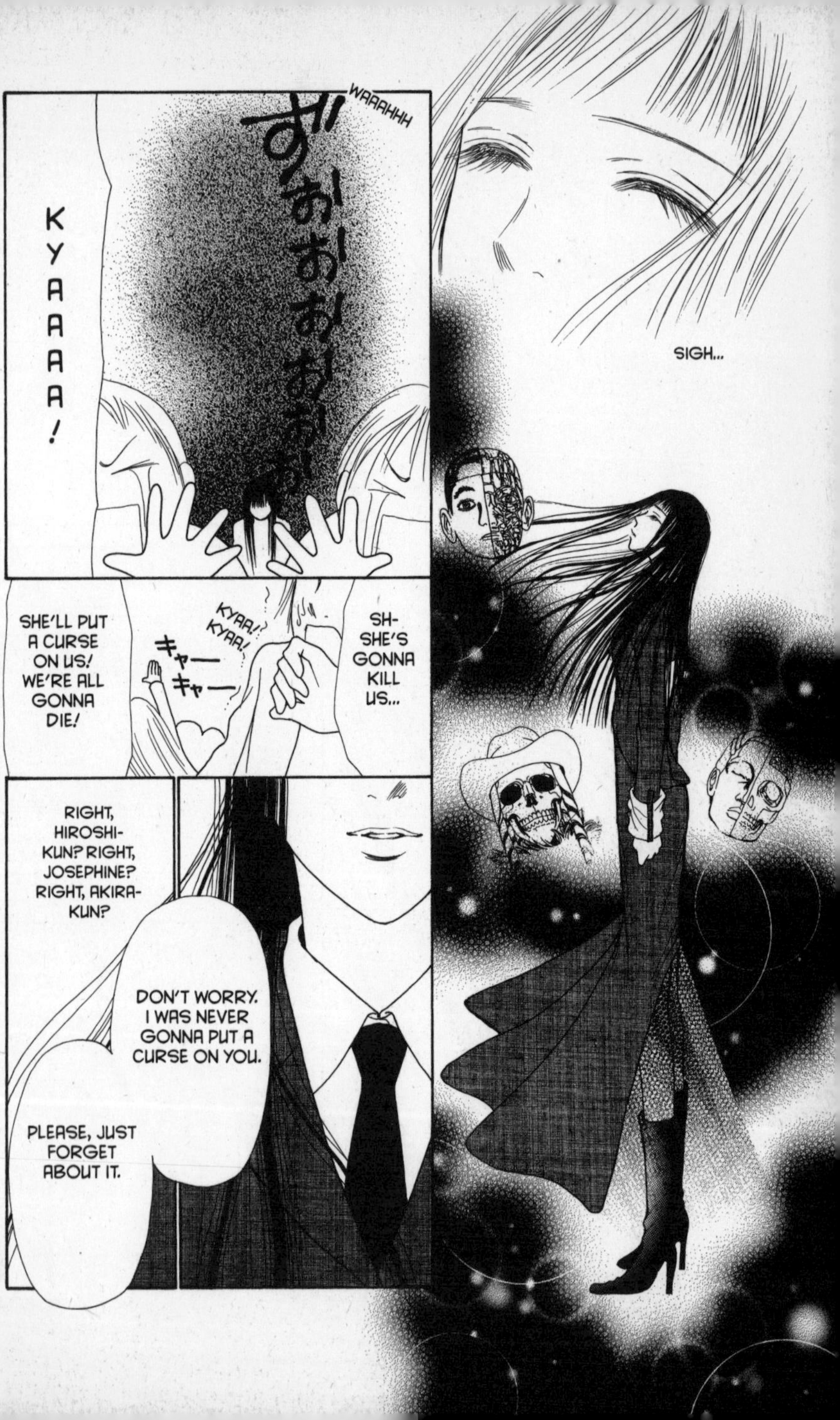
SIGH...
WAAAHHH
ずおおおお
KYAAAAA!
SH-SHE'S GONNA KILL US...
KYAA! KYAA!
キャーキャー
SHE'LL PUT A CURSE ON US! WE'RE ALL GONNA DIE!
DON'T WORRY. I WAS NEVER GONNA PUT A CURSE ON YOU.
PLEASE, JUST FORGET ABOUT IT.
RIGHT, HIROSHI-KUN? RIGHT, JOSEPHINE? RIGHT, AKIRA-KUN?

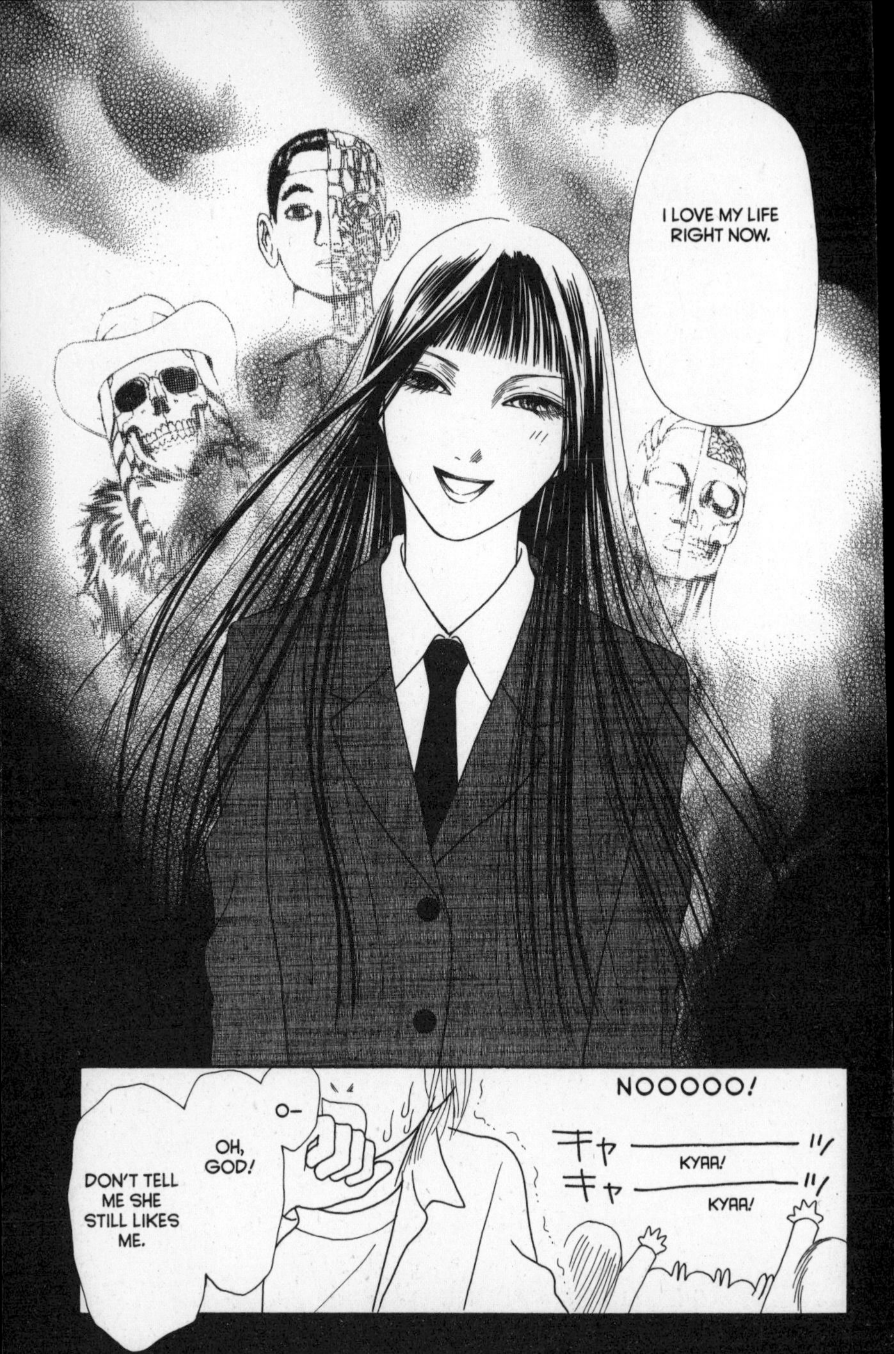
I LOVE MY LIFE RIGHT NOW.
NOOOOO!
キャ──!! KYAA!
キャ──!! KYAA!
O-
OH, GOD!
DON'T TELL ME SHE STILL LIKES ME.

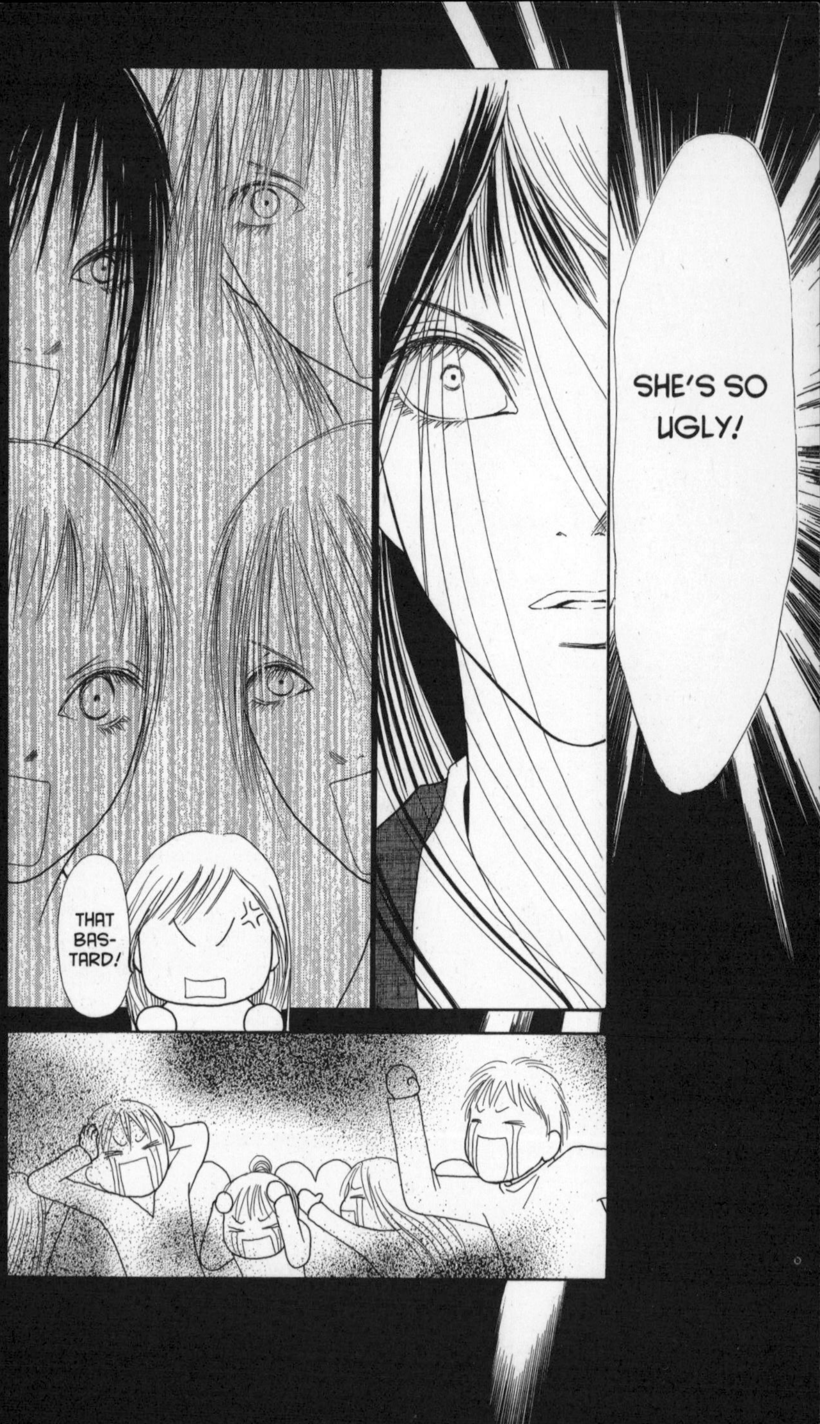
SHE'S SO UGLY!
THAT BAS-TARD!

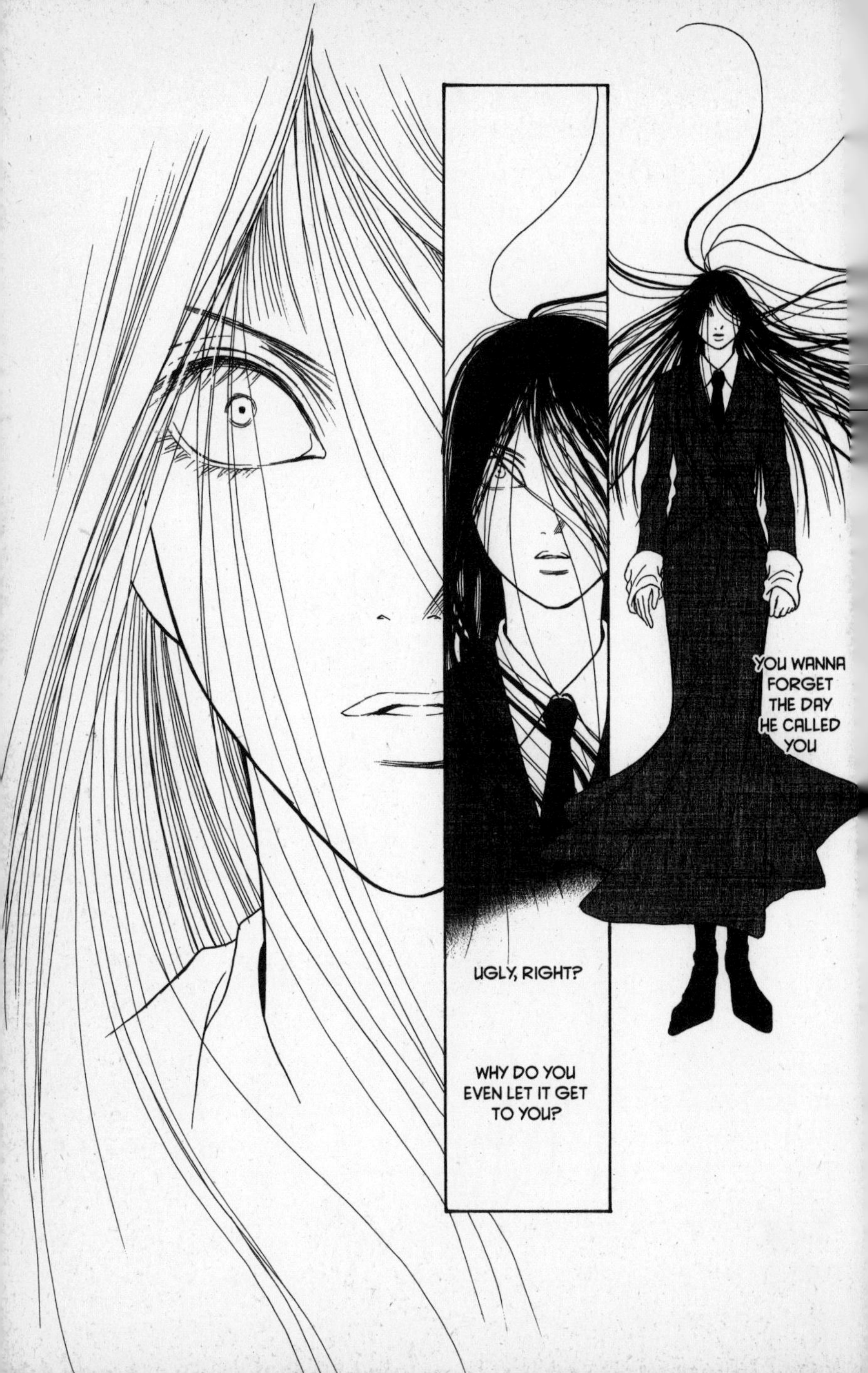
YOU WANNA FORGET THE DAY HE CALLED YOU
UGLY, RIGHT?
WHY DO YOU EVEN LET IT GET TO YOU?

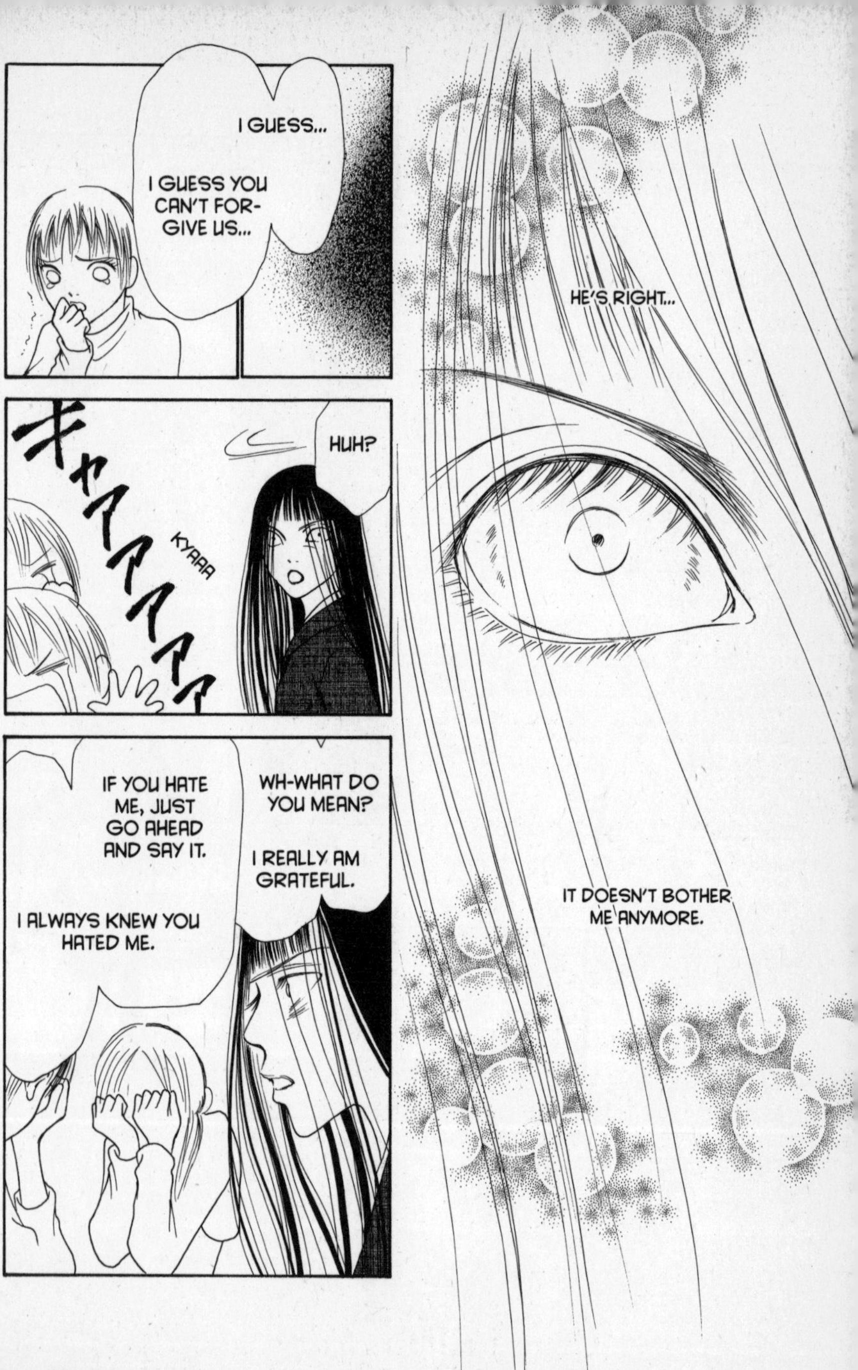
HE'S RIGHT...
IT DOESN'T BOTHER ME ANYMORE.
I GUESS...
I GUESS YOU CAN'T FOR-GIVE US...
HUH?
ギャアアアアア
KYAAA
WH-WHAT DO YOU MEAN?
I REALLY AM GRATEFUL.
IF YOU HATE ME, JUST GO AHEAD AND SAY IT.
I ALWAYS KNEW YOU HATED ME.

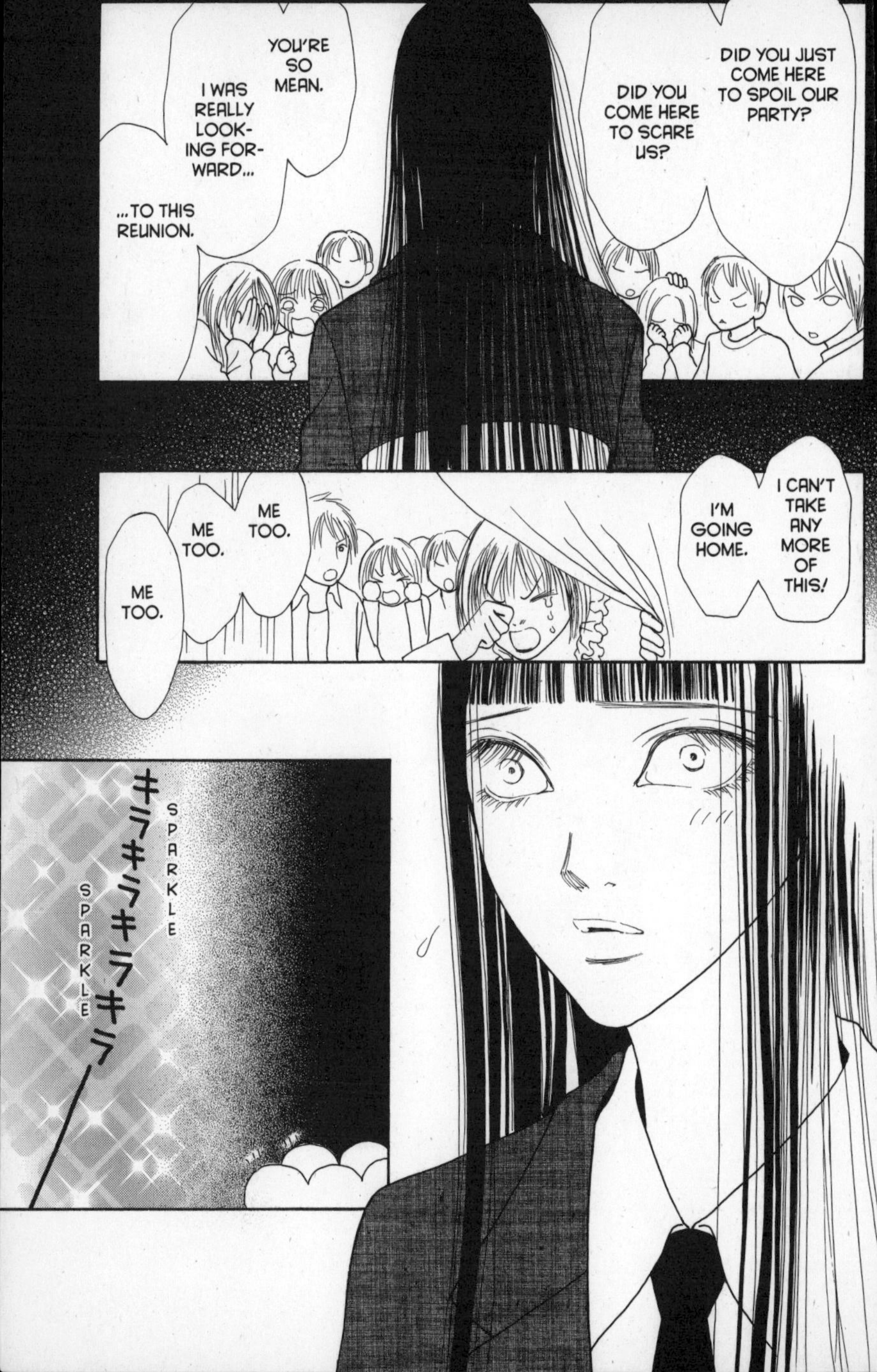
DID YOU JUST COME HERE TO SPOIL OUR PARTY?
DID YOU COME HERE TO SCARE US?
YOU'RE SO MEAN.
I WAS REALLY LOOKING FORWARD...
...TO THIS REUNION.
I CAN'T TAKE ANY MORE OF THIS!
I'M GOING HOME.
ME TOO.
ME TOO.
ME TOO.
キラキラキラ
SPARKLE
SPARKLE

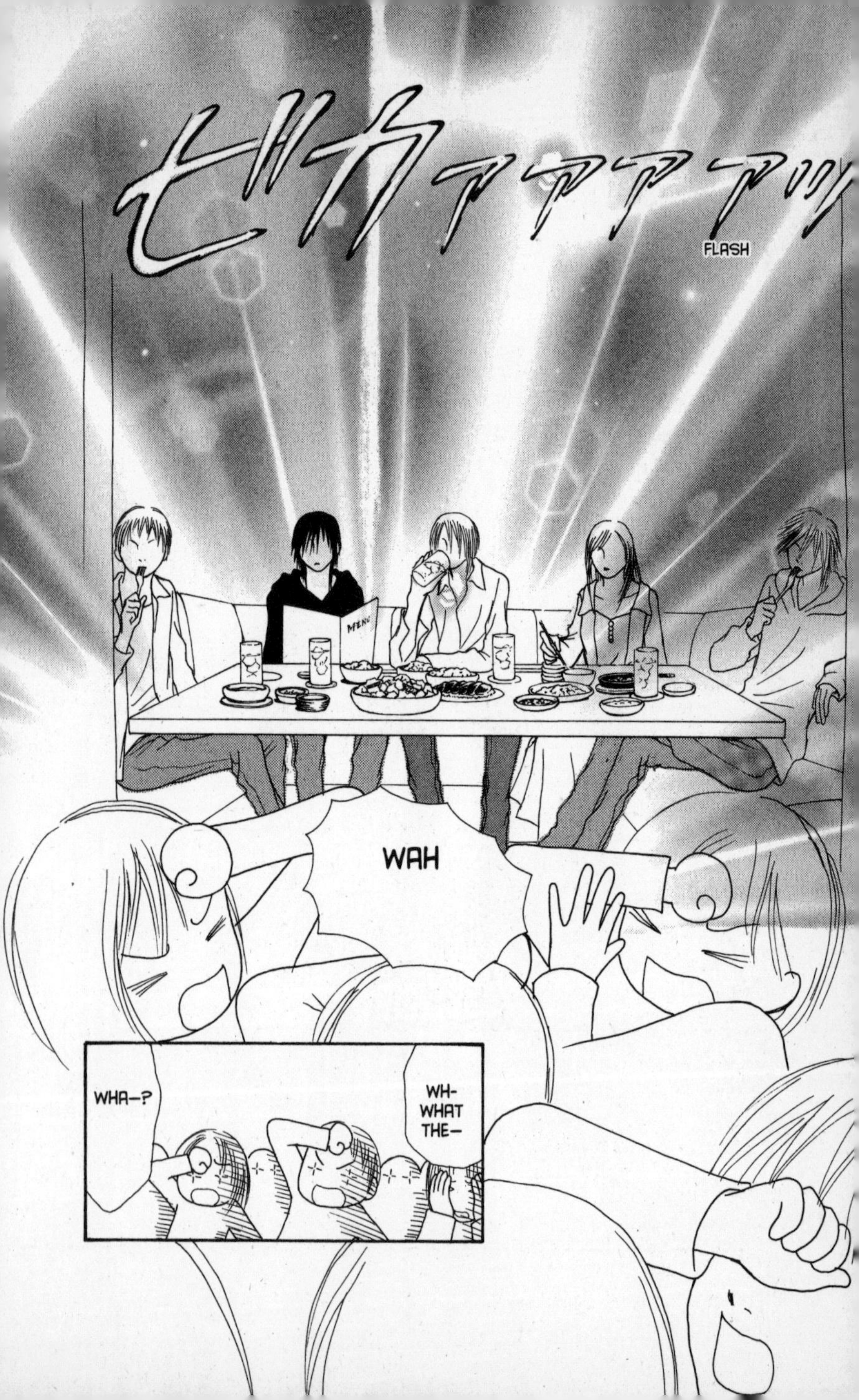
ピカァァァァッ
FLASH
MENU
WAH
WH-
WHAT
THE—
WHA—?

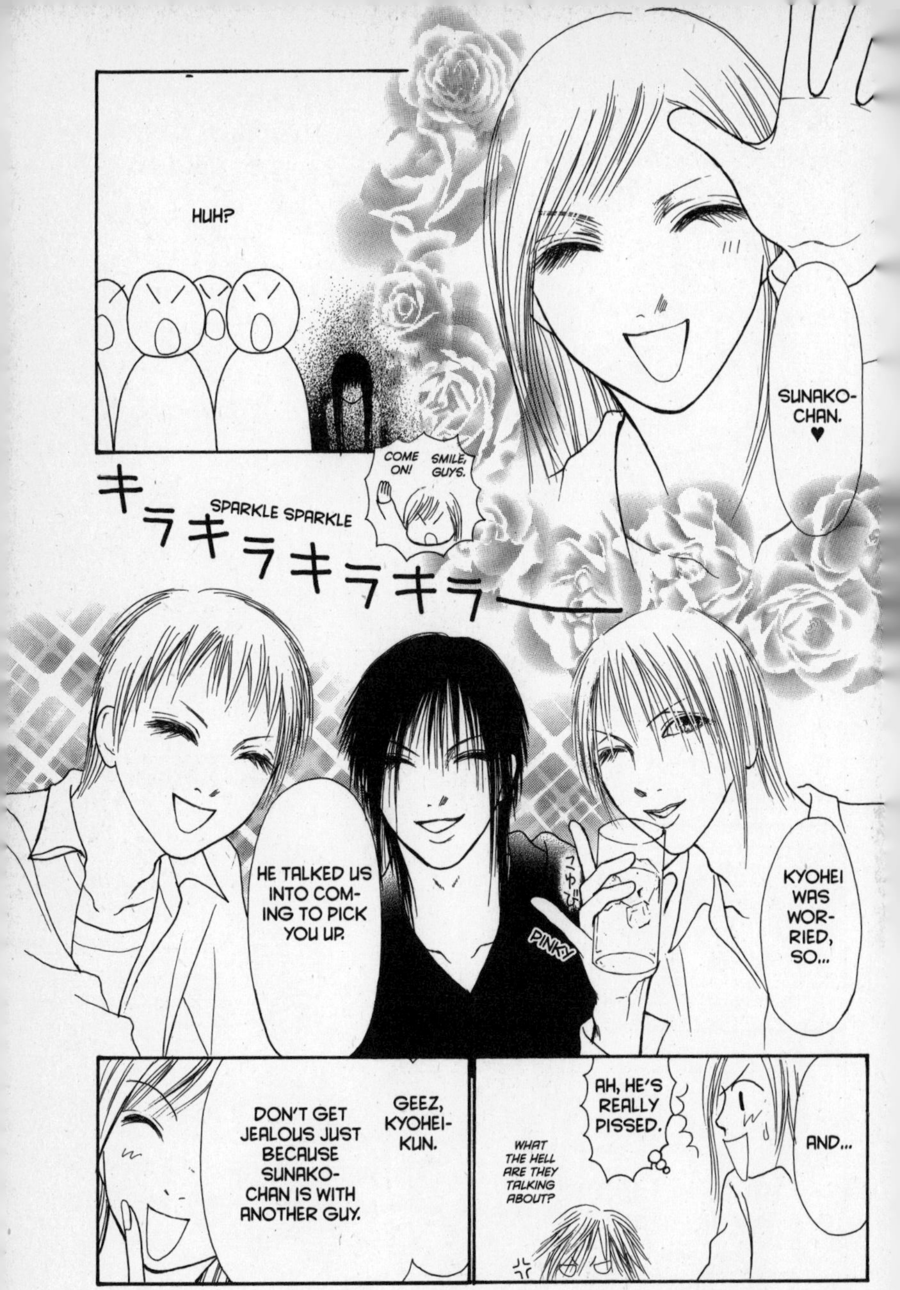
SUNAKO-CHAN. ♥
HUH?
COME ON! SMILE, GUYS.
キラキラキラキラー
SPARKLE SPARKLE
KYOHEI WAS WORRIED, SO...
HE TALKED US INTO COMING TO PICK YOU UP.
AND...
AH, HE'S REALLY PISSED.
WHAT THE HELL ARE THEY TALKING ABOUT?
GEEZ, KYOHEI-KUN.
DON'T GET JEALOUS JUST BECAUSE SUNAKO-CHAN IS WITH ANOTHER GUY.

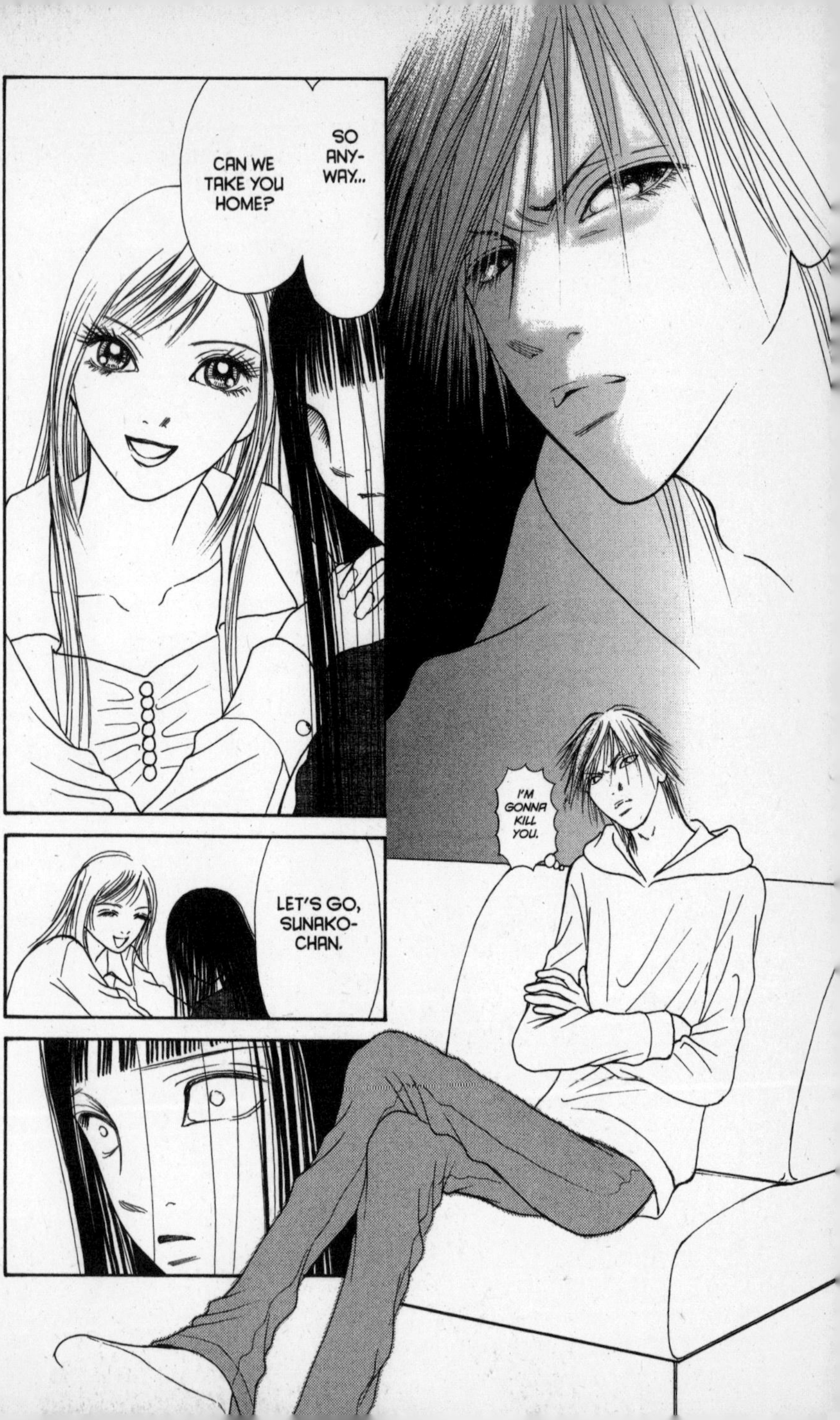
I'M GONNA KILL YOU.
SO ANYWAY...
CAN WE TAKE YOU HOME?
LET'S GO, SUNAKO-CHAN.

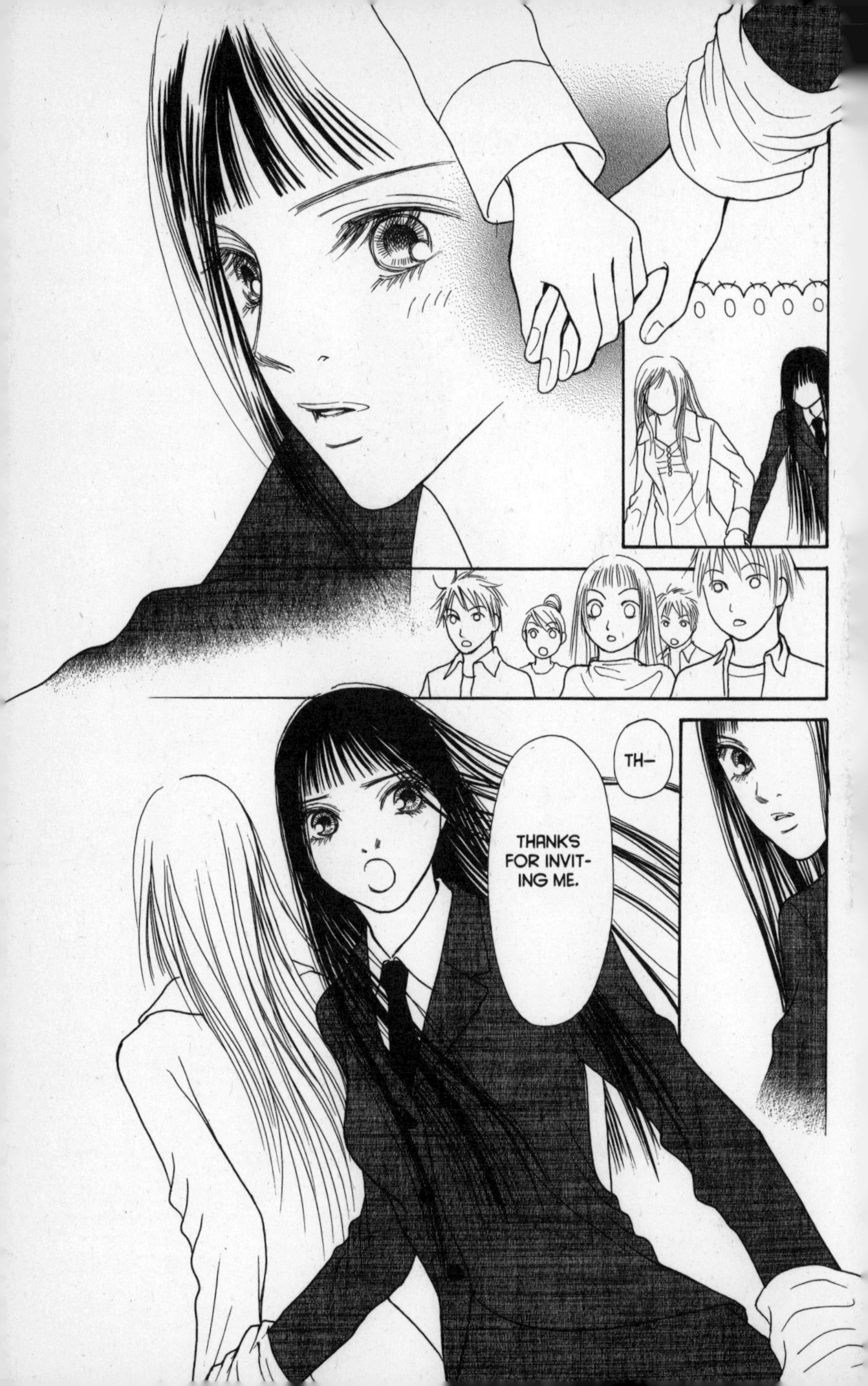
TH–
THANKS FOR INVIT- ING ME.

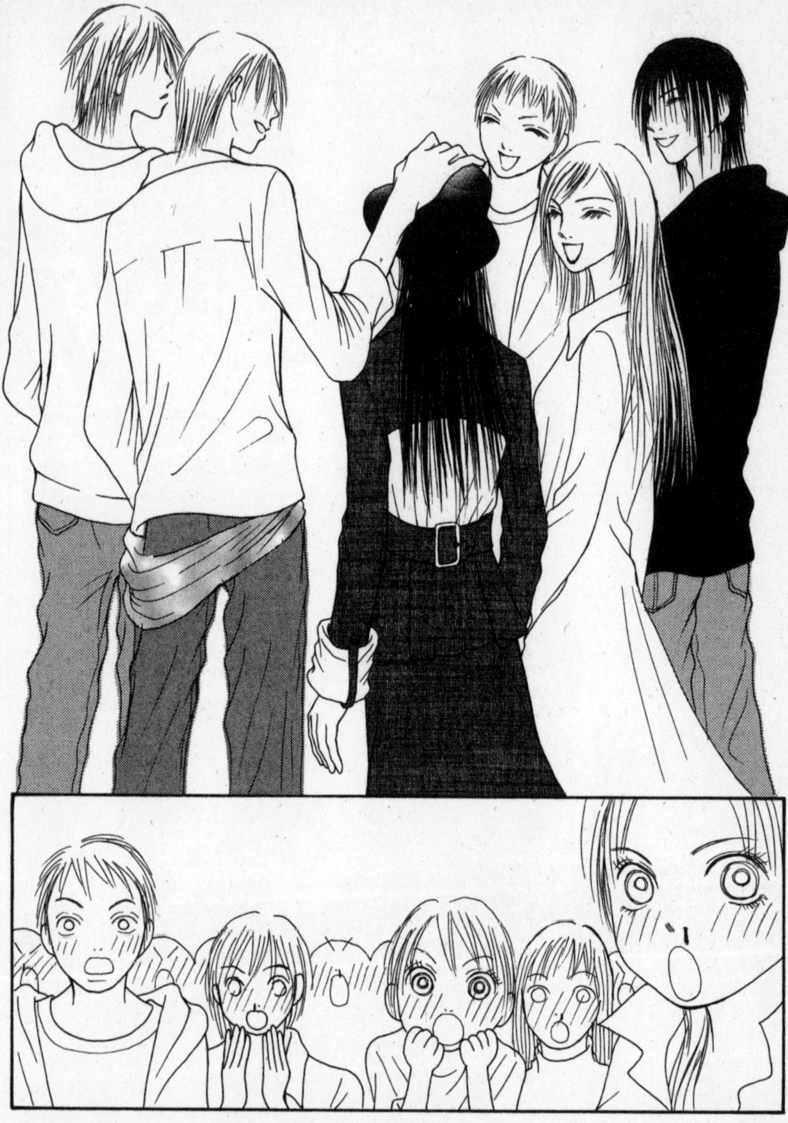

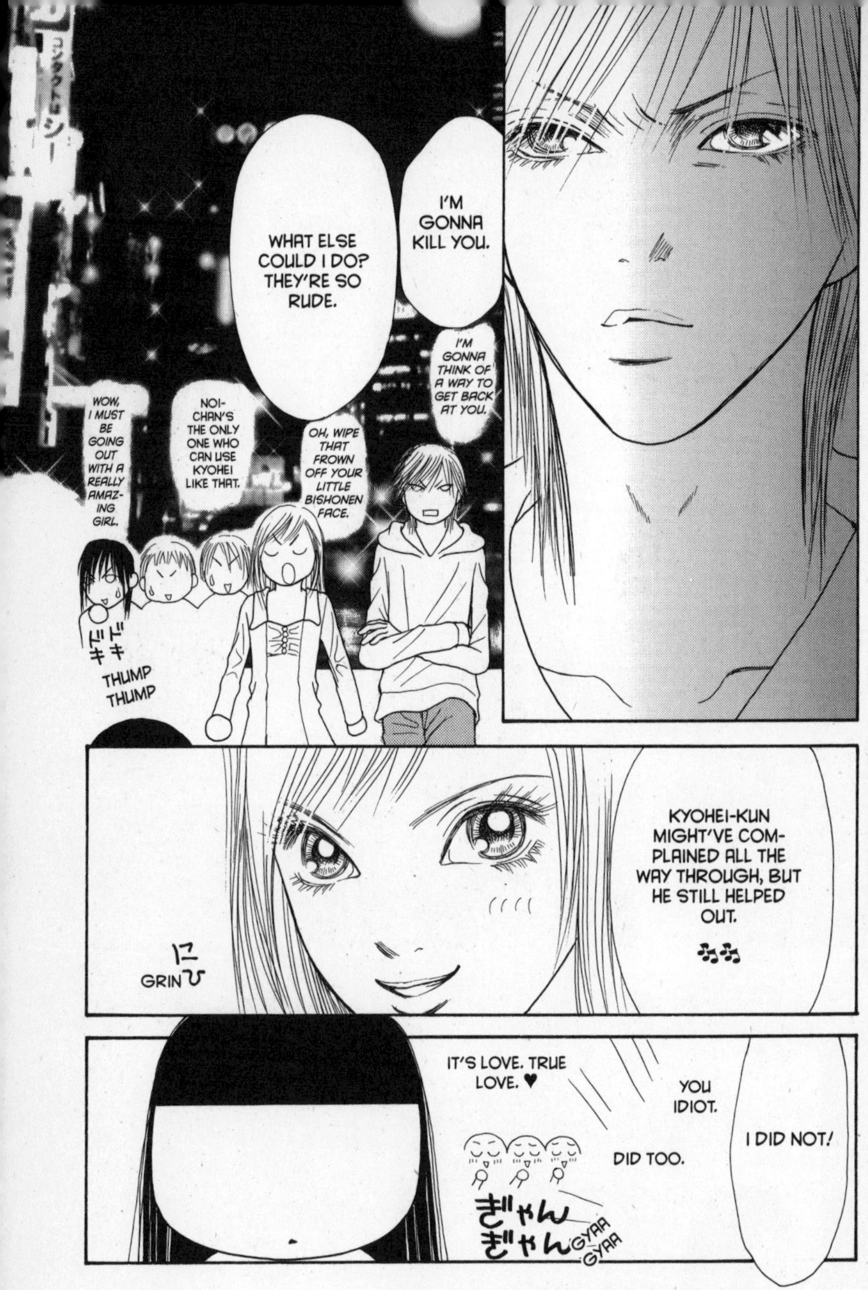
I'M GONNA KILL YOU.
WHAT ELSE COULD I DO? THEY'RE SO RUDE.
I'M GONNA THINK OF A WAY TO GET BACK AT YOU.
OH, WIPE THAT FROWN OFF YOUR LITTLE BISHONEN FACE.
NOI-CHAN'S THE ONLY ONE WHO CAN USE KYOHEI LIKE THAT.
WOW, I MUST BE GOING OUT WITH A REALLY AMAZING GIRL.
ドキドキ
THUMP THUMP
KYOHEI-KUN MIGHT'VE COMPLAINED ALL THE WAY THROUGH, BUT HE STILL HELPED OUT.
にひ
GRIN
I DID NOT!
YOU IDIOT.
IT'S LOVE. TRUE LOVE. ♥
DID TOO.
ぎゃんぎゃん
GYAA GYAA

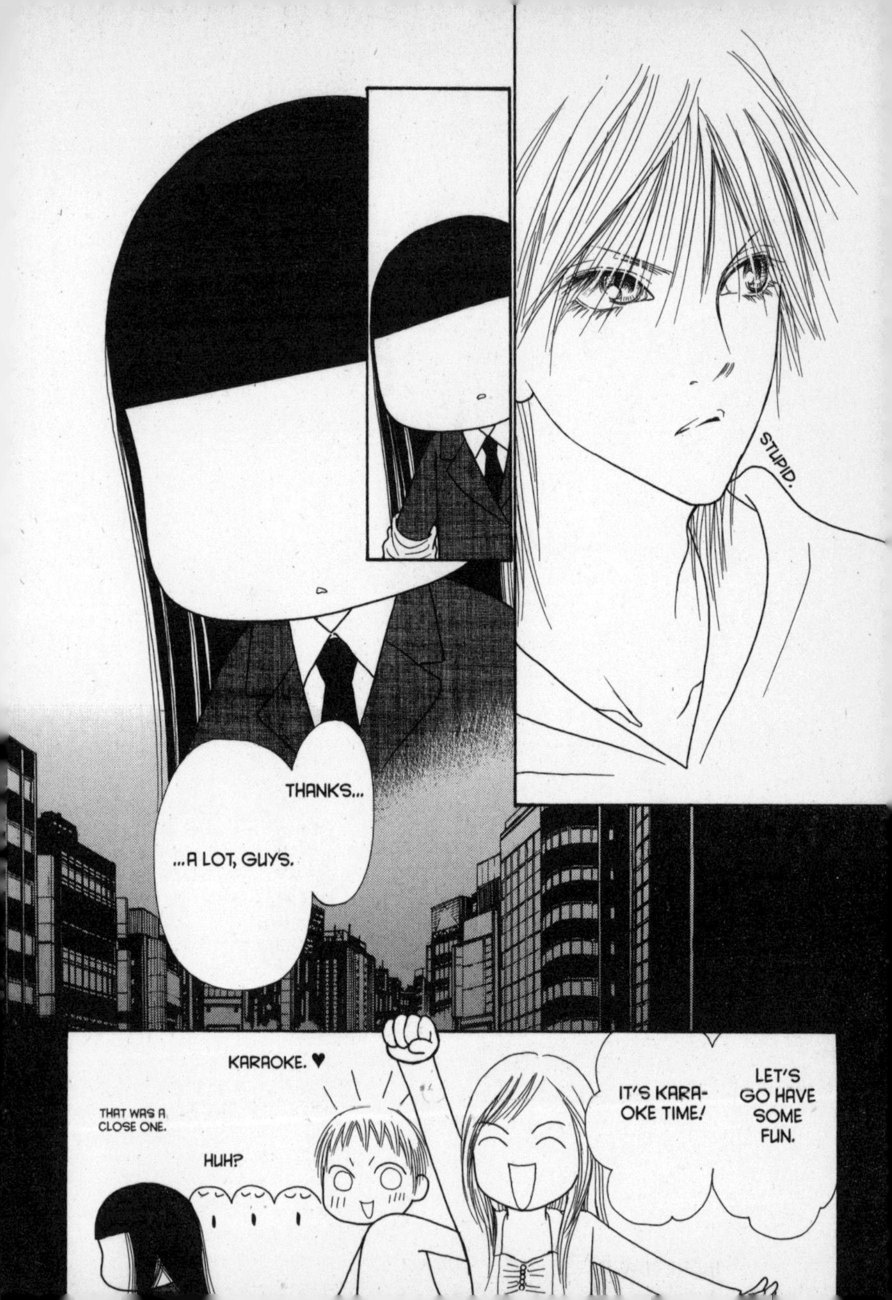
STUPID.
THANKS...
...A LOT, GUYS.
LET'S GO HAVE SOME FUN.
IT'S KARA-OKE TIME!
KARAOKE. ♥
HUH?
THAT WAS A CLOSE ONE.

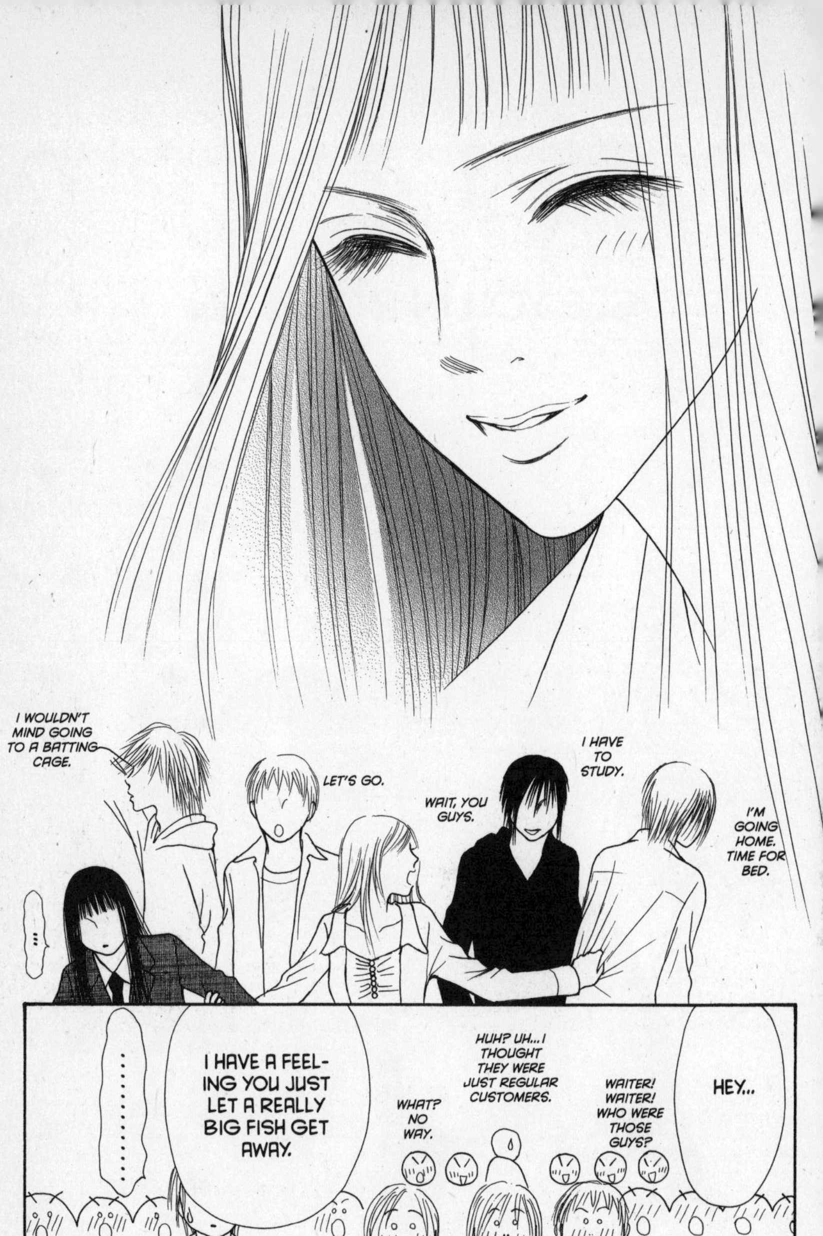
I'M GOING HOME. TIME FOR BED.
I HAVE TO STUDY.
WAIT, YOU GUYS.
LET'S GO.
I WOULDN'T MIND GOING TO A BATTING CAGE.
...
HEY...
WAITER! WAITER! WHO WERE THOSE GUYS?
HUH? UH...I THOUGHT THEY WERE JUST REGULAR CUSTOMERS.
WHAT? NO WAY.
I HAVE A FEEL-ING YOU JUST LET A REALLY BIG FISH GET AWAY.
....

CONTINUED IN *WALLFLOWER* BOOK 16

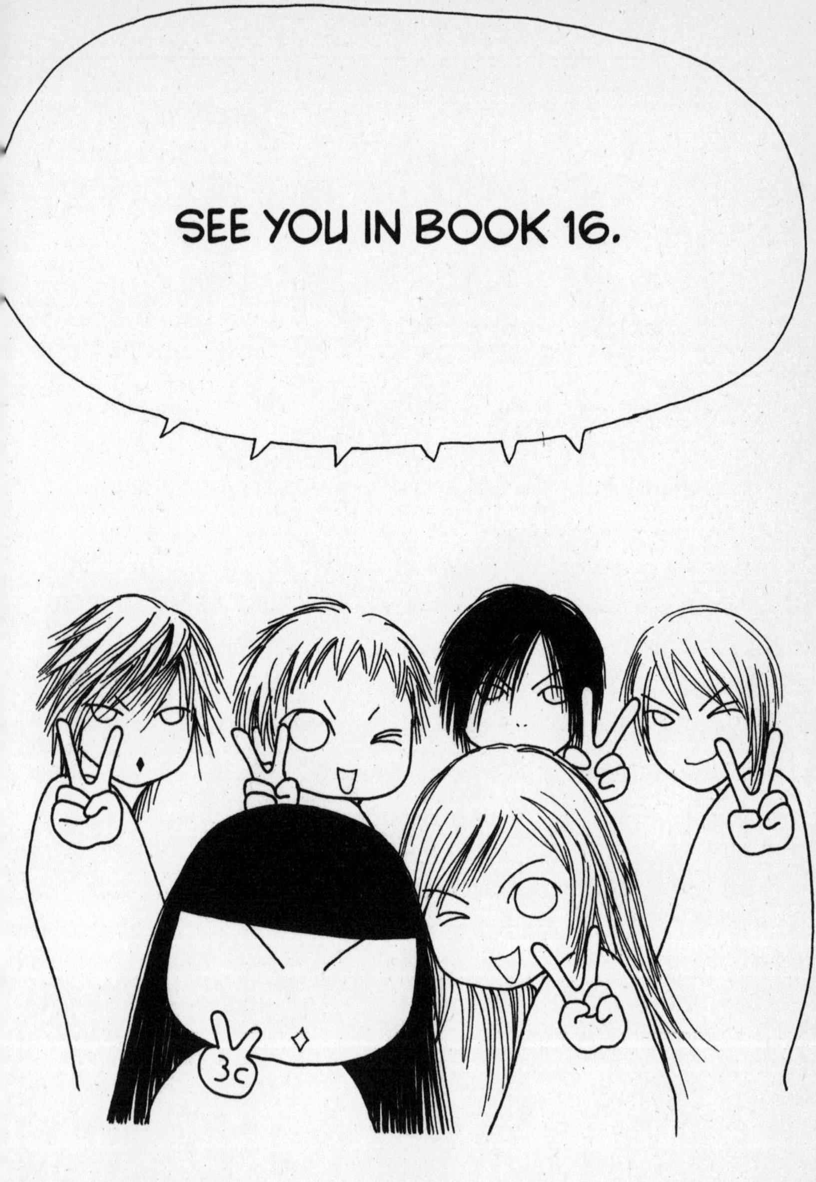
SEE YOU IN BOOK 16.

About the Creator

Tomoko Hayakawa was born on March 4.

Since her debut as a manga creator, Tomoko Hayakawa has worked on many *shojo* titles with the theme of romantic love—only to realize that she could write about other subjects as well. She decided to pack her newest story with the things she likes most, which led to her current, enormously popular series, *The Wallflower*.

Her favorite things are: Tim Burton's *The Nightmare Before Christmas,* Jean-Paul Gaultier, and samurai dramas on TV. Her hobbies are collecting items with skull designs and watching *bishonen* (beautiful boys). Her dream is to build a mansion like the one the Addams family lives in. Her favorite pastime is to lie around at home with her cat, Ten (whose full name is Tennosuke).

Her zodiac sign is Pisces, and her blood group is AB.

Translation Notes

Japanese is a tricky language for most Westerners, and translation is often more an art than a science. For your edification and reading pleasure, here are notes on some of the places where we could have gone in a different direction in our translation of the work, or where a Japanese cultural reference is used.

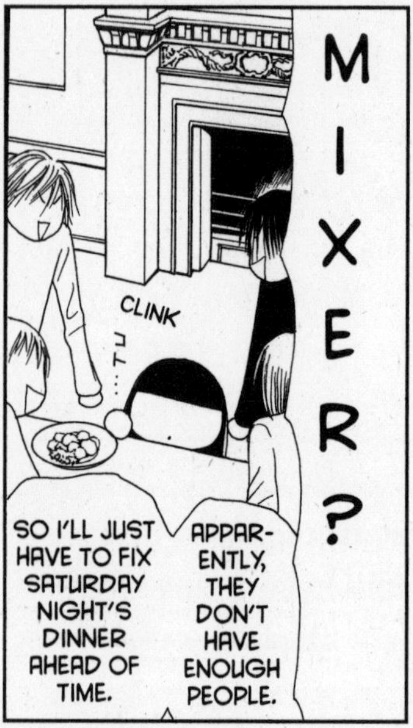
MIXER?
CLINK
...TU
APPARENTLY, THEY DON'T HAVE ENOUGH PEOPLE.
SO I'LL JUST HAVE TO FIX SATURDAY NIGHT'S DINNER AHEAD OF TIME.

Mixer, page 6

A "mixer" is called a *gokon* in Japanese. At a *gokon*, an equal number of single girls and guys go out for food and drinks and get to know each other.

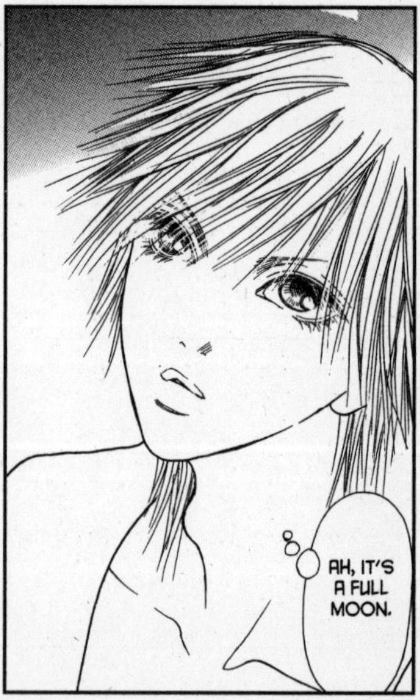
AH, IT'S A FULL MOON.

Moon rabbit, page 25

Kyohei is actually saying something like "Ah, the rabbit!" Japanese people say that if you look at the full moon you can see the image of a rabbit pounding rice cakes (mochi). It's sort of the Japanese version of the "man on the moon."

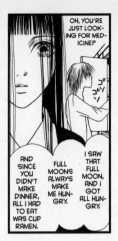

Full moon hunger, page 28

Kyohei actually says that seeing the rabbit making rice cakes has made him hungry.

OH, YOU'RE JUST LOOKING FOR MEDICINE?
ゴソゴソ
I SAW THAT FULL MOON, AND I GOT ALL HUNGRY.
FULL MOONS ALWAYS MAKE ME HUNGRY.
AND SINCE YOU DIDN'T MAKE DINNER, ALL I HAD TO EAT WAS CUP RAMEN.

Tooyama no kin san, page 46

Tooyama no kin San is a long-running television *jidaigeki* or "period piece" that takes place in the time of the samurai.

キャアアアアア
KYAAAAA
GHOSTS!
ちょこん
TINY
BEHIND YOU, YUKI!
WHAT IS THIS, SOME KIND OF DORIFU COMEDY SKETCH?

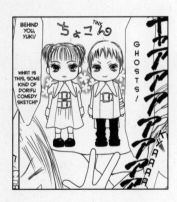

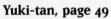

Dorifu, page 49

Dorifu, short for "drifters" is a popular Japanese sketch comedy troupe often referenced by Tomoko Hayakawa in *The Wallflower*.

Yuki-tan, page 49

Yuki-tan is baby talk for "Yuki-chan."

YUKI-TAN!

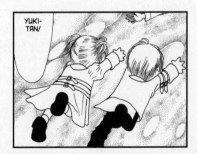

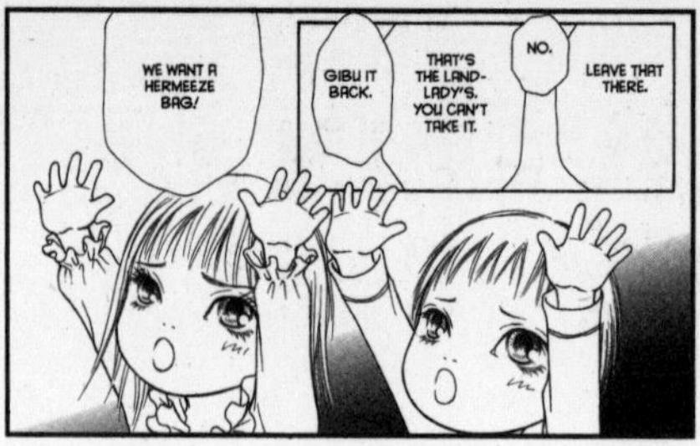
LEAVE THAT THERE.
NO.
THAT'S THE LAND-LADY'S. YOU CAN'T TAKE IT.
GIBU IT BACK.
WE WANT A HERMEEZE BAG!

Hermeeze, page 65

This is a little kid's way of pronouncing "Hermès," a luxury fashion brand that is extremely popular in Japan.

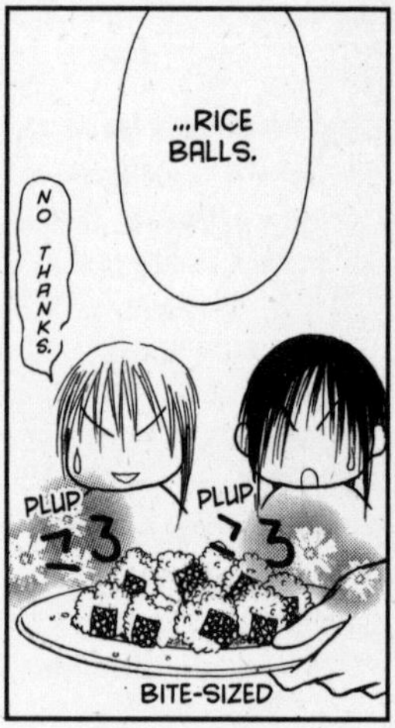
...RICE BALLS.
NO THANKS.
PLUP
PLUP
BITE-SIZED

Riceballs, page 74

The twins have made *Onigiri*—balls of rice covered with *nori* seaweed and stuffed with pickles or fish. They're not supposed to be sweet.

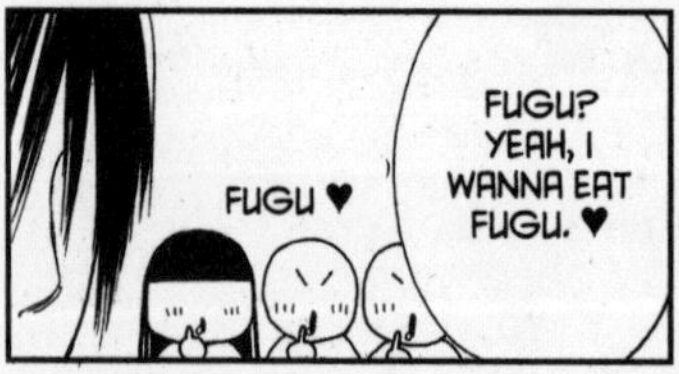
FUGU? YEAH, I WANNA EAT FUGU. ♥
FUGU ♥

Fugu, page 91

Fugu is the Japanese name for "puffer fish." *Fugu* is poisonous and can be deadly unless properly prepared. It is an expensive delicacy in Japan.

MY HEAVENLY HOCKEY CLUB

BY AI MORINAGA

WHERE THE BOYS ARE!

Hana Suzuki loves only two things in life: eating and sleeping. So when handsome classmate Izumi Oda asks Hana—his major crush—to join the school hockey club, convincing her proves to be a difficult task. True, the Grand Hockey Club is full of boys—and all the boys are super-cute—but, given a choice, Hana prefers a sizzling steak to a hot date. Then Izumi mentions the field trips to fancy resorts. Now Hana can't wait for the first away game, with its promise of delicious food and luxurious linens. Of course there's the getting up early, working hard, and playing well with others. How will Hana survive?

Special extras in each volume! Read them all!

TOMARE!

止まれ

[STOP!]

You're going the wrong way!

Manga is a completely different type of reading experience.

To start at the *beginning*,
go to the *end*!

That's right! Authentic manga is read the traditional Japanese way—from right to left. Exactly the *opposite* of how American books are read. It's easy to follow: Just go to the other end of the book, and read each page—and each panel—from right side to left side, starting at the top right. Now you're experiencing manga as it was meant to be!

OCT 11
CH